BUILDING BRITANNIA

STEVEN PARISSIEN

BUILDING
BRITANNIA

A HISTORY OF BRITAIN
IN TWENTY-FIVE BUILDINGS

HEAD
f ZEUS

An Apollo Book

Head of Zeus Ltd
First Floor East
5–8 Hardwick Street
London EC1R 4RG

WWW.HEADOFZEUS.COM

To Kerry

CONTENTS

Introduction

The history of Britain is, perhaps more than any other nation, defined by its architecture. This book seeks to examine not just *how* these twenty-five selected buildings were constructed, but *why*: for what reason or reasons they were built; what they were designed to do, and to mean, at the time of their creation; and, crucially, what they represented to subsequent generations eager to assign a new function, resonance or symbolism to their structure and their story.

All these buildings, to some extent or another, reflect and express their historical and social context: they all, to varying extents, say something about the nation's history or about specific developments. Many of them reveal something about not just the time of their creation but also the shifting sands of a more recent past. Some were specifically designed to signpost, mythologise or reinvent British history in order to proffer incarnations of assumed or perceived elements of national identity or 'British' character. And nearly all of them, in that sound British tradition, sought to encapsulate the latest social and technological advances in their design.

Everyone will naturally have their own twenty-five buildings. Many readers may, indeed, profoundly disagree with some of my choices. As with the music played on Britain's radio series *Desert Island Discs*, this selection is a personal one, which to some extent reflects my own story, background and experience. The same would be true of us all, I think.

The buildings I have selected for this particular journey are not necessarily the grandest or the most stylistically influential structures of their era. Instead, they represent a cross-section of interesting and, I hope, engaging building types, sizes and purposes. I have tried to avoid the usual suspects, whose overly familiar narratives may not bear another rehearsal and may have little to contribute in terms of a wider socio-political significance. I have also tried to ensure a reasonable chronological and geographical spread across Great Britain and have chosen buildings which can be visited by the public today, either by an impromptu visit or by a booked appointment.

Huge thanks go to all who advised on or helped in the planning of this book, especially Kerry Fretwell, Julian Holder and James Hulme. Particular thanks go to my editor and friend, Richard Milbank, with whom this book was devised and who has been such a stalwart supporter of my writing over the years. Thanks, too, to Ellie Jardine, Kate Wands, Kathryn Colwell and all of the HoZ team.

1

MAIDEN CASTLE, DORSET

C.600 BC

Summoning the British: conjuring a national identity from a mythical past

In the history of Britain, Maiden Castle has always occupied a central and commanding place. In an attempt to forge a British national identity out of so many disparate nations and narratives, historians, writers, poets and musicians have turned to the site to validate their fantasies or substantiate their beliefs. The 'Castle' has played a role as one of these islands' most important pre-Christian fortresses and, centuries later, as an inspiration for those seeking to disinter the ancient Britons; as symbol of British resistance and isolationism and as a cultural crucible for British 'values'. The reason why the fort is there has been long debated, but the power of its allegory endures.

What we do know is that Maiden Castle was an important Neolithic fortified hilltop settlement, built in around 600 BC by the Durotriges, a tribal confederation based in what is now Dorset and south Somerset. The Durotriges' name has been translated as 'hill-top dwellers', which would be highly appropriate for Maiden Castle, and their capital has been identified as the town the Romans named Durnovaria, now present-day Dorchester, which Maiden Castle guarded to the south-west.

Whether the Durotriges were able to resist the invading Roman legions of the Emperor Claudius, led by the future emperor Vespasian, in the years after AD 43 is debatable. Responding to Britain's stout resistance to Nazi Germany in the perilous summer of 1940, the archaeologist who had brought the site to national attention in the previous decade, Mortimer Wheeler, wove Maiden Castle into a stirring tale of a massive Roman attack on this British redoubt at the height of the first invasion, shortly after the disembarkation of the Roman fleet at the Durotriges' main port of Poole Harbour. However, later excavations have failed to find any evidence of this. Indeed, the Romanisation of the Durotriges – whether welcomed or enforced – continues to be a long-standing research project at Bournemouth University, near Poole. Certainly, following the Romans' withdrawal from Britain in the early years of the fifth century, the Romanised Durotriges appear to have fought off Saxon incursions for at least 200 years before succumbing to the Germanic raiders in the mid-seventh century. The Saxon county of Dorset, indeed, was only first recorded in 841.

However, Wheeler's story was a more resonant one. As a result of his conclusions, formed during his widely publicised excavation of the site after 1934, Maiden Castle became an evocative symbol of British defiance and endurance that inspired a generation of British artists.

The dig itself was part of a wider movement directed towards excavating ancient Britain's past which followed the carnage of the First World War and which was dubbed 'hill-fort mania' by the press. Nothing more typified the mania and the romantic claims being made for its finds than the work at Maiden Castle. The site's original name, though, has long been forgotten. 'Mayden Castell' is first recorded as late as 1607 and was a generic and possibly medieval label alternatively interpreted as 'a fortification that looks impregnable' or simply 'a great hill'.

Immortalising Maiden Castle

The 'Castle' was, by many reckonings, one of the most impressive fortifications in the western world – and certainly the largest in western Europe.

◁ *A contemporary aerial view of Maiden Castle, showing how modern agriculture has eroded the site's curtilage.*

It stretched across a saddle-backed chalk hilltop 914 metres long and by 450 BC occupied 47 acres (19 hectares). Such British hill forts were built either to resist incursions from European invaders or, as is more commonly held today, to control an expanding and restive population. Oxford University archaeologist Sir Barry Cunliffe has suggested that hill forts were proto-urban 'town-like settlements' which

> provided defensive possibilities for the community at those times when the stress [of an increasing population] burst out into open warfare. But I wouldn't see them as having been built because there was a state of war. They would be functional as defensive strongholds when there were tensions and undoubtedly some of them were attacked and destroyed, but this was not the only, or even the most significant, factor in their construction.

In the 1980s Cardiff University archaeologist Niall Sharples began new excavations at Maiden Castle, vastly extending the scope of Mortimer Wheeler's work, and subsequently suggested that ancient British hill forts such as this one had been built to control and defend agricultural land to support a large local community. This was later supported by Barry Cunliffe, who argued that the elaborate earthworks around the entrances to Maiden Castle were used to defend the weakest part of the hill fort, increasing the time the attackers took to reach the gateway and thus leaving them vulnerable to defenders armed with slings. (More than 20,000 'slingstones', small, rounded pebbles gathered from nearby Chesil Beach on the Dorset coast, have been found at the eastern entrance of the site. They were stored in large pits ready to be pitched at attackers.) Cunliffe has also pointed out that the hill fort's high, imposing banks and deep ditches would have represented formidable psychological as well as physical obstacles to any attacker.

The site had already become a beacon for romantics keen to reach back to the ancient Britons in the years before the Wheeler excavations. The celebrated Dorset novelist and poet Thomas Hardy (1840–1928) was infatuated with the castle. In 1885 he built his new home, Max Gate, at a location within sight of Maiden Castle, and cast the structure as a principal character in a short story of that year, 'Ancient Earthworks and What Two Enthusiastic Scientists Found Therein'. (A demonstration of how little was then known about the castle was that this first version posited the site as a Roman redoubt, not a

British hill fort.) Eight years later Hardy reworked this rather awkward tale into a shorter and more focused story, 'A Tryst at an Ancient Earthwork', in which the hill fort was pictured almost as a sentient being, looming out of the dark 'like a thing waking up and asking what I want here'. In many ways Maiden Castle was more vivid and alive than Hardy's ill-defined narrator:

> The position of the castle on this isolated hill bespeaks deliberate and strategic choice exercised by some remote mind capable of prospective reasoning to a far extent. The natural configuration of the surrounding country and its bearing upon such a stronghold were obviously long considered and viewed mentally before its extensive design was carried into execution. Who was the man that said, 'Let it be built here!' – not on that hill yonder, or on that ridge behind, but on this best spot of all? Whether he were some great one of the Belgae, or of the Durotriges, or the travelling engineer of Britain's united tribes, must for ever remain time's secret [...] Many a time must the king or leader have directed his keen eyes hence across the open lands towards the ancient road the Icening Way, still visible in the distance, on the watch for armed companies approaching either to succour or to attack.

After the First World War, other artists followed Hardy and seized on Maiden Castle as an incarnation of a simpler time and of noble 'British' virtues. In 1921 composer John Ireland wrote a 'symphonic rhapsody', *Mai-Dun*, about the fort. Like many artists of the day, Altrincham-born Ireland (1879–1962) was fascinated by Britain's distant past and in particular, as music historian James McCarthy has noted, 'Ancient sites with echoes of the supernatural'. *Mai-Dun* is a strong, forceful piece designed to echo the 'violent history' of the hill fort, the legend of which Mortimer Wheeler was subsequently to rekindle. Ireland was particularly susceptible to such tales, frequently exhibiting 'a yearning for long lost customs in ancient civilisations, pagan or occult'. In 1933 he claimed he had gone for a picnic on the South Downs by himself when he saw in front of him a group of children dressed in strange white clothes playing and dancing in silence, who suddenly vanished. It would be simple to set this incident within the disconcerting and magical folds of Maiden Castle.

Fifteen years after Ireland's rhapsody the author John Cowper Powys (1872–1963), an ardent admirer of Hardy, set the fourth of his Wessex novels near and at the site. The convoluted plot of *Maiden Castle*, which involved our

△ *An aerial view of Maiden Castle taken for Mortimer Wheeler in 1934.*

novelist-narrator, 'Dud No-Man', and his obsession with a circus performer, 'Wizzie', revolved around the hill fort and the religious beliefs of its imagined ancient British inhabitants. The castle was a brooding presence throughout the work – a feature which, on Candlemas Night, was reputed by the locals to 'come alive again':

> Dud stared in fascinated awe at the great earth monument. From this half-way distance it took all sorts of strange forms to his shameless mind. It took the shape of a huge dropping of super-mammoth dung. It took the shape of an enormous seaweed-encrusted shell... It took the shape of that vast planetary tortoise upon whose curved back, sealed with the convoluted inscriptions of the nameless Tao, rested the pillar of creation... 'I wonder,' he said to himself, 'whether it really is possible that if I'd come along this

16

road ten thousand years ago I should now be gazing up at the Cyclopean walls and towers and temples and parapets of a great peaceful city of a far nobler civilisation than ours, where war and torture and vivisection were unknown...'

To John Cowper Powys, Maiden Castle was a source of natural magic as well as ancient simplicity. Later in the novel Dud feels as if 'the powers of Mai-Dun were fusing him with his father', and Powys conjures the ghosts of the Arthurian court and a mystical wind to provide his bizarre, bickering characters with an enchanted canvas.

Powys had lived in Dorchester as a child – at exactly the same time, in fact, as Hardy was writing *Far From the Madding Crowd* and *The Mayor of Casterbridge* at Max Gate – and he returned there, after twenty years in America and with his American partner, Phyllis Playter, in order to attempt to reconnect with his English roots. After only ten months in Dorset, however, he abruptly moved to north Wales, where he finished the book.

Powys was at heart a primitivist, for whom virtually every modern invention was anathema. He never drove a car or used a typewriter. He thought television was pernicious. He rarely talked on the telephone because he did not want his words 'violated by a tangle of wires'. (Much of one chapter of *Maiden Castle* is taken up with a denunciation of electricity pylons.) So it is not surprising that he looked to his British ancestors, untouched by the complexities and technologies of modern life, for his inspiration. In the event, Powys' unironic, un-English prose style was much mocked – his earlier novels, along with the rural romances of Mary Webb, having already been skewered by Stella Gibbons in her satire *Cold Comfort Farm* of 1932 – although the novelist saw himself as a new Thomas Hardy. Even Glen Cavaliero of the Powys Society has more recently admitted that 'Certainly Maiden Castle... can induce impatience – "For God's sake, get on with it!" one tends to exclaim at times, largely as a result of the extraordinary length of Powys's chapters, which would benefit by an unobtrusive separation into sub-divisions.'

The mystic and ghostly aura of the site which had been suggestively conjured by Hardy, Ireland and Powys, and which was so successfully stoked by Mortimer Wheeler in 1940, formed the backdrop for John Schlesinger and Nicolas Roeg's evocative 1967 film adaptation of Hardy's 1874 novel *Far from the Madding Crowd*. Indeed, in the pivotal scene in which Sergeant Troy effectively seduces Bathsheba with a thrilling if frightening display of swordplay,

Maiden Castle becomes a character in itself, the violence of Troy's demonstration fuelled by the savagery of the site's history.

Mortimer Wheeler and Maiden Castle

Enthusiasm for ancient British sites such as Maiden Castle after the First World War, as Britons looked to the distant past for certainties and simplicities after the carnage of the Western Front and doubts grew about whether the enormous sacrifices had been worthwhile, in turn helped to make celebrities of the more media-friendly archaeologists. And none was so keen to seize the media spotlight as Mortimer Wheeler, the man who was judged to have 'rediscovered' Maiden Castle.

Robert Eric Mortimer Wheeler (1890–1976) had had a good First World War, reaching the rank of major and winning a Military Cross. After 1918 his career was similarly successful: having obtained a doctorate from University College London, he joined the National Museum of Wales as an archaeologist; there, largely thanks to his reforming ideas about his discipline as well as his talent for self-promotion, in a few years he became its director. His scientific and methodological approach to excavation, based on the pioneering digs of Augustus Pitt Rivers, both modernised the profession and brought it into the eye of a public hungry for colourful historical escapism in the vein of Walter Scott's evergreen novel *Ivanhoe* of 1819 and Elgar's ancient British cantata *Caractacus* of 1898. Pitt Rivers had also made some preliminary excavations at Maiden Castle in the 1880s.

Increasingly, however, Wheeler's innovations have been ascribed more to his first wife, Tessa Verney Wheeler (1893–1936), or Verney as she was generally known. A highly accomplished archaeologist in her own right who had helped to found the Institute of Archaeology and established a reputation as a brilliant teacher and public speaker, she inevitably remained in the shadow of her entrepreneurial husband. While she lived, the Wheelers' work was published in both of their names, but it was Mortimer who was given – and happily accepted – much of the credit, notably at Maiden Castle, where, although Mortimer basked in the subsequent media attention as the author

▷ *Archaeologist and media celebrity Sir Mortimer Wheeler greets Queen Elizabeth II at Maiden Castle in 1952, the year in which he was knighted.*

of the work, the dig appears to have been largely directed by Tessa.

Verney Wheeler died in 1936, aged only forty-six and during the latter stages of the Maiden Castle excavations. She was worn down by gastric illness – and by stress, caused partly by the well-publicised sexual exploits of her philandering husband. For Mortimer was that very twentieth-century phenomenon: the media celebrity who was at the same time a serial sexual predator. Young female researchers, friends' wives and archaeology colleagues were all fair game, however brief the liaison. Wheeler seemed to be attracted to the danger of illicit sex, indulging in casual copulations in very public places, despite his increasingly high public profile.

Openly distraught following Tessa's untimely death, in private Wheeler continued much as before. By the summer of 1937 he had become obsessed with the strikingly attractive blonde Mavis de Vere Cole (1908–70), whom he finally married in 1939. Mavis, née Wright, was as notorious a sexual adventurer as her new husband. A former maid and waitress at Veeraswamy, an Indian restaurant in London's Regent Street, she was the widow of the wealthy Horace

de Vere Cole, twenty-seven years her senior, whose bizarre career as a practical joker came to an untimely end when he died of a heart attack in France only months after Mavis has borne him a son. Mavis was clearly attracted to older men. She first met Wheeler at Maiden Castle when with her then-lover, the sybaritic painter Augustus John – who was thirty years older than her and was in truth the father of her young son, Tristan. Predictably, the marriage did not prosper, and Mavis' later diaries note that Wheeler frequently hit her. After Wheeler discovered Mavis in bed with one Clive Entwhistle, he initiated divorce proceedings, which were finalised in March 1942. Three years later Wheeler married his third wife, Margaret Norfolk, an Australian archaeologist who had worked with the Wheelers at Maiden Castle, and who had doubtless been one of Mortimer's many conquests there. In 1941 Margaret Collingridge, as she then was, had married a submariner, Robert Thorn; but his vessel, HMS *Thorn*, went down with all hands after being attacked by an Italian torpedo boat off Crete in August 1942. By 1956, however, partly as a result of Wheeler's incessant infidelities, the pair had become estranged, though Margaret's staunch Catholicism meant that they never divorced. (Meanwhile, Mavis had been back in the headlines in 1954 for having shot her then-lover in the groin, for which she was jailed for six months.) With three marriages behind him, for the rest of his life Wheeler continued in the same promiscuous fashion, exasperating friends and lovers alike.

Mortimer Wheeler's sexual adventures notwithstanding, his contribution to archaeology, and to the understanding of Britain's ancient past, was seminal. His excavations were impeccably recorded, and their results published as quickly as possible – with Wheeler taking to the media to ensure they were as widely publicised as was feasible.

It was Wheeler's publication of the findings at Maiden Castle which cemented his public reputation as Britain's premier archaeologist. Inspired by Hardy, Ireland and Powys, as well as by the RAF's dogged resistance to the Luftwaffe in the perilous summer of 1940, when he was writing up his conclusions, Wheeler wove Maiden Castle into a stirring tale of invasion and defiance, centred on a massive Roman attack on this brave British redoubt during Vespasian's invasion of Britain of AD 43. It was a moving story which owed as much to John Ireland and the Battle of Britain as to the events of the first century AD.

As Wheeler finished his account of the Maiden Castle dig, he was surrounded by and immersed in war. Volunteering for service, Wheeler was initially assigned to command the 48th Light Anti-Aircraft Battery at Enfield in Middlesex, subsequently becoming acting lieutenant-colonel of its expanded successor, the 42nd Mobile Light Anti-Aircraft Regiment of the Royal Artillery. (Heartily disliked by many serving in his unit, who nicknamed him 'Flash Alf', Wheeler was widely blamed for the death of a soldier from influenza during training.) Meanwhile, Spitfires and Hurricanes from the nearby RAF bases at Northolt, Hendon, North Weald and Hornchurch spiralled in the sky above north London, chasing after the Messerschmitts, Junkers, Heinkels and Dorniers. Following the British army's retreat from Dunkirk, a German invasion was regarded as imminent until October 1940, and still highly likely until Hitler embarked on his ill-fated Russian campaign in June 1941. Wheeler's war-torn Britain, much like the nation of the Durotriges almost two millennia before, was under siege, and the future of its civilisation imperilled. The ancient Britons had failed to fight the Romans on the beaches or the landing grounds; now they found themselves defending their ancestral hills.

Invasion and resistance were, unsurprisingly, very much on Wheeler's mind in 1940, and they undoubtedly influenced his interpretations of Maiden Castle. In the archaeologist's fertile imagination the vast hill fort was cast as one of the last true ancient British redoubts, standing alone against the tide of legionaries recruited from across the European continent – much like Hitler's Wehrmacht following its rapid conquests of 1939–40 in eastern and western Europe. His excavation of the cemetery in the castle's eastern gateway had revealed fifty-two burials, suggesting to Wheeler that the total number of burials was likely to be at least double this figure. Crucially, one of the excavated areas of the cemetery revealed the burials of fourteen people, all of whom had died in violent circumstances. One skeleton, much to Wheeler's delight, even had a Roman catapult bolt lodged in its spine. As a result, Wheeler labelled this feature of the site as a 'war cemetery' and promoted it as evidence of a major Roman attack on the British defensive position at Maiden Castle. From this starting point he conjured a narrative in which a Roman legion used primitive artillery fire to wreak destruction on the site, butchering men, women and children before setting fire to the fort and demilitarising its defences:

First, the regiment of artillery which usually accompanied a legion was ordered into action and put down a barrage of ballista arrows... Following the barrage, the Roman infantry advanced up the slope, cutting its way from rampart to rampart until it reached the innermost bay, where some circular huts had recently been built. These were set alight, and under the rising clouds of smoke the gates were stormed and the position carried. But resistance had been obstinate and the fury of the legionaries was aroused. For a space, confusion and massacre dominated the scene. Men and women, young and old, were savagely cut down before the troops were called to heel. A systematic slighting of the defences followed, whereafter the legion was withdrawn. Doubtless taking hostages with it, and the dazed inhabitants were left to bury the dead amongst the ashes of their huts beside the gates.

Reconstructing the past

Wheeler's story was, however, sheer fantasy. AD 43 was not 1940: late Iron Age Dorset was not Blitzkrieg Poland or France, and Maiden Castle was no Warsaw or Sedan. Caught up in the contemporary drama of seemingly unstoppable German victories and Britain's dogged but seemingly doomed attempt to stem the Nazi legions, Mortimer Wheeler the archaeologist became Colonel Wheeler the artilleryman, and wove a tale in which the ancient Britons of the Durotriges became the gallant Britons of Fortress Britain. He almost admitted as such when he later confessed in the dedication of his Maiden Castle report of August 1941 that 'the wreckage of the present has in these days been more instant to my mind than the wreckage of the past, and *inter arma* I have no heart for studentship'.

As Oxford Archaeological Unit's Neolithic expert and celebrity media archaeologist Dr Miles Russell observed in 2014:

> The account of a furious but futile defence of property, family and land by the local Iron Age tribe of the Durotriges, leading eventually to their slaughter or enslavement, is undeniably powerful and remains one of the more potent stories relating to the demise of British prehistory. A recent study of Dorset hillforts has, however, called this narrative into question, reassessing the evidence provided for the so-called Great Battle of Maiden Castle. The discrediting of the siege scenario has serious repercussions, not only as to how we interpret evidence revealed through excavation, especially in relation to perceived historical events, but also how archaeological discoveries are reported in the press.

Wheeler later described 'skeletons in tragic profusion, displaying the marks of battle and making actual one of the best-known events in British history: the Roman conquest'. As his biographer, Jacquetta Hawkes, later wrote, it was 'no wonder that press reports multiplied and the crowds came'. As Russell has recently noted, Wheeler's gripping narrative, which could have been written of events in France in 1917 or 1940, 'reads like a dispatch from the frontline... which also at once vividly sears itself into the mind of the reader'. Russell indeed attributes Wheeler's colourful tale as much with first service in the First World War as with the events of the Second:

> The masterstroke, of course, certainly as far as Wheeler was concerned, was the identification of residue relating to a Roman artillery barrage. During the war of 1914–18, Wheeler had seen at first hand the importance of artillery to soften up an enemy: the discovery of bodies buried in the Iron Age cemetery of Maiden Castle with injuries apparently consistent with catapult fire seemed, on the face of it, too good to be true. 'One skull', Wheeler remarked 'showed the square piercing of a quadrangular Roman ballista-bolt, whilst another skeleton – most vivid relic of all – had an iron arrow-head embedded deeply in a vertebra.' These sad remains, together with the ash of 'burnt huts', naturally led him to propose that an initial phase of attack upon the Iron Age stronghold had been heralded by ballistae, putting down 'a barrage across the gateway, causing casualties at the outset'.

However, as Russell went on to remark, 'This was no densely occupied tribal town then, whose inhabitants rallied *en masse* to protect their economic and spiritual centre from a Roman legion, but, rather a sparsely inhabited space, largely gone over to agriculture, set within the long-abandoned ramparts of a politically defunct hillfort.' Whether any of Maiden Castle's handful of inhabitants died fighting the Romans is now impossible to tell. Later analysis of the site suggested that there is actually little archaeological evidence to support Wheeler's melodramatic version of events, or even that the hill fort was ever attacked by the Romans. Although there is a layer of charcoal dating from the first decade of the Christian era, it is associated with the ironworks at the site, while the main evidence for slighting of defences comes from the collapse of an entranceway to the fort. And crucially, although fourteen bodies in the cemetery exhibited signs of a violent death, there is no evidence that they actually died at Maiden Castle; instead, they may have been brought here for burial in accordance with Durotrigian custom. Most of the discovered burials reveal people who had not been hastily buried in the midst of war but had been carefully interred with grave goods such as beads, brooches and rings, along with pottery and even joints of meat as food for the afterlife. (Wheeler's colourful account of an artillery bombardment and subsequent massacre and confusion hardly square with evidence of a couple being buried with a leg of lamb for the journey.) The handful of battle-scarred warriors Wheeler had found may indeed have been injured defending Maiden Castle from the Romans; but it is equally likely that they had been involved in local skirmishes between contending tribal factions.

In the 1980s Niall Sharples suggested, following much further excavation of the site, that the hill fort had already been largely abandoned by the time of the Roman invasion owing to 'a breakdown of the communal ownership', which was primarily a result of the expansion of craft industries such as ironworking, ceramic production and salt extraction as well as the creation of small, undefended farmsteads near water sources in the surrounding valleys. Sharples found that the bodies of those allegedly slain by Romans, discovered by Wheeler at the east gate, could have been 'brought from elsewhere to this cemetery and do not indicate death in the immediate vicinity of the graves'. And he politely refuted Wheeler's stirring tale, which, he concluded, was 'not altogether consistent with the evidence on the ground'. Instead, he suggested that Maiden Castle was, by AD 43, already a shrinking community in an outdated facility.

Ironically, rather than extinguishing a thriving British settlement, the Roman invasion appears to have given Maiden Castle a new lease of life. The site was repaired and extended, and large quantities of brooches, rings and imported Gaulish ceramics have been found dating from the first and second centuries AD. There is even evidence to suggest that the Romans themselves occupied this site for military purposes. However, the establishment of a Roman garrison at nearby Dorchester (*Durnovaria*) by AD 70 – later named by the Alexandrian geographer Ptolemy (*c*.100–170) as the capital of the Durotriges – meant that the castle's days were numbered, and by the mid-second century it was largely abandoned.

This was not, though, Maiden Castle's last service for the ancient Britons. In the late fourth century a temple complex was built on the site, whose eerie evocations must have provided an ideal setting for the celebration of a new pagan religion. The date of AD 367 for the foundation of this temple has been suggested, deduced from a hoard of coins discovered beneath a mosaic floor. Its plan, basically a central room surrounded by a passageway, was similar to many Romano-British temples found in the South of England of roughly the same date. Nearby were two other buildings: one rectangular with two rooms that may have been a house for a priest, the other circular, which may have been a shrine. At the same time as the temple was built, the fort's eastern gateway also appears to have been refurbished, suggesting that there was possibly another shrine inside the gateway. Around the end of the fourth century, as Romans troops were successively withdrawn from Britannia, fusions of native British and classical Roman gods were widespread, and it was common to find shrines located in remote rural locations. This particular temple did not, however, survive the later Saxon incorporation of the Dorchester area into the new county of Dorset, whose name was derived from the former Roman name for the town, *Durnovaria*.

Following the Norman Conquest, Dorchester grew into a respectably sized town, being provided with a castle and a priory (both of which have since disappeared). Up until the 1880s it was best known for hosting two notorious series of trials: the so-called 'Bloody Assizes', the show trials held by King James II's Lord Chancellor, George Jeffreys, which condemned so many of those who had fought with the Duke of Monmouth in 1685 against the Catholic king, and the Tolpuddle Martyrs' conviction in 1834, when six local agricultural labourers were sentenced to transportation for starting a union to protest at the lowering of agricultural wages. Dorchester only began to shed this infamous reputation when, in 1874, it appeared in the first novel to be written by an architect who had been born just outside the town. The novel was *Far from the Madding Crowd* and the author was Thomas Hardy. Dorchester appeared in many more of Hardy's novels, thinly disguised as Casterbridge.

Maiden Castle, meanwhile, had passed from recorded history after the Norman Conquest into the realms of myth and legend. In the sixteenth century a barn was built at the site's eastern entrance, and little heed was given to the massive but now long-deserted earthwork. By the eighteenth century the site had wholly reverted to pasture, its origins almost entirely forgotten. There it lay, waiting like a sleeping princess to be reawakened in the modern era by the unlikely quartet of Thomas Hardy, John Ireland, John Cowper Powysand Robert Eric Mortimer Wheeler.

2

THE ROMAN BATHS, BATH

BEGUN AD 65

What Did the Romans Ever Do for Us?

Ninety-five years after Julius Caesar had raided southern Britain and defeated the local British tribes, Gaius Caesar Augustus Germanicus – popularly known as 'Caligula' after the little boots his soldiers wore – waited at Boulogne (*Bononia*) on the Channel coast. Caligula (AD 12–41), Rome's third emperor, was a very different figure from the great Caesar and his two imperial predecessors. Restless and unbalanced, Caligula sought to eclipse his forebears by raiding Britain – and possibly even incorporating it into his empire, although there is no firm evidence to support this theory. In the event, though, the campaign was aborted some time in AD 40. Suetonius' traditional story, which Robert Graves cheerfully retold in his 1934 novel *I, Claudius*, was that the emperor had arranged his troops in battle order on the shore and then ordered

▷ *The Romans' Great Bath of the first century AD in its present guise. In the background looms the Perpendicular Gothic masterpiece of Bath Abbey.*

them to attack the sea and to gather seashells from the beach as 'fitting plunder'. In truth, this expedition may just have been a punitive exercise designed to discipline restive British tribes which was exaggerated by later historians to fit the image of a crazed and megalomaniacal ruler. Suetonius' tale could have resulted from the mistranslation of the word *musculi* as 'shells' when it was also army slang for military huts – suggesting that the Romans might have captured one or more British military encampments. Indeed, recent evidence excavated from the Roman palace at Fishbourne in Sussex – including the discovery of an early first-century Roman soldier's scabbard – suggests that, while a large-scale invasion was probably never attempted by Caligula's army, some units did actually cross the Channel in AD 39 or even earlier. Once here, they may have been used to reinforce the rulers of the Romans' client kingdoms in the south of the country, statelets which had originally been established by Julius Caesar during his raids-in-force of 55 and 54 BC.

Whatever the realities of Caligula's campaign, the histrionic emperor seems to have deserted his troops sometime during AD 40. A few months later, in January 41, he was dead: stabbed to death in his palace by exasperated senior officers of his own Praetorian Guard. Two years later, however, the new emperor, Caligula's uncle, Claudius, decided to revive the idea of invading Britannia. And this time the Romans stayed.

Claudius felt he had good reason to subjugate the Britons once and for all. By AD 43 anti-Roman protests across the client kingdoms and the ejection of a Roman client king, Verica of the Atrebates (a tribe which occupied modern-day Sussex and east Hampshire), by the aggressive Catuvellauni nation gave him a cast-iron excuse. In addition, civilised Romans were increasingly uneasy with the savage rites of British and Gallic Druidism, a faith they believed fostered anti-Roman sentiment and which they were accordingly determined to stamp out. Thus, in 43, four legions under the command of General Aulus Plautius, a former governor of Pannonia at the other end of the empire, were assembled once more at Boulogne. This was not, though, before an army mutiny had been suppressed, some of the soldiers believing that the Channel marked the boundary of the 'proper world' and that to go beyond this was to invite disaster.

Plautius' forces landed in Richborough in Kent and swiftly cowed the disunited British tribes. The Catuvellaunian kings Caractacus and Togodumnus were routed and withdrew beyond the Medway while the Dobunni, who occupied the lands north of the Durotriges – around what is now Gloucestershire, west Oxfordshire and south Warwickshire – quickly surrendered. After Plautius had inflicted a decisive defeat on the Catuvellauni, Claudius himself arrived to accompany Plautius into the Catuvellaunian capital Colchester (*Camulodunon*, which the Romans latinised to *Camulodunum*) in the late summer of 43.

By 47 Plautius' crack legion *Legio II*, under the command of the legate and future emperor Vespasian, had arrived in the territory of the Dobunni – although there they stopped, at least for the time being, by the banks of the Severn. It was not until after AD 58 that the Romans penetrated into Wales.

Here, nestling in a valley of the River Avon, the advancing Romans found a British temple based around a sacred hot spring.* And it was here that they founded a settlement devised more for rest and recuperation than to serve as a garrison town: *Aquae Sulis*, 'waters of Sulis', or, in modern English, Bath.

John Wood and Roman Bath

Roman Bath was, in historian David Mattingly's opinion, 'the prime example of a small town centred on a religious sanctuary'. The walled town they created was built around a classical temple and baths, itself based over a hot spring which may have already been a place of worship for the Dubonni. The sophisticated leisure complex and canalised reservoir the Romans built around AD 65–75 was unique in Britain: there was nothing else of this magnitude or ambition in the rest of the British Isles. Accordingly, it must have been a powerful testimony to Roman ingenuity and civilisation.

While some Romanised Britons did use the Baths complex, its principal audience was Roman. The Romans happily appropriated the Celtic goddess Sulis who had originally been worshipped here, identifying her with their own goddess Minerva and after whom they named their new city: *Aquae Sulis*. Around two-thirds of the dedications to Sulis Minerva at Bath were on behalf of Roman citizens serving with the occupying legions. Around 130 'curse tablets' have also been found, the object of which was to record binding spells in quasi-legal terms. Many were related to petty thefts, such as the one Mattingly cites which declares: 'The person who has lifted my bronze vessel is utterly accursed. I give [him] to the temple of Sulis... and let him who has done this spill his own blood into the vessel itself.' In the twelfth century, however, the Welsh chronicler Geoffrey of Monmouth popularised the alternative narrative that the spring had been discovered not by *Legio II* but – countless centuries

---

* 'Avon' is in fact tautological, since the word derives from the Celtic word for 'river'.

earlier – by the ancient British king Bladud; and that it was Bladud, not the Romans, who had built the Baths. Centuries later, after the original Baths had been largely destroyed, buried or built over, local architect John Wood (1704–54) seized on this story, deliberately ignoring any role the Romans might have played in their creation and instead emphasising that the city was actually an authentically British invention. Wood's heroes were not Plautius' cohorts but Bladud, the flying king who had created Stonehenge, and his Druidic people.

Wood anchored ancient Bath not to the Roman occupation but to a decidedly bizarre and eccentric vision of Britishness. Accordingly, the stone frieze of the elegant Circus that he designed for the centre of Bath, and which was completed in 1754, is covered with symbols of the supposed Druidic faith – oak leaves, the moon, the sun – and of Freemasonry, then so prevalent in Georgian Britain, which Wood understood to have evolved from ancient British foundations. In addition, the dimensions and the number of houses in the new Circus were directly based on those of the legendary stone circle at Stonehenge, which Wood believed Bladud and his Druids had built. Seen through the prism of British Freemasonry of the mid-eighteenth century, Wood's new Circus became the Freemasons' sun, his Royal Crescent their moon, and Queen Square and Gay Street a Masonic key.

Bath historian Dr Amy Frost has observed that 'Wood was a man whose mind was constantly in motion, filling his thoughts with new ideas, educating himself with different theories and facts, adapting his ideas accordingly and ultimately producing the outpouring of these ideas in stone'. There is no surviving Wood masterplan for Bath, but we presume that he had one – and that he intended to use his Palladian architecture to signal the glories of Bladud's Bath. More recently, architectural historian Dr Cathryn Spence has written:

> According to Wood, the entire history of architecture hinges on the presence of one individual – King Bladud. Wood believed that Bladud's heroic and sometimes totally impossible deeds led him to translate the art of building from the Temple of Solomon back to ancient Britain, where he founded a city around healing hot springs – the City of Bath.

Wood's interminable and rambling *Essay towards a description of Bath* of 1742 lauds Bladud (for whose existence there is, incidentally, no historical evidence) as a seminal Druidic king of the Britons who could fly, who was present at the building of the second temple of Jerusalem, who taught Pythagoras, who built Stonehenge and, influenced by the ancient Jewish models he had seen at first hand, was wholly responsible for developing architecture in Britain. The Romans, he asserted, had nothing to do with it. Britain's architectural past – from Stonehenge to Bath – was the product of British genius alone.

The context of Wood's assertions goes some way to explain his nationalistic fervour. The era during which Wood wrote his *Essay* was one of growing British confidence and self-importance. By 1748 the French had been defeated in the War of the Austrian Succession – the peace treaty of which, the Treaty of Aix-la-Chapelle, opened up Spanish South America to British traders, provided Britain with new colonial gains and bound Louis XV to eject the Jacobite pretender to the British throne, Prince Charles ('Bonnie Prince Charlie'), from his territories, thus neutering the Jacobite threat once and for all. For the first time since 1688, Britain no longer feared the prospect of a French invasion supporting a Catholic claimant to the throne.

The 1740s was also the decade of truly 'British' music such as Thomas Arne's 'Rule, Britannia!' and of Handel's *Messiah*, the last of which was first performed in the year of Wood's *Essay*. In the visual arts, British patrons were escaping from the cultural cringe that, twenty years before, had seen them aping the artistic and architectural precedents of sixteenth-century Italy. Now, in architects such as John Wood and painters such as William Hogarth – whose astonishing work *The Gate of Calais* of 1748 (popularly known, after the celebrated song of 1735, as *O, The Roast Beef of Old England!*) neatly set the nationalistic agenda for a century and a half – the nation boasted a new generation of cultural figures who no longer looked to France or Italy for their stylistic cues.

Wood's elaborate story of Bath's creation was thus a product of its age: a call for a new definition of nationhood, for recognition for a people whose culture and lifestyle were not forged by Roman (or indeed Norman) invaders but by the 'ancient British' – whom, we now know, were just as much 'incomers' to the British Isles as were the Romans.

Using sixteenth- and seventeenth-century sources such as William Camden's *Britannia* of 1586 – the first serious attempt at a history of Roman Britain – and Michael Drayton's mammoth historical poem *Poly-Olbion* of 1613, Wood traced the ancient kings of Britain back beyond ancient Rome to the mythical city of Troy. Daringly, he charted their origin to the descendants of the legendary Aeneas, who (Homer tells us) had fled Troy after its capture and sacking by Agamemnon's Greeks. In Wood's narrative it was Aeneas' great-grandson, Brutus, who founded the city of 'New Troy'. This was not, as

△ *The surround to the King's Bath was built by Thomas Baldwin after 1784 and, following Baldwin's disgrace and fall, completed by John Palmer in 1789.*

earlier British writers had wrongly alleged, London, but, Wood insisted, Bath.

In Wood's fanciful account it was thus not the Romans but the ancient Britons who had discovered Bath, many centuries before the Claudian invasion. And it was Brutus' descendant Bladud – not Plautius' *Legio II* – who had built a temple over Bath's hot springs. This temple, he confidently asserted, was dedicated to the Druidic version of the sun god Belin – an equivalent to the Romans' Apollo – and not Sulis Minerva. In his bizarre yet self-assured *Essay*, Wood transformed this anecdote into a remarkably precise narrative, by which Bladud built Bath's shrine in 483 BC and ruled over the city as a sort of priest-king, attracting many Athenian émigrés when that city was wrecked in 480 BC during the Persian Wars.

Bladud's legend would remain a powerful one right down to the eighteenth century. A medieval statue of the colourful king still survives in a niche in the King's Bath in the Baths complex; dated 1699, it is actually much older and may even predate the fanciful accounts of Bladud's life by fifteenth-century chronicler John Harding. (Thomas Johnson's 1675 view of the King's

Bath shows the statue already in place there.) Indeed, the legend of Bladud of Bath goes much further back in time. A 'Bleydiud', meaning 'wolf-lord', is first mentioned as the son of Caractacus in tenth-century documents now in the Harleian Collection of manuscripts in the British Library. The Welsh cleric-historian and author of the magisterial *History of the Kings of Britain* of the 1130s, Geoffrey of Monmouth (*c*.1100–*c*.1154), embroidered this story, declaring that Bladud was the son of the king Rud Hud Hudibras, founder of the cities of Canterbury and Winchester and the tenth ruler in line from the first British king, Brutus. Geoffrey also declared that Bladud had ruled at the same time as the prophet Elijah was preaching in Israel, i.e. in the ninth century BC, and that he was succeeded by his son Leir – subsequently immortalised by William Shakespeare as King Lear.

Six centuries after Geoffrey of Monmouth, John Wood took Geoffrey's tantalising account of Bladud's life and refashioned it into a far grander and more politically charged narrative. To cut a long story short, Wood claimed that, having spent some time in Athens (where he was also known, Wood boldly suggested, as the mythological priest-healer Abaris the Hyperborean), Bladud had contracted leprosy. Returning home to Britain, he was swiftly interned owing to his affliction. He then escaped from his confinement, went into hiding and found a job as a swineherd in the village of Swainswick. While pig-herding incognito in Swainswick, Bladud noticed that his pigs – which, he observed, liked to roll in the warm mud at the bottom of a nearby spring – did not suffer from skin diseases as the other pig herds did. Having wallowed in the spring's mud bath himself, Bladud found that he was magically cured of his leprosy. Now fully restored to health, he reappeared at court, quickly re-established himself as Hudibras' successor, and after his accession founded Bath near the site of the warm spring that had cured him, so that others might also benefit from its paranormal power.

Wood did not stop there, maintaining that Bladud also established a super-natural Druidic cult, whose operation subsequently enabled him to fly after he had handily fashioned a pair of wings for himself. The soaring monarch frequently flew to London, but on one trip he misjudged his landing, hit a wall and broke his neck. He was supposedly buried in London and was succeeded by his son, Leir.

In Wood's eyes, then, the foundation of Bath had nothing to do with the Romans. Even its architecture, he alleged, was pre-Roman: derived by the Druidic Britons directly from the Temple of Jerusalem, which had also served as the inspiration for the Britons' stone circles at Stonehenge, Stanton Drew and elsewhere in the region. Architectural historians Professor Timothy Mowl and Brian Earnshaw have noted that, at the King's Circus:

> [Wood was] deliberately deploying the classical orders to honour the men who he believed had created them: the Prophet Moses and the Jewish architects of the First and Second Temples of Jerusalem. The circular shape in which he cast them was not a reference to Rome but to the dimensions and form of the prehistoric stone circles at Stanton Drew and Stonehenge, a commemoration of a glorious native Druidic culture which he believed to have flourished in pre-Roman Bath.

The number of houses in the Circus, thirty, was deliberately equivalent to the number of stones calculated (by Wood, at least) to have formed the outer ring at Stanton Drew's 'Temple of the Moon' *and* at Stonehenge, while the dimensions of the Circus were based on the diameter of the same two monuments, i.e. sixty cubits (roughly 27 metres).

Wood constantly stressed the British, as opposed to the classical, heritage of the city and its Baths. As already noted, many of the decorations (metopes) which adorned the frieze at the Circus were not traditional classical motifs, taken from Roman or Renaissance sources, but ancient British and Druidic symbols, most of which he appears to have culled from George Wither's obscure guide of 1635, *Emblemes*, which the author appears to have 'borrowed' from an earlier Dutch title of 1611 and linked with some of his own mediocre doggerel. Thus the 'Roman' Circus (which decades of Bath tour guides had declared had been based on the Colosseum in Rome) was bedecked not with the usual classical designs but by Masonic devices, supposedly derived from the ancient Druidic practice – in particular the suns and moons of the ancient British temples at *Aquae Sulis* (the temple of the sun) and Stanton Drew (the moon). If anyone missed the significance of this carved thesis, it was rammed home by the circular form of the Circus itself, reproducing that of a sun temple, and the complementary crescent moon form of the Royal Crescent, planned by Wood and completed by his son John Wood the Younger (1728–82) in 1767–74.

Myth and reality

In truth, of course, Wood's incredible Celtic saga was pure fiction. The Baths complex was originally built, as we now know, not by the native British many centuries BC but by the occupying Romans in the second half of the first century. And its effect on Romans and British alike must have been staggering.

The original Great Bath was an immense structure for the time: 25 metres by 12 metres, and 1.5 metres deep, it would have been the biggest building ever seen by most of its Roman and Romano-British visitors. Supported on long wooden piles driven into the ground around the hot springs, it was made of local Bath limestone ashlar, its walls topped with Roman-style roofs of ceramic tiles and its courts and terraces asphalted and paved with stone. Nothing like it had ever been seen before in Britain. The stone bath had stepped sides, lined with sheets of locally mined lead, and around the bath, where now there is an open Tuscan colonnade of the 1890s, was originally a continuous arcade which supported a vast timber barrel vault. In the second century this roof was replaced with a heavier ceramic vault, which required the pillars to be thickened and extended into the waters of the bath itself.

By the tenth century the monks of nearby Bath Abbey – founded in 675 and rebuilt by King Offa of Mercia after 781 – ran what was left of the Roman Baths as a centre for bathing and recuperation. The monks built what later became known as the 'King's Bath', an open-air plunge bath, on Roman foundations over the hot spring at some time during the twelfth century. Here bathers sat happily in niches up to their necks in water. After the abbey was surrendered to the crown in 1539 as part of Henry VIII's ruthless Reformation, however, the abbey church itself faced ruin until rescued by Elizabeth I through a far-sighted initiative of 1574. The Baths were now under council control, and soon became notorious for mixed-gender nude bathing and licentious behaviour. A 'Queen's Bath' (since demolished) was added around 1576 and an adjacent 'Pump Room', to the design of one John Harvey, was opened in 1706, where visitors could actually drink the sulphurous spring water, and soon drinking the waters became an accepted part of any Bath 'cure'. In 1704 social entrepreneur Richard 'Beau' Nash was made the city's 'Master of Ceremonies' and resolved to clean up its act: nude bathing was prohibited in 1737 and genders were segregated in 1753. By the time Nash died in 1761 he had successfully made the city into the most fashionable social meeting place of its day and the nation's first true resort: a chic watering-hole famously visited by the likes of Jane Austen (1775–1817), who set her novels *Northanger Abbey* and *Persuasion* in the heart of Wood's crypto-Masonic terraces.

Wood was never to realise how wrong he had been about the Druidic origin of the Baths. The original fabric of the Roman Baths was only discovered a year after his death, in 1755, when Abbey House, a surviving part of the monastic establishment which had owned the site until its dissolution in 1540, was demolished. In the years after his death John Wood the Elder was, even within Bath, viewed to some extent as a gifted crank – albeit one who had left the city with a splendid architectural legacy – and his eccentric *Essay* was quietly forgotten as an embarrassing aberration. The Baths that Jane Austen would have seen and swum in was, at least above ground level, largely the work of another, equally controversial yet wholly different Georgian architect: the notorious Thomas Baldwin.

The disgrace of Thomas Baldwin

Baldwin owed his meteoric rise, as well as his precipitous fall, to the Bath Improvement Act of 1789. This ground-breaking piece of planning legislation sought to give the complex now revealed as ancient Roman Baths an appropriate architectural setting by protecting the site from encroachment from development and enhancing the remains and their approaches with an appropriately complementary classical context. The man chosen to lead this ambitious and very forward-thinking project – one which anticipated the urban *grands projets* of the nineteenth and twentieth centuries – was Thomas Baldwin, who had only been living in the city for fifteen years but who had, soon after his arrival, inveigled himself into the lucrative position of Bath's City Architect. Like Wood, Baldwin was an accomplished architect and planner. The Bath Improvement Act, like Wood's masonically driven plan for the King's Circus and the Royal Crescent, offered him the perfect opportunity to create a masterpiece of urban planning. It also, however, allowed him to defraud his employers.

Baldwin was a sharp and canny professional whose architectural talent temporarily blinded the city authorities to his pecuniary greed. He ensured that he was appointed as the Architect and Surveyor for the Improvement Commissioners – a post created by the Act – and, having already been given the go-ahead by a compliant administration two years before the Act was passed by parliament, proceeded to design highly impressive, seven-bay colonnades which led both to the ancient Baths and to a new addition, an austerely noble Grand Pump Room of 1790–5 – whose north front would have looked still more imposing had Baldwin's more expensive detached portico been executed, instead of the cheaper version the city insisted upon, with attached columns.

Baldwin's work was much admired. However, almost from the word go he began to siphon off some of the project budget straight into his own pockets. As Baldwin's biographer, Jane Root, has observed: 'he had a history not merely of imprudence, but of deliberate dishonesty.' Overly confident in the trust the City Corporation had blithely reposed in him, between 1790 and 1792 Baldwin refused to provide any financial accounts to the Improvement Commissioners or the Corporation. The Commissioners smelled a rat and, urged on by Baldwin's son-in-law, architect John Palmer, judged in May 1793 that he had been guilty of serious financial speculation. He was dismissed from this and all his other city posts and was arrested – although he was released after only three days, presumably in order to whitewash the city's reputation. In a similar vein, while Baldwin was declared bankrupt in 1794, eight years later an embarrassed City Corporation formally discharged him from his bankruptcy and, astonishingly, allowed him to relaunch his architectural career. Even then Baldwin's influence was not over: the man who replaced him as the architect to the Baths was his ambitious son-in-law, John Palmer, who completed the scheme to Baldwin's designs.

Almost a century later Baldwin's work was extended to take advantage of the hundreds of tourists who were now arriving by train to 'take the waters'. Isambard Kingdom Brunel's remarkable, Tudoresque railway station was built in 1840–1, at Temple Meads, to serve as a grand terminus for the newly opened Great Western Railway (GWR) which now connected Bristol with London. The GWR's first major stop eastbound was Bath Station, which boasted a wooden, all-over 'Tudor' hammerbeam roof spanning both platforms until this splendid feature was unceremoniously removed in 1897 when re-gauging works were taking place.

Defending the Baths in the twentieth century

By the 1880s Bath had become one of the GWR's most popular destinations, and Bath – unlike many of the old spa towns, eclipsed by the new seaside resorts which were now easily accessible by railway – prospered accordingly. In 1889 City Architect and spa specialist Charles Edward Davis (1827–1902) added fine Douche and Massage Baths to Baldwin's complex. Davis had already excavated much of the Roman structures on the site, including the Great Bath, the Circular Bath and the reservoir, and although most of his additions were unnecessarily demolished in 1972 – at a torrid time for Bath, when many of its venerable Georgian terraces were being torn down – a fragment of his work still survives as the west wall of the Great Bath.

In 1894 an architectural competition was held for a new building to house and safeguard the Great Bath, which Davis had left uncovered, and to add a Museum and a Concert Room. Yet the winner was not Davis, the local man. Davis had shot his bolt with his new Queen's Bath of 1886–9, which had met with much local criticism both for its inappropriate design, as many saw it, and for the damage its construction had done to the Roman work that Davis himself had recently revealed. Instead, the competition's first prize went to Scottish architect John McKean Brydon (1840–1901), a former pupil of the celebrated Richard Norman Shaw who had been working, with Shaw and then independently, in London since 1866. However, just as Baldwin's Pump Room had been emasculated by the local council a century earlier in order to save money, so Brydon's impressive and respectful winning scheme was also seriously diluted after its acceptance. The cheaper version that the council insisted upon did include a Concert Room and Brydon's impressive colonnaded approach to the Great Bath but omitted the overall roof for the Great Bath, which was attempting to reproduce the original Roman structure and which would have made the bath more commercially viable. Brydon's colonnade was designed to be as much like the old Roman one as possible and was topped by a pierced parapet which carried life-size statues – carved by another Scot, the sculptor George Lawson (1832–1904) – of the Roman emperors and generals who had exerted a major influence on British history, an illustrious gallery which included Julius Caesar, Claudius, Hadrian and Vespasian.

The Roman Baths continued to prosper until the 1970s, when bathing in the ancient Baths itself finally ceased. Now even the historic Baths site was affected by the mania for demolition which had seized Bath – and much of Britain. The city council's policy was to preserve the city's architectural 'set pieces' at the expense of much of the outlying Georgian fabric of the city, leading to the demolition of streets which had housed the working-class men and women who had made Georgian Bath what it was and which provided such an important context for the city's development and success. This appalling piece of architectural vandalism was forcefully and famously denounced in Adam Fergusson's 1973 polemical book *The Sack of Bath*, which became an instant classic. Nor were the depredations which Fergusson had detailed over by the 1980s, as Fergusson and Tim Mowl's equally incensed sequel of

Drawn & Engraved by Robt Cruikshank

Published by Sherwood & C.º August 1 1825

Public Bathing at Bath, or Stewing Alive.

△ The social whirl at the baths in 1825, Jane Austen was just one of hundreds of fashionable men and women who came here in the late Georgian period for the 'cure'.

1989, *The Sack of Bath – and After*, amply demonstrated. Yet Bath City Council still continued to demolish historic parts of the city well into the 1990s, while persisting in erecting bland and occasionally offensive new additions which would have looked out of place in any old British town, let alone in the historic core of Britain's Georgian jewel – a city of which Jane Austen famously said, 'Oh! Who could ever be tired of Bath?'

Perhaps predictably, the Sack of the Seventies embraced Charles Davis' fine though now rather unfashionably muscular additions to the Baths complex of 1889. In 1976 the nearby Hot Bath, too, was closed, followed by the Victorian Tepid Bath and Beau Street Baths in 1978. At the same time, new development around the Roman Baths site merely served to rob the Baths of much of its Georgian context. To add insult to injury, in 1972 the visually contemptuous new Southgate Shopping Centre and Bus Station, designed by Owen Luder in an uncompromisingly Brutalist idiom, was built only 200 yards away from the Baths. One of Luder's best-known buildings, the Tricorn Shopping Centre in Portsmouth, was once voted one of the ugliest buildings in Britain

41

and was demolished with little protest in 2004. Rather more fondly remembered was the same architect's vast multi-storey car park in Gateshead; in this case, though, only because this was the spot where Michael Caine's Jack Carter threw sleazy businessman Cliff Brumby to his death in the classic British gangster film *Get Carter* of 1971. The Gateshead car park, too, went in 2010, while Luder's Bath complex had been razed – to widespread applause – three years earlier.

Nor was insensitive development the only threat to the complex's survival. In 1969 Professor Barry Cunliffe and the Bath Archaeological Trust had lowered the water levels in the Baths in order to expose more of the Roman fabric, launching a six-year archaeological programme. Yet just three years after this was finished, in October 1978, something nasty was found in the water. A young girl swimming with the Bath Dolphins Club in the newly restored Roman Bath contracted meningitis and died. The Baths complex was immediately closed, and remained so for several years, while tests showed that the water now contained a brain-eating amoeba, *Naegleria fowleri*, which appears to have originated in America but which was only identified in Australia in the 1960s by the pathologist Malcolm Fowler.

When the original Baths were reopened in 1983, swimming was still prohibited, and that is still the case today, but it is permitted in the nearby hot springs of what was once the Cross Bath. In 1987, the city council's belated recognition of the contribution that the whole of the historic city lends to its Roman and Georgian heritage was rewarded with the bestowal of World Heritage Status for the city centre by UNESCO.

The present-day city of Bath reflects two great eras in British history: Roman and Georgian. As Historic England have noted, the Roman complex makes 'a significant contribution to the understanding and appreciation of Roman social and religious society', while the eighteenth-century redevelopment of the city by the Woods, father and son, Thomas Baldwin and others 'is a unique combination of outstanding urban architecture, spatial arrangement, and social history':

> Bath exemplifies the main themes of the 18th century neoclassical city; the monumentalisation of ordinary houses, the integration of landscape and town, and the creation and interlinking of urban spaces, designed and developed as a response to the growing popularity of Bath as a society and spa destination and to provide an appropriate picturesque setting

and facilities for the cure takers and social visitors.

While John Wood the Elder's attempt to brand the city as a creation of the ancient Britons never gained traction, his replanning of the ancient city influenced architecture throughout Britain and beyond. After Wood's death in 1754, as we have seen, the Baths became one of the country's most fashionable social resorts, attracting artists as celebrated as Thomas Gainsborough and Jane Austen. Today the Baths is once again accepted and celebrated worldwide as a symbol of British history and British taste – as appropriately epitomised by the city's starring role in Netflix's TV series *Bridgerton*, a fittingly bizarre mash-up of Georgian culture, contemporary pop references and sexual politics of which John Wood, if not Jane Austen, would have surely approved.

3

MUCKING VILLAGE, ESSEX

BEGUN C. AD 500

Settling with the Saxons

By the dawn of the fifth century AD the Roman occupiers of Britannia had been living happily alongside the native British for over 300 years. By now, though, Romanised Britons increasingly realised that they would soon have to cope on their own. In December 406 the ambitious Roman general Flavius Claudius Constantinus, who was stationed in Britain and was soon to be acclaimed by his British legions as Emperor Constantine III (and reluctantly endorsed as such by Rome in 408), crossed to Boulogne (*Bononia*) with the last of the army units stationed in Britain – troops who had recently mutinied after remaining unpaid for some time. His aims were twofold: to confront a new invasion of Gaul by a confederation of Germanic tribes and to establish his imperial bid by force. In the event, though, neither Constantine nor his legions ever returned to Britain. Constantine himself was captured and beheaded by a rival Roman general in 411, while, a year earlier, Constantine's rival and (briefly) co-emperor, Honorius, wrote a general letter to the British administrators telling them that the Roman empire could no longer help them to resist foreign incursions and that they should henceforward look to their own defence.

△ *The English historian Bede, a monk at the monastery of Wearmouth-Jarrow, remains one of our principal sources for the development of early Saxon England. We have no idea how he looked, though; this is a wholly conjectural portrait.*

After the disappearance of Constantine's troops, and seemingly helpless in the face of armed attack, Romano-British leaders decided to enlist Anglo-Saxon mercenaries from across the North Sea to help them fight off the Pictish raiders from the north. These mercenaries were largely Angles, Saxons, Jutes and Frisians (collectively called 'Anglo-Saxons' and simply 'Saxons' by modern-day historians), and came from the flat, monotonous landscapes of present-day north Germany, west Holland and Denmark. And they liked what they saw.

46

The arrival of the Anglo-Saxons

The origins of the Anglo-Saxon peoples who settled in Britain are still uncertain. In his landmark *Ecclesiastical History of the English People*, completed in around 731 and for centuries one of the principal sources for Anglo-Saxon historiography, the middle-Saxon Tyneside monk-historian Bede (*c*.673–735) was very precise, if at the same time rather confusing, about the Saxons' background and destinations:

> They came from three very powerful nations of the Germans; that is, from the Saxones, Angli and Iutae. Of the stock of the Iutae are the Cantuarii and Uictuarii; that is, the race which holds the Isle of Wight... From the Saxones; that is, from the country now called the land of the Old Saxons, came the East Saxons, South Saxons, and West Saxons. From the Angli; that is, from the country called Angulus, which is said to have lain deserted from that time to this between the country of the Iutae and Saxones, are sprung the east Angles, Middle Angles, the whole Northumbrian race – that is, the people living to the north of the river Humber – and the other peoples of the Angli.

So that's all cleared up, then. In fact, as the celebrated historian Sir Frank Stenton observed, Bede over-emphasised the distinction between these Germanic peoples. What we do know is that by the end of the fifth century Germanic raiders were attacking eastern Britain via both the Thames estuary and the Wash, with a view not just to plundering the comfortable British communities they encountered but also to gaining a foothold in this green and pleasant land.

From the time the last Romans departed the British paid their German mercenaries not just in money but also, when money was scarce, in land. This policy predictably proved a dangerous hostage to fortune. In about 442 the Anglo-Saxon mercenaries mutinied, apparently because they had not been paid for some time, sparking fifty years of fighting between the Germans and their British hosts. This in turn prompted a large number of British families to emigrate to the more peaceful environments of Brittany and Galicia (originally called *Britonia* after its British settlers) in modern-day Spain. The conflict was temporarily halted by a major British victory of the Battle of Mount Badon, which may have occurred at any time between 493 and 516; but by the end of the sixth century the Saxons and their Germanic cousins the Frisians, Anglians and Jutes (tribes which all became homogenised in Anglo-Saxon England, so we shall simply call them all 'Saxons' from now on) had seized control of most of eastern England, leaving the Britons with just modern-day Devon and Cornwall, Wales, north-west England and south-west and northern Scotland.

Re-evaluating the Saxons

Whether the arrival of the Anglo-Saxons in Britain was peaceful or violent, sudden or gradual, is still being argued. The traditional view was based on Bede, whose *Ecclesiastical History of the English People* spoke of the Britons being slaughtered by the Saxon invaders or being forced into 'perpetual servitude'. This in turn encouraged a narrative which depicted a vicious struggle between soft, unmilitary Romano-Britons and hardened Saxon warriors that plunged Britain into what were long called the 'Dark Ages'.

However, more recent assessments, based on archaeological investigations at sites such as Mucking in Essex, were that, while certain Saxon incursions may not have been welcomed and were fiercely resisted, in some areas the transition was peaceable. Saxons joined and modified existing Romano-British communities much as Roman soldiers had been accepted into British families four or more centuries earlier. Dr Heinrich Härke, formerly of Reading University, suggested that in many places the two races happily co-existed – although he concludes that, while it was possible for Romanised Britons to become rich freemen in Anglo-Saxon society (rather than Bede's vision of perpetual slaves), they seemed to be given a lower status than that of their Anglo-Saxon neighbours. Even the British historian-monk Gildas (*c*.500–*c*.570), who dolefully recorded the Britons' internal quarrels in his uncompromising polemic *De Excidio et Conquestu Britanniae*, admitted that the fifty years that followed the Battle of Mount Badon in *c*.500 were a time of comparative peace and prosperity.

By the middle of the seventh century, Saxon England had settled down into a hierarchy of kingdoms and sub-kingdoms based around the 'big four' statelets of East Anglia, Mercia, Northumbria and Wessex. Each of these big kingdoms exercised sway over the others for a time, at least until Wessex incorporated them all into the first English kingdom in 829. After 616 the most powerful of the Saxon state monarchs – subsequently titled a *bretwalda* or 'Britain-ruler', the first suzerain of Britain since the days of Roman empire –

was King Rædwald of East Anglia (reigned *c*.597–*c*.624). Rædwald appears to have acted as kingmaker for the newly unified state of Northumbria, converted himself and his kingdom to Christianity (although he continued to worship the pagan Germanic gods, too, just in case) and founded the international port of Ipswich. Rædwald may also be the occupant of the sumptuous ship burial at Sutton Hoo in Suffolk, whose discovery in 1939 was highlighted in the 2021 film *The Dig*. The richness and magnificence of the findings, all originally held in a large, 27-metre-long ship (although today the discoveries are mostly to be found in the British Museum in London), certainly suggest that it was the burial site of a great king. Gold objects were found in profusion, while one object may be a royal sceptre befitting an Anglo-Saxon *bretwalda*. Raedwald suffered from a bad press for centuries, having been excoriated by Bede for his equivocal attitude to Christianity, but if it was indeed he who was buried at Sutton Hoo then by 624 the English certainly had come of age as one of the first European races to weld some sort of unity out of the ruins of the Roman empire.

In the last fifty years we have learned far more about these early Saxons. Far from being the brutal, backward aggressors of Georgian and Victorian historiography, they appear to have been domesticated settlers who were cultured, family-oriented and for the most part lived contentedly alongside their British neighbours.

The Grubenhäuser

Perhaps the most convincing proof of the civilised lifestyles of the early Saxons came with the archaeological discoveries made at Mucking, where more than 200 Saxon 'pit homes' (*Grubenhäuser*) were discovered by pioneering archaeologist Margaret Jones in the years after 1965, in what still remains the largest excavation site ever worked in Britain. These homes defined a new sense of 'Englishness' and community as the epicentre of Saxon life: the place where families lived with their livestock and where they entertained, crafted, cooked and told stories.

In contrast to the well-publicised finds of King Rædwald's possible burial site at Sutton Hoo in Suffolk, the Mucking dig, further south in Essex, provided significant information about living and working conditions for everyday people from the fifth to seventh centuries – not kings or nobles but ordinary families.

49

Mucking was – and remains – a small settlement on the coast of Essex, at the point where the Thames estuary narrows, between Canvey Island to the east and what became the Saxon port of Tilbury to the west. It occupies a highly strategic position: looking out across the Thames to Cliffe, another key Saxon foothold on the Hoo peninsula in Kent, with an excellent vista of the Thames estuary as it straightens out in its last rush to the North Sea. Mucking was thus well placed to observe all shipping entering or leaving the estuary. It may have taken its name from the first headman, Mucca, with 'Mucking' describing either Mucca's home or his family. By the nineteenth century it was a thriving village, complete with a church, a large rectory and shops. Today, though, it has shrunk to its middle-Saxon size of around a hundred inhabitants. Nevertheless, it remains celebrated for the much-publicised archaeological dig which took place here in the 1960s and did so much to challenge established myths about the Saxons and of the supposed origins of 'Englishness'.

In its day the Mucking excavation became perhaps the most celebrated British archaeological project of the century. During the very dry summer of 1959, the Director of Aerial Photography at Cambridge University noted crop marks showing through the barley fields above the Saxon village where extensive gravel extraction was about to begin. It was not until 1965, however, with the expansion of Hoveringham's gravel workings, that the Ancient Monuments Branch of the Department of the Environment, supported by the local council, Thurrock Museum and the British Museum, finally commissioned an archaeological investigation of the site, which was to be led by Margaret Jones.

Margaret Jones and the Mucking dig

The subsequent dig was huge and lasted for fourteen years. More than 3,000 students from across the world came to enlist, living in tents during the summer and old caravans and sheds during the winter. As Mike Pitts wrote in his *Guardian* obituary of the excavation's leader, Margaret Jones:

> The conditions were tough: accommodation ranged from your own tent to leaking huts; food was the cheapest line from the cash and carry, creatively supplemented with wild gleanings (I once asked the cook what was for supper, to learn she had spent her afternoon removing, as instructed, mouse-droppings from a sack of rice); and entertainment consisted of a

△ *Archaeologist Margaret Jones at Mucking.*

night-time drive round one of the uncannily-automated oil-refining stations along the coast.

Margaret Jones (1916–2001) was a formidable figure. Many were intimidated by 'Mrs. Margaret U Jones', as she habitually signed herself, and the time-worn euphemism that 'she did not suffer fools gladly' was frequently applied to her. (When she worked at the Ministry of Works in London her nickname had been 'Boadicea'.) Jones was not a formally trained archaeologist, a factor which

51

prompted many an academic to disparage her work, then and now. During the Second World War she had worked as a postal censor and after 1945 she and her husband, Tom, ran a photography business in Birmingham, with Margaret selling Tom's photographs. Nevertheless, her attitude to excavation – and in particular the immense project at Mucking – was impeccably professional. As her obituarist wrote: 'She bridged the eras of amateur and modern institutional archaeology; through dogged salvage excavation on a grand scale, saving remains before sites were disturbed, her influence was quiet but profound.'

Margaret's husband, Tom, was very much in her shadow – as was everyone else. He officially served as the site's photographer, but basically did whatever he was told. The Joneses lived in a small caravan, from where Margaret directed their huge but ever-changing volunteer workforce all year round, even in the most atrocious weather. As Pitts noted, 'Living among the graves and houses of hundreds of prehistoric, Roman and, especially, Anglo-Saxon villagers, Margaret could not see the point of spending months in an office while large chunks of her site vanished, unrecorded, into the gravel graders. So she continued to dig.' Even as the rain and snow swirled around her caravan and the money ran out once again. The excavation continued through the winter, in contravention of the custom that archaeological digs were only staged in the summer. The need to stay ahead of the gravel extraction sometimes meant softening the frozen ground with a blow torch in the depths of winter. And everyone who worked at Mucking recalled the windswept site, the cold, the basic living conditions, the ragged site dog, Reject, and even the time when Tom Jones scavenged hundreds of pounds of bananas from the Tilbury Docks and everyone lived on them for days on end.

When it was finally completed in 1978, the excavation covered 44 acres and had recorded 44,000 archaeological features, from Beaker burials of c.2,500 BC to a Roman villa and cemetery and, most importantly, one of the most significant Anglo-Saxon settlements ever discovered in Britain. As the *Independent* later observed, 'for a generation of respectable middle-aged archaeologists... to have dug with Margaret Jones at Mucking remains a badge of honour'.

Jones's work at Mucking helped both to professionalise and to raise the profile of archaeology. In 1973 she helped to found the campaign group Rescue, which lobbied for increased government funding for rescue archaeology of the sort she had pioneered at Mucking. This initiative was successful, its messages ultimately enshrined in the pages of the government's official *Planning Policy Guidance Note 16* of 1991.

Academic archaeologists subsequently criticised Jones's work at Mucking as one of the prime examples of 'excavation without publication', given that she only disseminated a single, short paper on the results of her trial excavations in 1965. Jones sensibly argued that, as the site was being constantly threatened by the gravel extraction, she simply could not afford to take time out for the lengthy process of writing up, editing and publishing. It was only long after the project was completed in 1978 that the final, detailed publication of the work at Mucking saw the light of day.

Jones and her considerable team of freelance archaeologists and volunteers made countless discoveries. The site dated back to the Neolithic period, i.e. around 10,000–5,000 BC. By the sixth century BC there were two small, circular hill forts there, one facing the river, presumably to guard against foreign attackers, and one overlooking Mucking Creek, possibly to deter local incursions. By the time of the Roman occupation the site included more than 100 round houses, Romano-British cemeteries and evidence of livestock farming. Most importantly, however, was the early Saxon settlement of what is now called Mucking Village: more than 200 sunken houses, 12 large halls and two cemeteries, one of which contained nearly 800 burials. Nothing in British archaeology is comparable to Mucking, with an estimated 44,000 features in total, including more than 400 structures and 1,145 burials.

The 200 or so buildings that were excavated – variously called pit houses, grubhouses, or *Grubenhäuser*, after their German origin (*Grube* means a pit) – were revelatory. This type of wooden, roofed hall with supporting posts at the corners, a centrally located entrance, a prominent hearth and a sunken floor in the middle was built in many parts of northern Europe between the fifth and seventh centuries; indeed, the type is still found today in many cultures, such as the indigenous peoples of the American Southwest. They were first identified in Britain in 1921, by the archaeologist E. T. Leeds during his excavation of a site at Sutton Courtenay in Oxfordshire. Their discovery disproved the long-held thory that the early Saxons had ignored the civilised towns and villas of the Romans to eke out a meagre existence in small, squalid huts. However, they had never been found with such frequency as at Mucking, where a whole village community was uncovered.

Grubenhäuser were multi-purpose: they could act as family homes, as stores for food or as centres of communal activity, from storytelling to dancing. They were of simple construction that could easily be dismantled – a form of building which has given rise, as we shall see, to theories about constant

△ *The Mucking dig, photographed sometime in the 1970s.*

migration. Those at Mucking were around 4 metres long and 3 metres wide, and were built over a pit, their gabled roof supported by two stout wooden posts. Some archaeologists have suggested that a suspended wooden floor lay over the pit and that the cavity beneath was used for storage or to control dampness. Inside was often a hearth, suggesting that the idea of a suspended floor is indeed correct.

The Mucking settlements changed our perceptions of early Saxon civilisation. The fact that the main focus of the settlement shifted northwards during the seventh century, and that the village was totally abandoned soon afterwards, has given credence to the theory that the early Saxons were to some extent nomadic, wandering across the English landscape as circumstances changed and threats and opportunities appeared. There was, it seems, no attempt by these settlers to revive or recreate the Romans' substantial urban centres. Instead, they simply ignored them, occasionally using their ruins as battlegrounds or as sources of building materials.

In addition, it has been frequently pointed out by archaeologists that all the houses and burials at Mucking were of a similar type, suggesting a markedly egalitarian community which regarded everyone as the same, no matter how wealthy or important they were. As Max Adams has written, these structures represent 'an architecture of very limited privacy and of external social equality, entirely compatible with the undifferentiated special ranking apparent in cremation cemeteries'.

There is no clear evidence for high-status or low-status dwellings before the late sixth century at the earliest. Status in early Saxon communities does not appear to have been expressed by the ability to support large numbers of people in a single household, as became the norm in the Middle Ages. This actually seems to bear out some of the strands in eighteenth- and nineteenth-century literature and historiography, which harked back to the Saxon era as one of relatively classlessness: an idyllic English democracy which was brought to a brusque and brutal end by the Normans' forcible introduction of the rigidly hierarchical and tyrannical feudal system.

The Norman Yoke

The concept of the Saxons as egalitarian democrats, whose individual liberties and democratic institutions were ruthlessly suppressed by the imposition of Norman feudalism after 1066, a development which was derisively summarised as the 'Norman Yoke', originally surfaced during the English Revolution of the 1640s. The concept seems to have been first employed in a polemic of 1642, *The Mirror of Justices* (which purported to be a work of a fourteenth-century lawyer but was palpably a fake), and it was subsequently expanded in the writings of contemporary radicals such as Gerard Winstanley and his Digger followers. Winstanley's *The True Levellers Standard Advanced* of 1649 declared:

> Seeing the common people of England by joynt consent of person and purse have caste out Charles our Norman oppressor, wee have by this victory recovered ourselves from under his Norman yoake... O what mighty Delusion, do you, who are the powers of England live in! That while you pretend to throw down that Norman yoke, and Babylonish power, and have promised to make the groaning people of England a Free People; yet you still lift up that Norman yoke, and slavish Tyranny, and holds the People as much in bondage, as the Bastard Conquerour himself, and his Councel of War.

The vision of a 'Norman Yoke' which crushed indigenous Saxon liberties gained further credence following the toppling of King James II in the 'Glorious Revolution' of 1688, during which the king was compared to the Normans and his subjects to the freedom-loving Saxons. In the following century, it was cited by the polemicist and philosopher Thomas Paine (1737–1809) in England, comparing George III's oppressive governments with the regimes of the conquering Normans, and it was also cited by Thomas Jefferson in America. Sharon Turner's *History of the Anglo-Saxons* of 1799 was the first focused attempt to dispel the Norman 'falsehood' that the Saxons had been violent barbarians, while Sir Walter Scott's enormously successful novel *Ivanhoe* of 1819 also cast the egalitarian if doomed Saxons as the founders of Britain's democratic English traditions. As Chris Worth of Monash University has noted, *Ivanhoe* is 'a memorable narrative of a national myth, the synthesis of England from Norman and Saxon peoples'.

> It contributed to the making and circulation of the analogous idea of a 'British' nation during the imperial era. Highly popular in Europe, it provided a paradigm for imagining a synthetic nation bringing apparently opposed interests together... Scott's use of the Robin Hood legend demonstrates how he adapted his material: the first writer to link Robin Hood to a surviving Saxon resistance, Scott appears to combat Ritson's account of Robin as radical folk-hero by presenting him as a figure co-operating in a natural community linking all levels of society in resistance to that which is foreign, cosmopolitan, without stake in the land.

By the middle of the eighteenth century this popular idea had blossomed into the cult of the late Saxon king Alfred the Great (848–899), whom historians such as Simon Keynes, and more recently Joanne Parker and Oliver Cox, have come to regard as a powerful symbol of the English nation's perception of itself: as the incarnation and defender of the nation's egalitarian values and liberties. The result was, as Parker has noted, that by the Regency era 'it was preferable to celebrate modern English culture, institutions and ethnicity as essentially Saxon', and that historians and politicians alike boasted that the roots of national liberty lay in the Saxon era. At the turn of the century the 11th Duke of Norfolk remodelled his ancestral seat of Arundel Castle in Sussex to 'provide a narrative in stone' celebrating what were supposed to be ancient Saxon virtues. Historian Dr Oliver Cox has written of Arundel:

The mixed constitution of king and parliament, as created by the Glorious Revolution, was not a recent invention but was a Teutonic creation brought over by the Saxons from Northern Europe. Ancient liberties, including trial by jury, frequent parliaments and common law, were codified by King Alfred but came under threat from the 'Norman Yoke'. Liberty could only be maintained through the even balance between the 'prerogatives' of the sovereign and the 'privileges' of the people. Accordingly, the signing of Magna Carta was crucial as an affirmation of both common law over feudal law and the privileges of the people over the prerogatives of kings.

The idealisation and idolisation of 'Saxon' liberties continued throughout the Victorian era. It was his enthusiasm for Saxon 'democracy' which prompted Charles Kingsley to shape his highly successful novel of 1866, *Hereward the Wake*, as a parable of traditional liberties destroyed in the vein of Scott's *Ivanhoe*. Influential historian Thomas Carlyle (1795–1881), however, was having none of this: he derided fashionable Saxonism, preferring to hymn the order and civilised habits the Normans had brought to England.

Carlyle notwithstanding, by the end of the nineteenth century commentators were linking British identity with that of the United States, then emerging as a world power, under the catch-all term of the 'Anglo-Saxon race' – a phrase still in use, albeit largely pejoratively, by the French today. In a surprising repudiation of the events of 1066, Queen Victoria was, by the time of her Diamond Jubilee of 1897, being hailed as the reincarnation of Saxon values 'after many years of Norman usurpation'. By 1892, as Parker points out, the notion of Britain's royal family as Saxon was underscored by the commissioning of a commemorative statue for St George's Chapel at Windsor Castle which 'presented Victoria as a Saxon queen and Albert as a ninth-century king making his last farewell'.

Mucking about in Essex

Mucking's findings have shed much light on the nature of the arrival of the Saxons in Britain. As we have seen, it was built on a site commanding an important strategic position in the lower Thames region. Accordingly, some have argued that it may have functioned as a meeting place and market for surrounding areas on both sides of the Thames. The site also allowed ready access to both seasonal pastures for cattle grazing and tidal creeks for salt-

△ *Re-creation of a* Grubenhaus *at Jarrow Hall, north-east England.*

making – both fundamental occupations for both Romans and Saxons. However, it was also very vulnerable to both raiders and the weather. Some archaeologists have cited the poor quality of soil at Mucking to suggest that arriving Saxons were forced by the local Romano-British inhabitants to settle on the poorest agricultural land in an area which they recognised was dangerously exposed – although others have argued it could have been an important 'early warning' installation to warn those in Colchester or London of ominous vessels sailing up the river. Related theories posited that Mucking was a settlement of Germanic mercenaries, engaged by the British, in Max Adams's words, 'to protect London and its hinterland against raiders from the same Germanic homeland'.

Crucially, the discovery of a Roman military buckle in a Saxon grave at Mucking, together with Romano-British pottery in some of the Saxon homes, suggests there was some continuity between the Romanised British and Saxon settlements (or indeed that some of these sites were simply 'borrowed' from the Britons). There were some Roman burials of the early third century there, in cemeteries later used by the Saxons, implying a good deal of continuity between the Romano-British and Saxon inhabitants. (In 2004 Roger Massey-Ryan produced a very plausible and fetching watercolour of how a Roman villa at Mucking might have looked.) Interestingly, though, the Romano-British settlements and cemeteries largely avoided the sites to the west inhabited by the earlier, Iron Age settlers there.

However, more recent research suggests not just that Mucking's *Grubenhäuser* were far larger than their sunken storage or refuse pits might indicate but that they were *not* designed as communal homes. Some excavated *Grubenhäuser* sites have yielded clay loom weights from a vertically oriented frame loom. This strongly indicates that these particular buildings were used as weaving sheds – as relatively sophisticated centres of domestically scaled industry. The pits below the suspended plank floors would also have been ideal for grain storage – and indeed cereal grains have been found in voids and holes of some of the excavated sites. Others appear to have been used to house animals. More significantly, some have given up human bones, animal remains and pottery shards, alongside debris from the building itself – 'closure deposits' which intimate that, when the structure was dismantled, a ritual closure feast was followed by community burials.

Even if the *Grubenhäuser* were not in fact Saxon homes – the inhabitants of Mucking would have lived in smaller, far less substantial dwellings erected round the periphery of the *Grubenhäuser* – the existence of such an array of sophisticated workshops suggests that Mucking was a self-sufficient community of *c*.100–150 people – a 'self-consciously coherent settlement with a life spanning two centuries', as Max Adams has observed – whose village lives were not much different from those of the Romano-British population with which they mingled.

The vulnerability of the site meant that, during or shortly after the eighth century, the settlement at Mucking was seemingly abandoned – either as part of the community's 'wandering' or forced inland by repeated attacks from the sea. By this time the Danes were raiding the east coast in large numbers. The first Danish raiders appeared in the Thames estuary in 835 and targeted Sheppey, just across the river from Mucking in Kent. From then on their incursions became increasingly regular, with the English seemingly unable to resist them – not helped by the lack of an English navy to challenge the Danish ships while they were at sea (it was King Alfred who finally built an English navy in the 870s) and by the uncoordinated responses from the various Saxon king-doms. English victories were few and far between, and by the 850s a Danish army was wintering in Kent. Finally, in 865 a vast Danish force – jointly led by the eccentrically named Ivar the Boneless – landed on the East Anglian coast north of Mucking and proceeded rapidly inland. Within ten years nearly all of the Saxon kingdoms had fallen to the marauding Danes: Northumbria in 867, East Anglia in 869, and eastern and central Mercia in 874–7. In 878 King Alfred of Wessex, who had retreated into the Somerset marshes to escape the invad-ers, defeated the Danes at the Battle of Edington and forced them to accept a settlement by which the Vikings were confined to East Anglia (including the now-abandoned site of Mucking) and the north.

By the time of the Norman Conquest of 1066 the village of Mucking had been deserted for two and a half centuries. In the Domesday Book of 1068 – an astonishing achievement that is effectively the nation's first census and which tells us much about both the late-Saxon nation and the Normans' imposition of the feudal system – the site was soon being recorded merely as being part of an old field system. The village revived in the Middle Ages and, as we have seen, by Queen Victoria's reign even boasted a sizeable parish church – redun-dant since 1982 and now privately owned.

Today, ancient landscapes such as that at Mucking are at risk not from seaward raids but from urbanisation, agribusiness or gravel extraction. However, gravel quarrying can, as Margaret Jones demonstrated, lead to dis-covery as well as to destruction. The rest of the Mucking site is still out there, challenging the archaeologists of the future to uncover more of our actual past and to challenge accepted myths about our origins.

4

CHEPSTOW CASTLE, GWENT

BEGUN 1067

Romancing the Stone: from Norman fortress to film set

One of the first and most important of the early Noman castles, begun only a year after William the Conqueror's invasion of England, Chepstow was not just the country's first stone-built castle. It was also a highly visible reminder of the military subjugation of the indigenous Welsh, as well as the Saxon English, by the Norman military machine – and, indeed, the subsequent, comprehensive transformation of England, from its language to its field systems, through the Normans' brutal imposition of the feudal system. The castle remained a potent symbol of regional policing until the 1680s. Today, perhaps predictably, it has become an epitome of Heritage Britain as a major tourist destination and as an ideal film location for romantic evocations of Britain's 'Norman' past.

Construction of the castle, located on cliffs above the River Wye, overlooking an important crossing point and a major communications artery, began in 1067 under the direction of the new Norman *seigneur* Lord William

▷ *The ruined façade of Chepstow Castle on its majestic site above the River Wye.*

FitzOsbern (*c*.1030–71), a relative, boyhood friend and close counsellor of William the Conqueror. He had been made Earl of Hereford (or, as more recent scholarship suggests, earl of the Marches region from Shropshire down to Hereford) and was later to be made Earl of Wessex before his untimely death at the Battle of Cassel in 1071.

There had been a large Roman town about five miles away at what is now Caerwent, but no record of occupation at Chepstow until the Normans arrived. William I and FitzOsbern doubtless chose the site not just because of its commanding position above the Wye. Chepstow was, and is, the gateway to South Wales, and of great strategic importance. The Wye itself was the main communications artery between Bristol, Monmouth and the cathedral city of Hereford. Moreover, evidence suggests that the Welsh rulers of the neighbouring kingdom of Gwent – until then wholly independent of the English crown – were on friendly terms with the Normans, and had recently risen against the last Saxon king, Harold II.

Suppressing the Saxons

The defeat of King Harold by the Normans under William the Conqueror in 1066 is one of Britain's best-known historical tales. The 'Normans' were Scandinavian Vikings who had settled in Normandy, on the north coast of France, after 911 and who had converted to Christianity. The penultimate Saxon king, Edward the Confessor, was the son of Emma of Normandy, sister of Duke Richard II of Normandy, and spent much time in the dukedom. As a result, many of his political and clerical appointments were not Saxons but Normans; thus England could have been said to have been at least partly Normanised before 1066.

On Edward's death on 5 January 1066, Harold Godwinson, Earl of Wessex and the most powerful of the Saxon aristocrats (and himself the ethnically diverse child of a Saxon father and Danish mother), ensured that he was swiftly elected by the national council or *Witan*. William, however, maintained that Edward had promised *him* the throne, and that Harold, when in France, had actually agreed to this. To make things even more complicated, King Harald of Norway also claimed the English throne. While Harold was watching the Channel coast with a large army, expecting a Norman invasion at any moment, Harald of Norway invaded East Yorkshire with 15,000 men. Harold sped his army northwards in one of the most spectacular marches of

British history and, taking the Norwegians by surprise, defeated them and killed Harald and the bulk of his army at the Battle of Stamford Bridge. Only twenty-four of the original 300 Norwegian ships were needed to transport the survivors back across the North Sea.

Three days after Stamford Bridge, William finally landed his Norman army on the Sussex coast. By the time Harold's victorious but exhausted army had retraced their long march south they were in no state to fight. In the subsequent battle not only Harold but two of his brothers were killed. (Harold's embittered, exiled brother Tostig had already been killed at Stamford Bridge, fighting for the Norwegians.) Whether or not Harold met his death by an arrow in the eye is still moot: the Bayeux Tapestry, woven after the battle, features the legend 'Here King Harold has been killed' above depictions of a soldier holding an arrow sticking out of his eye and a falling man being hit with a sword.

Following his victory at Hastings, William advanced towards London but found his army unable to take London Bridge. Instead he crossed the River Thames at Wallingford, 30 miles to the west of London, and then moved north-east to Berkhamsted – building castles in both locations. There he received the surrender of most of the English nobles and leading clerics before being crowned by the Archbishop of York at Westminster Abbey on 25 December 1066.

Saxon England did not go down without a fight. Rebellions broke out in the south-west and north of England annually until 1070 – all of which were savagely put down by the Norman forces. Wherever they went, the Normans imposed their order on the subjugated counties through the establishment of a garrison housed in a castle – a building designed both to awe the locals as well as to resist attack. Early wooden fortifications were replaced by durable and seemingly impregnable stone castles as soon as was feasible.

The Norman order

As we have seen, in *Ivanhoe* Walter Scott wove a romantic fantasy about the Saxons' suppression, transposing the undoubted tensions between Saxon and Norman during the last decades of the eleventh century rather improbably to the last years of the twelfth:

> A circumstance which greatly tended to enhance the tyranny of the nobility, and the sufferings of the inferior classes, arose from the consequences of the conquest by Duke William of Normandy. Four generations had not

67

sufficed to blend the hostile blood of the Normans and Anglo-Saxons, or to unite, by a common language and mutual interests, two hostile races, one of which still felt the elation of triumph, while the other groaned under all the consequences of defeat. The power had been completely placed in the hands of the Norman nobility, by the event of the battle of Hastings, and it had been used, as our histories assure us, with no moderate hand. The whole race of Saxon princes and nobles had been extirpated or disinherited, with few or no exceptions; nor were the numbers great who possessed land in the country of their fathers, even as proprietors of the second, or of yet inferior classes. The royal policy had long been to weaken, by every means, legal or illegal, the strength of a part of the population which was justly considered as nourishing the most inveterate antipathy to their victors. All the monarchs of the Norman race had shewn the most marked predilection for their Norman subjects; the laws of the chase, and many others, equally unknown to the milder and more free spirit of the Saxon constitution, had been fixed upon the necks of the subjugated inhabitants, to add weight, as it were, to the feudal chains with which they were loaded. At court, and in the castles of the great nobles, where the pomp and state of a court was emulated, Norman French was the only language employed.

Chepstow Castle was the epitome of Scott's alien castles of the Norman race. No such stone fortresses had ever been seen in Britain before, and they were to prove their military worth both as a deterrent and as a defence for six centuries. Yet, despite Scott's claim that Saxons and Normans were still bitterly divided even by the time of King Richard I, in truth the local population of border English and Welsh areas accommodated themselves to the new order remarkably rapidly. Originally known as 'Estrighoiel', Chepstow Castle's construction encouraged many to build new homes beside its formidable walls – both for their own security and to exploit the trading opportunities which the fortress would spawn. This castle-side settlement quickly developed into a thriving town which was called 'Chepstow', an Anglo-Saxon term meaning an important trading centre. Ironically, by the fourteenth century the Normans' castle had adopted the adjoining town's Old English name, too.

As Chepstow Castle was the physical embodiment of the new Norman order, so its founder was the stereotypical Norman noble. And in William FitzOsbern, King William I had no more loyal or successful lieutenant.

FitzOsbern's rise to prominence in the decades prior to the invasion of England had been swift and spectacular, and by 1066 he had become of the most prominent of Duke William's Norman aristocrats. FitzOsbern had already inherited lands across the breadth of Normandy; now he sought land and power further afield, and as a result was one of the most forceful advocates of the English invasion in 1066. Within three years he was being described as *comes palatii*, 'Count of the Palace', at William's Anglo-Norman court, a title which suggests that he was, by then, effectively the king's deputy. William reposed little trust in his eldest son, Robert, who was an embittered exile in Flanders after 1077 and who received only the Duchy of Normandy on his father's death in 1087. It was FitzOsbern, and not Robert nor any other member of the king's family, who accompanied William on the military expeditions of 1067–70 designed to subjugate the north and the south-west. And it was FitzOsbern who was deputed to ensure that England's crucial border with the small Welsh kingdom of Gwent was secure. In this he and his new castle were wholly successful: thanks to Norman military might, the kingdom of Gwent had ceased to exist by 1091 and for centuries after was called by the English name of 'Monmouthshire' by the Anglo-Normans.*

FitzOsbern, more than any other of the Norman invaders, was the man on whom William relied to keep the English and their Welsh neighbours quiet. In 1069 FitzOsbern was at the royal court at Winchester; later that year he marched north as one of the leaders of the military expedition which successfully recaptured York from the Danes and the local Saxons. During this ruthless and unforgiving campaign much of the city was razed by FitzOsbern's army, presumably on King William's orders, and he himself was installed as castellan – the regional military commander.

FitzOsbern was not just King William's right-hand man. He was also the greatest castle-builder Britain had ever seen – or indeed was to see until King Edward I constructed his mighty chain of castles in North Wales over a century later. FitzOsbern built a chain of fortresses across the Welsh Marches to keep the vanquished Welsh in check: from Wigmore near Ludlow to Chepstow by

---

* The status of Monmouthshire was confirmed in 1542, but thereafter it was a popular subject of debate whether the county was part of England or Wales. This argument was resolved when the 1974 Local Government Act created a new Welsh county named 'Gwent' after the old Welsh kingdom, only for 'Monmouthshire' to reappear when the new county was summarily dissolved in 1996.

the Severn. Yet although the Normans made inroads into south-east Wales, they initially preferred to defend their new English kingdom against major Welsh incursions rather than venture any further west. FitzOsbern's plan was evidently to hold what the Normans already had and to contain the south Welsh princes within their own kingdom.

The Norman castle

Chepstow Castle – and in particular its tall Great Tower, which rose so impos-ingly above the river's bluff – was a highly visible and effective symbol for both Saxons and Welsh of the reach and power of the Norman armies, as well as of the strength and influence of FitzOsbern himself. The fact that the great Norman tower was constructed in stone from the very beginning – as opposed to wood, the material customarily used to establish most other forts and castles of this period – emphasised both Chepstow's importance as a border stronghold and the permanence of Norman occupation.

FitzOsbern's tenure of Chepstow Castle was, however, remarkably short. At the end of 1070 he crossed to Normandy to support King William's queen, Matilda, in her duchy, and as part of his duties there soon found him-self fighting on the Franco-Flemish border. It was here that he met his un-timely death – fighting, once more, for King William. As Turner and Johnson observed, 'FitzOsbern's death at the Battle of Cassel on 20 or 21 February 1071... removed a man who had been of the utmost importance to the Norman Conquest of England.'

William FitzOsbern may have founded Chepstow Castle but his prema-ture death meant that others built it. After FitzOsbern's death in 1071 King William took matters into his own hands and divided the former's inheritance between the oldest son, William de Breteuil, who received FitzOsbern's lands in Normandy, and his younger son, Roger de Breteuil, who was given his father's English lands. Roger chafed at this reduction in status and in 1075 allied with the Norman Earl of Norfolk and the Saxon Earl of Northumberland to rebel against the king while William was away in Normandy. The revolt was swiftly crushed and Roger was imprisoned and stripped of both his earldom and his lands, including Chepstow Castle, all of which reverted to the crown. Following William I's death in 1087 Roger de Breteuil was released by the old king's successor, the duplicitous and quarrelsome William II, but then abruptly executed. With Roger's death the earldom of Hereford became extinct, since

Roger had no legitimate sons. Thirteen years later de Breteuil gained some posthumous revenge when the unpopular William II was killed – most likely assassinated by one of his hunting companions.

Roger de Breteuil's imprisonment and execution did not, however, interrupt the construction of Chepstow Castle. By 1093 the castle was largely complete and was used as a base to overrun the rest of Gwent, a campaign which reached its zenith with the capture and murder at Brecon of the king of the south-western Welsh kingdom of Deheubarth, Rhys ap Tewdwr, ancestor of the Tudor kings of England after 1485. The Welsh had initially supported the Norman subjugation of their Saxon neighbours but now found that they had backed the wrong horse and that their own independence was threatened.

The centrepiece of the new castle at Chepstow was the Great Tower, completed by about 1090 and intended by the Normans as an unmistakeable symbol of strength and wealth. Its first-floor room was unparalleled in either Britain or France: a vast, seven-bay space lined with niches and lit by circular and round-headed windows. The interior was originally plastered and decorated with bands of Roman tiles, possibly as a deliberate reference to the great Roman buildings raised ten centuries earlier at nearby Caerwent and Caerleon. Access to the hall, however, was, for security reasons, only possible via a dog-leg staircase or through a north door – which was only served by temporary wooden stairs to the ground below when demanded by the castle's lord.

Around 1115 the third and most durable of William I's sons, King Henry I, granted Chepstow Castle to Walter FitzRichard de Clare, a powerful baron who had frequently conspired with Henry against his late brother, the ill-fated William Rufus. De Clare's family held the castle until 1189, when it passed to the formidable figure of William Marshal on his marriage to the last de Clare heir, Isabel.

Marshal's inheritance of Chepstow Castle put the fortress firmly back into the limelight. Marshal was a figure whose national significance matched that of William FitzOsbern over a century earlier. Arguably the most important

▷ *The thirteenth-century Marten's Tower, named after the seventeenth-century regicide Henry Marten, who died here in 1680, and the castle's outer gatehouse, built after 1219 by the ill-fated Bigod earls of Norfolk.*

man in Angevin England* after King Henry II and his immediate family, Marshal was *the* man of the age. He was an experienced courtier, soldier and administrator who had supported Henry II and his sons in various campaigns and who had even been on crusade in Palestine for two years. Marshal was also a kingmaker, responsible for the smooth accessions of Richard I in 1189, John in 1199 and the young Henry III in 1216. A mere knight by birth, Marshal had made his fortune from his lucrative royal service – initially with Henry II's fractious son and heir, Prince Henry ('the Young King') until the latter's premature death in 1183, aged only twenty-eight. When Richard I became king on the death of his father, Henry II, in 1189, Marshal was granted permission to marry Isabel de Clare, a union which instantly made him one of the wealthiest and most powerful magnates in the kingdom. His marriage to Isabel bought him not only Chepstow Castle but also extensive lands across the Welsh Marches. Ten years later he was able to add the earldom of Pembroke when it was gifted to him by a grateful King John at the latter's coronation.

During the 1190s, under Marshal's direction Chepstow Castle was substantially enlarged to reflect its national significance, the strategic importance of its location between England and Wales and Marshal's own power and wealth. Marshal added new outer defences, increased the height of the original Norman walls, strengthened the Middle Bailey, enlarged the Upper Bailey – a project which included the provision of a vast rectangular tower, subsequently known as 'Marshal's Tower', complete with fireplaces and a kitchen – and built an impressively large gatehouse, whose size and sophistication were rare for any European fortification of this date, let alone a British castle. The gatehouse was constructed of two massive, linked round towers, a new French fashion of which Marshal could have learned through his many campaigns across the Channel. The gatehouse doors have been dated by dendrochronology to the 1190s and have been hailed as the oldest castle doors in Europe. Their outer faces were covered in iron plates to make them impermeable to battering as well as fire; inside, their latticework decoration features what may be the oldest surviving mortise-and-tenon joints in Britain. (Today the original doors are in storage while replicas guard the castle entrance.)

---

* The Angevin kings of England were those twelfth- and early thirteenth-century monarchs – Henry II, Richard I and John – who were descended from Henry II's father, Geoffrey, Count of Anjou.

Marshal died in 1219, the most famous man in the kingdom as well as one of the richest. Only three years earlier he had crowned a lifetime of achievement by successfully engineering the peaceful and uncontested accession of King John's young son to the throne of England as Henry III, at a time of internal unrest and foreign invasion. His fortress of Chepstow Castle, one of the nation's most effective and sophisticated strongholds, stood as a proud testimony to his influence, authority and affluence. Within thirty years of his death, however, Marshal's legacy had completely evaporated with the death of all of his five sons. Marshal's fourth son, Walter, enjoyed the title of 5th Earl of Pembroke for only four years following the death of his elder brother, Earl Gilbert, at a tournament; Walter himself died of illness in November 1245. Walter's younger and last surviving brother, Anselm, was 6th Earl of Pembroke for only twenty-six days before he, too, died – this time at Chepstow Castle itself. He was only thirty-seven.

The Bigods' castle

This astonishingly rapid reversal of fortunes, which resulted in the sudden extinction of the male line of the all-powerful Marshal family, was later credited by the thirteenth-century monk-historian Matthew Paris to a curse bestowed upon the family in 1218 by the Bishop of Ferns (a small diocese in Co. Wexford in Ireland) as a result of what the locals had viewed as unjustly heavy taxes levied on the bishop's flock by William Marshal. Paris also repeated the (presumably apocryphal) story that the five boys' mother, Countess Isabel, had once tearfully foretold that each of her sons would in turn be holders of the same earldom.

On Anselm's death, the title of Earl of Pembroke went into abeyance. (It was later revived numerous times through the centuries: the current holders of the title, the Herbert family, are of the tenth creation.) Chepstow Castle and the office of Marshal of England passed instead to Roger Bigod, 4th Earl of Norfolk, a vastly wealthy aristocrat whose mother was William Marshal's eldest daughter, Matilda.

As the Marshal line withered and died and Norfolk took possession, work still continued apace on extending and strengthening Chepstow Castle. The early Norman Great Tower was heightened and extended to become one of the most luxurious castle interiors of its day, decorated by virtuoso stone carving and punctuated by large Gothic windows which looked out high above the River Wye. This stone carving was of a quality also found in contemporary decoration at both Llandaff and Gloucester cathedrals, suggesting a common and presumably local hand for all three.

After 1245, the 4th and 5th earls of Norfolk, already very rich men in their own right, were perfectly able to fund ambitious improvements to the castle fabric. The 5th Earl (another Roger Bigod) even used the castle to threaten his monarch, Edward I, when in 1297 he refused to serve at the king's command in Gascony. This was the last time an English subject openly invoked the defence of Magna Carta against the sovereign until the revolution of the 1640s. The 5th Earl, a powerful and proud man, added giant crossbows or 'springalds' to the castle's newly enlarged Great Tower to underline his defiance of Edward's authority. He also chose to live like a king in great luxury, adding a well-lit and sumptuously furnished new range to the castle which he called the 'Gloriette' and which was built by his master mason Ralph Gogun after 1270. The gloriette's main feature was a vast new Great Hall, on the dais of which sat Norfolk's high table. From here, Norfolk, sitting at the head of his luxurious Hall in the depths of the Marches, far from London, presided over his own court, dining from silver and gilt dishes and flanked by colourful Italian silks and paintings of biblical or Arthurian scenes. Only two other contemporary castles in Britain – Corfe in Dorset and Leeds in Kent – boasted gloriettes of such magnificence and size. Here Norfolk was literally king of his own castle.

To complement the gloriette the earl also added a new tower at the south-eastern corner of the Lower Bailey: of semi-circular design and presenting a massive, flat-fronted aspect to the river, its inner elevation was, in a step away from conventional castle design, copiously fenestrated. Inside these windows were yet more lavishly appointed interiors, whose walls were painted in (paint research of 2000 has discovered) a rich scheme of deep yellow ochre and red. Historians have suggested this New Tower, as it was originally called, was used to house important guests in great style. (The feature was later renamed the Marten Tower after its most notorious prisoner, the regicide Henry Marten, who was lodged here with his common-law wife for twelve years before his death in 1680.) At the same time Norfolk added another storey to the Great Tower, which he appears to have used as a ceremonial and administrative centre as well as an armoury and possibly also as a chapel.

As with the lurid tales of the sad fates of the children of William FitzOsbern and William Marshal, however, at Chepstow Castle pride always seemed to precipitate a fall. By 1302 the tables had turned and the 5th Earl of

Norfolk, unwell and childless, saw no alternative but to surrender his castle to the king if he was to disinherit his hated brother. As a result, when the earl died four years later, the castle passed once more to the crown and the earldom of Norfolk – as the FitzOsbern earldom of Hereford and the Marshal earldom of Pembroke before it – became extinct.

A century later Chepstow Castle was still a formidable deterrent. In 1400 the Welsh independence fighter Owain Glyndŵr, the last native Welshman to bear the title Prince of Wales, raised much of Wales against the English monarch Henry IV. In 1403 his army captured nearby Newport Castle and defeated a royal force led by Henry IV himself at the Battle of Stalling Down. However, Chepstow Castle, hastily garrisoned with twenty men-at-arms and sixty archers, was deemed too tough a nut to crack, and was carefully avoided by Glyndŵr's army. The brave but doomed prince was finally driven further back into Wales by the English until he escaped from the siege of Harlech Castle disguised as an old man. Glyndŵr died, in hiding in mid-Wales, in 1415.

Decline and fall

In the decades after the defeat of Glyndŵr's army, the development of artillery and the pacification of Wales meant that Chepstow Castle's defensive significance gradually declined. However, the castle was besieged by the parliamentarians twice in the English Civil War: in 1645 and again in 1648. Much of Wales had declared for Charles I at the outbreak of hostilities in 1642, and Harlech Castle was the last royalist stronghold to surrender, in March 1647. When war broke out again in May 1648, Chepstow Castle became one of the flashpoints of the renewed struggle. The local royalist landowner Sir Nicholas Kemeys held the castle for the king, refusing General Oliver Cromwell's demand that he surrender to parliamentary forces. Cromwell occupied the town of Chepstow on 11 May and directed Colonel Isaac Ewer to besiege the castle. Ewer's modern artillery made short work of the castle's imposing stone walls and on 25 May the castle was stormed. Kemeys was killed in the subsequent fighting, along with many of his men. Only 120 royalists survived; one of these was Kemeys's son, Charles, the 2nd baronet, who was spared but was heavily fined and exiled for two years.

The storming of Chepstow Castle in 1648 demonstrated that medieval fortifications, however redoubtable and intimidating they may look, were of little use in the age of artillery. However, the castle still had a role to play:

77

this time as a barracks and a political prison. (It was in the latter capacity that the castle hosted Henry Marten after 1668.) Nevertheless, on the accession of King James II in 1685 the castle's garrison was disbanded and the castle fabric leased to tenants and left to decay. During the early decades of the eighteenth century, as Chepstow's economy prospered, the castle's grounds became an extension of the town's industry, serving as a makeshift farmyard, a workshop and a glass factory.

Georgian Chepstow soon eclipsed the decaying castle from which it had originally sprung, and became a major economic force in the region. By 1790 the town port was handling more trade than Swansea, Cardiff and Newport combined, and its exports of timber, wire and paper were proving particularly lucrative. The town had also become a crucial stopping point between Bristol, Gloucester and, further up the Wye, Hereford.

In the last years of the eighteenth century the river also created another benefit for the town – and, this time, for the castle, too. In 1782 the artist, cleric and travel writer the Reverend William Gilpin published a travel guide which expounded the new concept of the 'picturesque', which held that beauty and the 'sublime' could be found in everyday nature, in painting and in music as well as in the revered classical achievements of antiquity. In Britain this developed, in the minds of Gilpin and others, into the idea that great pleasure could be derived from scenic tours of the beauties of the British countryside and its buildings. The sublime could be found, they argued, as much in the irregularities of a ruined abbey or castle, in the folds of a valley or the bend of a river. The judgement and enjoyment of beauty should not be just the preserve of rich Grand Tourists strolling among – and then pronouncing upon – the monuments of ancient Rome. It could be discerned by anyone, classically educated or not, in their own backyard. Nor did it depend on the symmetrical geometries so beloved of Renaissance followers and their Palladian disciples in early Georgian Britain: the irregular, the naturally formed and even the accidental could prove just as visually rewarding as the artificially contrived.

This novel and egalitarian view of humankind's natural and built environments formed the basis for the Romanticism of the early nineteenth century, a cultural revolution which saw British novelists, dramatists, painters and architects looking to nature for inspiration rather than, as had been the case for much of the preceding century, to the much-admired proportions of classical art. More particularly, Gilpin's theories also provided a timely lifeline for the decaying fabric of Chepstow Castle. Building on the foundations already laid

△ Paul Sandby's evocatively romantic view of the entrance to Chepstow Castle of 1777.

by watercolourist Paul Sandby's evocative views of Chepstow Castle which he published between 1775 and 1777, Gilpin used his tour of the River Wye of 1770 to promote his picturesque ideals in a book catchily titled *Observations on the River Wye, and Several Parts of South Wales, etc. Relative Chiefly to Picturesque Beauty; made in the Summer of the Year 1770*, published in 1782. Gilpin exhorted his readership to revisit Britain, or simply their own backyard, using the precepts of the picturesque: discovering beauty in, as architectural historian Christopher Hussey wrote in 1927, 'roughness and sudden variation joined to irregularity of form, colour, lighting, and even sound'.

The fact that Gilpin, in promoting the picturesque in his book, used as his prime examples the majestic River Wye and the romantic ruins of Chepstow Castle conjured the spectacle of popular tourism in Britain almost overnight. In 1793 the radical Monmouth writer and printer Charles Heath sought to exploit the growing interest in visiting the castle by publishing the first guidebook to the contents of both castle and town. By 1800 the castle had become a key destination for artists and tourists, and the Wye Tour was a must for every cultural tourist. With the completion of Isambard Kingdom Brunel's

79

Great Western Railway terminal of Bristol Temple Meads in 1841, visitors from London and the south-east could arrive at Bristol and catch a day-tripping steamboat to Chepstow and the Wye. In 1850 Chepstow gained its own station – designed by Lancaster Owen for Brunel's South Wales Railway – bringing the castle even nearer to the popular tourist market.

Lights, camera, action

While Chepstow town became a thriving industrial centre in the nineteenth and early twentieth centuries – developing shipbuilding and clock-making industries, both of which flourished during the two world wars, and becoming the epicentre of the Red and White Service's regional bus empire in 1938 – the castle from which it had originated was celebrated as a romantic icon of Britain's medieval past, as seen through the rose-tinted spectacles of Walter Scott and his many Victorian imitators. The farmyards and work-shops were banished from the castle precincts; in their place came horticultural shows, fêtes, balloon ascents (from 1862), donkey polo matches (from 1900) and, increasingly, grand historical pageants recreating a mythical Middle Ages straight out of the pages of *Ivanhoe* or *Kenilworth*. In 1884 the annual summer fête was transformed by the castle's then owner, Henry Somerset, the 8th Duke of Beaufort, and his wife Georgiana. The Beauforts introduced tableaux of locals dressed as characters from various episodes in the castle's alleged history, from Arthurian legend through to the Civil Wars of the 1640s. The part-time soldiers of the Chepstow Volunteers were dressed up as parliamentarian troops, besieging the castle in 1648, while the seventeenth-century theme was continued with a display called 'Prisoner in the Dungeon', a highly romanticised and inappropriately gruesome take on Henry Marten's incarceration, for which an extra charge was made. Following the success of this pageant, similar events were staged on numerous occasions before the First World War, including a Norman- and Elizabethan-themed spectacular in 1889, an oriental carnival in 1907 (which admittedly had precious little to do with the history of the castle in which it was set) and, even more bizarrely, 'The Siege of Troy' in 1909.

The story of Chepstow Castle's Edwardian Summer was not entirely one of fancy-dress fêtes and historical extravaganzas. In 1904 the respected antiquary William St John Hope published the first serious study of the castle's architectural development in the *Archaeological Journal*, laying the basis for

John Clifford Perks's authoritative guides for the Ministry of Works of 1955 and 1967 and for the building's Grade I listing of 1950. More eccentrically, in 1909–10 sites across the castle and the adjoining riverbed were excavated by the highly peculiar and undoubtedly obsessed American physician Dr Orville Ward Owen, who believed he would find documents that would prove his theory that all Shakespeare's plays had in fact been written by a contemporary of the bard, the Jacobean philosopher Francis Bacon. Owen's book *Sir Francis Bacon's Cipher Story*, published in two volumes in 1893 and 1895, posited that Queen Elizabeth I had been secretly married to Robert Dudley, the Earl of Leicester, and that Francis Bacon was their son. (The queen was said to have confessed that Bacon was her son on her deathbed but was then poisoned and strangled by her first minister Robert Cecil, to prevent her proclaiming Bacon and not James VI of Scotland as her successor.) Bacon had written all the plays erroneously attributed to Shakespeare (*Romeo and Juliet* was allegedly the story of Bacon's own romance with Queen Margaret of France), the original manuscripts of which were buried in sixty-six iron boxes near Chepstow Castle.

The fact that Owen's theories were taken even half seriously says much about the broad-mindedness, or perhaps sheer credulity, of Edwardian Britain. Unsurprisingly, Owen found nothing to support his barmy hypothesis, although he did find some valuable Roman and medieval remains in the process. He died penniless in 1924, regretting that he had spent all of his money on his fruitless search for Bacon's plays.

Rather more appropriately for the castle's role in British history, in 1913 the newly founded American film studio Universal Pictures released a silent film of *Ivanhoe*, which had been almost entirely filmed on location in the castle. The wheel had thus come full circle: Chepstow Castle was once more the setting for the old story of Saxons versus Normans, as adapted by Sir Walter Scott into a timeless historical romance. Directed by Irish-born Herbert Brenon (later to achieve fame as the director of Paramount's 1926 film of *Beau Geste*, with Ronald Colman) and produced by Universal's founder Carl Laemmle, *Ivanhoe* starred King Baggot in the title role. Baggot may be largely forgotten today but in 1913 he was the world's most famous film star: 'The King of the Movies'. After the First World War he reinvented himself as a director but his career was wrecked by his alcoholism: before his death in 1948 the most renowned film actor of his day was reduced to playing small bit parts in B-movies.

In 1914, with the castle still basking in its publicity as the setting for Brenon and Baggot's *Ivanhoe* of the previous year, Chepstow Castle at last found a saviour in the Black Country steel tycoon William Royse Lysaght. Lysaght, better known to posterity as a collector of bird specimens on an industrial scale, was the first owner of the castle since the Bigod earls of Norfolk to properly care for the castle's fabric. A programme of serious building conservation was begun, funded by Lysaght's successful sale of his steel concerns to Guest, Keen and Nettlefolds in 1920. Decay was arrested and a historically informed process of repair and restoration was begun.

Eight years after Lysaght's death in Chepstow his family gave the castle to the government's Ministry of Works in lieu of death duties. Today the castle remains in the hands of the Ministry's Welsh successor, Cadw, but its forbidding stone ramparts still continue to take centre stage on film. In modern times the castle has starred in Terry Gilliam's film *Jabberwocky*, as one of the principal locations for the HTV series *Robin of Sherwood* and has even earned the accolade of being used for the flagship Welsh-produced series of BBC's *Dr Who*. Historical romance never lurks too far behind its lowering parapets.

5

LINCOLN CATHEDRAL

BEGUN 1072

Vaulting Ambition:
Britain's greatest Gothic monument?

By 1066 almost every parish in Saxon England had its own church. The nomadic traditions of the former German and Danish tribes who had settled in England had, by the beginning of the eighth century, been replaced by a trend towards permanent settlement. And at the heart of these Saxon towns and villages was the church. As Christianity spread across Britain from the seventh century onwards, churches became ever-larger and more substantial, a symbol both of the piety and of the wealth of the communities they served.

Anglo-Saxon churches grew higher, too. The tall church tower was by no means a Norman innovation. Ecclesiastical towers began climbing skywards at the end of the tenth century: examples survive today at Earls Barton in Northamptonshire, Barton-upon-Humber in Lincolnshire and Sompting in West Sussex. The Normans built even higher than their Saxon predecessors.

▷ *Wenceslaus Hollar's view of Lincoln Cathedral from the west of 1672, dedicated to the cathedral's Dean, Michael Honywood. The spires still survive on the west towers.*

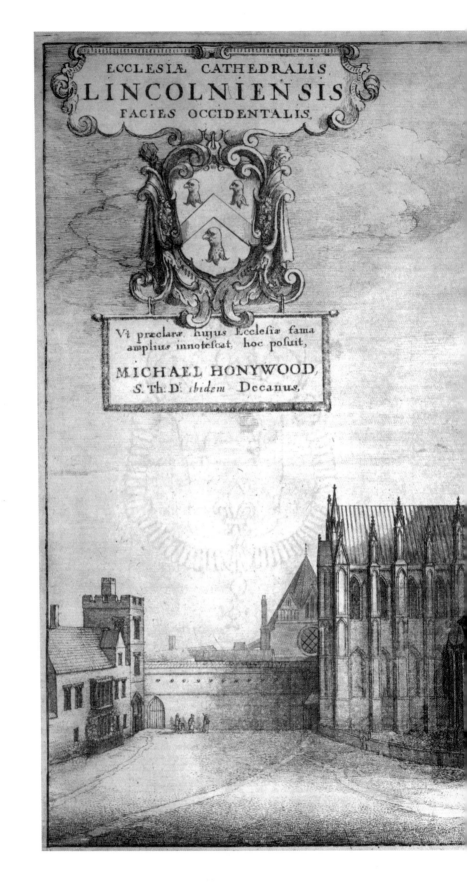

ECCLESIÆ CATHEDRALIS
LINCOLNIENSIS
FACIES OCCIDENTALIS.

Vt præclaræ, hujus Ecclesiæ fama
amplius innotescat, hoc posuit,

MICHAEL HONYWOOD,
S. Th. D: ibidem Decanus.

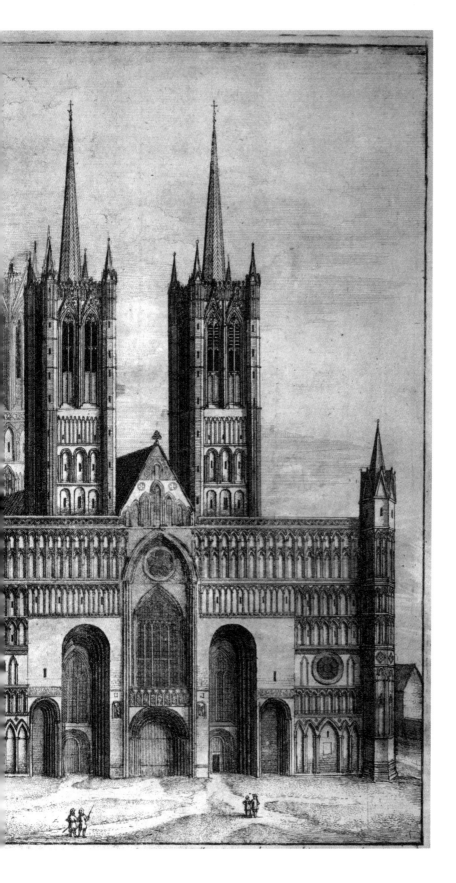

However, their ambitions were often founded on uncertain foundations, since the massive round arches which characterised early Norman architecture in Britain were not as structurally stable as they looked. Unlike the pointed Gothic idiom of the late twelfth century (subsequently labelled the 'Early English' style by the Regency architect-antiquary Thomas Rickman), the Normans' fat, solid-looking columns and arches that lent their naves such an impressively robust aspect were not as strong as they seemed: the thick cylindrical columns were actually hollow, and filled with rubble, and neither the columns nor the arches that linked them were designed to support heavy weights. The result was that ambitious Norman churches and cathedrals, after adding a tall tower at the intersection of the nave and the transepts, all too often suffered from major collapse. This was certainly true of Winchester Cathedral, which suffered just such a calamitous collapse of the crossing tower in 1107. Amusingly, and presumably to the relief of the masons involved in the project, contemporary chroniclers were quick to fix the blame for the collapse not on the errant master mason responsible for the build but on the personal failings of William the Conqueror's son King William II (c.1056–1110), a dissolute, controversial and little-loved figure nicknamed 'William Rufus' on account of his red hair, who had been buried in the cathedral seven years earlier. Similarly, at Ely Cathedral in 1322 the Norman crossing tower imploded with such a noise that the townsfolk believed it augured an earthquake. Further north, it was the added impetus of a genuine earthquake that precipitated the dramatic fall of Lincoln Cathedral's central tower in 1185 – a collapse that took much of the Norman building with it. The tower had just been rebuilt when it fell yet again, in 1237. The subsequent rebuild, though, was to produce one of the finest and most inspiring religious buildings in Europe.

Lincoln Cathedral is in many ways a palimpsest of medieval England. It commanded the largest diocese in the nation, while four of its post-Conquest bishops were leading English statesmen who played a major role in building not just the diocese but the whole nation and who stood beside – or, on some occasions, in audacious opposition to – the national monarch. As a result of the eminence of its bishops, the cathedral received original copies of those touchstones of British civil liberties: the Magna Carta of 1215 and the Charter of the Forests of 1217, both of which survive in the cathedral today.

Lincoln Cathedral also represents one of the high points of British architectural achievement. The Victorian art critic John Ruskin called Lincoln 'the most precious piece of architecture in the British Isles' which was 'roughly speaking worth any two other cathedrals we have'. Its architectural ambition and confidence were astonishing. Reflecting the new-found assurance of King Edward I's reign, which sought to reverse decades of losses of French territory and influence and to subdue its British neighbours in Scotland and Wales, the cathedral's third central tower in a century was designed to soar upwards to unprecedented heights. The tallest building in the world for 238 years – from 1311 until the central spire collapsed in an extraordinary storm in 1548 – Lincoln rivalled or even eclipsed the best French cathedrals of the time. In its aisle vaults, too, its gifted master masons introduced something wholly original: an English vault which was both aesthetically pleasing and structurally support-ive, enabling the tower to rocket skywards.

The Norman cathedral

The first incumbent of the post-Conquest diocese was the Norman fighting cleric Bishop Remigius of Fécamp (d. 1092). A close friend and ally of William the Conqueror, he had stood with him at the Battle of Hastings. Indeed, Remigius' material contributions to the invasion, in the form of a ship and a score of knights, were subsequently to earn him a summons to visit Pope Alexander II in Rome to face charges of simony – his critics arguing that, effec-tively, his military support had bought him his lucrative bishopric. Although Remigius survived his papal interrogation, it was undeniable that he had been rewarded by William I with the largest and richest see in England (then based at Dorchester in Oxfordshire rather than Lincoln) on the convenient death of its last Saxon incumbent, Bishop Wulwig, in 1067. Remigius was William's first Norman appointment to what was still a largely Saxon epis-copacy; it even predated the king's installation of his close friend, the Italo-Norman lawyer-scholar Lanfranc, as Archbishop of Canterbury in 1070. Abiding by Lanfranc's Accord of Winchester of 1072, which decreed that bish-oprics should henceforth be sited in substantial towns rather than rural sites, Remigius transferred the episcopal seat from the small town of Dorchester to the far larger community of Lincoln, at the northern end of the diocese.

In the early years of William I's reign, Remigius was always at the epicentre of events. He appeared with his sovereign at every court William held in England and was central to the creation and implementation of the national census of 1085–6, a project called the Domesday Book ('dome' or 'doom' was Anglo-Saxon for law or judgement), for which he acted as one of the survey's principal county commissioners.

Bishop Remigius addressed the construction of his new cathedral with the same rigour with which he addressed statecraft. He built a church in the contemporary French manner of the abbeys of Jumièges and Caen, with a tall nave and two lower aisles, resulting in a composition which, either deliberately or coincidentally, recalled the triumphal arches of ancient Rome in what might have been an allusion to Lincoln's pre-eminence in Roman Britain. Indeed, architectural historian Dr Anthony Quiney suggests that the whole west front of Remigius' new cathedral was a homage to the Arch of Constantine in Rome of AD 315, a monument the bishop would undoubtedly have seen during his visits to Rome of 1071 and 1076. As the historian has noted: 'What better way to symbolize his secular power as the Conqueror's lieutenant in Lincoln and affirm his ecclesiastical power as bishop of the immense Midlands see than to refer to an ancient conquest by which Christianity triumphed?'

The nave and aisles originally terminated to the west in a large, battlemented tower which, both Richard Gem and Anthony Quiney have suggested, may have served as a defensive bastion in the manner of a castle keep and also as the bishop's residence, since it included a garderobe and a privy. This bastion came in handy when it was besieged during the bitter civil war of the 1140s between King Stephen and the Empress Matilda.

Remigius' two great aisle portals are still evident in the west front today, and his cathedral was complete by the time of his death in 1092. Sadly, though, the bishop died a day or two before its scheduled consecration. It was long said that he was buried behind its altar – a theory which was proved correct when, during building work in 1927, his tomb was found underneath the Angel Choir, on the site of what had been the original cathedral's east end. Covered with an intricately carved marble slab, the grave contained not just the bishop's bones but also his chalice, his paten and half of his pastoral staff. Not long after his death, the contemporary chronicler Gerald of Wales (c.1146–1223) attempted to make a case for Remigius' canonisation in his optimistically titled *Vita Sancti Remigii*, which detailed the many miracles supposed to have taken place by the late bishop's tomb. However, the papacy remained unimpressed and refused all approaches on Remigius's behalf. Less than ninety years later, a local earthquake caused the tower of Remigius' cathedral to topple 'from top to bottom'. The subsequent rebuilding only incorporated elements of the Norman west end in the new structure.

St Hugh of Avalon

As Remigius was a pillar of strength for the first two Norman kings, so the third post-Conquest Bishop of Lincoln, Hugh of Avalon (*c*.1135–1200), was a leading supporter of the Angevin monarchs. Unlike Remigius, however, Bishop Hugh *was* subsequently canonised, becoming St Hugh of Lincoln twenty years after his death. Until the English Reformation of the 1530s he was the best-known saint in England after Thomas Becket. Today, though, he is little remembered outside Lincoln.

French-born Hugh of Avalon had already become celebrated as a trouble-shooter for failing clerical foundations when he was brought over to England by King Henry II (1133–89) in 1179 to establish the Carthusian charterhouse at Witham in Somerset, a foundation that had long been promised by the king as penance for Archbishop Becket's notorious murder in 1170. Having successfully achieved his goal, in 1186 Henry transferred Hugh to the see of Lincoln to sort out the cathedral in the wake of the tower's recent collapse.

Bishop Hugh was much respected by Henry II but remained, throughout his life, his own man. He rebuked the sovereign for keeping sees vacant while the crown pocketed their incomes, resisted the appointment of royal nominees after arriving at Lincoln and opposed Henry's demands for knights to serve in France. However, Hugh's legendary tact, diplomacy and good humour always prevented a lasting breach with the monarchy. The same qualities proved invaluable when he became bishop. Although he came from the distant south-eastern borders of France, Hugh immediately won over the local population with his generosity and sincerity as he reformed the cathedral school and protected the city's Jewish population from attacks. Lincolnshire folk* were also enchanted by the fact that he kept a pet swan, which would follow him about, eat from his hand and even sleep near him, but which would attack anyone else who came near. (His saintly attribute was, inevitably, a white swan.)

Bishop Hugh was, his independence notwithstanding, frequently asked to serve as a royal ambassador by King Henry and his sons. It was while conducting a diplomatic mission for King John in London that he died in 1200; it

---

*   The term 'yellowbellies', referring to the inhabitants of Lincolnshire, does not seem to have been used until the later eighteenth century. The name appears to have derived from the yellow facings and frogging on the uniforms of the North Lincolnshire Regiment.

was said that the king himself helped to carry his coffin to its last resting place. Almost Hugh's last task before he left was to consecrate the church of St Giles in Oxford in the south of his diocese, and the medieval fair held to commemorate that day has taken place every September since.

St Hugh's new cathedral was a predictably ambitious project. Remodelled between 1180 and 1200 by Richard 'the Mason' (who was probably the site architect) and Geoffrey de Noiers, it introduced something completely new in European architecture: a building that seemed to reflect English ingenuity and the English sense of humour. No longer were the masons of Lincoln content with quadripartite roof vaults which simply followed the lines of construction. The new nave at Lincoln featured a familiar longitudinal ridge rib and the transverse and diagonal ribs of a typical quadripartite vault. However, it also included something new: additional vaulting ribs that both helped to support the structure above – giving much-needed relief for the weight of the crossing tower – and which made the vault more decorative and aesthetically pleasing. The new ribs were called 'tiercerons', literally 'third ribs', and created a star pattern around the central boss affixed to the ridge rib of each bay. Four tierceron ribs connected to two pairs of shorter tierceron ribs, which were in turn joined to the central roof boss on the central rib. The result was a very English compromise: a ceiling that was both structurally sound and at the same time visually entertaining.

In the choir vault Geoffrey de Noiers's craftsmen went even further, creating something entirely novel which was never repeated anywhere else. Transverse tierceron ribs were inserted to create an asymmetrical, eight-panel pattern for each bay. The result was unusual, bizarre – and fun. In 1848 the pioneering architectural historian Robert Willis declared that the vault had been the result of 'a mad Frenchman', i.e. de Noiers. (In fact de Noiers's family had been in England since the Conquest, while Geoffrey himself was most likely what we would today call the supervising architect, the vault itself having probably been constructed by local masons.) The highly influential French architect-restorer Eugène Viollet-le-Duc took great exception to Willis' epithet, which clearly implied that the words 'mad' and 'Frenchman' were synonymous, and in a furious letter of 1861 declared the work to be unmistakeably English –

▷ *Looking down Bishop Hugh's nave at Lincoln Cathedral, constructed between 1180 and 1200 by Richard 'the Mason' and Geoffrey de Noiers. The vault includes the novel tierceron ribs.*

'or Norman, if you will'. (The Parisian architect clearly thought Normandy was half-English anyway.) In 1907 British architect and critic W. R. Lethaby termed the vault 'eccentric' while in 1953 historian Paul Frankl transposed Willis' slur on the French to the structure itself, labelling the choir vault 'crazy' – a term which stuck, although Historic England's list description prefers the more polite term 'syncopated'.

The new vaulting at Lincoln, combined with the unprecedently large window area of the nave and choir, must have made a great impression on thirteenth-century contemporaries. As recent historians have commented, 'The new treatment of natural daylight reflecting through the large windows to the vaults, the scale and rhythm of the new roof, the influence on the liturgical rituals and the use of music must have left a strong impression of progress and prosperity to the ecclesiastical patrons, the faithful and the masons.' And, as Paul Frankl noted in 1953, the style of the new cathedral was 'unquestionably English in character'. However, even the revolutionary new vault was not strong enough to support the weight of Bishop Hugh's ambitious new tower, as the dramatic events of forty years later would show.

Some authorities have suggested that Lincoln's radical vaults were far too revolutionary to have belonged to the 1190s and must have been executed, possibly with French help, fifty or so years later. In 1911 historian John Bilson firmly attributed the choir's 'crazy vault' to the 1140s, a theory which was rehearsed by other writers during the ensuing century. However, evidence for this chronology so far remains inconclusive. In 1861 Viollet-le-Duc had not only judged of the choir that 'The construction is English; the profiles of the mouldings are English; the ornaments are English' but that 'the execution of the work belongs to the English school of workmen of the beginning of the thirteenth century'. The great French architect and restorer also refused to believe that such avant-garde work could date from the last years of the preceding century – and thus was far more advanced than anything French Gothic had yet devised.

Hugh of Wells, King John and Magna Carta

Hugh of Avalon was ultimately succeeded by a nine-year hiatus which saw the see vacant for six years. He was then succeeded by a namesake, Hugh of Wells (d. 1235). This second Hugh, however, was very different from his saintly predecessor. He was a thrusting and ebullient figure who may well have had two daughters – a persistent rumour which led to the postponement of his consecration – and who ran his diocese in a robust manner. He was, like Remigius before him, a strong supporter of the monarch, for whom he acted as ambassador and adviser. This in turn led to his exile from England in 1209–13, following King John's excommunication by the pope, and his excoriation by the barons in 1215. He worked hard to secure the canonisation of Hugh of Avalon and acted as a conspicuously successful fundraiser for the new cathedral at Salisbury, begun in 1220. But he displayed none of St Hugh's tolerance, ordering in 1222 that everyone in his diocese refrain from contact with Jews – a decree that was swiftly countermanded by Henry III's Chief Justiciar Hubert de Burgh.

Hugh of Wells's close identification with King John (reigned 1199–1216) was little help to him during the years of baronial rebellion. This aristocratic unrest had crystallised around the monarch's perceived misrule, his loss of the rich provinces of Normandy and Anjou to the French and his abysmal relations with the papacy. When in 1213 a party of rebel barons met with Bishop Hugh's ally and supporter, Lincolnshire-born Stephen Langton, Archbishop of Canterbury, to air their grievances and to ask Langton to lead their protest, Hugh decided to follow his ecclesiastical master into the rebel fold. Langton had been elected pope in 1207 with the express support of his friend Pope Innocent III. King John raged at the failure to elect his own nominee and declared that anyone who sided with Langton would be regarded as the king's enemy. Such childish bravado got him nowhere: despite Bishop Hugh's advice to settle matters with the pope quickly, John continued his defiance of both Canterbury and Rome. As a result, the powerful Innocent III placed England under an interdict in 1208 (an order which, in theory, barred heaven to English men and women), excommunicated the king in 1209 and formally declared John deposed as monarch in January 1213. The last measure was accompanied by a frank invitation to King Philip II of France to unseat John and take the English throne himself. Hugh was the last bishop standing by the king; but at the end of 1209 even he decided to retire from the political stage. Fearing a less than ecstatic welcome in Lincoln, he fled to France.

The depictions of British history purveyed by Hollywood during the twentieth century have invariably presented us with a series of over-simplified narratives peopled by black and white characters who are generally either heroes or villains. King John has suffered particularly in this regard, with most writers and filmmakers taking their cue from Shakespeare and Walter Scott's unflattering pen portraits in, respectively, *King John* of *c.*1595 and *Ivanhoe* of 1819 to portray him as a scheming rogue (such as epitomised by Guy Rolfe in MGM's 1952 film) or a simple-minded yet treacherous glutton (as played by Nigel Terry in Anthony Harvey and James Goldman's superb 1968 movie *The Lion in Winter*). In John's case, however, the screenwriters appear to have been largely correct.

John's reign was a disaster from the start. It was not his fault that he was invariably compared unfavourably to his legendary predecessors: his empire-building father Henry II and his fearless (but largely absent) brother, the warrior-king Richard I. Yet John always managed to live down to that reputation. The new king was notoriously duplicitous, suspicious and vindictive – qualities that his contemporaries cheerfully advertised with little respect for his royal status. After his accession in 1199, John was universally assumed to have had his young nephew and rival claimant to the throne, Arthur of Brittany, murdered – possibly in Rouen in 1203. In a few years, too, his lack of military prowess instantly earned him, according to the contemporary chronicler Gervase of Canterbury, the soubriquet Johannem molle gladium, 'John Softsword'. John taxed his subjects far more vehemently than his father or brother, exacting 'scutage', a tax paid in lieu of military service, eleven times during his seventeen-year reign – it had been levied only eleven times in the previous forty-four years. Only five years after his accession John also proceeded to lose the rich French territories of Anjou, Maine, Touraine, Normandy and most of Aquitaine – a cross-Channel empire which his father had painstakingly assembled over thirty years – with, in the words of historian Dan Jones, 'almost bewildering speed'. The loss of Normandy was particularly damaging to the king's reputation, as many English nobles had earned much of their income from their lands on the opposite side of the Channel.

John finally made peace with the pope in 1213, effectively placing England under papal control and guaranteeing the English church freedom to appoint without royal interference. With this accord, Bishop Hugh agreed to return to Lincoln from France. However, typically John backed the wrong horse in the epic struggle between the Holy Roman Empire and France of the following year. The imperial rout at the Battle of Bouvines in Flanders made John's position even more untenable, as any recovery of French lands now seemed a distant prospect. Yet John still shrank from meeting Archbishop Langton and his fractious English nobles. He finally promised to meet them at Northampton over the Easter weekend of 1215, so as to allow them to air their grievances;

but, predictably, he failed to turn up. The enraged rebels seized London, and John had no option but to confront them and their self-appointed mediator, Archbishop Langton, at a spot by the River Thames between Windsor and Staines ('Windlesoram et Stanes') called Runnymede, in June 1215.

The result of that momentous meeting was a document, agreed by affixed seal by the king and the rebels on 15 June, which has been hailed as the first constitution in European history and the cornerstone of western liberties: Magna Carta. ('Magna' or 'Great' was added after 1217 to distinguish it from that year's equally influential Charter of the Forest.) A process which started out as a litany of specific complaints by the highest echelon of society was to become an articulation of timeless concepts which, in the words of the British Library's archivist-historians, 'both challenged the autocracy of the king and proved highly adaptable in future centuries':

> Most famously, the 39th clause gave all 'free men' the right to justice and a fair trial. In 1776 rebellious American colonists looked to the Magna Carta as a model for their demands of liberty from the English crown [while] some of Magna Carta's core principles are echoed in the United States Bill of Rights (1791) and in many other constitutional documents around the world, as well as in the Universal Declaration of Human Rights (1948) and the European Convention on Human Rights (1950).

Despite the fact that the vast majority of its clauses have now been repealed or superseded by other legislation, Magna Carta still retains enormous symbolic power as an ancient defence against arbitrary and tyrannical rulers and as a guarantor of individual liberties. Since 1215 it has been a beacon for democracy the world over.

For many of the barons, though, signing Magna Carta was the end of the whole episode. On 19 June the rebels made their formal peace with King John and renewed their oaths of allegiance. For Bishop Hugh, however, his travails were by no means over. As one of the leaders of the episcopacy he had been a signatory to Magna Carta; however, even as the two sides signed the document at Runnymede, 120 miles further north the city of Lincoln was convulsed by anti-government riots. In the ensuing weeks, John predictably tried to persuade the pope to annul Magna Carta; in response, the barons refused to surrender the City of London to the king until Magna Carta had been implemented. Hugh, meanwhile, hastened back to his see to try to restore order in the city, taking one of the copies of Magna Carta with him. This copy still remains in the city today – though at the castle rather than the cathedral. It has for decades been toured around the world; in 1941, indeed, the Lincoln Cathedral copy was even offered to the United States as an inducement to enter the war at Britain's side.

Invasion

For both England and Lincoln, things were to get worse before they got better. Touched by the king's pleas to free him from his aristocratic shackles, Pope Innocent III excommunicated the rebel barons by name. The result was outright civil war, with the barons inviting Philip II of France's heir, Prince Louis (later King Louis VIII), to invade England and assume the throne in John's place. This Louis duly did: only a month after his landing in Kent in May 1216, to England's everlasting shame, Louis of France controlled the entire southern half of the kingdom. However, Lincoln Cathedral and its neighbouring castle continued to hold out against a combined force of baronial and French troops. Attempting to raise the rebel siege of Lincoln by cutting across the estuarine corner of north-west Norfolk, an area known for its tidal streams and treacherous currents, King John suffered a final ignominy when his baggage train became swallowed up in the marshes – a train that included the royal crown jewels, valued today at a hundred million pounds. As W.C. Sellar and R.J. Yeatman memorably put it in 1930's classic satire *1066 and All That*, 'John finally demonstrated his utter incompetence by losing the crown and all his clothes in the wash.' A month later, in October 1216, John died of dysentery in Newark, 16 miles to the south-west of Lincoln.

Lincoln's troubles were by no means over. The New Year saw the French and rebel army still besieging both castle and cathedral. Resistance was led by the formidable female Constable of the Castle, Nichola de la Haye, who was then well into her sixties. Then in May 1217 another remarkable English leader of advancing years – William Marshal, the septuagenarian 1st Earl of Pembroke, paragon of knightly virtues and regent to John's ten-year-old heir, King Henry III – led an impressive relieving force from Newark to help the dauntless Nichola. What followed was one of the most important battles ever to take place on English soil – second only, perhaps, to Hastings in 1066. If the rebels had won, it is possible that Britons would be speaking French today. It is certainly the only major battle in the British Isles which was fought around

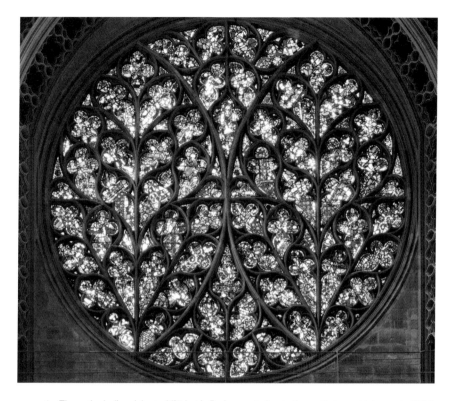

△ *The cathedral's celebrated 'Bishop's Eye' rose window in the south transept, begun in 1325.*

a cathedral. Yet despite these distinctions, the Battle of Lincoln remains little known.

Soon after their arrival outside Lincoln, Marshal's forces retook the castle through a shrewd pincer movement. They entered the castle bailey from the west thanks to a timely feint by Nichola's defenders, while another royalist force drove down towards the cathedral from the north-west. The French and rebel troops were then forced back towards the cathedral precincts, their backs to the cathedral's formidable west front. The French commander was actually killed fighting directly in front of the cathedral's west door, after which the French contingent fled and the surviving English rebels were chased round the cathedral or down aptly named Steep Hill. While Bishop Hugh remained a helpless bystander, Marshal's victorious men then sacked the city for having helped the rebels – a series of outrages which were subsequently dubbed, with bitter irony, the 'Lincoln Fair'. Contemporary chronicler Roger of Wendover described this ruthless pillaging of the city, which did not even spare the half-rebuilt cathedral:

> After the battle was thus ended, the king's soldiers found in the city the waggons of the barons and the French, with the sumpter-horses, loaded with baggage, silver vessels, and various kinds of furniture and utensils, all which fell into their possession without opposition. Having then plundered the whole city to the last farthing, they next pillaged the churches throughout the city, and broke open the chests and store-rooms with axes and hammers, seizing on the gold and silver in them, clothes of all colours, women's ornaments, gold rings, goblets, and jewels. Nor did the cathedral church escape this destruction, but underwent the same punishment as the rest, for the legate had given orders to the knights to treat all the clergy as excommunicated men, inasmuch as they had been enemies to the church of Rome and to the king of England from the commencement of the war.

The victorious troops drunkenly looted the city. To escape their predations, many of Lincoln's women took to the river in boats with their children; but, overloaded as most of these vessels were with families and their household goods, many of their passengers drowned and 'were afterwards found in the river by the searchers, goblets of silver, and many other articles of great benefit to the finders'. It was a dark time for Lincoln and for England.

The Battle of Lincoln was a major turning point for the French invasion and, indeed, for English history. Prince Louis, having lost many of his English allies, accepted a massive bribe from Marshal's government – equivalent to a quarter of England's annual revenue – and returned home to France. Lincoln Cathedral returned to its rebuilding project, completing the new choir and nave.

Robert Grosseteste

In 1237 further structural disaster befell the cathedral. Barely two years after the election of yet another statesmanlike Bishop of Lincoln, the philosopher-theologian and de facto Chancellor of Oxford University, Robert Grosseteste (*c*.1168–1253), St Hugh's new crossing tower came tumbling down. Thankfully, this time the tower appears to have collapsed vertically downwards, demolishing only the first two bays of the choir.

Bishop Grosseteste directed that the cathedral's central tower be immediately rebuilt – and, most importantly, that it should be higher than any of its predecessors. As a result, from around 1240 the bishop's master mason, whom we only know as Alexander, started building skywards again. While England continued to lose more of her former French possessions, the Suffolk-born philosopher-bishop was determined to enhance the prestige of his diocese and his nation by building a tower the likes of which the world had never seen. After Grosseteste's death, his tower was heightened yet further by Richard of Stow after 1307. Stow also added a tall, lead-encased wooden spire to make the cathedral the tallest building in the world.

Grosseteste did not stop at adding a new tower to his cathedral. He remodelled the Chapter House, providing it with blind arcading and a central pillar supporting a lierne vault. 'Lierne' ribs were the next evolutionary step from tiercerons: smaller, linking ribs which serve no structural purpose at all. The whole building was topped by a pyramidal roof and supported, unusually, by eight dramatic, freestanding flying buttresses in its mesmerising, swooping naturalistic design. Academic John Hendrix has detected the geometrical expression of Bishop Grosseteste's theories of structural geometry, as expressed in his treatise *De Lineis, Angulis et Figuris seu Fractionibus et Reflexionibus Radiorum*, which was written shortly before his consecration at Lincoln.

After Grosseteste, building work continued in a similarly ambitious manner. The five-bay Angel Choir added to the east to house the shrine of St Hugh between 1256 and 1280 was, again, emphatically English – borrowing, as Jennifer Alexander notes, from Westminster Abbey, Ely Cathedral and the old cathedral of St Paul's in London. In its massive clustered piers and tall triforium it featured the new architectural fashion for combining pale limestone and dark Purbeck marble to produce an engaging contrast in tones. And by the mid-fourteenth century the building featured not one but two outstanding rose windows – a rarity in English medieval architecture. The 'Dean's Eye' of the early thirteenth century and the 'Bishop's Eye' begun in 1325 are outstanding examples of English skill and ambition. The Bishop's Eye was created just before the pestilence later dubbed the Black Death decimated the country's population by over a third and robbed the nation of many skilled craftsmen. In particular, the window dubbed the 'Bishop's Eye', added to the rebuilt south transept after 1325, introduced something wholly new in medieval stained-glass design. As the art critic Tom Lubbock has noted:

> To put it geometrically: the circle of this window has been intersected by two arcs with the same diameter. The centres of these arcs lie on opposite sides of the window's circumference. The two arcs touch at the window's centre. They create a pair of upright almond forms. Each almond is then bisected vertically – almost all the way – by a straight line. Within these forms there's a network of tracery, its shapes mainly irregular long-tailed quatrefoils. So the layout is essentially binary.

Sadly, today it is impossible to discern the significance of these two mandorlae, since both rose windows were smashed during the English Revolution and their component pieces later reassembled haphazardly. They could have represented the Old and the New Testaments or, as Lubbock suggests, the saved and the damned; or even the Christian fish symbol. Whatever their original narrative, there has been nothing like them before or since.

Today Lincoln Cathedral remains one of the most outstanding examples of Gothic architecture in Europe, and one of England's most magnificent churches. Fittingly, it is among the few English cathedrals to be built from the rock it was standing on – and to still own the quarry from which the original building stone was hewn. It may no longer be the tallest building in the world (in 1548 the spire of its central tower collapsed in a gale, while in 1807 the cathedral chapter removed the two smaller spires from the west towers, its stained glass was mutilated in the seventeenth century, and some of its fabric over-restored in the nineteenth) but it remains an astonishing tribute to Gothic workmanship, ecclesiastical hubris and the national aspirations of medieval England. It is also a superb example of what can be conjured from apparent disaster.

Lincoln Cathedral is frequently filmed as a stand-in for Westminster Abbey. Yet in many ways it eclipses that great national storehouse of people and memories in showcasing some of the most audacious medieval Gothic architecture to be seen anywhere in Britain. It is not only a testimony to native craftsmanship and invention: the resources expended on this vast and magnificent building also show the immense resources of finance and labour that the church could command in the centuries before the English Reformation.

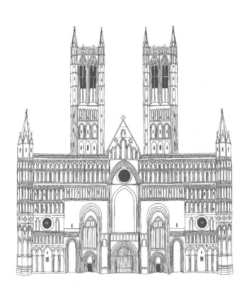

6

GREAT COXWELL BARN, OXFORDSHIRE

1292

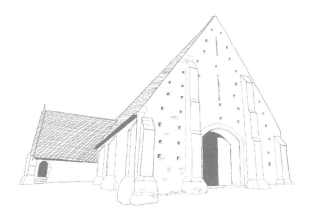

Back to the Land: from the Cistercians to National Trust

The great medieval barn was the economic driver of the medieval community and one of the linchpins (or perhaps we should say king posts) of the feudal system. Here locals stored their tithes – a tenth of their crop – for the use of the church and the village. Along with the parish church, it formed one of the two main focuses of the medieval village until the arrival of the pub – which, as the social and economic power of the church waned while that of the local brewer waxed, gradually supplanted it as a community hub.

It was no different at Great Coxwell, a village which lay at the foot of Badbury Hill in the Vale of the White Horse in the county of Berkshire for centuries – at least before the ill-advised and much-derided local government changes of 1974 moved it into Oxfordshire. Here the great barn and the parish church of St Giles stood at opposite ends of the village: moral and economic guardians keeping watch over the faith and prosperity of the inhabitants. For most English villages during the Middle Ages it was much the same – though few, if any, of Britain's manor barns were as ambitious as that built at Great Coxwell.

Great Coxwell Barn's significance in the history of England lies not just in its sheer survival. Its looming presence at the village's northern perimeter is a lasting testimony to the power of the church over every community, at least until the English Reformation of the 1530s. Its role as an economic generator for a faraway Cistercian monastery demonstrates the supra-national nature of royal and ecclesiastical patronage as well as the many ties of power, money and allegiance that held medieval Britain together. Bereft of a role by the mid-nineteenth century, largely thanks to the increasing mechanisation of British agriculture, Great Coxwell's venerable barn was then adopted by local sage, critic, socialist and designer William Morris as an archetype of the classless medieval utopia he so extolled. Decades later, its safeguarding by the National Trust not only exemplified the excellent work that the Trust was undertaking after 1945 to protect the nation's built heritage from serious damage or disappearance; their ownership also prevented this highly significant structure from disfigurement or dismemberment during the barn conversion craze of the late twentieth century.

The Cistercians

Great Coxwell was an established village by the time of the Norman Conquest. (The hamlet of Little Coxwell lies about a mile to the east, on the other side of the Faringdon–Swindon road.) It was, evidence suggests, once owned by the late Saxon kings. The village's vast barn was built more than two centuries after the Conquest, however, being raised in or around 1292 for the benefit of both the village and the clergy. It was not necessarily designed to enrich the local clerics, though: the manor of Great Coxwell as a whole, including its magnificent barn, was owned by and subject to a monastic foundation sited on the Hampshire coast. This arrangement was by no means uncommon in medieval Britain: many manors were owned by far-flung monasteries which, in turn, had often been founded by, and were accordingly subject to the orders of, a mother house across the Channel in France.

When the Cistercian monastery of Beaulieu was founded in 1204, King John, eager to find helpful new friends now that he had just lost most of his

◁ *The fabulous 'nave' of the agrarian cathedral that is Great Coxwell Barn.*

father's rich Angevin empire in France* and antagonised his own aristoc-
racy, eagerly gifted the order a clutch of manors in what was then north-west
Berkshire. The Cistercian order was a relatively recent foundation, created so
as to provide an example to the rest of the Roman church of the benefits of
avoiding the temptations to which other, older monastic orders had allegedly
fallen prey. Its members were known as Bernardines, after their early champion (St) Bernard of Clairvaux, or as the 'White Monks' after the white colour
of their cowls – which had been chosen as a deliberate contrast to the black
cowl of the long-established Benedictines. The word 'Cistercian' derives from
Cistercium, the Latin name for the town of Cîteaux, near Dijon in Burgundy. It
was here in 1098 that a group of reformist Benedictine monks founded a new
abbey, in which they aimed to eschew the perceived corruption of their fellow
Benedictines by following the original, sixth-century Rule of St Benedict to
the letter. Bernard of Clairvaux helped to spread the order's influence and by
the end of the century the Cistercian order had spread throughout Europe.
The foundation at Beaulieu was, like all the other Cistercian houses, subject to
the supervision of the Abbot of Cîteaux; thus so were, indirectly, the church
of St Giles and the barn at Great Coxwell.

Cistercians led a harsher life than other monastic orders, seeking to focus
on a regime of austerity, prayer and manual labour. Many of the new British
Cistercian foundations were deliberately sited in remote areas, far away
from the enticements of the town. Among the most celebrated today are the
now-ruined abbeys of Fountains and Rievaulx in North Yorkshire, founded
in 1131 and 1143 respectively and deliberately sited well away from any urban
temptations. Rievaulx, built in a hidden valley by the River Rye, not only
provided the seclusion the Cistercians sought; its remoteness also ensured
that, after the Reformation had forced its closure, its ruins survived in better
condition than many other dissolved religious foundations, the vast majority
of which were ruthlessly pillaged for their valuable stone and glass. At isolated
abbeys such as Rievaulx and Beaulieu, the monks worked hard to improve the
land and to make even the most unlikely landscape fully productive.

Appropriately for Great Coxwell Barn, one of the cornerstones of the
Cistercians' doctrine was their emphasis on manual agricultural work. As a

---

* The Angevin empire comprised the massive territorial gains that flowed from the
marriage of Henry Plantagenet (son of Count Geoffrey of Anjou and the Empress Matilda),
subsequently Henry II, to Eleanor of Aquitaine.

result, Cistercian houses became the 'model farms' of their day – seven centuries before the Victorians coined the term to denote exemplars of agrarian reform. This in turn led to many Cistercian foundations developing highly successful agricultural, winemaking and brewing businesses. In the seventeenth century a breakaway sect of French Cistercians founded a new house at La Trappe Abbey in Normandy. Known, inevitably, as Trappists, this new Order of Cistercians of the Strict Observance sought, like their Cistercian forebears four centuries earlier, to ensure they remained distant from fleshly temptations – but, famously, not from alcoholic ones. Today they are rather better known for their beer than for their strict observance.

King John's patronage

Beaulieu was a wealthy foundation from the start. It was also no ordinary abbey. It occupied possibly the largest Cistercian site in the country and assumed a political role out of all proportion to its acreage. Historic England has called its creation 'one of the greatest acts of English monastic establishment in the High Middle Ages' and has noted that, 'as one of the most significant medieval Cistercian monasteries in England, [it] was built on a grand scale, hosted royal visitations and [its] abbots represented the Crown on diplomatic missions'. Already in 1208, only four years after its foundation, Beaulieu's abbot was serving as an intermediary between the king and the pope during the time of the Papal Interdict.

The abbey was originally intended to be sited near Faringdon, close to Great Coxwell, but King John translated it to a more remote spot in the royal-owned New Forest. (One of the principal baronial complaints against John and his Norman and Angevin ancestors was that they had appropriated nearly a third of the nation's farmable land as privately owned 'royal forest'.) The king christened it Beaulieu – a name derived from *bellus locus regis*, the 'king's beautiful place'. (Beaulieu was, incidentally, also the name of a sixty-year-old Cistercian establishment in the Rouergue, in south-central France.) King John originally intended to be buried there, but shortly before his death resolved instead to be interred beside the shrine of his personal patron saint, St Wulfstan, in Worcester Cathedral. Twelve years later the monks of Beaulieu – evidently with short memories of John's appalling reputation and pitiable legacy – petitioned to have the late king's body translated to their monastery, but their pleas were ignored.

John granted the new, 58-acre abbey a clutch of west Berkshire manors, including Great Coxwell, and a series of villages across southern England. He also granted it a comfortable supply of corn and cash, copious building materials for further extensions, 120 cows, twelve bulls, a golden chalice and an annual gift of a tun of wine.[*] For good measure, John additionally left the abbey a massive £2,000[†] in his will of 1216.

The abbey grounds included a cloister, a refectory, a chapter house and living and sleeping quarters for the abbot and monks. It was surrounded by workshops, a weaving shed, farm buildings, guesthouses, a mill and extensive gardens and fishponds. A water gate allowed access for boats and ships from the Beaulieu River, which ran into the Solent and thence into the English Channel. All this took over forty years to build: the abbey was finally consecrated in 1246 in the presence of King Henry III and his eldest son, the future King Edward I.

Beaulieu was also special in that it was an 'exempt abbey' – meaning that the abbot had to answer only to the pope and not to the local bishop, in this case of Winchester – and was given special privileges of sanctuary. In 1471, after her husband's death at the Battle of Barnet during the Wars of the Roses, Anne, Countess of Warwick, sought sanctuary here, as did the pretender to the throne, Perkin Warbeck, in 1497.

The Reformation

Beaulieu's high profile was its undoing during the Reformation, when it became one of the first large monasteries to be closed, in 1538. Its abbey church was almost entirely dismantled to provide building stone for the region. (In contrast, secluded Cistercian foundations such as Rievaulx were largely left to decay in their own time.) The site then passed to Henrician courtier Thomas Wriothesley, the 1st Earl of Southampton, who converted the Great Gatehouse into his own residence. Wriothesley's descendants, the Montagus, still live there today.

The English Reformation was an unmitigated disaster for Britain's architectural and educational pre-eminence. The so-called 'Dissolution of the Monasteries' was, as the architectural historian Sir Howard Colvin wrote in

---

[*]   A 'tun' comprised around 210 modern gallons or 950 litres. In case you were wondering, two butts made a tun, three puncheons also made a tun, while two hogsheads made a butt.

[†]   The modern equivalent would be c. £12 million.

1999, 'the greatest single act of vandalism in English, and perhaps European history', undertaken by 'a grasping and tyrannical king, and effected through... ruthless, cynical and philistine men'. Some of the most impressive buildings and the most advanced centres of learning in Europe were extinguished in order to enrich the coffers of the crown and inflate the purses and augment the estates of Henry VIII's sycophantic courtiers. The establishment of some new 'public' schools by Henry's heirs, Edward VI and Elizabeth I, after the royal tyrant's death in 1547 went some way towards alleviating the dramatic impoverishment of England's learning infrastructure. However, the loss of the abbeys and monasteries was a cultural holocaust from which it took Britain three centuries to recover.

Recent scholarship has also suggested that the dissolution strangled a nascent industrial revolution at birth. By the 1530s the Cistercian monks at Rievaulx had established a blast furnace at the nearby hamlet of Laskill to produce cast iron. In 1998 Gerry McDonnell and his colleagues at the University of Bradford discovered that the Tudor furnace's slag was low in iron content and thus must have produced a refined cast iron similar in quality to that created by a modern blast furnace, suggesting a much more efficient blast furnace technology than otherwise existed. The suppression of Rievaulx, at the same time as that of Beaulieu, prevented the monks from developing and sharing this new technology. If this had not occurred, Britain could have embarked on an industrial revolution two centuries earlier, and the world might have been very different today.

The Great Barn at Great Coxwell was also included in the vast fire sale which followed the Dissolution. Thankfully, though, it continued to serve the purpose for which it had been built. In 1540 the crown sold the manor of Great Coxwell to a local landowner, William Morys or Morris – a famous name which was to resurface in the building's history over three centuries later. As the nation was precariously balanced between Protestantism and Catholicism, however, the Morris family stayed obdurately Catholic. In 1580 – by which time the Protestant ascendancy had been conclusively established by Elizabeth I and Catholicism was illegal – a Catholic mass was secretly celebrated at Court House Farm opposite Great Coxwell Barn. The following year a member of the Morris family was imprisoned in London for sheltering the celebrated Jesuit priest Edmund Campion.

In 1638 the Morrises sold Great Coxwell to a neighbouring landowner, Sir George Pratt, Bt, who already held the neighbouring estate of Coleshill.

It was at Coleshill that Inigo Jones and George's cousin, the amateur architect Roger Pratt, built one of the most advanced mansions of its day. (Coleshill House was, though, tragically destroyed by fire in 1952.) By 1939 the combined estate was owned by Ernest Cook, the grandson of the travel trade pioneer Thomas Cook. Ernest had made a fortune when he and his brother had sold the Thomas Cook travel business to the French Compagnie Internationale des Wagons-Lits in 1928 – just a year before the Wall Street Crash devastated the travel industry in particular and the world economy in general. During the 1930s Ernest Cook bought up a number of historic estates, including Coleshill, and on his death in 1955 bequeathed most of them to the National Trust. As a result, the Great Barn is now in the care of the National Trust – whose membership has risen from under 8,000 in 1945 to almost six million today.

Construction

Great Coxwell Barn was built of local limestone, with a roof of limestone slates from nearby Stonesfield. The site selected for the barn, however, was one of the very few in the area where stone lay immediately below the ground surface. To conform to the contours of this site, the barn's axis was forced to run from north to south, instead of the more usual east to west. An east–west orientation allowed for the maximising of daylight to illuminate the barn's interior as well as for good ventilation from prevailing westerly winds, creating a draught which helped the labourers separate the grain from the chaff. Accordingly, the unconventionally sited barn at Great Coxwell was provided, unusually, with two large east and west doors, added to help admit light and air.

Great Coxwell Barn's timber-framed interior is a rare survival of top-class medieval joinery. It is, moreover, a meticulously engineered and peculiarly English composition which architectural historian Sir Nikolaus Pevsner lauded as the finest of any barn in England. The oak timbers of the barn's interior have been dated by dendrochronology to the winter of 1291–2 – although, as was often the case in this period, both seasoned and unseasoned wood was used for construction, and the same dendrochronological tests have dated some of the barn's timbers to trees felled in 1253. This in turn corresponds to the build date proposed by celebrity University of California historian Walter Horn,[*] in

---

[*]   Professor Horn was the expert who recovered the crown jewels of the Holy Roman Empire in 1945 after they had been looted by the Nazis during the Second World War.

his definitive study of the barn of 1965, which suggested that previous esti-
mates citing the mid-fourteenth century were incorrect. Horn and his collaborator, draughtsman Ernest Born, categorised Great Coxwell as 'the finest of the
surviving mediaeval barns in England, and one of the most impressive structures of its kind in the whole of Europe'.

The barn was very large by the standards of the late thirteenth century.
One hundred and fifty feet long, it was originally entered through the gabled
porches on the east and west sides. The large north and south entrances are
more recent; they were probably added to accommodate the larger wagons
and bigger loads that resulted from the rapid advance of wheeled vehicle
technology in the later Georgian era. These four ample entrances – unusually large even for a barn of this great size – were also able to admit the new-
fangled farm machinery of the Victorian era which effectively spelled the
death knell for the barn as a working farm building.

Inside, the barn has the proportions of a cathedral. The 'nave' is divided
into seven bays which are roughly square in plan. The cruck-like timber frame
is supported on principal posts which rise from tall stone bases, nearly seven
feet high, creating column-like vertical elements which effectively separate the internal space into nave and aisles. Between the stone pedestals and
the vertical oak posts were small oak fillers or templates, laid sideways to the
direction of their grain so that moisture would not rise from the stone below
to rot the fibres of the wooden posts above. (The barn's carpenters clearly knew
what they were doing.) The posts were then braced securely by tie-beams just
below the rafters. From the top of these aisle posts, pairs of straight braces
extend diagonally in three directions, supporting both the tie-beams and
the outer wall plates and creating an aesthetic composition which suggests the
ribbed vaulting of a large church or cathedral. The tie also supports the foot
of a secondary rafter that extends to a smaller, higher collar sited just below
the apex of the roof and is itself secured to the vertical post by two pairs of
diagonal struts. This higher collar in turn supports a king strut (a miniature
king post: the central vertical support of a wooden frame) which rises to carry a
yoke for the ridge-purlin – the long axial beam which anchors the barn's rafters.

As in any large church, the structure of the barn's side aisles – which
are supported on a frame of tie-beams and secondary rafters – is a miniature
version of the construction of the nave roof. Each aisle tie is supported by a
curved brace springing from a wall post, carried on stone corbels with distinctive keeled profiles. These have been compared by historians to examples

at Rievaulx Abbey of a roughly similar date. This suggests that the Cistercians' English masons were asked to work at the order's sites all over the country. Certainly the excellence of the timber framing and the seamless integration of carpentry and masonry at Great Coxwell Barn suggest experienced hands used to working on similarly ambitious buildings, and not just local workmen. Up above, the considerable weight of the roof is carried by two rows of slender oak posts which have been so ingeniously woven together that, after 700 years of wind, rain and ground movement, not one has been dislodged from its original position.

There was originally also a 'tallat loft"' above the west porch. This feature was probably destroyed in the eighteenth century, when the original west door was bricked up following the provision of new openings at the north and south ends and the porch was converted into a stable. These later additions were themselves removed by the National Trust in 1962.

In the centre of the barn is the extensive threshing floor, on which grain was once threshed by hand with flails – wooden staffs with a shorter swinging stick attached – to separate the grain from the chaff. After threshing, the barn was used for storing the crop. Before 1538 this grain was intended not just for the residents of the local manor but also for the monks of Beaulieu. From 1538 until the abolition of tithes in 1836, the tithe grain was allocated to the Church of England in general.

The death of the barn

By the end of the eighteenth century agrarian reform and the industrial revolution had caught up with the medieval barn. An agricultural engineer named Michael Stirling was said to have invented a rotary threshing machine which, for forty years after 1758, was used to process all the corn on his farm at Gateside in Fife, Scotland. However, there is no documentary evidence for this. Instead, the palm for creating the first working threshing machine goes to Stirling's fellow Scottish engineer Andrew Meikle for this invention of 1786.

The use of mechanical threshing spread rapidly in Regency England, drastically reducing the number of farm labourers who needed to be paid to process the harvest. As early as 1797 the Devonian brewer William Spicer Dix

---

*   A tallat loft was the accommodation provided for the hapless monk (the *grangerius*) in charge of guarding and overseeing the barn.

△ *The barn from the south. The gable end is pockmarked with ventilation holes, essential for storing large amounts of grain.*

was urging farmers to adopt the threshing machine: 'By this Machine one man, or a woman, can clear as much grain in one day, as can be done with the flail in ten days, without bruising, injuring, or leaving any ears... [while the farmers] will be able to carry to market nearly every grain grown on their farms.' The result was that, in 1830, farm labourers across southern England, already incensed by the rising tide of enclosures, rampaged across towns and villages in what were dubbed the 'Captain Swing' riots, after the authorial pseudonym used on several of the anonymous threatening letters sent to prominent landowners. The Swing Rioters smashed threshing machines and threatened farmers who had bought them. However, local militias and magistrates dealt with them severely: 644 rioters were imprisoned, 505 were transported to Australia and 19 were sentenced to hang –the very fate 'Captain Swing' had threatened to mete out to the modernising farmers.

115

Early threshing machines were small, hand-fed and horse- or water-powered, while the engines or mills required to operate them were often housed in bespoke buildings adjacent to the barn. Following the Captain Swing Riots, however, the portable, steam-powered thresher became more common. This could be brought into the heart of the barn, making these venerable structures into what were now called 'mixing barns': simple areas for processing and storing grain which either temporarily (via a hired machine) or permanently (through installed equipment) shared their space with steam engines. Threshing machines were in turn replaced by self-propelled combine harvesters, which both harvested and threshed the crop while on the move. Combine harvesters were first developed in the 1920s, but the Great Depression limited their spread, and they were only fully adopted in Europe during the 1950s. This made the traditional barn largely redundant, as the harvested grain was stored for as short a time as possible before being shipped out to buyers.

The spread of the threshing machine was not the only threat to the traditional barn in the mid-nineteenth century. The abolition of tithes in 1836, a long-overdue piece of legislation which demolished the final prop of the Norman feudal system, was the death knell for large community barns such as that at Great Coxwell, since farmers began to store all, rather than just part, of their crop at their own farms. Not only had the barn's threshing floor lost its original purpose: by the time of agriculture's Great Depression of the 1870s the whole barn had become a relic of a bygone age.

The threshing machine brought the industrial revolution into the heart of the British countryside. By 1830, the year of the first Swing Riots, there were over a thousand threshing machines in use across southern England, while fifty years later the medieval flail had virtually disappeared from the larger farms. Thomas Hardy's *Tess of the D'Urbervilles* of 1891, set among the sheep and arable farmsteads of southern Dorset, directed the reader's eye towards an alien object among the corn:

> Close under the eaves of the stack, and as yet barely visible was the red tyrant that the women had come to serve – a timber-framed construction, with straps and wheels appertaining – the threshing-machine, which, whilst it was going, kept up a despotic demand upon the endurance of their muscles and nerves.

When Hardy wrote these lines Britain's Great Agricultural Depression had already smothered lowland farms in its asphyxiating embrace. During the 1870s, as the American prairies opened up in the wake of the Civil War, while advances in British steamship technology meant quicker transatlantic crossings, imports of cheap American grain became a common sight on British wharves. Coupled with the global warming of the mid-1870s, which led to appalling harvests in Britain and devastating famine in the hotter parts of the world, this led to disaster for many British arable farmers. Many did not recover until 1939; and only then thanks to the artificial stimulus of the wartime government's policy to maximise the production of home-grown food.

As a consequence of this downward economic spiral in rural areas, innovative agricultural architecture in Britain came to a halt. No more exemplar Model Farms were built; no more mechanised barns were created. As the large wooden barn became a relic of a barely remembered past, farmers turned to the cheapest means possible of storing crops and animals and housing their new machinery. Many turned not to wood or brick but to corrugated iron. First invented (naturally, in Britain) by engineer Thomas Telford's assistant Henry Palmer as a way of providing a cheap, fireproof and water-resistant roof for a London warehouse, by the 1850s corrugated iron roofs and walls were trendily fashionable. The material was even used by Prince Albert to create a temporary room at Balmoral in 1851. By 1880 corrugated iron sheds were common in British farms – which, aside from the advent of American-influenced concrete silos from the 1910s, rarely saw the addition of buildings of any architectural merit.

William Morris and Great Coxwell

Great Coxwell Barn's subsequent survival in something like its original form following the redundancy of its threshing floor and the late Victorian agricultural depression was largely due to the prominence and publicity given to the building by one highly influential individual: a figure who was to exert a monumental influence on British interior decoration which is almost as strong today as it was in 1870.*

William Morris (1834–96) went up to Exeter College, Oxford, as an undergraduate in 1852 and was immediately drawn to Oxford's medieval heritage – which he saw at a time before much of it had been reimagined by the college architects of the late Victorian era. (Twenty years earlier his own college had

---

*   He also termed the proliferation of corrugated iron a 'pestilence'.

been re-Gothicised under the direction of architect H. J. Underwood, completing the Tudorisation of the medieval thoroughfare of Turl Street.) After his graduation later Morris joined the neo-Gothic Oxford office of the prolific High Victorian architect G. E. Street, where he befriended the young architect Philip Webb. Tiring of their architectural apprenticeship, Morris and Webb then redirected their enthusiasm towards furniture-making and decorative painting, with mixed results. Morris was wealthy and thus able to fund his design work and his forays into poetry publication himself without fear of financial ruin if the enterprise failed. It also enabled him to stick to his principles when others suggested compromise.

In 1859 Morris married a working-class girl, Jane Burden, the daughter of an Oxford stableman and a servant. Jane became the muse of and model for both Morris and his close friend and artistic collaborator, Dante Gabriel Rossetti (1828–82).* Then in 1861 Morris founded the furniture-making and interior decoration firm Morris, Marshall, Faulkner and Co. with Rossetti, Webb, Oxford contemporary Edward Burne-Jones and the eponymous P. P., Marshall and Charles Faulkner. The company's ambition was to restore handmade craft and domestic decoration as one of the country's great art forms, as it had been before the industrial revolution.

Morris's increasing public profile and his distaste at London's crowds and dirt encouraged him to look for a house in the country as a refuge. He found one in 1871 at Kelmscott, a village to the west of Faringdon and only six miles from Great Coxwell. Here the Morrises lived for a time with Rossetti, which enabled Jane Morris and her husband's friend to consummate their love affair right under William's nose.

Kelmscott House was an Elizabethan house relatively untouched by the succeeding centuries. Built around 1570 in the distinctively English late Tudor idiom, with proto-classical additions of a century later, its rubbled walls of local Cotswold limestone, tall gables and grid windows with prominent dripmoulds were typical of the English great houses of the sixteenth century, before the alien classicism of Andrea Palladio and Inigo Jones supplanted those very English traditions of architectural compromise and technological evolution.

---

*   Jane Burden's rise to social prominence was said to have been the inspiration for George Bernard Shaw's play *Pygmalion*, which appeared three months after her death in 1914. Forty years later, *Pygmalion* was adapted into a hugely successful Broadway musical, *My Fair Lady*, by Alan Jay Lerner and Frederick Loewe which was in turn, in 1964, turned into an immensely successful film directed by the evergreen George Cukor.

△ G. F. Watts's portrait of conservationist, designer, poet and socialist William Morris, which is now in the National Portrait Gallery. It was painted in 1870, although not exhibited until a decade later.

Morris called it 'a heaven on earth' and although he was just a tenant – the house was only bought outright by his widow after his death – he continued to rent the house and spend increasing amounts of time there until his death in 1896 at the age of only sixty-two.

Any visitors to Kelmscott were invariably taken to see the nearby barn at Great Coxwell. For Morris it was the epitome of English ingenuity and craftsmanship, an agrarian cathedral which prioritised function and

119

workmanship to create something of beauty. He was delighted that its simple design exactly reflected the precepts of his mentor, John Ruskin (1819–1900): its decoration was its structure, it incorporated nothing which did not have a function or role, and both its design and its purpose dignified the labour of the agriculture worker – exactly as the Cistercians had intended. For Morris it was a rural masterpiece which deserved to be ranked alongside the very best buildings of Oxford University, 'unapproachable in its dignity, as noble as a cathedral'.

The threats posed to this now largely redundant building would undoubtedly have helped to inform Morris' greatest contribution to Britain's built heritage: the foundation of the Society for the Protection of Ancient Buildings (SPAB) in 1877. In a letter to the Athenaeum Club of London of 10 March 1877 Morris had protested against the growing trend towards invasive and insensitive 'restoration' of historic buildings and pleaded for a society to be formed to protect old structures such as Great Coxwell from these 'acts of barbarism'. The germ of what followed twelve days later, the *Manifesto of the Society for the Protection of Ancient Buildings*, was surely grown from the seed of Great Coxwell Barn. The text of the *Manifesto*, which may have been written at Kelmscott following a visit to Great Coxwell, declared of recent restorations:

> [I]n the course of this double process of destruction and addition, the whole surface of the building is necessarily tampered with; so that the appearance of antiquity is taken away from such old parts of the fabric as are left, and there is no laying to rest in the spectator the suspicion of what may have been lost; and in short, a feeble and lifeless forgery is the final result of all the wasted labour.

Morris demanded instead that contemporary Britons 'treat our ancient buildings as monuments of a bygone art, created by bygone manners, that modern art cannot meddle with without destroying':

> Thus, and thus only, shall we escape the reproach of our learning being turned into a snare to us; thus, and thus only can we protect our ancient buildings, and hand them down instructive and venerable to those that come after us.

With this treatise, with which he laid the foundation not just of the SPAB* but of the global building conservation philosophy of the next 150 years, Morris used the example of Great Coxwell Barn to inspire and inform the conservation movement. Today the National Trust's continued protection of this rural cathedral still shines as a beacon of best practice of which the Cistercians would have been proud.

---

* The SPAB is alive and well in London today and continues as the torchbearer of informed and honest building conservation.

7

LITTLE MORETON HALL, CHESHIRE

BEGUN 1504

Reframing the Elizabethans

Begun in 1504 and augmented in stages by successive generations of the family over the next century, Little Moreton Hall in Cheshire represents the apogee of the Tudor half-timbered house. Its precariously jettied floors, its complex plan, its 'gingerbread-house' timber-framing and its large areas of window glass all testify to the technological prowess of its builders and of its age. Even the National Trust's own guidebook describes the Hall as 'lifted straight from a fairy story'. To modern eyes its wood-framed engineering may appear hazardous and unstable; yet it has lasted for five centuries and will doubtless last many more.

Little Moreton also highlights essential concepts that recur throughout British history: continuity in an age of change; the love of adapting traditional forms and methods to create something which at the same time is both wholly new and yet fundamentally reassuring; and a lingering scepticism of what

▷ *The virtuoso carpentry and window-glazing at Little Moreton makes it an outstanding example of – and survivor from – its period.*

lies beyond the English Channel. And the survival of its original sixteenth-century plan and elevations makes Little Moreton Hall one of the most valuable buildings in the whole of Britain.

Tudor who?

Little Moreton Hall was rebuilt for the prosperous Cheshire landowner William Moreton towards the end of the reign of the founder of what we now know as the Tudor dynasty, King Henry VII. In 2012 the late lamented Oxford historian Dr Cliff Davies published a seminal article pointing out that the 'Tudor' name for the royal family was hardly known in the sixteenth century, and that 'The almost obsessive use of the term by historians is therefore profoundly misleading about how English people of the time thought of themselves and of their world, the more so given the overtones of glamour associated with it':

> The royal surname was never used in official publications, and hardly in 'histories' of various sorts before 1584. Monarchs were not anxious to publicize their descent in the paternal line from a Welsh adventurer, stressing instead continuity with the historic English and French royal families. Their subjects did not think of them as 'Tudors', or of themselves as 'Tudor people'... Nor did they situate themselves in a distinct 'Tudor' period of history, differentiated from a hypothetical 'middle ages'.

Davies' point applies equally well to British architecture. Little Moreton Hall, while incorporating some impressive new technological features – notably the profuse use of window glass and the engineering of the projecting, jettied floors – should not be seen as a particularly 'Tudor' building. Rather, it should be seen, as late, lamented architectural historian Dr Mark Girouard has remarked, 'as a magnificent last flowering' of the English medieval tradition and a building which looks both backwards to the past and forwards to the future.

Most crucially, the Hall's style and materials signally refused to respond to contemporary classical developments in continental Europe – despite the fact that, by the time the building was completed during the reign of King James I, the vocabulary of Italian classicism had become a significant influence on the design of many of the large 'prodigy' homes of the period. As such, the

Hall's style and form have been belittled by generations of architectural historians, for whom an organic, native tradition was no substitute for the antique erudition of continental classicism and was, as a result, viewed with amused condescension as a charming but hopelessly outmoded stylistic dead end. While 'Tudor' great houses such as Burghley and Longleat were seen as helpful steps on the staircase to the inevitable 'triumph of classicism', as the architectural history of the following century is invariably called, less pretentious (and far less costly) homes such as Little Moreton were dismissed as mere footnotes.

Origins of the Hall

Built as a testimony to economic and social success, Little Moreton Hall is frequently cited as an indication of the upward social mobility of the period – one of the key elements in the traditional conception of the Golden Age of Tudor England. However, while it was built in an idiom which has been belittled as reactionary and unsophisticated by generations of British historians, it can now be recognised not just as a proud survivor of a typically British craft tradition, but also as a reflection of a peculiarly English identity during the Elizabethan age.

As at Coxwell, there are actually two Moretons in this part of south Cheshire. (The name Moreton, incidentally, comes from the Old English *mor* or *more* ('moor'), or marshy area, and 'ton', or town.) Illogically, the Moreton family lived at Little Moreton while, from 1606, it was the Bellot family which lived at Great Moreton (also known, in the fine British tradition of weird and wonderful place names, as Moreton-cum-Alcumlow), which lies a mile to the east of its Little sibling. Great Moreton Hall, also known as Moreton Magna, appears to have been a timber-framed structure which may not have been too dissimilar to the Hall at Little Moreton. However, in 1814 the Great Moreton estate was sold to the cotton tycoon George Ackers, whose son demolished the Jacobean house in 1840 and commissioned the highly successful royal architect Edward Blore to build a vast, stone-walled replacement.

Like many of the landed gentry of the 1530s and 1540s, the Moretons did well out of Henry VIII's ruthless suppression of religious houses, later dignified by the title of the English Reformation,* and by 1560 William Moreton II

---

* The more emotive term the 'Dissolution of the Monasteries' derives from Henry VIII's Dissolution of the Lesser Monasteries Act of 1535.

△ *Interior of Little Moreton's astonishing Long Gallery. The prolific use of window glass in such a domestic context was a bold statement for sixteenth-century England.*

owned two watermills and 1,360 acres (550 hectares) of land. The first William Moreton (d. 1526) built the Great Hall and the rooms immediately to the east, including what became the Parlour, the Chapel the Withdrawing Room, and added a service wing to the west to create a highly fashionable and avant-garde H-plan house. In 1546 William Moreton's son, also called William (*c.*1510–63), replaced the original west wing with a new range, added a new floor at gallery level in the Great Hall and, in 1559, two large, linked bay windows looking onto the courtyard. By 1600 the Great Hall was entered through a porch on the left of the main courtyard while the Chapel was not, as was often the case on the Continent, afforded a prominent position at the centre of the composition, but was instead squashed into the south-east corner of the court. To add to the confusion, the gabled bay window overlooking the courtyard, added in 1559, competed with that projecting from the adjacent Great Hall. Two of the bay's decorated facing-boards carry bold inscriptions (made even more visible by the modern black and white paint scheme) which brazenly namecheck the Hall's builders: 'GOD IS AL IN AL THING: THIS WINDOVS WHIRE

128

MADE BY WILLIAM MORETON IN THE YEARE OF OURE LORDE MDLIX' and 'RICHARDE DALE CARPEDER. MADE THIES WINDOVS BY THE GRAC OF GOD'.

Having been extended at numerous times over a century and a half, the Hall was full of contradictions which often made no sense. The family would have sat at the far end of the Great Hall; but right behind them was a door which led to what was originally known as the Little Parlour. In the 1640s William Moreton III used what is today known as the Exhibition Room as a bedroom, entered through a doorway from the adjoining Withdrawing Room, but following his death in 1654 his children Ann, Jane and Philip divided the house into three separate living areas and Ann, who had already converted the Prayer Room above into a bedroom, used the Exhibition Room as a kitchen. The Hall's plan may have been incomprehensible to those looking for the rigid classical symmetry of a contemporary Italian villa, but its haphazard and flexible nature enabled it to grow organically in response to its inhabitants' whims and circumstances.

The 'Tudor' Hall seems to have been a very colourful home. The original wooden panelling of the Great Hall, rediscovered during the repairs of 1976, was, in typically sixteenth-century style, painted in a cheerful imitation of marble.* Some walls in both the Great Hall and the Chapel (which was begun in 1508) also featured crude biblical scenes – many featuring the story of Susannah and the Elders, a moral yet also rather licentious story from the Book of Daniel – which were painted directly onto the plaster or onto paper that was then pasted to the wall.

It was presumably William Moreton II who added the large chimney surround in the Parlour, which was re-Gothicised in the eighteenth century. Its plaster overmantel is original, though, and features the royal arms flanked by two vaguely classical caryatids – an assertively patriotic gesture in the uncertain period after Elizabeth I's succession to the throne in 1558, when Britain was still riven by religious disputes and the imposition of Protestantism (as indeed happened in 1559) might encourage an attack from any of Europe's three great Catholic powers. A south wing was also added early in Elizabeth's reign by William Moreton II's son, John (1541–98), which included the Gatehouse and a third storey comprising the celebrated, 68-foot Long Gallery. A further

---

*   The concept of bare, unpainted deal panelling is very much a twentieth-century one, born of a confusion between historical practice and Scandinavian Modernism.

range of service rooms was added to the north-western corner of the Long Gallery around 1600 while the provision of a brewhouse and kitchen around 1610 completed the original work.

The Civil War and after

Any happiness the Moretons might have felt at the completion of their century-long building programme was, however, sadly short-lived. From the outbreak of the English Civil War in 1642, the Moretons were never to enjoy a glad confident morning again. Having chosen to advertise their royalist sympathies in a staunchly parliamentarian region – an act which prompted parliamentary troops to brusquely requisition the house to billet soldiers in 1643 – in 1654 the fifth-generation head of the family, William Moreton, died leaving crippling debts to his family. Twenty years later the Moretons found they simply could not afford to repair or even to live in the house their ancestors had so painstakingly built, and instead rented it to a series of tenants. In 1841 – the year in which work began on Edward Blore's new Great Moreton Hall, just a mile away – the Dale family took over the lease on what was becoming an increasingly decrepit structure. The Dales chose only to live in one corner of the property, leaving the rest of the Hall to moulder away, its fine Elizabethan windows boarded up. As early as 1847 the deconsecrated Chapel was being used as a coal bunker.

In retrospect, however, the Moretons' neglect and the Dales' indifference did the house a favour. Little Moreton Hall did not suffer the ignominy of demolition, as its Great Moreton neighbour was to; nor was it modernised beyond all recognition. Instead, it retained the same basic layout of 1610 throughout the next four centuries.

As the Hall was not particularly remote – it lay just to the east of the main Stoke–Manchester road, now the A34 – its picturesque if parlous condition soon attracted the attention of artists and writers looking for a romantic ruin to depict. In 1880 the indefatigable artist, novelist, traveller and pioneering Egyptologist Amelia Edwards (1831–92) – hailed as 'the most learned woman in the world' when she toured New England towards the end of her life and the founder of the first English university Chair in Egyptology – used Little Moreton as a setting for her 1880 novel *Lord Brackenbury*, her last and most successful book, published in numerous editions. The success of Edwards's popular novel in turn attracted more curious visitors to Moreton, which was now on the point of collapse.

Structural salvation came after 1892, when Elizabeth Moreton inherited the freehold of the semi-derelict house and began to repair it, conserving and refurnishing the Chapel and stabilising the structure of the Long Gallery. In 1912 she bequeathed the house to a cousin, Charles Abraham, the Bishop of Derby (1857–1945), on the condition that it must never be sold. Abraham continued Elizabeth's restoration programme; however, his work corresponded to a Victorian ideal of the 'Tudor' house that in truth was as contrived as the Victorian concept of the 'Tudor dynasty'. The sixteenth-century Moretons would have built a house whose exteriors comprised oak beams, designed to silver with age, and Flemish-bond brick or plaster panels, the latter painted off-white or a more yellowish ochre. The 'black and white' colour scheme we so associate with sixteenth-century buildings is mostly a late Victorian invention. By the 1920s the blackening of external woodwork and the painting of plaster infill with bright white paint (or, worse still, the plastering and painting of original herringbone brick panels) was becoming standard across the country. Towns and cities across Britain – most notably the city centre of Chester, 'Tudorised' in the 1890s at the whim of the fabulously wealthy Grosvenors – were inspired by this historicist fashion, which celebrated the age of Good Queen Bess and all her colourful courtiers so beloved by school textbooks of the time and made for picturesque book illustrations if not for authentic architectural practice. On occasion, where money was tight (as, for example, the King's Arms Hotel in Amersham, Buckinghamshire), the building's façade was converted into a black and white 'Tudor' confection while the side elevations were left in its original state (in the King's Arms' case, with infill panels of attractively weathered local brick). In Little Moreton Hall's case, its current owners, the National Trust, are gradually returning the building to something approaching its original, pre-Victorian appearance.

On his retirement in 1927, Bishop Abraham opened up Little Moreton Hall to the public, charging an entrance fee of sixpence. The house's tenants – still the Dale family – both collected the money and conducted guided tours. However, the Hall's fabric continued to need constant attention. As a result, encouraged by the favourable terms of the National Trust Act of the previous year, in 1938 the eighty-one-year-old retired bishop bravely and wisely transferred the house to the National Trust.

The National Trust, justly called the most successful and influential private membership organisation in the world, is a peculiarly British construct. It was founded in 1895 by a trio of private individuals – social reformer Octavia Hill, preservationist lawyer Robert Hunter and yet another conservation-minded cleric, Canon Hardwicke Rawnsley – yet its status is also enshrined in law. The Trust's earliest acquisitions on behalf of the nation were of tracts of threatened countryside and seashore, and by 1930 they owned only a handful of buildings, acquired more by accident than design. However, the donation to the Trust by the Royal Society of Arts of the entire estate village of West Wycombe in Buckinghamshire in 1934 marked a change of direction. The Trust's management worked with Stanley Baldwin's National Government (a Conservative-dominated coalition) to frame and pass the National Trust Act, by which a family donating their property to the Trust did not have to pay death duties but, by the terms of the Trust's new Country Houses Scheme, could continue to live in the property rent free for two generations. In return the property would be at least partly opened to the public – although interpretations of this clause were to vary widely. The Trust was mandated to meet the costs of maintenance and repair, although these could, of course, be very substantial. By 1968 – the year in which the 'Chorley Formula' was devised to calculate the long-term cost of custodianship – the Trust was acknowledging that any future donations of historic buildings would have to be accompanied by large and sustainable endowments.

Little Moreton Hall was one of the first homes to be offered to the Trust under the Act of 1937. By the terms of the Act the Hall's tenants, the Dale family, continued to farm the estate until 1945, and acted as site caretakers for a further decade. Meanwhile, the Trust began a systematic programme of urgent repairs to the building which lasted well into the 1970s.

In the post-war years Little Moreton Hall was regarded with affection by locals and visitors and was in much demand as a film and television setting. Yet it was not held in high esteem by most historians, other than those interested in British timber vernacular architecture. More recently, journalist and cultural historian Simon Jenkins has rightly lauded the Hall's virtuoso wooden structure, calling it 'a feast of medieval carpentry', but until the late twentieth century few shared his opinion.

Beyond the cringe

Little Moreton Hall was built during a period which has been unhelpfully called the 'English Renaissance', when classical forms from the Continent began to be absorbed, little by little, into native Tudor buildings. However, as we have seen, the Hall was firmly rooted in the medieval English tradition of timber-framing – aside, that is, from a few obligatory classical motifs, added in the interior to demonstrate that the Moretons were no provincial hicks. The Hall was, in a sense, a reflection of the Elizabethan regime's splendid iso-lation, during which the monarch and her government successfully kept all the continental powers at arm's length: not just the Catholic Spain of Philip II, the Counter-Reformationist Habsburg empire and the perennially unsta-ble France of the last Valois kings but also the new Protestant, republican re-gime of the United Provinces (today's Kingdom of the Netherlands), to which Elizabeth I sent half-hearted support in 1585 (which achieved nothing) and to which she continued to pay lip service largely to keep the Spanish distracted across the sea.

While Little Moreton Hall and other timber-framed great houses of the sixteenth century have always been admired for their picturesque qualities, they have long been dismissed from the canon of British architectural history as they did not – or, as many historians saw it, simply failed or refused to – reflect the classical developments of continental Europe. In his magisterial work of 1953, the Pelican History of Art's *Architecture in Britain 1530–1830*, architectural historian Sir John Summerson followed contemporary commen-tators in applauding what he called 'the infiltration of the Antique taste' into British architectural design of the sixteenth century, but dismissed the native tradition of half-timbering, preferring to highlight Italian decoration of 'qual-ity'. This illustration of the classic British 'cultural cringe' saw Tudor timber vernacular as an attractive yet quaint sideshow that was more craft than architecture, an amusing pastime in which to indulge while Britons expect-antly waited for the advent of classicism. More recently, though, it has been suggested that the imported, Italianate neo-Palladianism of Inigo Jones* and his classically inspired followers in the early seventeenth century was actually an alien incursion into the British architectural tradition.

Little Moreton Hall was certainly not in the forefront of Renaissance design. Its use of timber-framing and reliance on traditional craftsman-ship was firmly set in the past. In many ways, however, the hall was a very modern building. Its emblazoning of the identities of both owner and prin-cipal carpenter (Richard Dale of the ubiquitous local clan) reflected the new secular trend towards self-advertisement rather than retiring Christian

---

*   See the following chapter for a detailed discussion of Jones.

humility in architecture. (This type of secular celebration was most famously expressed in the parapets of Hardwick Hall in Derbyshire, built in the 1590s to the designs of Robert Smythson, whose openwork parapet repeatedly carries the initials of its proud and ambitious owner, Elizabeth, Dowager Countess of Shrewsbury.)

Equally modern was the Hall's prolific use of window glass – again, as also seen at Smythson's new house for Bess of Hardwick in the neighbouring county. In the secular age which followed the English Reformation, house builders followed the ecclesiastical masons of the fifteenth and early sixteenth centuries in engineering their homes to admit as much glass as possible (or, rather, as much as they could afford). At Little Moreton, as at Hardwick, this depended on making the load-bearing timber or stone walls take the strain rather than the vulnerable grids of fragile external glazing.

Improvements in glass technology

The provision of large areas of window glazing, as at Little Moreton, was still a symbol of status when the house was begun in 1504. But by 1600 Britain led the world in the manufacture of domestic window glass, which could be found even in the poorer English homes.

This does not mean that it was cheap. Yet even in France, widely celebrated for high-quality mirror-glass manufacture throughout the seventeenth and eighteenth centuries, oiled paper or cloth was, as Colin Clark has cited, still being used to cover French window openings by the end of the eighteenth century. King James I's proclamation of 1615 prohibiting the use of oak as a fuel for glassmaking furnaces seemed at first something of a blow to British glass manufacturers (particularly in areas such as the Sussex Weald, where glassmaking and ironmaking never recovered); but in the longer term it actually proved a boon. The higher temperatures afforded by the use of coal – a fuel that was widely abundant across the British Isles – enabled the glass industry to make stronger, thicker and more durable glass. This gave the English a head start not just in making sturdy window glass but also in the manufacture of glass bottles, which in turn led indirectly to the English invention of champagne in the 1660s,

◁ *The half-timbered gables and gallery may look precarious but they have withstood the Cheshire elements for five centuries.*

135

since the robust bottles made in Sir Robert Mansell's Newcastle and London glass factories were able to withstand the pressure of the secondary fermentation occurring in the hitherto unremarkable Champenois wines.

In 1600, however, window glass could still not be made in very large panes. That did not come until the seventeenth century, with the development of new casting and blowing techniques to make larger, stronger crown glass. As a result, the large windows at Little Moreton Hall comprised around 30,000 small, rectangular, square, circular, triangular or octagonal panes or 'quarries', held together by an intricate spider's web of lead cames.* On some of these panes historic graffiti still survives.

Little Moreton's prolifically glazed bay and oriel windows took as their model the profusely fenestrated aristocratic great houses of sixteenth-century Britain: vast creations such as Hardwick Hall (famously 'more glass than wall'), Thornbury Castle, Montacute House, Worksop Manor and, in the opinion of Mark Girouard, 'the most swagger of Elizabethan creations: the two bay windows of the Hall [at] Bradford-on-Avon'. All of these paradigms, however, were couched in a stone-built rather than a timber-framed context. Little Moreton's bombastic glazing was a version of Hardwick or Montacute suitable for the upwardly mobile upper-middle classes: families such as the Moretons, who had done well out of the Reformation and who preferred to use local materials to build their own testaments of success.

Such great windows, Girouard admitted, had little to do with the Renaissance. They could also be found in houses of the late Gothic period in England – the later fifteenth century and earlier sixteenth century. However, Little Moreton Hall's exceptional glazed Long Gallery, jettied out beyond its supporting floors and extending almost the whole length of the building, has no direct medieval precedent. It is a bold statement of what new technology could do within the confines of traditional building methods. Running the entire length of the south range, the Long Gallery was roofed with heavy stone slabs, the weight of which has over the years caused the supporting floors below to buckle. Nevertheless, although the Gallery may not meet modern engineering standards, it still survives after five centuries. Cheshire architectural historians Peter de Figueiredo and Julian Treuherz have celebrated this astonishing room as 'a gloriously long and crooked space, the wide floorboards

---

*   Cames are the thin metal strips which held window panes together before the advent of wooden glazing bars in the later seventeenth century.

rising up and down like waves and the walls leaning outwards at different angles'. The cross-beams between the braced roof trusses were probably added later to prevent the structure from bursting apart under the weight of its roof, and the two tympana at either end of the Gallery have plaster panels with depictions of Destiny and Fortune, subjects which must have seemed bleakly ironic to the Moreton family after 1642. The images featured in the panels were taken from Robert Recorde's astronomical treatise of 1556, *The Castle of Knowledge*, and are accompanied by appropriate, improving inscriptions: 'The wheel of fortune, whose rule is ignorance' and 'The speare of destiny, whose rule is knowledge'. Like many similar spaces in British great houses, the actual function of the Long Gallery – apart from impressing visitors – is still uncertain. But we do know that it was sometimes used as a games room, as two Jacobean tennis balls have been discovered behind the wood panelling.

With its ostentatious glazing and flamboyant carpentry, Little Moreton Hall can be seen as the latest expression of the ingenuity and resourcefulness of English medieval architecture – part of, as Mark Girouard put it, 'a living Gothic tradition' which persisted from the thirteenth century until the middle of the seventeenth. This was the sort of house to which most wealthy Elizabethans aspired: something adaptable yet at the same time ostentatious, which reflected local building traditions and employed local resources of materials and crafts-manship yet at the same time made a bold statement that combined cutting-edge technology with unapologetic ostentation and the public flaunting of symbols of success. 'Elizabethan Renaissance' masterpieces such as Somerset House and Longleat may have been much acclaimed by generations of histo-rians for their transcultural sophistication, yet they were atypical of the main-stream of British building of the time – not just because of their size and cost but also in their incorporation of classical idioms. Girouard, inverting the inherent Italianate bias of Summerson's era, has suggested that this was simply 'because the Elizabethan upper classes found that their own Gothic tradition was better fitted to supply the particular kind of magnificence which they wanted'.

A celebrated survival

Little Moreton Hall is special – but not much more than many timber-framed homes of its time. Its uniqueness comes in its survival, thanks to the impecu-nity and indolence of its owners and tenants. It has been said that the build-ing technique it employs – an oak frame on stone footings – is unremarkable for Cheshire houses of the period; diagonal oak braces that create chevron, lozenge and quatrefoil patterns were not uncommon in homes of all sizes during the sixteenth century. Inside, the Hall showed no evidence of conforming to the symmetrical villa planning then becoming prevalent in Italy and France; instead, as architectural historian Lydia Greeves has noted, the interior of Little Moreton Hall was a 'corridor-less warren, with one room leading into another, and four staircases linking different levels', with some of the smaller rooms representing 'little more than cupboards'. The Hall obviously grew organically over decades, in response to the needs of successive generations of Moretons, rather than being logically planned from the start. There are few examples of homes as diametrically different from the contemporary, geometrically ordered Veneto villas of Andrea Palladio as Cheshire's Little Moreton Hall.

It was not just the fashionability of Italianate classicism, however, which ultimately caused the disappearance of timber framing. The replacement of the English vernacular tradition of timber-framed houses, even those as spectacular as Little Moreton Hall, may well have had more to do with practicality rather than fashion. By the time the house was finished in James I's reign, Britain faced a crisis in sourcing the building material on which the Hall and its timber-framed contemporaries had relied: old English oak. Homes such as the Hall had been viable as they sat amid a well-wooded area, where oak was plentiful. Only in densely wooded parts of the country such as south Cheshire did the availability of good-quality timber make possible large, expertly carpentered structures such as Little Moreton Hall. (Inevitably, in stone-rich upland areas of Britain local stone replaced timber as the principal material used for external walling.) In areas such as Cheshire, oak remained the building material of choice until the second half of the seventeenth century. But by the eighteenth century it was no longer considered fashionable or practicable. Not only were classical models and fireproof materials more in vogue – resulting in the widespread refronting of timber-framed buildings in brick or stone and the disappearance of jettied elevations under symmetrical façades – but oak was no longer freely available.

Part of the reason for the British revolution in building materials was the need to reserve oak for the nation's ever-growing navy and merchant marine. During the Middle Ages England's standing navy had been negligible, reliant during time of war – which was invariably with France – on the widespread commandeering of ships from the country's merchant fleet. However, Henry

VIII's brutal Reformation, which detached Britain from Catholic Europe, raised the prospect that England could now be invaded by an alliance of Catholic powers from the Continent – a combination (or indeed all) of Spain, France and the Holy Roman Empire, backed morally and financially by the papacy. Henry VIII responded by strengthening the defences of England's south coast and developing a permanent navy. His children Edward VI and Elizabeth I continued the process; as a result, in the fifty years after the Reformation, from the Dissolution of the Monasteries to the defeat of the Spanish Armada, 131 ships were added to the Royal Navy (although admittedly some of these were appropriated prizes). Yet in 1559 Elizabeth I's unsteady new government prohibited the sale of 'any seaworthy vessels' to foreigners 'on account of the scarcity of timber'.

At the same time as meeting naval demands, there was a growing need for more oak-built merchant ships to serve the English coast. These were particularly needed to supply London, which had grown astronomically during this period, from around 70,000 residents at the beginning of the sixteenth century to 200,000 by the end, with food, fuel and consumer goods. The growth of London also inevitably increased the demand for timber for building purposes. As a result, country landowners became increasingly aware of the value of timber.

The medieval concept of the forest as a reserve for the hunting of deer had long vanished, its legitimacy fatally undermined by the great Charters of 1215 and 1217. Now the typical English landowner, particularly after both the Reformation and the gathering pace of the enclosure movement had redistributed thousands of acres to him and his kind, adopted a more cost-efficient approach to land and timber management. Landowners now began to employ professional surveyors to record land use and timber stocks. For the first time, the sustainability of English oak reserves was being called into question.

Acknowledging the finite nature of the nation's timber resources was nothing new. Since the second half of the fifteenth century there had been a reduction in the size of timbers used in house building – possibly not just to conserve stocks but also for aesthetic reasons or, as Paul Barnwell has argued, the realisation that the use of substantial timbers was not always structurally necessary. However, by the middle of the sixteenth century this concern was being translated into legislation. As early as 1543 an attempt was made by Henry VIII's government to establish a system of woodland management in an Act designed to arrest:

... the greate decay of Tymber and Woodes universally within this Realme of Englande to be suche that unlesse speedy remedy in that behalfe be provided there is great and manifest likelyhood of scarcity and lacke as well of Tymber for building, making, repayringe and maynteyninge of Houses and Shippes, as also for fewell and firewood.

However, the phenomenal increase in naval construction and house building during the later sixteenth century put further pressure on these precious stocks. In 1960 J. L. M. Gulley concluded that, in the prosperous Sussex Weald, there were 'many more houses built between 1570 and 1640 than in any other period of comparable length before or afterwards'. At the same time, the Elizabethan navy continued to expand both before and after the Armada of 1588.

Elizabeth I's unloved successor, King James I and VI of Scotland, was hardly a warmonger. He purposely (and wisely) kept Britain out of the ruinous, pan-European Thirty Years War that erupted in 1618, much to many of his subjects' disgust. However, he was sufficiently concerned about preserving oak reserves for the Royal Navy to resort to new legislation. In 1611 James issued a 'Proclamation for Restraint of Building in and about London' which advocated the greater use of brick in building, 'which is safer and reduces use of timber, which needs to be preserved'. Without anyone to enforce this measure, however, the proclamation was largely ignored. (Fifty-five years later, after the Great Fire of London had burned much of timber-framed London to the ground, it was to be a different story.) In 1615, though, King James found an easier target: the fledgling glass industry rather than the nation's myriad house builder. Accordingly, he issued a 'Proclamation touching Glasses' banning the use of wood as industrial fuel. The official reason given for this policy was to protect 'Wood and Timber':

... that timber thereof is not only great and large in height and bulk, but hath also that toughnesse and heart, as it is not subject to rive or cleave, and thereby of excellent bie for shipping, as if God Almightie which had ordained this Nation to be mighty by Sea and navigation.

James's concern was that the 'wastfull destruction and consumption of them... hath been exceeding great and intolerable by the Glass-houses and Glasse-workes, of late in divers parts erected'. Helpfully, the proclamation directed glassmakers to newly perfected ways of manufacturing glass with 'sea-cole, pit-cole and other fewell, without any manner of wood' – although glass-houses were strictly forbidden from importing 'any manner, kind, or fashion of Glasse or Glasses whatsoever'. As noted, while many smaller glassmaking concerns folded as a result of this royal decree, the use of coal furnaces actually provided the larger glass manufacturers with the catalyst they needed to make a better, stronger material.

The scene was set not just for ground-breaking improvements in British glass and iron technology. It also laid the basis for the industrial revolution which was to propel Britain to astonishing wealth and global pre-eminence. At the same time, in architecture the scarcity of oak spelled the end of the medieval timber tradition and finally opened the door to the continental classicists.

8

THE QUEEN'S CHAPEL, ST JAMES'S PALACE, LONDON

1623–5

Inigo Jones and the Temple of Doom: how classical architecture led to civil war

The expansion of trade between Britain and Europe in the early seventeenth century inevitably encouraged Britons to adopt technological and stylistic influences from Europe – among them the new-fangled French invention of the sash window[*] and a taste for pure, pristine, Italianate classical architecture. But perhaps the most important factor in ensuring the instant fashionability of classical design in post-Elizabethan Britain was the royal patronage of the nation's early Stuart kings, now ruling over a united monarchy of both England and Scotland. The Stuarts' facilitator in accelerating the importation of full-blooded Italianate classicism into Britain was one Inigo Jones, court architect first to King James I, then to James's eldest son and heir, Prince Henry of Wales, and lastly, after Henry's death, to the latter's younger brother, Prince Charles – King Charles I from 1625 until his death in 1649.

---

[*]   Recent research suggests that the (single-hung) sash window was invented by the French in the 1650s but swiftly abandoned by them and, instead, developed by the British.

However, in Jones's unapologetic introduction of classical forms, using a style grounded in the works of a Catholic Italian architect who had been dead for forty years, lay the seeds of Charles I's downfall and execution. No better was this transition from soffit to scaffold exemplified in a building which, to many Britons on the outbreak of war in 1642, incarnated what they perceived as the insidious Catholic and absolutist influences undermining the royal court: the Queen's Chapel at St James's Palace.

Inigo Jones and British classicism

Inigo Jones was a humbly born artist, the son of a Welsh clothworker who had moved to Smithfield in the City of London. His rapid ascent in fashionable circles was prompted by two factors: his skill at draughtsmanship and his ability to ingratiate himself with influential patrons at the sexually fluid court of James I. As a young man he may have worked as an apprentice joiner at nearby St Paul's Cathedral; then, he was sent by a rich patron – we have no idea who, or how Jones cultivated him or her – to study in Italy and then in Denmark. While in Copenhagen he managed to inveigle his way into the design team working on new palace architecture for the Danish king, Christian IV. This was in turn to open doors in Britain: on his return to London, Jones seemingly used his experience of the Danish court to obtain an appointment as a designer of royal masques for King Christian's sister, Anne, the long-suffering wife of King James I. In this capacity Jones worked alongside (though rarely in accord with) the playwright Ben Jonson and is credited with introducing the concept of moveable scenery and the proscenium arch to the British theatre. A later visit to Italy in 1606 saw Jones learn Italian and buy a book by the late Padua-born architect Andrea Palladio (1508–80): *Il quattro libri dell'architettura* of 1570. This purchase was to be of enormous significance not just to Jones's own artistic development but also to the history of British architecture in the eighteenth century. It was also a crucial influence on the history of Britain in the 1640s, a time which saw a king tried and executed and a republic established. In some senses, Palladio and Jones can be said to have inadvertently stoked the fires of revolution.

◁ *The Queen's Chapel from the west, sundered from the rest of St James's Palace by Marlborough Road.*

146

Jones was always adept at securing lucrative patronage. In Jacobean London he quickly attached himself to James I's Lord Treasurer and (in all but name) first minister, Robert Cecil, 1st Earl of Salisbury. Jones appears in the accounts as an architect at Salisbury's new country house at Hatfield, Hertfordshire, and in 1610 – presumably thanks to Salisbury's influence – was appointed Surveyor to Prince Henry, the heir to the throne, on the latter's investiture as Prince of Wales.

Henry and Charles

Prince Henry was a young man of enormous promise, in which many British hopes were vested. A strongly moral figure of a Calvinist disposition who excelled at sport and music – and who also clearly despised his undersized younger brother, Charles, whom he made the butt of countless practical jokes – it is possible that, had he lived, Britain would have avoided the ruinous civil wars of the 1640s. The country might also have weighed in on the 'Protestant' side of the Thirty Years War, involvement in which Henry's father, James I, had carefully evaded after international hostilities began in 1618. However, all these counter-factual scenarios must remain conjectural 'what ifs'. For in 1612 Prince Henry died of typhoid, leaving his shy, undersized and nervous younger brother as heir to the throne.

Prince Charles – King Charles I after 1625 – was, unlike his elder brother, very much in his father's shadow. He continued his father's policy of splendid isolation at the periphery of the Thirty Years War, prompting many Britons to question the young king's commitment to Protestantism and the Church of England. In 1639, indeed, the English navy came close to entering the war on the side of the Catholic Spanish, following the decisive Dutch victory of the Battle of the Downs without any intervention on either side from King Charles's fleet, a lost opportunity which many Britons found deeply humiliating. Such national embarrassments fostered suspicions of Charles's secret Catholic predilections, misgivings which were to find a solid focus in the chapel Charles was to build for his Catholic queen at St James's.

In 1613 Jones travelled to Italy yet again, this time in the company of the greatest British artistic patron of the day: Thomas Howard, the Catholic 14th Earl of Arundel. In Arundel's company Jones met numerous artists and architects, including the great Vincenzo Scamozzi (1548–1616), and was able to study the ruins of ancient Rome at first hand. After his return he was (probably thanks

△ *Inigo Jones's Banqueting House of 1619–22 was the first wholly classical building to be completed in Britain and almost the only survivor of the Whitehall Palace Fire of 1698. It was surely no accident that Parliament chose to execute King Charles I at this particular building on 30 January 1649.*

to Arundel's advocacy) elevated to the peak of the architectural profession – despite having had little experience of building – as Surveyor-General of the King's Works. It was in this capacity that he designed Britain's first flagrantly classical buildings: the Queen's House at Greenwich Palace, begun in 1616 for Queen Anne of Denmark, and the Banqueting House at the Palace of Whitehall, built in 1619–22. Thereafter the majority of Jones's works were commissioned by the royal family, a factor which proved to be the architect's undoing during the ensuing Civil War.

Jones's immaculately proportioned, stone-walled Banqueting House was easily visible to any visitor to Westminster, and landed like an alien spacecraft in the midst of low-rise, timber-framed Tudor London. We know from contemporary paintings of the visual impact the building had on its surroundings, its pale, two-tone, neo-Palladian façade towering over the adjacent brick and timber buildings. The cool classicism of the Banqueting House appeared to augur a new era not just of Italian influence but, to many, of the preferment of Catholics, too. These suspicions were hardly allayed when, in 1638, exquisite painted panels were finally installed in the ceiling of the Banqueting

House, featuring *The Apotheosis of James I*. These had been created not by a British artist but by the legendary Flemish painter Sir Peter Paul Rubens, the Catholic diplomat-artist who had been ostentatiously knighted by Charles I in 1630. It should not perhaps come as much of a surprise to learn that, barely eleven years after this cultural inauguration, King Charles I was to be led to his execution through one of Jones's classically proportioned windows in the very same building.

Creating the chapel

In 1623 work began on a new classical chapel by Jones, the purest expression of Italianate classicism that he had yet devised. It was built at the western edge of the royal palace of St James's, half a mile north of the cold and damp regal residence at Whitehall. (Whitehall Palace was, with the exception of Jones's stone Banqueting House and its two sixteenth-century gates, to burn to the ground in 1698.) The new chapel was designed for and named after Charles's Catholic wife, Queen Henrietta Maria, and its primary purpose was to serve as a centre for royal Catholic worship at the heart of a Protestant country in which the profession of Catholicism was technically illegal and punishable by death. Of the three Catholic Chapels Royal constructed after 1620 for Henrietta Maria – at St James's Palace, Somerset House and Whitehall – only that at St James's has survived relatively intact.

The Queen's Chapel has been described by architectural historian John Harris as a building which 'expresses of the quintessential Jones [more] than any other surviving building'. Yet, as historian and *The Buildings of England* editor-in-chief Simon Bradley has commented, while the Queen's Chapel 'is cherished as perhaps the most intact of all Inigo Jones's works... its importance was established beyond doubt only during the scholarly restoration begun in 1937'. In this case the building's notorious reputation appears to have obscured its architectural merits to later generations.

In form the Queen's Chapel was a simple double cube, a disposition beloved of Jones which he took straight from the sixteenth-century Italian models of architects Andrea Palladio and Vincenzo Scamozzi. It lacked the transepts or choir of a traditional English Gothic church; instead, it featured shallow lateral galleries and a spacious Royal Closet at the west end, which was accessed through a screen of Corinthian columns. At the east end it was lit by a large Venetian window which occupied almost the whole of the wall space.

149

Jones had borrowed this motif from the early sixteenth-century Bolognese architect Sebastiano Serlio (1475–c.1554), and this was possibly the first use of this feature in a properly classical context in London, if not in Britain.

Built by Jones's own Office of the Royal Works, the Chapel was a simple and inexpensive structure. Built of brick that was then rendered and incised to look like stone (no doubt Protestant critics found much to ridicule in this gentle dissimulation), it was in essence a plain classical box topped with a large pediment. Modest in its construction it may have been, but its Italianate symmetry and elegance looked completely alien amid the haphazard, brick-walled components of Henry VIII's palace of St James's. Equally unusual was its purpose.

A Catholic court?

From the very start, the Queen's Chapel was destined to serve as a cockpit for Catholics. A royal Catholic chapel initially formed an integral part of a draft treaty intended to reunite England and Spain by means of a marriage between Prince Charles (as he was then) and the Spanish Infanta, Maria Anna, daughter of King Philip III of Spain. James I was exceedingly keen to pursue this alliance even after the renewal of war between Counter-Reformation Spain and the Protestant Netherlands in 1618 had made such a putative diplomatic realignment geopolitically embarrassing. Yet James desired to make European peace his principal legacy to the world. As historian Kyle Leyden has observed, James had, on his accession to the English throne in 1603, been keen to end the financial drain of the long war with Spain while also characterising himself 'as a bringer of peace and prosperity to his newly united Kingdoms'. Twenty years after his accession, and now significantly in debt, the financial imperative for such an alliance was now even stronger for James, who was doubtless attracted by the Spanish promise of a £600,000 dowry should the marriage to his son go ahead. The Spanish ambassador to the Court of St James's, Count Gondomar, even paid for and laid the foundation stone of the new Catholic chapel on 16 May 1623, whose inscription read:

> The Spanish ambassador made a cross on the first stone, laid it in mortar, made a prayer in French, that God would dispose of that foundation to his glory, and the good of his Church, and

△ *A copy of Van Dyck's double portrait of King Charles I and Queen Henrietta Maria. Despite what this allegorical composition suggests, the royal couple were in fact married by proxy in 1625.*

the universal good of all Christians and gave £80 to the workmen; his son laid the second stone and also gave them £30.

Gondomar's zeal for an Anglo-Spanish match was, however, premature. There was, unsurprisingly, substantial opposition to the idea in England,
which only three decades before had been expecting a hostile Spanish invasion
of its shores and the deposition of its Protestant sovereign. These fears were
now stoked by the unnecessarily provocative terms demanded by the Spanish,
which included the upbringing of any royal children as Roman Catholics, the
suspension of the Elizabethan anti-Catholic Penal Laws, the appointment
of Catholic priests as royal advisers and permission for the priests of the new
Roman Catholic Chapel (which was to be a public church, not just a royal
chapel) to wear their habits in the street. To many, it looked like the Counter-
Reformationist purges of Mary I's bitter and divisive reign of seventy years
before had come again. Such fears were heightened by the fact that the original
plan for the Chapel was based on that sanctioned by Philip II of Spain for his
royal wife Queen Mary in the form of the Chapel Royal of 1554.

By the end of 1623, however, the court of Philip IV of Spain suddenly rejected both the match and the alliance – a decision which they announced, embarrassingly for the newly arrived delegates, while receiving a British embassy led by the Prince of Wales himself. Charles thus returned empty-handed to Britain (securing perhaps the only rapturous public welcome he ever earned); Gondomar retired, and the field was accordingly left open for French diplomats to secure the hand of King Henry IV's daughter, Princess Henrietta Maria. By the time the Chapel was finished in 1626, James I was dead, his son Charles was on the throne, and Charles had been married to his (Catholic) French wife for over a year.

The image of cool, sophisticated beauty which shines out from Anthony van Dyck's luminous portraits of Queen Henrietta Maria was somewhat at variance with reality. In truth, the new queen was ungainly and awkward, with teeth allegedly protruding from her mouth 'like tusks'. Crucially, she was certainly no diplomat. A pious and evangelical Catholic, she remained blind to the distress and anger that her proselytising for the Catholic cause would create and the damage that it would do to the crown. Her chapel was insensitively adorned with French fittings and, as David Baldwin has noted, was even provided with services set to French music:

> [The chapel] soon developed a musical tradition akin to that which Henrietta Maria knew in Paris, alongside a form of Catholic preaching and quasi-monastic observance that was distinctly different from that of the ancient Chapel Royal which operated within the Church of England. While treaty obligations ensured that the Queen's Chapel was well protected from its critics, it became bound up intimately in the Stuart family's problems of a political, military and religious nature... antagonising many in Parliament over its relationship to Rome and France.

More importantly, the queen also used the building for promulgating the Catholic faith. In her hands the Chapel became a vehicle for converting men of influence, men who saw preferment and wealth at Charles's increasingly ecumenical court as the inevitable reward for a convenient conversion to papism. It did not help that the senior clerical figure in the Church of England, the current Archbishop of Canterbury, William Laud, was already seen by many as a crypto-Catholic on account of his Arminian* reforms, which sought to reverse the Puritanical ordering of churches by bringing back stained glass, colourful vestments, raised, east-end altars, altar rails and music. Laud in truth remained a staunch defender of Protestantism; yet his Arminian belief in the freedom of will was erroneously interpreted by many as the re-Catholicisation of England by stealth.

There were other supposed portents of a Catholic hegemony in England. In 1623, the year in which work was begun on the Queen's Chapel, Pope Paul V appointed the first Vicar Apostolic to England and Wales since the Reformation. (The second appointee, though, was forced to leave London after being attacked in the street.) Ten years later Pope Urban VIII actually offered Laud a cardinal's hat on his elevation to the archiepiscopacy. Laud immediately rejected the overture – although he privately admitted that he was prepared to reconsider the concept if the papacy was 'purged of errors'.

If even the Vatican believed that England was on the road back to Catholicism, it was unsurprising that many of Charles's subjects did so, too. Sadly, Laud was to find that his rejection of the pope's offer cut no ice with either his critics or his monarch. At the beginning of the English Revolution, King Charles lamely abandoned his tainted archbishop to become one of the first victims of a vengeful parliament. Accused of treason by parliament in 1640, Laud was imprisoned in the Tower of London in 1641 and finally executed in January 1645.

Feeding these anti-Catholic suspicions was the fact that Charles's Catholic queen was genuinely using her chapels at St James's Palace and Somerset House (the latter completed, also to the designs of Inigo Jones, in 1635) to convert key members of Charles's government. The government's deeply unpopular Lord Treasurer, Richard Weston, Earl of Portland, publicly accepted the Catholic sacraments in Jones's St James's Chapel, followed in 1636 by the nation's Chancellor, Lord Cottington.

Henrietta Maria also intervened very publicly on behalf of persecuted Catholics. Leyden cites the example of an incident in 1626 in which the queen 'had attracted flagrant outrage by walking barefoot in peasant's clothing to Tyburn to pray at the feet of a Jesuit priest put to death without trial on the

---

*   The Arminian faction within the Church of England, named for the Dutch theologian Jacobus Arminius (1560–1609), rejected the concept of predestination and was opposed by the Puritans.

orders of her husband and courted great controversy by flouting laws forbidding the celebration of marriage according to Catholic rites by facilitating the marriages of several Catholics within the growing Queen's Chapel community'. Worse still, in 1637 the queen appointed an agent to represent England at the Papal Court and invited the pope to appoint the first Papal Legate to England since the reign of Henry VIII. It was almost a deliberate invitation to rebellion.

Such activities appeared to be mirrored in the unapologetically Italian design of a chapel which acted as a nucleus of re-Catholicism. As David Baldwin has noted:

> The Queen's Chapel was a startlingly bold statement by Inigo Jones of Palladian classical architecture reminiscent of Rome, and stood, intentionally or otherwise, as an embodiment and public statement announcing the arrival/re-establishment of Catholicism at least in London at the heart of the Court, if not of the monarchy – in some eyes perhaps as a prelude to legal re-establishment of Catholicism throughout the Realm.

This was clearly no peripheral, furtive refuge for surreptitious or clandestine worship. Henrietta Maria, with her husband's apparent blessing, ensured that this small, box-like building occupied a crucial space in British politics out of all proportion to its size and location. Historian Simon Thurley has noted how the Queen's Chapel and the other Catholic Chapels Royal held 'a central position in the choreography of the Court' while Kyle Leyden has observed that they were all 'politically charged spaces' which, as a result, 'became a primary nexus for Protestant hostility which was to spill over into the wider malaise felt towards Stuart rule'. Leyden concluded that 'in the end they proved to be at the centre of what became an aesthetic undoing of the Stuart dynasty itself'.

The conversion of key members of Charles I's government in 1635–6 seemed to confirm what many feared for years. In 1629 Charles I had abruptly dissolved what turned out to be his last pre-revolutionary parliament and imprisoned nine leading 'opposition' parliamentarians after MPs had protested against Laud's Arminianism, the Catholic freedoms allowed to the community of the Queen's Chapel and excessive taxation. (The leading opposition politician and celebrated orator Sir John Eliot was to die in prison in the Tower in 1632.) For the next eleven years Charles ruled without a parliament at all, in what has been termed the 'eleven years' tyranny'. Bereft of the funds which would normally have been granted to the crown by parliament, Charles resorted to unusual measures to raise money, most notoriously the ship money levied after 1634 ostensibly to secure funding for British naval expansion.

Freed of his parliamentary shackles, King Charles also began to reorient his nation's foreign policy. In 1630, in the midst of the Thirty Years War in which the Spanish fought as one of the principal oppressors of continental Protestantism, the king concluded peace with the Spanish in a treaty which included the promise that London would re-mint Spanish coinage in order to pay Spanish troops fighting the Protestant Dutch across the North Sea. Yet again, Charles's personal rule was viewed by many as an underhand way of introducing yet another continental fashion: absolutist monarchy, by which the sovereign ruled at the behest of God without the checks of a representative body. France was already an absolutist state: no parliamentary equivalent had been summoned there since 1614, and was not to be recalled until the fateful year of 1789. Most German and Italian states – including, significantly, the Papal States – were similarly ruled without recourse to a representative assembly; while in Spain the Cortes had, since the days of Ferdinand and Isabella at the end of the fifteenth century, merely rubber-stamped the policies of the monarch or the chief minister. It seemed as if Charles was merely following the example of his European contemporaries in seeking to establish England as an absolutist Catholic state.

The road to war

Would-be absolutist he may have been, but in truth Charles was no closet Catholic. In 1626 he had three hundred of his wife's Catholic priests forcibly ejected from the country and subsequently refused to allow the imposition of a Catholic episcopacy on England and Wales. However, many Britons would have agreed with the contemporary diarist Lucy Hutchinson, who alleged that the queen's 'prelates... meditated re-union with the Popish faction' and that following Charles's marriage to Henrietta Maria 'the court was replenished with papists'.

Inigo Jones's debt to the later Italian Renaissance in general and to the long-dead Veneto architect Andrea Palladio in particular may have appeared the height of sophistication to Charles's court, but for many this very Italian style of building amplified fears that the king was trying to impose a Catholic absolutism of the type common on the Continent. This concern indeed became the most frequently cited reason why Britons took up arms against the king in 1642. And nowhere was this suspicion more acute than in the case of Jones's Queen's Chapel. A direct thread can thus be drawn from the completion of this building to Charles's trial and execution twenty-six years later.

When the floodgates of revolution opened in 1640 following the summoning of parliament, reluctantly recalled by a king now desperate for parliamentary funding for his unsuccessful Scottish wars, all the perceived props of Charles I's personal rule were cheerfully tossed onto the bonfire. And once the genie was out of the bottle, it could not be coaxed back. Charles pusillanimously sacrificed both Archbishop Laud and his close adviser the Earl of Strafford to his baying critics; Laud ended up in the Tower (for now) and Strafford, once a promising opposition MP, on the scaffold. Significantly, parliament also turned on the queen and her chapels. In June 1641 parliament enacted the Ten Propositions and the Grand Remonstrance, which together blamed the current sorry state of national affairs on the court's apparent Catholicism. The Propositions alleged that court favours were being offered in return for Catholic influence in the queen's chapels and was specifically designed to censure both the queen and her chapel communities, whom it demanded be either banished or executed. Parliament was particularly vehement in demanding the dispersal of the Capuchin monks the queen had introduced into London to operate the Chapels.

The king's refusal to grant the necessary royal assent to the Grand Remonstrance made armed conflict more likely. And when war did break out, the much-expected royal victory failed to materialise. The first big encounter of the First Civil War, the Battle of Edgehill of 23 October 1642, was inconclusive, and with further royalist reverses the prospect of a royal triumph receded.

When Britons went to war in 1642, religion was the factor most commonly cited by those who joined the two armies: defence of the monarchy and the Church of England against a supposed Puritan onslaught for the royalists, and the defence of the church and state against Catholic infiltration by those who sided with parliament. For the latter, nothing encapsulated the insidious influence of the papacy on the crown better than the Queen's Chapel.

As the revolution gathered pace, the apparatus of the Queen's Chapel was rapidly extinguished. In October 1642, the month of Edgehill, some of the queen's now unemployed Catholic priests who had previously officiated at the Queen's Chapel and Somerset House were publicly executed, to enthusiastic applause. The queen herself was not there to protect them: she had fled to the Continent in February to raise money for her husband's cause. In March 1643 parliamentarian troops forced their way into Inigo Jones's chapel at Somerset House and smashed the statues, threw the queen's fittings and books and the priests' vestments onto a bonfire, and stabbed Rubens's fine altarpiece with a pike and threw it in the Thames.

The more secluded Queen's Chapel survived for now. However, in March 1644 parliament passed an Ordinance demanding that the royal chapels be 'clensed from all Popish Reliques and superstitions'. The interior of the St James's Chapel was now looted and destroyed, too. After the fighting ended in 1645, and the chapel's interior had been converted into a plain, white-walled Puritan space, it was, with a deliberate irony, presented to a group of Huguenots, French Protestants who had fled France to escape persecution from their Catholic government.

Inigo Jones's time had come, too. When he was finally captured by parliamentarian forces at the siege of Basing House in 1645 – bundled ignominiously out of the blazing ruins in a blanket – it is significant that the parliamentary pamphlet celebrating the event named him as 'the queen's architect', explicitly associating Jones with the perceived papism of the fallen court.

The Republic and after

By January 1649 Charles I was a prisoner at Windsor Castle; his queen an embittered exile presiding over a fractious court at Saint-Germain-en-Laye, to the west of Paris; and Inigo Jones a half-forgotten figure trying to piece together some semblance of an architectural practice from his apartments at Somerset House. We have no record of Jones's reaction to his former royal master's trial and execution, but the site chosen for the spectacle of his sovereign's decapitation on 30 January 1649 would have doubtless left him shocked and appalled.

Oliver Cromwell and the other parliamentary leaders knew that the execution of the king would be an act that would reverberate around Europe for decades, outraging, horrifying and inspiring in equal measure. The symbolism to be invested in the event was thus of paramount importance. As a result, the venue they chose to stage the execution was designed to emphatically underline to a global audience exactly why they had gone to war, deposed their monarch and established a republic. It was the king's apparent drift towards a continental culture of Catholicism and absolutism – unwelcome developments best exemplified in the alien, neo-Palladian classicism of Charles and Henrietta

Prospectus interior Sacelli Serenissimæ Mariæ Magnæ Britanniæ Reginæ. Londini ad Sanctum Jacobum

△ Jan Kip's 1688 view of the interior of the Queen's Chapel. In that year the new monarchs, William III and Mary II, convened parliament here in an ostentatious break with the building's Catholic past.

Maria's faithful court architect, Inigo Jones – which they chose as a backdrop for his public demise.

Jones's Queen's Chapel would clearly represent the most obviously resonant location to perform Charles's beheading. However, as a small building hemmed in by the neighbouring brick-built ranges of St James's Palace, it was evidently unsuitable for a public ceremony at which a large crowd was expected. Jones's contemporary Banqueting House at Whitehall Palace, though, was ideal. The first of Jones's Italianate intrusions into London's brick-and-timber cityscape, the building with its two, tall storeys allowed for the erection of a substantial stage to enable the crowd to witness the spectacle properly, while the broad expanse of Whitehall in front of the building's main elevation facilitated the assembly of a large audience. The highly symbolic image of King Charles I stepping out to his scaffold through the classical architrave of one of Jones's 'Italian' windows was surely premeditated. In this manner was the link between Charles and his Catholic wife – their patronage of Jones, their supposed promotion of Catholicism, their suspected absolutist ambitions – grimly underscored.

The Queen's Chapel's role in symbolising the threat of a return to Catholicism did not cease in 1649. On the restoration of the monarchy in 1660 the reinstated sovereign – Charles I's son, now crowned King Charles II – was controversially married to the Catholic, Portuguese princess Catherine of Braganza. Catherine was as deeply pious as Henrietta Maria had been. Fortunately for her husband, though, she was also shy and reserved, and had none of her mother-in-law's obdurate will. The marriage treaty of 1662, like that of thirty-seven years before, required 'a private Chapel in [the queen's] residence with the right to practice her Catholic religion'. Jones's forlorn, emptied chapel at St James's Palace was accordingly restored: an organ loft, a tall pulpit and a confessional box were reintroduced; a silver tabernacle was constructed in the chancel; a new royal closet was added to the west end and upholstered with crimson damask; while Jones's great Venetian window was reglazed with stained glass by Thomas Bagley, who included 'a Crucifix of paynted glass iii foot broad and four foot deep'. In 1669 the new Surveyor-General of the King's Works, Christopher Wren – then better known as an academic scientist than an architect – extended the friars' accommodation at the rear of the chapel, adding a semi-circular apse which actually blocked Jones's great Venetian window, which was instead hung with tapestries.

By 1679 Queen Catherine had migrated to Somerset House and St James's Palace was home to the Duke and Duchess of York. James, Duke of York, was not only the king's brother and heir presumptive but also a Catholic convert – having been brought up by his mother, Henrietta Maria, in the Catholic faith. After his first wife died in 1671, James chose as his new bride the deeply religious, fifteen-year-old Italian princess Mary of Modena. He married her in a secret Catholic service on 23 November – a wedding which parliament later vainly attempted to have annulled. Thereafter the pair turned their attention to Jones's palace chapel. As Leyden notes, 'The quiet politic adopted by Catherine of Bragança in her architectural works and furnishings was abandoned by the politically naïve couple who instead decided to lavish the interior with vastly expensive furnishings and plate.' An unapologetically Baroque high altar was constructed, which Simon Thurley has convincingly suggested was designed by Wren. This featured woodcarving by Grinling Gibbons and was designed to accommodate a painting of the Holy Family by Benedetto Gennari.

On his accession in 1685, King James II, as the former Duke of York now became, made no secret of his Catholic ambitions, which included making the Queen's Chapel into a public place of worship and building a vast Catholic Chapel Royal at Whitehall. The birth of a son to Queen Mary, bringing with it the prospect of a perpetual Catholic succession, was the last straw for parliament, which set in motion the events leading to William of Orange's 'invasion' of England in 1688 and the subsequent ignominious flight of James II to Louis XIV's France. As James's royal family fled into exile, they took with them much of the moveable art in the Queen's Chapel, including Gennari's *Holy Family*.

William III took care that the Queen's Chapel never again became a prop for popish ambitions. David Baldwin has suggested that it was deliberately used as the venue for the parliamentary assembly of December 1688 ordered by the new (joint) monarch to legitimise his rule, observing that 'William would have seen the political and Protestant triumphalism of using the Queen's Chapel, of all places, as the venue for having his military victory legitimised, and a wholly Protestant order reinstated'. Subsequently William granted the chapel to the French Huguenot and Dutch Protestant refugees who had settled in London to escape persecution in the wake of Louis XIV's revocation of the Edict of Nantes in 1685. The chapel's interior was stripped of its existing statues, relics, side altars and paintings, though much of Gibbons' work on the High Altar was to survive intact. In 1709 Wren's French Baroque east end was demolished and Jones's original east window uncovered.

Modern times

By the end of the eighteenth century the politically charged symbolism of the Queen's Chapel's origins had made it something of an architectural embarrassment. Given that the need for a Huguenot chapel had now waned, as London's Huguenot communities were moving eastwards, in 1781 the chapel was presented to the capital's German Lutheran community. When its interior was illustrated in W. H. Pyne's *Royal Residences* of 1819, no mention was made either of Inigo Jones or of Charles I's infamous queen. Simon Bradley notes that E. W. Brayley's *Londiniana* of 1829 'muddied the water still further by alleging that the chapel had been "newly built" in 1662'.

In 1809 a fire destroyed the royal apartments adjacent to the chapel and, rather than rebuild them, King George III decided to connect Pall Mall to the Mall by constructing Marlborough Road over the site of the destroyed buildings. This had the effect of severing the palace from its chapel, which now appeared to be connected not to the Tudor royal palace but to the London home of the Dukes of Marlborough behind it.

Thereafter the Queen's Chapel was extremely lucky to survive at all: it was slated for demolition in 1856 to make way for a new road while in the following year the *Building News* urged the wholesale removal of 'the great ugly packing-box-looking chapel'. The *Building News* did not even say who had designed the chapel. By then Inigo Jones's career was mostly forgotten, and even when it was remembered, it was with little affection. The Stuart architect's reputation was only revived with J. A. Gotch's monograph of 1928; even then, however, Gotch inexplicably declared that the Queen's Chapel had been demolished.

German services in the chapel had ceased on Queen Victoria's death in 1901, when the name of the building was changed from the German Royal Chapel to Marlborough House Chapel. Services in Danish, for the benefit of the Danish-born Princess of Wales, Alexandra, were introduced in 1881; they ended in 1938, thirteen years after Alexandra's death at Marlborough House. That same year the chapel was closed, as Simon Bradley notes, 'for its first major restoration since William III purged it of its Catholic past'. The impetus for the work came from its new royal neighbour, George V's formidable widow Queen Mary, who had withdrawn to Marlborough House after her husband's death in 1936. Three years later she insisted that the building's old name of the Queen's Chapel be revived.

As Simon Bradley relates, the men largely responsible for restoring the chapel to something approaching its Stuart condition were the Office of Works architect George Chettle, already very familiar with Jones's work, having recently restored his Queen's House at Greenwich, and ecclesiastical specialist W. H. Randoll Blacking. Chettle was adept at balancing the evaluation of Jones's architecture with the historical importance of later accretions, as well as with Queen Mary's firm opinions on all matters aesthetic. Following significant bomb damage in 1944, further work was conducted by F. L. Rothwell, who restored Chettle's internal colour scheme of light olive-green and white.

Today the Queen's Chapel sits perched uneasily beside Marlborough House, looking across the road to the sprawling palace complex of which it was once an integral part. As a passing feature on the link road between Pall Mall and St James's, it is little noticed. Only in 2002 was it dragged into the limelight as the temporary resting place for the coffins of Princess Margaret and, later in the year, Queen Elizabeth the Queen Mother. Few of those who pass quickly by today have any idea of the significance this small, unpretentious building – the chapel that caused a war – once had for the entire kingdom.

9

HERIOT'S HOSPITAL, EDINBURGH

1628–59

The Auld Alliance in Stone

Heriot's Hospital is an astonishing building in so many ways. In design terms, it is an expression in stone of the Auld Alliance between Scotland and France. Yet it is also a very British synthesis of old and new, a stylistic fusion which demonstrates the assurance, wealth, independence and aspirations of seventeenth-century Scotland. It was the first wholly symmetrical building in Scotland – architectural historian Alistair Rowan called it 'a revolutionary structure... a great Renaissance palace riding proudly above the town' – and it is still cited as an expression of a distinctive and resonant Scottish identity. However, its significance as an institution lies in its pioneering role as one of the first real expressions in Britain of philanthropic social welfare.

The fact that the Hospital was begun during the reign of Charles I led some in the eighteenth century and after to attribute the building's design to Charles's court architect, Inigo Jones. However, Scottish architects had no need to employ an English intermediary to source European influences. Nor was the Hospital's architect in thrall to sixteenth-century Italian fashions, as Jones's London buildings had evidently been. Sir John Summerson insisted

that the form of the hospital had been inspired by a plate from Sebastiano Serlio's *I sette libri dell'architettura*, published posthumously in 1575. Yet in truth the two designs have, aside from the two tall corner pavilions, little in common. The building compares more favourably with French châteaux of the time, while its decoration appears to have been sourced from sixteenth-century French publications such as the prints of Jacques Androuet du Cerceau, *architecte du roi* to the house of Valois and author of the influential *Livre d'architecture* of 1559. The sixteenth century saw what has been called the Auld Alliance between the Scots and the French reach its zenith, and it was this emotive axis that defined Heriot's Hospital.

The role of the jeweller

The man behind the idea of the Hospital was George Heriot, a successful Edinburgh goldsmith whose business brought him close to James VI and his queen, Anne of Denmark. Heriot played the role of court jeweller and by 1603, when he accompanied King James to London, he had become an invaluable prop to the royal couple as one of their principal moneylenders. Queen Anne's love of jewellery was legendary, and by late 1600 both she and the king were taking out sizeable loans from Heriot, now effectively their private banker, to support their substantial spending. By 1609 Queen Anne's debt to Heriot was £18,000 – around £1.2 million in today's money. And these royal loans in turn guaranteed the shrewd goldsmith considerable interest.

By the time Heriot died in February 1624 he had amassed a cash fortune and property in London, Surrey and Edinburgh. He had had at least four children by his first wife, although all predeceased him, including two sons who may have been drowned at sea. The majority of his estate, valued at £23,625, he left to the city of Edinburgh to establish a hospital for the free education of the 'puir, faitherless bairns' of deceased Edinburghians.

◁ *P. R. Montford's splendid statue of George Heriot of 1909, installed on the façade of the Victoria and Albert Museum in London. Heriot is commemorated here as a jeweller rather than as a patron.*

Building the hospital

The Hospital was begun in 1628 and was effectively completed by 1659, when it received its first pupils and orphans. It represented something wholly new: not a hospital in the modern sense, but a refuge for the orphaned and destitute. Much has been written about the Foundling Hospital in London, founded in 1739 by the philanthropic sea captain Thomas Coram, but surprisingly little about Heriot's vision. The Foundling Hospital was designed to do just what its title implied: provide a home, a school and the basis of employment for destitute children abandoned by their parent or parents. Heriot's brief was similar – but his institution was founded over a century before Coram's. It represents the first major attempt in Britain to provide a future for poor orphans, who otherwise would have been left to fend for themselves on the streets.

It may have been French in influence, but the Hospital's design and construction were entirely the work of Scots. Heriot's nephew, Walter Balcanquhall, who was one of his executors, allegedly provided a 'patterne' for the new project – which, it has been suggested, leaned more heavily on the pattern books of Sebastiano Serlio than the design of the executed building. The Hospital's principal architect, William Wallace, was well known to James VI, too, as the king's master mason in Scotland. He worked on such royal residences as Edinburgh Castle (in 1615), Linlithgow Palace (1618), Stirling Castle (1625) and Holyrood Palace (1627), while simultaneously running a lucrative private practice based on his intimacy with members of the Scottish court. Unlike Heriot, though, Wallace never followed his royal masters south of the border and died in Scotland in 1631.

Wallace's style was based on French precedent. It was not couched in a particularly 'Anglo-Flemish' style – an inappropriate label which has often been reapplied to the Hospital without question. Nor was it based on Italian precedents, as Jones's architecture was. As Alistair Rowan declared in 1975: 'there can be no case of an exact pattern-book model here.' The building was instead designed as a fusion of the Scottish castle style – an evocative, romantic idiom which was successfully revived in the nineteenth century as 'Scots Baronial' – with contemporary Renaissance châteaux of France. This combination was then overlaid with strapwork decoration derived from the sixteenth-century Flemish pattern books which proved so influential on northern European architecture well into the next century. Historic Scotland's list description calls it 'Scots Renaissance/Northern Mannerist', which sounds about right.

As a result of this stylistic synthesis, there is far more life and exuberance in the Hospital than in any of Inigo Jones's pedantic Palladian derivatives. The future architect Hippolyte Blanc, born and bred an Edinburghian despite his francophone name, counted 209 profusely decorated pediments on the building when he was a pupil there in the 1850s; and no two, he declared, were ever the same. As Rowan noted, a few of the details on the main elevations are culled from popular Italian manuals by Giacomo da Vignola and Serlio, but equal use is made of contemporary French sources such as Alexandre Francine's *Livre d'architecture* of 1631. It was the Auld Alliance commemorated in stone.

The English and Scottish crowns may have merged with the accession of King James VI and I to the English throne in 1603, but the two kingdoms remained wholly separate until the Act of Union of 1707. (Admittedly, from 1606 James I did order the creation of a composite 'British flag', the ancestor of today's Union Flag or Jack, which melded the red cross of St George with the saltire of St Andrew.) Indeed, the two nations were still at war with each other as late as 1651.

Rather closer to Scotland for the past few centuries had been France – largely on the practical assumption that my enemy's enemy is my friend. If allied, the two countries' armies could theoretically coordinate an attack on their traditional foe, England, from both north and south. Such coordination, in the event, largely seemed to elude both monarchies over the centuries, and the Scots rarely seemed to profit by their much-vaunted compact.

The Auld Alliance

The term 'Auld Alliance' was coined in the sixteenth century to refer to the Franco-Scottish amity originally concluded in 1295, when King John Balliol of Scotland and Philip IV of France made common cause against the England of Edward I, then fighting in both Scotland and in Wales. The result was ignominious for the Scots: after a series of military defeats John Balliol was forced to abdicate in 1296, imprisoned in the Tower of London for three years and then spent the rest of his life in continental exile. Fifty years later the result was much the same: two months after overwhelming the superior French army at the Battle of Crécy in 1346, Edward III's northern army captured King David II of Scotland at the Battle of Neville's Cross. Edward held him captive for eleven years before finally agreeing that the Scots could pay a sizeable ransom for his return.

Such disasters, however, rarely seemed to diminish Scottish enthusiasm for the Auld Alliance. The terms of the Treaty of Paris were still being enacted as late as 1513, when the Scots invaded England in response to Henry VIII's campaign in France. The result, predictably, again proved disastrous for the Scots: King James IV and a swathe of Scottish nobles were killed and the larger Scots army routed. Thirty-four years later James IV's son and heir, King James V – the only child of James IV to survive infancy – reignited the Auld Alliance by marrying a daughter of the French king, Francis I. Once more, though, Scottish ambitions were crushed by an English army: the Scots were heavily defeated by an English force at Solway Moss on the Anglo-Scottish border in November 1542. The following month James V died of a fever, leaving as his successor a six-day-old daughter, Mary.

Despite the fact that the agreement with the French seemed to have brought Scotland nothing but grief, Mary, Queen of Scots's ill-starred life constantly revolved around the Auld Alliance. She spent most of her childhood years in France while Scotland was ruled by a succession of regents, and in 1558 was married to the French Dauphin, the future King Francis II, whose sixteen-month reign ended with his premature death in December 1560. After two disastrous further marriages Mary herself was forced to abdicate her throne in favour of her year-old son, James VI. She sought protection from her cousin, Elizabeth I of England, but this soon turned to custody when Mary was exploited by English Catholic plotters as a rival claimant to Elizabeth's throne. After one such plot, Mary was executed in February 1587.

Mary's son had no intention of perpetuating the French alliance, which he acknowledged had brought little of lasting value to his ancestral kingdom, and his succession to the English throne merely accentuated his calculated pacificism. However, thanks to his benefactor George Heriot, the symbolism of the Auld Alliance lived on into another era of Anglo-Scottish conflict. Indeed, just as the Hospital was being built, the Scottish seizure of Newcastle in 1640 forced King Charles I not just to grant a humiliating peace to the Scots Presbyterians but to recall parliament after a twelve-year absence – an action which, as we have seen, effectively opened the floodgates to revolution. As J. H. Elliott has observed, 'In effect the Scots handed a lifeline to the English opposition, and the Long Parliament would seize the opportunities to wrest the concessions it demanded of Charles and dismantle a regime which threatened England and Scotland alike with the loss of their treasured liberties.'

Heriot's Hospital was devised by William Wallace to combine Scotland's fine 'castle Gothic' tradition of high walls, corner pavilions, turrets and bartizans with the vocabulary and exuberance of the French Renaissance. On Wallace's death the building was continued by his former assistant, William Ayton, and subsequently by John Mylne, uncle of the more famous Scots architect Robert. John Mylne's chapel, to use Rowan's colourful phrase, 'plummets back into the late Gothic world' of ogee domes, large arched windows and rose-shaped openings – a deliberately reactionary affirmation of traditional Scottish design which Rowan opines may have been suggested by Charles I's conservative Archbishop of Canterbury, William Laud.

Heriot's patronage

In marked contrast to the austere Palladian solemnity of Theodore Jacobsen's Foundling Hospital complex in London of a century later, the architecture and embellishment of Wallace's Heriot's Hospital was lively and fun. The aedicule between the first-floor windows which contains Heriot's statue is, for example, flanked by playful, twisted Solomonic or 'barley-sugar' Corinthian columns, while the plethora of ogee-roofed bartizans suggests a rather exotic citadel. Inside the building, the pediment inscription GEORGE HERIOT JEWELLER is accompanied by a panel which carries the delightful motto I DISTRIBUTE CHEARFULLIE. Wallace and Ayton's building, too, is unmistakeably cheerful.

Many other inscriptions can be found inside and outside the building, leaving the visitor in no doubt as to Heriot's intentions and munificence. Indeed, the building is covered with them. The carved panels in the frieze over the entrance show a goldsmith in his workshop accompanied by the inscription FUNDENDO FUNDAVI ('by founding I have founded'); Charity with a widow and her children, together with the legend HIS COR INCALUIT ('towards these my heart has warmed'); five boys dressed in the uniform of Christ's Hospital, London – an institution of similar charitable intent – and the motto SIC DEUS, UT VOS EOS ('may God treat you as you treat them'); and a class of eager pupils and their teachers described, presumably with no intended irony, DEUS NOBIS HAEC OTIA FECIT ('God hath given us this leisure'). Robert Mylne's statue of Heriot, copied from a portrait by James I's accomplished and unjustly forgotten court portraitist Paul van Somer, is accompanied by an inscription which reads CORPORIS HAEC, ANIMI EST HOC

OPUS EFIGIES ('this statue represents my body, this work my soul'), while over the chapel entrance are carved the words AURIFICI DEDERAT MIHI VIS DIVINA PERENNEM ET FACERE IN TERRIS IN CAELO ET FERRE {CORONAM} ('Power divine hath granted it to me, a goldsmith, to make on earth, and to wear in heaven, an everlasting crown'). Inside the chapel there is, for the first time, an inscription in English on the aedicule to the east, which reads HONOUR THE LORD WITH THY RICHES AND WITH THE FIRST OF ALL THINE INCREASE SO SHALL THY BARNES BE FILLED WITH ABUNDANCE; TO DO GOOD & TO DISTRIBUTE FORGETT NOT FOR WITH SUCH SACRIFICES GOD IS PLEASED.

Three nations

God may not have been too pleased when, in 1650, the first inhabitants moved into the still-unfinished building. For they were not the 'puire father-less bairnes' Heriot had anticipated; they were, instead, wounded parliamentarian soldiers, brought to recuperate in the half-completed school following Cromwell's unexpected but overwhelming victory over the royalist Scots

▽ *The western elevation of Heriot's Hospital, photographed in 1923.*

army at Dunbar on 1 and 2 September and General John Lambert's subsequent capture of the city of Edinburgh on the 7th. Oliver Cromwell's triumph at Dunbar had confirmed his position as the leading figure in the new Republic and made him the obvious choice to be created Lord Protector in 1653, while his loyal lieutenant General John Lambert (1619–84) was to draw up Britain's first written constitution, the Instrument of Government, to define the fledgling Protectorate. Lambert was a man of dazzling talents but, having fallen out with Cromwell before his death in 1658, he was arraigned for treason two years after the restoration of the monarchy in 1660 and died in exile on an island off Plymouth Sound in 1684.

Shortly after the end of the Third Civil War in 1651, and just as work recommenced on the Hospital, the English parliament proposed that Scotland be incorporated into 'the free state and Commonwealth of England'. The Scots' coronation of King Charles II at Scone in January 1651 directly threatened the infant Republic, a danger the English were determined to extinguish. In 1654 Cromwell's Council of State finally enacted the necessary legislation to absorb Scotland into their kingdom. At a stroke of a pen the Scottish parliament, which traced its origins back to 1235, disappeared.

Scotland was henceforward ruled as an English province by a committee of eight, which included Generals Lambert and George Monck (1608–70), a former royalist soldier who had commanded a regiment at Dunbar for Cromwell. Monck had returned to Scotland that same year as military commander following a rebellion in the Highlands and quickly earned a reputation for efficiency, pragmatism and ruthlessness. After Cromwell's death in September 1658 it was Monck who seized the initiative, filling the power vacuum which was paralysing the government by publicly opposing Lambert's Republican faction, bringing his army south and entering London to great acclaim in April 1660. Although, unlike Lambert, Monck seemed to harbour few political convictions or interests, his actions were essential in paving the way for the return of the monarchy. And one of the first actions of the restored Charles II was to order the restoration of the Scottish parliament, kirk and legal system. At its first session in January 1661, the revived parliament tried to put the clock back not just to 1640 but as far back as 1633, in an attempt to wipe out the influence of the Presbyterian Covenanters. In practice, though, Scotland was, in those precarious post-Restoration years, governed by the crown in the person of Charles II's callous and unsavoury Secretary of State for Scotland, John Maitland, 2nd Earl and 1st Duke of Lauderdale.

It was in the midst of these dramatic events, and not long before Monck's army left Edinburgh for London, that Heriot's Hospital finally opened its doors. On its inauguration in 1659 it boasted thirty male pupils and, from the autumn of 1661, a garden 'planted with herbs sort of phisical, medicinal and other herbs such as the country can afford, conform to the fullest catalogue that can be had, that such who intend to studie herbs may have full access there' – making this one of the earliest botanic gardens in Britain.

By 1695 the Hospital had a complement of 130 – all Foundation and bursarial students who had lost a parent. And during these first thirty-six years of the school's history, too, relations with France had continued to dominate Anglo-Scottish politics. In 1670 Charles II signed a compact with Louis XIV of France, the Treaty of Dover, which showed just how politically and fiscally weak the post-Restoration monarchy had become. By the treaty – whose highly contentious religious clauses remained secret from all but a few of Charles's closest advisers until after the Glorious Revolution of 1688 – Charles was to receive £1 million in cash immediately, followed by £600,000 per annum and the promised support of 6,000 French troops so that he might declare himself a Roman Catholic. Charles also agreed to support French claims to the Spanish throne once the seemingly terminally unwell Charles II of Spain died. (In the event, the sickly Spanish sovereign outlasted the Merry Monarch by fifteen years.) As historian Ronald Hutton has written, 'Few international agreements have provoked more controversy among historians than that concluded at Dover on 22 May 1670... The existence of this treaty was concealed not only from the other European states and the subjects of the respective monarchs, but from the greater number of their own ministers.'

Charles's anticipated windfall was prodigious: to put the treaty's offer in context, during 1667 – the third *annus horribilis* in a row, which had added ignominious military defeat at Dutch hands to the Great Plague and the Great Fire of London – the regular revenue of the crown had yielded less than £900,000, while a subsequent report commissioned for the English Treasury on possible economies in expenditure could not find a way to reduce the annual total below £1,200,000. Louis's tempting terms gave Charles a financial lifeline, which allowed him to indulge his expensive tastes for gambling, jewels, buildings – and mistresses. Nevertheless, only eighteen months later the crown suspended all payments for a year in what became known as the Stop of the Exchequer, which ruined many of Heriot's successors now acting as the crown's goldsmith-bankers.

In signing the Treaty of Dover, Charles had just made, in Hutton's words, 'the most serious error of his reign'. He seriously underestimated the French 'Sun King', Louis XIV, who merely sought to entice his fellow sovereign into what turned out to be, for the English at least, an unsuccessful and fiscally ruinous war with the Dutch. Not only would the Dutch survive the combined onslaught of Britain and France; as Hutton observes, 'after two more decades and a few more mistakes, one of them [i.e. the Dutchman William III] would sit upon his throne'. By the time of the Anglo-Scottish Union of 1707, which formally united the nations' two parliaments under what was now a constitutional monarchy, Britain was once again at war with France – as she was to be for thirty-nine years of the eighteenth century. The Scots now hoped that the commercial advantages of throwing in their lot with their southern neighbour would outweigh their loss of political independence.

The nineteenth and twentieth centuries

During the nineteenth century Heriot's Hospital expanded exponentially. In 1829 the London-born though Edinburgh-educated Greek Revival specialist William Henry Playfair added a north gatehouse to the Hospital on Lauriston Place. Eight years later the Scots architect William Gillespie Graham redesigned the Hospital's Gothic chapel, leaning heavily on the academic Gothic style recently popularised by A. W. N. Pugin and eradicating much of the more playful Commonwealth Gothic of John Mylne. In 1893 the Foundation's in-house surveyor Donald Gow designed a new examination hall, while in the early years of the twentieth century much work was done to the site by the eminent Glaswegian architect John Macvicar Anderson. Anderson had built a highly successful practice designing bank and auction house headquarters in an austerely Caledonian Arts and Crafts manner, had been responsible for the celebrated church of St Columba in Pont Street, in London's Belgravia, for the Church of Scotland, and had been President of the Royal Institute of British Architects in 1891–4. At Heriot's Hospital Anderson made many alterations and additions for the new day pupils, including the creation of a new chemistry block.

Not all of these years were trouble-free for the school. In 1846 pupils mutinied against the Hospital's notoriously overcrowded and austere conditions. The school now housed 180 pupils in a building which had originally welcomed thirty; but fifty-two of these were now expelled as a result of the insurrection. The new Provost of Edinburgh and Chairman of the Hospital Governors, Duncan McLaren, demanded that the number of boys in the Hospital be reduced, and he worked hard to expand the number of 'outdoor' (i.e. off-site) schools, relieving pressure on Wallace's building. Many of these spin-off schools, incidentally, had been built in an idiom which deliberately cited that of Wallace's Franco-Scottish parent foundation.

Forster's Education Act of 1870 – a momentous piece of legislation which changed the educational landscape in Britain for ever – provided state support for the schooling of English children up to the age of twelve for the first time. (A similar statute for Scotland was enacted in 1872.) Heriot Hospital Trust's response of 1885 was to become a day school, to start charging fees – although children of a deceased parent were still admitted free – and to sell off the 'outdoor' schools. At the same time, the school took over the nearby Watt Institution and School of Arts. The Watt was a forward-thinking college which had admitted women in 1869, twenty years before other Scottish universities and colleges did the same and seven years before the first English university, Bristol, became co-educational. The resulting merged institution, Heriot-Watt College, was directly supported by the Trust until 1927 and was granted university status in 1966. Disappointingly, though, the main school failed to follow Heriot-Watt's lead and only became co-educational over a century later, in 1979.

Unlike London's Foundling Hospital, which was scandalously demolished in 1926, Heriot's noble foundation – now called George Heriot's School – is still with us in the shape of a highly successful independent school with 1,600 pupils, 155 teaching staff and 80 support staff. It still serves its original charitable goal, providing free education to a large number of children of deceased parents, who are still referred to as 'Foundationers'. On 15 June every year the school celebrates Heriot's birthday by adorning Robert Mylne's statue of the founder with garlands of flowers.

Remembering the past

In many ways, the Auld Alliance is still with us, too. As historian Siobhan Talbott has commented, 'The traditional view that the Auld Alliance was brought to an end in 1560 – taking any vestige of the Franco-Scottish commercial relationship with it – continues to proliferate' yet 'recent archival research demonstrates that Franco-Scottish commerce continued to flourish after 1560

△ George Winter's 1847 engraving of R. W. Billings's view of the north-west corner of the Hospital's inner courtyard. The exuberance of the richly carved pediments transforms what otherwise could have been mundane elevations into something uniquely distinctive.

and throughout the long seventeenth century'. Even after the Act of Union of 1707, successive French administrations sought to exploit Scottish resentment of their seemingly subservient status in order to destabilise the common enemy, England. In 1701 Prince James, son of the late King James II who had been ousted from his native land in 1688, was, on the death of his father in 1701, accordingly styled James III of England and James VIII of Scotland by his French and Scottish supporters. Seven years later 'King James' was launched towards Scotland in French ships at the height of the War of the Spanish Succession and just months after the signing of the Act of Union. His small force was driven off by the Royal Navy before he had chance to land, but he subsequently served with great distinction in Louis XIV's French army until the peace of 1713, when his removal from French territory was a key clause in the Treaty of Utrecht. The defeated French had no option but to agree to the dissolution of James's alternative court: what had once been Henrietta Maria's fractious court-in-exile at the palace of Saint-Germain-en-Laye was dissolved and James was banished to the then-independent Duchy of Lorraine.

Eight years after his first attempt to regain Scotland, however, Prince James – subsequently dubbed by satirical Whigs as 'the Old Pretender' – did finally make landfall in Scotland, at Aberdeen. His aim this time was to lend the weight of his royal presence to the Jacobite rebellion (the word 'Jacobite' comes from the Latin for James, 'Jacobus'), led by the 6th Earl of Mar against the new Hanoverian monarchy of George I. James had previously declined the offer of both thrones by London's Tory ministers in 1714, as it would have meant renouncing his Catholicism. It was a decision many of his Scottish adherents would come to regret.

The rebellion did not go well from the start. Arriving after the Jacobite rebel army had suffered two major defeats at the hands of government forces, James was struck down with fever in the midst of the freezing Scottish winter. In January 1716 he summoned a court to Scone Palace, near Perth, but fled ignominiously from Scone just four weeks later on hearing of the approach of government troops – a shameful retreat which lost him much respect across the kingdom. On his arrival in France he found the new regency government determined to keep the peace with England. (King Louis XV had succeeded his great-grandfather Louis XIV the previous year at only five years old.) James was, as a result, this time shunted off to the Papal States. He died in Rome in 1766 and, along with his sons Charles ('Bonnie Prince Charlie') and Henry (a solemn, devout man who became a cardinal), was commemorated in St Peter's Basilica with the splendid Monument to the Royal Stuarts, completed by Antonio Canova in 1819.

Having been at peace with their cross-Channel neighbours since 1713, in the 1740s the British government found itself dragged into the pan-European conflict later dignified by the title of the War of the Austrian Succession, and once again fighting France. The French government now took advantage of British distractions in Germany to stir the embers of the Auld Alliance and support James Stuart's son, Prince Charles, in a new attempt to invade England via Scotland. In July 1745 Charles landed on Eriskay in the Outer Hebrides and rapidly won support from disaffected clans.

The Edinburgh government was caught with its trousers down. As historian Matthew Dziennik has commented, 'The raising of the Jacobite standard at Glenfinnan on 19 August 1745 found the British state woefully ill-prepared':

The wider War of the Austrian Succession had seen the withdrawal of several regiments to Flanders including the 43rd Foot (Black Watch), a collection of independent Highland companies regimented as a regular force for overseas service in 1739. Only three additional companies of the Black Watch were based in Scotland when the rebellion began but they were painfully short of experienced officers and soldiers... To defend Whig Scotland, the commander-in-chief, Sir John Cope, could call upon no more than two and a half battalions of newly raised infantry and two regiments of dragoons – fewer than 3,000 men – most of which were distributed in garrisons throughout Scotland. They had little experience and were in a shambolic state.

Cope's ramshackle army was shattered by the Jacobites at Prestonpans in September and then headed south as London quaked. Charles's bold force got as far as Derby in December 1745 when, faced with the reluctance of the indolent Duke of Richelieu's French army at Dunkirk to invade the south coast of England (a hesitancy which had been so common throughout the history of the Auld Alliance), along with the marked absence of support from the anticipated legions of English Jacobites, the decision was taken to retreat back to Scotland. Here the Jacobite army was annihilated at Culloden in April 1746. Had Charles continued his march and taken London, prompting the unpopular King George II to bolt back to Hanover, the aims of the Auld Alliance might finally have been realised. The Stuarts would have been restored to the throne; the Seven Years War would never have happened; Canada would have become entirely French, as would much of India; and the American colonies might have remained British possessions – or, indeed, become French.

After Culloden the Auld Alliance appeared well and truly buried. Scottish regiments played a prominent part in the British army during the Napoleonic Wars and particularly at Waterloo, where the famous charge of the Royal Scots Greys cavalry (later immortalised in the evocative 1881 canvas *Scotland Forever!* by Elizabeth Thompson, Lady Butler) was one of the principal turning points of this epic battle. Indeed, for the next century Scottish units appeared to feature in British military history in disproportionate ratio to their country's size. However, it was only with the Entente Cordiale of 1904 that the threat of another war between the British and French was finally averted.

Nevertheless, over the last century the spectre of the Auld Alliance has been repeatedly conjured. While in Edinburgh in June 1942 to visit Free French military establishments, and still smarting over the perceived lack of support he was being given by his British and American premiers, General Charles de Gaulle mischievously disinterred the concept of the Auld Alliance, describing it as 'the oldest alliance in the world' and declaring:

In every combat where for five centuries the destiny of France was at stake, there were always men of Scotland to fight side by side with men of France, and what Frenchmen feel is that no people has ever been more generous than yours with its friendship.

Even as de Gaulle was sulking at home in Colombey-les-Deux-Églises after the Second World War, evaluating the prospects of his return to a frontline role in politics, the rapturous reception given to the Franco-Scottish Exhibition held at the Palace of Rohan in Paris in 1956 (opened by the Queen Mother) demonstrated that the great affection between the two nations still endured. In 1995 celebrations were held in both countries to mark the 700th anniversary of the original Auld Alliance treaty, signed in Paris on 23 October 1295. Four years later, the first Scottish parliament to meet since 1707 assembled in Edinburgh. In 2004 it moved into its permanent new home at Enric Miralles's expressive if eccentric new parliament complex in Holyrood.

Nor has interest in the historic Franco-Scottish axis waned in recent years. Indeed, at the time of writing it is once more receiving the attention of the international media. Following the controversial Brexit vote of 2016, when Scotland – in which every single council returned 'remain' majorities – voted overwhelmingly to stay in the European Union while Britain as a whole voted to leave, the prospect of an independent Scotland reviving the French alliance as a means of re-entering the EU was widely mooted in the media and in the corridors of Holyrood. This prospect prompted the Scottish government to issue a lamentably straight-laced denial that it had any intention of proceeding down this route, having 'no plans to restore the Auld Alliance in the event of Scotland becoming an independent country'. Such public protestations aside, if – or perhaps when – a sovereign Scotland is successful in restoring direct ties with France and the rest of Europe, it would be most fitting if the agreement could be signed in the joyously Francophile environment of that enduring symbol of the Auld Alliance, the hall at George Heriot's School.

10

PECKWATER QUAD, CHRIST CHURCH, OXFORD

1706–14

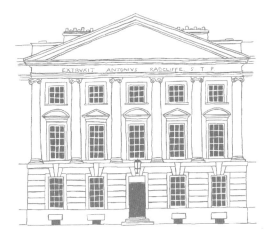

An Oxford Quad Becomes the Model for Georgian Britain

Begun in 1706 and completed by the time of the accession of George I, the first of Britain's Hanoverian kings, in 1714, the three ranges of Henry Aldrich's Peckwater Quadrangle can be found at Christ Church in Oxford. Designed by an Oxford college dean, an amateur architect better known as a logician and musical composer, they deserve to be far more widely known as the ancestor of the Georgian terrace houses of the British Isles and North America, from Bath and Newcastle to Boston and New Orleans.

Henry Aldrich

Aldrich (1647–1710) was an astonishing polymath. A witty Oxford University don who rarely ventured outside the city's walls, his expansive range of interests appeared to encompass almost every element of the British

▷ *The central portico of Aldrich's north range today.*

intellectual revolution of the late Stuart period, from poetry and music to logic and architecture. What he created at his own college had no precedent in British or indeed northern European architecture. At Peckwater Quad he grouped modest residential units into the first, Renaissance-style 'palace front', dignifying student rooms and dons' quarters with a 'giant order' of columns and unifying each façade with continuous rustication on the ground floor and, above the second floor, a massive pediment. Everyday housing was thus transformed into a grand, unified architectural composition with social as well as architectural aspirations: a Roman palace imported into the dense urban grain of a British city.

The integrated Georgian terrace has rightly been called one of Britain's most visible architectural exports to the world – and Peckwater was its godfather. Aldrich's quad not only directly influenced one of the first civic terraces of the Georgian era, John Wood's Queen Square in Bath, but shaped the form of every terrace, square and crescent built across Britain and America during the eighteenth and nineteenth centuries. Aldrich's fusion of Italian style and British rationality established just the right tone for a Britain which, following the conclusion of peace in Europe in 1713, was established as the Continent's rising power, with a growing reputation for concealing its political and economic aggression beneath a veneer of understated sophistication.

Aldrich came up to Christ Church, Oxford, in 1662 and never left. His college was, by Oxford standards, fairly new when he arrived as a freshman. It had been founded by Cardinal Wolsey in 1525 using the proceeds of dissolved religious houses and, following Wolsey's fall from power in 1529, was refounded by Henry VIII in 1532. Henry, however, never bothered to release funds to complete the college's Great Quadrangle, and its planned cloister remained unbuilt – giving the quad a less intimate feel than most older college equivalents. In 1546 the now ageing and virtually immobile king did, though, enhance the college's status and influence within the university by making its fine Norman and late Gothic chapel – around which Wolsey had originally arranged his new college and to which he had appointed the illustrious composer John Taverner as Director of Music – into a fully fledged cathedral, transferring the see of Oxford from the recently reprieved former abbey at Osney in west Oxford. From that time onwards the Head of House at Christ Church was also Dean of the cathedral, appointed by the crown, and thus had to be an Anglican cleric. The former cathedral at Osney, meanwhile, was pillaged by locals for its valuable stone, and what was once Oxfordshire's largest abbey church soon became a picturesque ruin. Today only a remnant of its fifteenth-century refectory survives above ground.

Aldrich progressed from student to don at the same college. He was a member of the college's governing body which invited his friend the Oxford scientist and now Surveyor-General of the King's Works, Sir Christopher Wren, to convert the Great Quad's unfinished gatehouse into a soaring composition in an exuberant if not strictly academic Gothick style in 1681–2. The main quad was subsequently rechristened 'Tom Quad' after the six and a quarter ton great bell, named 'Great Tom', which hung inside Wren's new tower and which had been salvaged from Osney Abbey. Today Great Tom still tolls 101 times every night for the 101 college fellows of 1680. It rings at 9.05 p.m., Oxford Time – the time Oxford kept before the advent of the railways cajoled the country into accepting London's Greenwich Mean Time as the national standard.

At the time of the ousting of the Catholic monarch James II in 1688, in what was later dubbed, somewhat inappropriately, 'the Glorious Revolution', a number of Catholic converts were at the helm of Oxford and Cambridge colleges. One of these was John Massey, appointed to the Deanship of Christ Church in haste in 1686 and who now fled even more hastily to Europe in the wake of his royal master. Hugely embarrassed by the whole incident, in 1689 the college persuaded the new joint monarchs – the Dutch *stadhouder* who had been invited to safeguard the Protestant succession, William III, and his Stuart wife and daughter of James II, Mary II – to elevate one of their own. Henry Aldrich duly became the new college dean, exploiting his position not just to indulge his many cultural and intellectual interests but also to contribute to the college one of the country's most influential new architectural designs. Six years later Aldrich was advanced yet further, to the *de facto* headship of the whole university, when he was appointed vice-chancellor. Yet he still found time to translate Greek, publish on logic, write poetry, compose music (he penned a number of choral anthems and hymns and adapted works by Palestrina and Carissimi) and to design two major additions to Oxford's architectural canon. On his retirement in 1702 Aldrich was provided with a lucrative church benefice in Shropshire. Nevertheless, he still preferred to remain in Oxford, where he could keep an eye on his new architectural projects. When he died in 1710, he was, at his own request, buried in Christ Church Cathedral. A modest man to the very end, Aldrich asked that no memorial be erected to him. His monument was, in truth, the new quadrangle that was being built at the rear of the college. This splendid creation deserves to bear Aldrich's name; instead, puzzlingly,

△ An amateur copy of Godfrey Kneller's 1699 portrait of Dean Henry Aldrich.

the college took the new quad's title from the medieval inn which had once stood on the site.

Aldrich personified that very British tradition the gifted amateur. The celebration of cheerful, inspired amateurism rather than calculated and practised professionalism has both enriched and bedevilled British history from the time the Saxon monk Bede began to scribble down his *Ecclesiastical History of the English People* in his spare time during the early years of the eighth century.

It was a tradition which particularly appealed to the dons of Oxford University, who believed – then as now – that their academic talents qualified them to tackle anything that was thrown at them. From the days of King James I, the university had preferred to entrust its major architectural commissions to amenable, local master masons who would be able, if necessary, to convert the port-fuelled architectural visions of college dons into solid masonry or, in instances where the task was deemed beyond even the wit and wisdom of the college fellows, to execute, adapt and, if necessary, dilute the designs produced *in absentia* by recognised architects. Generally these professional architects were local men, or at least metropolitan names who had fallen out of stylistic favour and consequently were more likely to acquiesce to dons' whims and would be less taxing to college budgets than their more fashionable equivalents in London.

The amateur tradition

By 1700 Oxford could already boast a long tradition of using master masons or building contractors to refine and augment as well as to construct architectural designs. It was John Townesend (1648–1728) – who, antiquary Thomas Hearne approvingly noted in 1720, 'hath a hand in all the Buildings in Oxford' of the first decades of the eighteenth century (and, Hearne added, 'gets a vast deal of Money that way') – who cornered the market in Baroque Oxford, earning himself the mayoralty of the city in the process. Hearne's accolade was fully deserved: Townesend not only built Aldrich's Peckwater Quad after 1706 – and, in 1707–8, rebuilt Aldrich's All Saints Church, adding a tower and spire to his own, Wren-inspired design in 1718–20. He also both designed and built the Fellows' Building at Corpus Christi of 1706–12 – for the elevations of which he adapted one of Aldrich's novel Peckwater ranges – and, after 1711, Lord Willoughby de Broke's new country house at Compton Verney. There he employed Vanbrughian Baroque elevations of the sort he was then erecting in his capacity as Master Mason at Blenheim Palace. In addition, he built Hawksmoor's Clarendon Building in 1712–13; the same architect's North Quadrangle at All Souls College (a 'Gothic' extension which included the magnificent Codrington Library) after 1716; as well as the west range of the Front Quad and much of the other new work then being undertaken at Queen's College between 1709 and 1719. There he was nominally under the direction of yet another amateur architect-don, Dr George Clarke of All Souls

College, next door. The deliberately archaic compositions of the Radcliffe Quad at University College in 1717–19 and the Robinson Building at Oriel College in 1719–20 were also realised by the Townesends* in an idiom which, to the dons' evident delight, evoked the era of the later Plantagenets rather than of the new Hanoverian dynasty.

In a rather more contemporary vein, father and son collaborated with George Clarke at his monumental Library at Christ Church – begun in 1717 but which, by the time it was finished in 1772, was something of an architectural dinosaur – and, from 1720, on Nicholas Hawksmoor's design for a new entrance at Worcester College, which they and Clarke substantially revised.

Many of the Townesends' new Oxford buildings – particularly the quads at University and Oriel – were couched in a deliberately archaic idiom, be it the late Gothic of the fifteenth century or the Baroque expressionism of the early eighteenth. At University College's Radcliffe Quad, John Townesend even included a stone-vaulted ceiling in the form of a fan vault, of the type first used in Oxford in *c.*1480. The fan vault had been used repeatedly as a eurosceptic symbol of Oxford's determined adherence to traditional English Gothic (as opposed to the pernicious classicism of the Continent) throughout the seventeenth century. In 1640 fan vaults were installed in the staircase hall at Christ Church, a symbol of the college's disregard of the classicism of Inigo Jones that was now all the rage in London. Today both the staircase hall and the dining hall itself are global celebrities, not because they constituted the epicentre of Charles I's makeshift court during the Revolution – the king's 'parliament' met in Christ Church's hall – but because they featured prominently in the Harry Potter film series from 2001.

Equally outdated was the classical Radcliffe Camera, completed by the Townesends to James Gibbs's design in 1748. In London, Palladianism – the proportional Georgian style which spawned countless squares, terraces, villas and mansions across the English-speaking world – had long been accepted as the default idiom for public and private buildings. Yet in Oxford, Palladianism barely registered among the conservative college dons – aside, that is, from at Peckwater Quad. The unmistakeably Baroque lines of Gibbs's Camera came from another era and had little to do with the proportionality of Palladian masters such as Colen Campbell, Lord Burlington, William Kent or Isaac Ware – leading lights of British architecture who were, notwithstanding their

*   John Townesend was aided and succeeded in his practice by his son William (1669–1739).

190

national reputations, wholly ignored by the university city.

Not only did Oxford largely turn its back on the Palladianism of the mid-eighteenth century. It also barely noticed the neoclassical revolution of the 1760s, a movement led by Robert Adam and William Chambers, pan-British architectural stars who, like their Palladian predecessors, were never invited into the hushed precincts of Oxford's ancient quads. Indeed, during the decades after the completion of the Radcliffe Camera, both the city and university effectively went to sleep. Almost nothing of any significance was built in Oxford after 1748 apart from Henry Keene's eccentric, antiquari-an-Gothick Hall at University College of the mid-1760s and James Wyatt's lofty Observatory of 1773. The dreaming spires slumbered on, largely oblivious to the passing fashions of the outside world. The innate conservatism of eighteenth-century Oxford thus made Henry Aldrich's achievement even more astounding – even if, with typical Oxonian modesty, his seminal role in the Palladian revolution was overlooked for centuries.

English Palladianism

What became known as 'English Palladianism' or just 'Palladianism' was an architectural revolution born of commercial success and new-found aesthetic confidence. During the last years of Queen Anne's reign, Britain's self-confidence rose as its wealth and military potential increased. Its armed forces and its well-stocked Treasury became the arbiter of Europe: Marlborough's epic victories at Blenheim in 1704 and Ramillies in 1706 electrified not only the British nation (as it was from 1707) but the whole of Europe, while the British government effectively subsidised the allied armies of the Austrians and Dutch during the bitter, twelve-year-long War of the Spanish Succession – which, after Louis XIV recognised James II's heir as James III of England and VIII of Scotland in 1701, became a War of the British Succession, too. Louis's act was largely designed to ensure that young James Stuart was accorded a high degree of royal precedence at court. But its effect across the Channel was to reignite fears that the French sought to establish England and Scotland as Catholic satellites ruled by a puppet monarch in the person of 'James III' – or 'the Old Pretender', as he was later dubbed by British Whigs.

Nationalistic sentiment spilled over into the world of architecture. In the years after Marlborough's great military victories there were calls by British architectural cognoscenti for a new 'national taste' to supplant the

△ Peckwater Quad from the south, in a watercolour painting.

Italian- and Catholic-inflected Baroque idioms of Wren, Hawksmoor and Sir John Vanbrugh. What this 'national taste' was to constitute, though, was never properly defined. In the event, the 'Palladian' style which, by the mid-1720s, was dominating the mainstream of British architectural design was just as dependent on Italian models (if not more so) than the Stuart Baroque of the previous decades.

In truth, what was more powerful than stylistic ambitions was personal preferment: the familiar Georgian refrain of 'places not principles'. In 1714 the accession of King George I triggered a general election which unseated the Tories on whom Sir Christopher Wren and his Office of the Royal Works had heavily depended and established a definitive Whig majority. Wren had been Surveyor-General of the King's Works since 1669, and in 1714 was a ripe eighty-two years old. A younger generation of architects were itching to get their hands on the levers of royal and governmental architectural patronage which the Office of Works controlled. With the advent of an unassailable Whig majority in parliament in 1714, the tainting of many Tories as Jacobite rebels, following the flight of prominent Queen Anne Tories such as Lord Bolingbroke to James VII's court at Saint-Germain-en-Laye and the abortive 1715 invasion of Scotland by the Old Pretender, this was no time to have a Tory-leaning architect at the helm of British architecture, no matter how illustrious his past achievements.

Wren's days were thus clearly numbered. He was old, he was ailing – his signature on the Works' minutes became increasingly shaky at this time – and he was even faintly tainted with Jacobitism, having been a Tory MP in 1689–90. (Wren had stood firstly for Plympton in Devon and then for New Windsor, the royal constituency. His son Christopher attempted to win New Windsor in 1713 but was unseated by the Whig government in 1715.) Younger architects such as Thomas Hewett, William Benson and Colen Campbell, along with power-ful and wealthy Whig architectural patrons such as the earls of Burlington and Pembroke, believed their time had now come. The election of 1714 and the accession of a pliable Hanoverian monarch who could barely speak English and who had no opinions whatsoever on cultural patronage (and, it turned out, no interest in culture at all) gave them the tools to do just that. Or so they thought. In 1714 Wren's job as Surveyor-General was put into commis-sion, and four years later he was dispensed with altogether. William Benson, an impeccably Whig gentleman-architect who had already ingratiated himself with George I in Hanover, was installed as Wren's unlikely replacement. When Benson proved himself to be appallingly incompetent, he was substituted by Sir Thomas Hewett, who had been elevated at the whim of his patron and effec-tive British prime minister, the 3rd Earl of Sunderland, in 1719.

In 1712 the celebrated philosopher Anthony Ashley Cooper, 3rd Earl of Shaftesbury, wrote to his friend the Whig politician Lord Somers from Naples. Shaftesbury (1671–1713) was even in his day regarded as a major voice in philoso-phy. His reputation remained high throughout the rest of the Georgian era, his three-volume work of 1711, *Characteristicks*, becoming the second best-selling book of the entire century. In his note, subsequently dignified by the title of *A Letter Concerning Design*, Shaftesbury decried the current state of architec-ture in Britain. The French government – with which Britain was still techni-cally at war in 1712 – stood, in his view, for 'slavish hierarchalism and insidious courtliness', while Britain's constitutional monarchy shone as a global exemplar of how to run a complex nation. Architecture in Britain, though, was, in Shaftesbury's opinion, still in thrall to the French and the Italians:

> 'tis no wonder if so many noble designs... have miscarry'd amongst us; since the genius of our nation has hitherto been so little tum'd this way, that thro' several reigns we have patiently seen the noblest publick buildings perish (if I may say so) under the hand of one single court-architect; who, if he had been able to profit by experience, wou'd long since, at our expence, have prov'd the greatest master in the world. But I question whether our patience is like to hold much longer.

The earl then went on to call for a renewal in British architecture: for the establishment of the balance and good taste for which the British constitution was celebrated.

According to the traditional historiographical narrative of the twentieth century, Shaftesbury's call for a British 'national style' of architecture, one which reflected the nation's commercial success, recent military achievements and its new-found prominence on the world stage, was a formative influence on the young and fabulously wealthy Whig landowner Richard Boyle, 3rd Earl of Burlington. In the familiar story of English Palladianism it was Burlington who, spurred on by Shaftesbury's epistolary call to arms, engineered the capture of the Office of Works in 1714 for the architectural radicals and leveraged this power base to bring the proportional classicism of Andrea Palladio and Inigo Jones to Britain. In this scenario, however, there was no place for Henry Aldrich, and Peckwater Quad was relegated to a mere footnote in history.

However, recent research suggests that this may not quite be the case. As we have seen, despite his challenge to the architectural status quo, Shaftesbury never suggested what form this new 'national style' might actually take. And, most crucially, there is no evidence that Burlington ever read Shaftesbury's letter. As Alexander Echlin and William Kelly have observed: 'Shaftesbury retired, ill, to Naples in 1711. Burlington was then just sixteen and had shown little interest in art or architecture. Shaftesbury composed the Letter in 1712, and then died in 1713, the year before Burlington's first journey to Italy.'

It is undeniable that Scots architect Colen Campbell, then Lord Burlington's leading protégé, was employed by the publishers of the ambitious new guide of 1715 to English great houses, *Vitruvius Britannicus*, to pen a hurried foreword and insert a variety of neo-Palladian schemes into their ambitious new book. However, this was not born out of a desire to produce a Palladian polemic. It was a hasty move by desperate publishers to harness a wealthy subscriber (Burlington) and fill up the many empty pages of what was planned to be the first of a multi-volume series with actual or conjectural schemes (by Campbell). Campbell's introduction is full of nationalist, anti-Baroque invective: he damns the 'capricious Ornaments' of contemporary Italian design and lambasts the masters of Italian Baroque such as Bernini ('affected and licentious') and Borromini ('who has endeavour'd to debauch Mankind with his odd and chimerical Beauties'). However, Campbell's involvement was only proposed at the last minute – his name can be seen hurriedly added to the side of the already typeset and centred title page – and was not part of any planned Palladian programme. And while William Benson, Burlington's proposed replacement for Wren, can certainly be described as Burlington's creature, Thomas Hewett, Benson's successor at the Office of Works, most certainly was not. Hewett's architectural vision, such as it was, seemed to encompass more general neoclassical influences rather than a prescription to adhere to the Renaissance models of Andrea Palladio and Inigo Jones.

The Godfather

As a result of this revisionism, Dean Henry Aldrich – rather than Shaftesbury or Burlington – can be cast as one of the principal godfathers of early English Palladianism. His coolly proportioned Peckwater Quad became a touchstone for those who were looking for a more sedate and polite alternative to the eccentric mannerism of the English Baroque of Hawksmoor, Vanbrugh and Thomas Archer. Aldrich's inclusion at Peckwater of a rusticated ground floor, large windows on the *piano nobile* and giant-order pilasters which tied the first and second floors together harked back not just to the Veneto palaces of the sixteenth century – although his alternating pointed and segmented pediments do appear to be directly influenced by Palladio himself – but also to seventeenth-century works by Inigo Jones such as Lindsey House in London's Lincoln's Inn Fields, built in *c*.1640. Furthermore, Aldrich's use of a giant pediment atop an engaged hexastyle portico at the centre of each of the three completed ranges unified what was, in reality, an everyday housing terrace, giving the whole composition the air of an Italian palace. This concept was entirely novel, and showed how brave even the amateur architects of early eighteenth-century Britain could be.

Aldrich's fourth range was designed to be a freestanding accommodation block, built in the same idiom but detached from the other three to enable easy access across the college to Merton Street. After the dean's death, however, this fourth range was completed as a new Library in a grander, more muscularly Baroque manner under the supervision of Aldrich's friend Dr George Clarke. In this Clarke was, as usual, abetted by the Townesends. The Library's soaring giant-order columns and pilasters, however, unify the building in a manner more reminiscent of Nicholas Hawksmoor than Inigo Jones.

Peckwater's influence was soon felt across the country. One of the most important early expressions of 'Palladianism', the new wing built at Narford Hall, Norfolk, by the amateur architect Sir Andrew Fountaine (1676–1753) in 1716, was directly inspired by Aldrich and by Peckwater, for Fountaine had been the dean's prize pupil. Born in 1676, Andrew Fountaine took his degree from Christ Church, Oxford, in 1696 and was knighted three years later for having performed the Latin oration as King William III entered Oxford. As a student at Christ Church, Fountaine had formed a close relationship with Dean Aldrich. As Echlin and Kelley have pointed out:

Aldrich was much impressed by the young Fountaine, nominating him first as a 'Canoneer Student' and then as 'the best classical scholar in the University'. It was Aldrich who selected Fountaine to deliver the Latin oration as William III entered Oxford in 1698, for which he was knighted the next year. Contemporaries, it seems, saw Fountaine as a devoted follower and even puppet of Aldrich, even long after he had left Christ Church. In November 1704, the Bishop of Norwich warned the Bishop of Carlisle 'against too great freedom in the company of Sir A. Fountain (a bigoted creature of the Dean of Christ Church)'. Francis Blomefield, writing in the 1740s, tells us that in Fountaine's library he hung portraits of Aldrich, Palladio and Jones.

Fountaine made at least two Grand Tours of Europe, in 1701 and again in 1714, and anticipated Burlington in bringing back a vast haul of drawings, paintings, books and sculptures. Some years later the inveterate gossip Lord Hervey declared Fountaine's home at Narford to be 'absolutely the prettiest trinket I ever saw. My Lord Burlington could not make a better ragoust [*sic*] of paintings, statues, gilding and virtù!' Clearly inspired by Aldrich, Fountaine also demonstrated that he could be a skilled amateur architect. A trio of distinguished architectural historians have called his Library 'a surprisingly sophisticated piece of work' which testified to his 'advanced Palladian taste'. And he looked not just to Aldrich, Jones or Palladio but to ancient Rome, too, in the neoclassical garden follies he built on his estate after Roman temples. The prolific pattern-book author and architect William Halfpenny dedicated his *The Art of Sound Building* of 1732 to Fountaine, mentioning his 'uncommon Penetration... exquisite Judgment... delicate Taste, and... thorough acquaintance with the Subject'. This dedication came just as Fountaine retired to his country house, remodelling it with the help of his friend the Earl of Pembroke's architectural amanuensis, Roger Morris. A year later, Lord Burlington did the same, retiring to his Middlesex retreat at Chiswick in the wake of rising condemnation of his failed attempt to remould British culture in an Italian vein.

Another of Aldrich's pupils who was to lead the new Palladian revolution was Henry Herbert, later the 9th Earl of Pembroke. The earl had studied at Christ Church a few years after Fountaine, matriculating in 1705 when Aldrich was still dean, and both he and his father were friends of Fountaine and his family. As John Harris has written of Aldrich: 'it cannot be a coincidence that two amateurs in Palladian architecture were taught by him.' Pembroke went on to design a few structures himself, including that flagrant expression of national triumphalism, the Column of Victory at Blenheim Palace. (The erection of the column was, inevitably, overseen by the Townesends.) But he is better known as the sponsor of architect Roger Morris, whose Palladian-proportioned villa Marble Hill House in Middlesex of 1724–9 became the prototype for compact classical villas across Britain and America throughout the Georgian era.

Christ Church during Aldrich's long tenure was clearly a centre of architectural study. Fuelled by the dean's extensive architectural library, the college can be seen as the engine room for the Palladian style that had swept the country by 1740. Everywhere, that is, except, with delicious irony, the city of Oxford itself. Another of Aldrich's pupils, Charles Brandon Fairfax, later noted that Aldrich had always acknowledged that Palladio had been the dean's 'master in architecture', while Aldrich himself wrote: 'we are much indebted to Palladio for his beautiful selections from the remains of ancient artists, which he has made with so much taste... wherefore in gratitude to his services, we will pass by other writers, and cheerfully follow his footsteps.' However, outside Christ Church there was little trace of Palladio in Georgian Oxford. The nineteenth and early twentieth centuries, too, had little time for Palladianism and even less for Dean Aldrich, who slipped back into Oxonian obscurity. By the end of Queen Victoria's long reign, his magnificent Peckwater Quad was better known as a symbol of aristocratic excess than as a foundation stone of the Palladian movement.

The Bullingdon Club had been founded in Oxford as a sporting society at the end of the eighteenth century. But by the 1890s the society had degenerated into a riotous dining club, whose vastly wealthy members were notorious for destroying the venues in which they dined. Their activities often centred on Christ Church, and in particular on Peckwater Quad. In 1894 and again in 1927 Bullingdon members smashed almost all the 468 perfectly proportioned windows in Peckwater, along with all the quad's blinds and doors. In 2005 the club was again in the national news when its members ransacked the fine Fyfield pub the White Hart, to the west of Oxford, smashing seventeen bottles of wine. After this incident four of the Bullingdon members were arrested.

The Bullingdon, and Peckwater Quad, hit the front pages again in 2007, when a twenty-year-old photograph was discovered of club members posing languidly on the steps at the south-east corner of Aldrich's quad. The poseurs included two future Conservative prime ministers: David Cameron and Boris Johnson. The media seized on this image with delight, citing it as proof that modern, supposedly egalitarian Britain still harboured anachronistic islands of unearned privilege and hidden influence. Subsequently, the Bullingdon's notoriety as a male bastion of privately educated anti-intellectualism and thuggish vandalism was sealed with the staging of Laura Wade's play *Posh* in 2010. This was subsequently made into a film, *The Riot Club*, which was given a worldwide release in 2014.

Soon after the media frenzy of 2007, and under pressure from its subjects, Oxford photographers Gillman and Soame, who owned the copyright of the original Peckwater picture, withdrew permission to use the image. However, this did not stop local artist Rona producing a version of the original picture in oils in 2019, thus providing the media with an image which *could* be published or filmed.

In the meantime, the photograph's subjects themselves tried desperately to distance themselves from this egregious snapshot. Boris Johnson was, predictably, the first to attempt to distance himself from his former clubmates, dubbing the notorious image 'a truly shameful vignette of almost superhuman undergraduate arrogance, toffishness and twittishness'. Five years later the Oxford University Conservative Association declared that the Bullingdon's 'values and activities had no place in the modern Conservative Party'. By 2016 it was reported that the Bullingdon Club retained only around five postgraduate members, and the following year an attempt to photograph the rump of the club in Peckwater resulted in the students being escorted out of the college by the porters of Christ Church, accompanied by heckling from the quad's undergraduates and the playing from a Peckwater window of Homer 'Boots' Randolph's 'Yakety Sax', which Britons young and old remember as the theme tune for the anachronistic and shamelessly sexist comedy TV show of the 1970s and 1980s, *The Benny Hill Show*. There was no protest four years later when a group of black students at Oxford posed confidently on the steps of George Clarke's Library in Peckwater as a riposte to the infamous Bullingdon image.

None of these stories seemed to affect the political landscape, however. David Cameron became prime minister in the year that *Posh* was produced, and nine years later he was succeeded in this office by his mop-topped Bullingdon crony, Boris Johnson, whose chaotic premiership ended in the ignominy of enforced resignation in September 2022. At the time of writing, however, Johnson evidently still harbours ambitions of a return to prime ministerial office. And Henry Aldrich's Peckwater Quad? It is still waiting to receive appropriate recognition for the role it played as a torchbearer for a new architectural style designed to encapsulate the nation's cultural and economic aspirations.

11

19 PRINCELET STREET, SPITALFIELDS, LONDON

BEGUN 1718

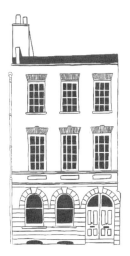

Immigration and Industry

Spitalfields, a working-class district just to the east of the City of London bordering the Roman road of Ermine Street, has been a centre of immigration since the sixteenth century. Indeed, as the district's biographer, the celebrated architectural historian Dan Cruickshank, has declared: 'The history of Spitalfields is a direct and dramatic echo of the history... of England.' To historian and author Raphael Samuel it was 'a weavers' parish, throbbing with industry and toil – one of the great manufacturing centres of the country'.

The origin of Spitalfields

The Romans had founded Spitalfields in the first century AD and burial remains suggest that citizens of Rome continued to come here until the turn of the fifth century, i.e. until the very end of Roman rule. In 1197 an Augustinian priory was founded here, dedicated to St Mary. Its priory hospital gave its name to the area, as 'the hospital in the fields'. At the time of its dissolution in 1535 the hospital precincts occupied a large site, extending south from Folgate Street

across what later became Spital Square and almost reaching what is now Brushfield Street. During an archaeological dig on the priory site, before the erection of the new market development, the skeletal remains of more than 10,000 bodies were found in the burial ground, mostly in the ancient charnel house. Many of these appear to have died following some cataclysmic event in the mid-thirteenth century – possibly the result of a volcanic explosion somewhere else in the world.

By 1685 Spitalfields was largely urbanised, although there were still many large open areas available for would-be house builders such as the Old Artillery Ground, just to the east of Bishopsgate. Many of these new houses had been built according to the 'speculative' system devised by the medically trained property developer Dr Nicholas Barbon (*c*.1640–*c*.1698) after the Great Fire of London of 1666. Barbon – who also launched a successful fire insurance business in 1680 and died worth around £326 million at today's rates – correctly thought that it would speed building development up if the ground landlord sold the development area off to a team of tradesmen. This professional group would generally be led by a surveyor, builder or architect who would allocate individual plots to different members of the team to get the carcasses of the new homes built. The homes were invariably terraced: packed tightly together with as little street frontage as possible. Each team member – be he a bricklayer, carpenter or leadworker – would then rent his skills out to his fellows working on adjacent plots. All would have a strong incentive to build quickly: the team would be charged a minimal rent for a short while, usually defined as two or three years. By the end of that period – and here's where the speculative bit comes in – the landowner assumed that the building team would have sold the houses on to the first tenant or 'leaseholder', who would agree to lease (a type of long-term rental) the property for a defined term, usually ninety-nine years. The house would then be completed to the wishes of the first owner, who would determine the level (and expense) of the home's decoration and what fixtures and fittings to install.

The problem with speculative development came with the sale of the house to its first occupier. On occasion, owing to external events over which the development team might have no control, such as war or economic depression, their homes could not be sold during the period of peppercorn rent. If the builder was left with the house or houses still on his hands when the commercial lease-rent kicked in, then he might well be ruined. Many a speculative building team came a cropper in this way during the late Stuart and Georgian periods.

These new houses were built, or at the very least externally faced, with fireproof materials: brick and, where the developer or owner could afford it, imported stone. The 1667 Rebuilding Act passed after the Great Fire of London stipulated that all new homes should restrict the use of external timberwork so as to prevent a future conflagration and required that all new construction should be of restricted height and confined to one of four predetermined 'rates' of houses. And all of these rates were to be faced with masonry, and not with inflammable timber. Strictly speaking, this Act only applied to the City of London, but soon the developments of Spitalfields, and indeed the rest of Britain, were following its guidelines in order to create a fireproof future for the nation. By the 1720s additional acts restricted the use of external timber still further, banning its use from eaves cornices and demanding that sash window boxes be recessed at least four inches into the wall and their woodwork be protected by a skin of masonry. As Dan Cruickshank has observed, though, 'The fact that in virtually all surviving Spitalfields houses of the 1720s timber sash boxes are still set flush with the elevations confirms forcefully... that the writ of the early Acts was not observed in early-Georgian Spitalfields.'

The Huguenots

In 1685 Louis XIV of France dramatically ended the toleration for Protestant worshippers that had been guaranteed by his grandfather, Henry IV, by the Edict of Nantes of 1598. Louis chose to expel what the republican historian Jules Michelet has called 'les meilleurs Français de France' – decades after German chancellor Otto von Bismarck had called the German Huguenot communities 'the best of Germans' – in order to eradicate what he saw as an inherent weakness and source of future friction and challenge to his Catholic absolutist state. Four years earlier Louis had initiated a campaign of intimidation against the largely Calvinist Protestants of France – or 'Huguenots' as they were known. (The exact origin of this proud name has sadly been lost.) Troops were billeted in homes in Huguenot communities to 'persuade' the inhabitants to convert to Catholicism, an exercise which was soon being called the *Dragonnades* after the dragoon regiments which formed the backbone of this military occupation. The revocation of 1685 sought to marginalise and eradicate what had previously been a privileged minority community in the nation. But Louis did not want them to leave: if they tried to escape France, they could be imprisoned, enslaved or even executed. Nevertheless, despite the introduction of such terrifying punishments, tens of thousands of Huguenots took the risk and fled to more tolerant countries – Holland, Switzerland, Northern Germany and Britain and its American colonies. By December 1687 it was calculated that 13,050 Huguenots had settled in England's capital, most of them in Spitalfields. The district held obvious attractions for the French immigrants: it was near the French Protestant church in Threadneedle Street in the City of London, there were new houses being built by speculative developers that they could occupy, and – given that many of these French arrivals were silk-weavers – there was already a tradition of textile production in the area, then dominated by the weaving of silk ribbons for women's dresses. This, then, seemed the ideal place from which to build a domestic silk industry in London.

As early as 1681 King Charles II was offering his support for the newly arrived refugees, raising funds to relieve those who were 'not only distressed strangers but chiefly persecuted Protestants' who had been 'forced to abandon their native abodes'. James II's accession in 1685, and his well-advertised Catholicism, seems to have deterred some Huguenots from coming to Britain after the Revocation – many chose Holland or Prussia instead – but thousands did still make the journey to Spitalfields. And following James II's Declaration of Indulgence of 1687 – a measure designed to allow British Catholics freedom of worship, freeing dissenters from having to adhere to the Anglican rite – a new flood of Huguenots arrived in the country.

The tightly knit Huguenot community were used to self-reliance and mutual support in France. As Menna Prestwich has written, in France 'The Huguenots were increasingly an alien and friendless minority whose enemies ranged from the parlements and magistrates to street gangs in the towns'. In Spitalfields they kept their French names and their French identity, marrying within the community during the eighteenth century and even changing the street names to French. Thus Church Street became Fournier Street, while the road which ran parallel to it to the north was called Princesse Street. (The name may have originated from the developers' surveyor, John Prince. It was only renamed Princelet Street in the 1890s.)

Two London lawyers, Charles Wood and Simon Michell, had bought the land on which Princesse Street stood and acted as the speculative developers. Local builder Samuel Worrall and bricklayer Samuel Phipps were two of the principal craftsmen they hired to erect the actual homes, which were begun in 1718. Numbers 17 and 19 both featured tall first-floor windows whose status on the *piano nobile* was emphasised by prominent brick keystones, presumably created by Phipps and his team. Ben Truman the brewer occupied the grander house at number 4 from 1724, while Worrall himself bought numbers 18 and 19 in February 1722. Unusually for the speculative system, Wood and Michell sold the freehold, and not the leasehold, of the houses; thus Worrall owned both the houses and their land outright.

Worrall, who occupied number 18 himself, successively sublet number 19 across the road to a druggist, a draper, a glover and a needlemaker – a fine indication of the range of Spitalfields's crafts. In 1743 it was occupied by the silk-weaver Peter Ogier, who in 1745 was recorded undertaking to raise a body of twenty-eight of his weavers to resist the Young Pretender, then advancing on the capital through northern England.

Peter Abraham Ogier was born in Poitou in 1690 and, aged only seven, was taken to England by his Protestant mother, Jeanne. Ogier became a successful silk-weaver: a freeman of the Weavers' Company in 1716, he became a full liveryman in 1741, by which point he and his family were living at 19 Princesse Street.

Princelet Street

Dan Cruickshank has noted of the street that:

> When completed in the mid-1720s, Princelet Street with its tall houses of regular design and relatively large rear gardens was one of the best streets in Spitalfields. For a successful master weaver and silk merchant such as Peter Abraham Ogier it was therefore a suitably prestigious address.

Number 19 was a medium-sized house by Spitalfields standards: one room wide, two rooms deep and three storeys high, with a kitchen pantry and scullery in the basement. The ground and first floors were provided with wood-panelled walls with Doric cornices. The wood of which they were made would have been deal (fir or pine), which was invariably painted a 'stone' colour derived from earthen and other organic pigments. And the staircase to the first floor was set with finely turned classical balusters. In the most important room of the house, the 'drawing room' at the front of the first floor, Ogier subsequently installed a French-style Rococo chimneypiece, all the rage around 1750. This was stolen from the house in 1980 but was later returned, and is now awaiting conservation. Number 19 also had a large rear garden, at the end of which would have stood the 'house of office' over a cesspit. Unlike some of the smaller weaving businesses of the district, however, number 19 did not contain a weavers' attic. (That feature was added to the house later.) Weaving for the Ogier firm went on in other premises; number 19 was instead reserved as Ogier's well-equipped home as well as the centre of his business activities.

In the meantime, the future Princelet Street had acquired a prominent near-neighbour: the towering spire of Christ Church, Spitalfields. The Tory government's Fifty New Churches Act of 1711 made certain that the dissenting Huguenots had an Anglican church they could attend. On a greenfield site at the western end of what became Fournier Street, architect Nicholas Hawksmoor built an astonishing, cavernous church, with a massive, freestanding tripartite portico and a soaring Gothic spire. By the time it was completed in 1729, Christ Church had become a major London landmark and the sort of building Burlington and his Palladian followers loved to hate. By 1743, however, the Huguenot community had funded the building of their own, plain Calvinist chapel at the eastern end of Fournier Street. This modest brick building, whose erection was supervised by the local surveyor Thomas Stibbs, survived to serve other Spitalfields immigrant communities by becoming a synagogue in 1897 and a mosque in 1976.

The peace and prosperity which followed the ending of the war with France in 1713, the accession of George I in 1714 and the abject failure of the 1715 Scots rising benefitted the Spitalfields silk industry enormously. By the time Peter Ogier died in 1757 he had become very rich. His descendants intermarried with other local artisan families and prospered. Peter Ogier III expanded the business into west Essex and even established a trading house for his products in Canada in 1767. He died at 37 Spital Square – now the home of the venerable and much-respected Society for the Protection of Ancient Buildings – in 1775.

Fluctuating fortunes

The Ogiers were not alone in building a successful business empire out of silk-weaving. The meritocratic Huguenot community in Spitalfields contained many successful silk-weaving families, master-weaving dynasties which included the Paroissiens at Spital Square,* the Symondses in Elder Street, the Sauberes in what became Hanbury Street and the Sabatiers as well as the Ogiers in Princelet Street. Their Spitalfields silks became celebrated across Europe and North America. From the 1740s – by which time the development of Spitalfields was almost complete – Spitalfields's floral designs became more naturalistic and more famous than their more stylised French competitors. As Dan Cruickshank has noted, flowers were very important to the inhabitants of the cramped Spitalfields lanes, and many artisans grew prize-winning tulips, fuchsias, auriculas or dahlias in window boxes or in their backyards. Indeed, the Huguenots of Spitalfields continued producing flowered silk well into the nineteenth century, by which time its market had shrunk considerably.

The outbreak of war with France in 1793 severely dented the appeal of Spitalfields silk, a market which was already shrinking thanks to the popularity and availability of cheap cottons. The end of the war at the Battle of Waterloo in 1815 seemed to hail a golden age for the area's silk-weavers, but it was a false dawn. Just nine years later the future of the Huguenot community was sealed when the Georgian acts of parliament prohibiting the import of French silks were repealed. From then on the Spitalfields silk industry went into a terminal decline, buffeted both by French imports and the fashionability of cheaper and easily washable printed cottons.

As the silk trade collapsed in the face of the onward march of Lancashire cotton, the Huguenots moved east. In their place came poor Jewish immigrants, fleeing the persecutions and pogroms of central Europe. Small-scale textile firms still characterised the area – although now silk production had largely been replaced by general tailoring – but the old merchant dwellings typified by number 19 now degenerated into multi-occupied slums as Spitalfields became a byword for urban deprivation. The wealthier families had already moved out: the Ogiers had seemingly foreseen this downturn and had moved out of Princelet Street as early as 1810. Meanwhile, the wealth of the remaining weavers declined.

---

* The spelling of their surname was only changed to Parissien in 1960, thirty years after their former Spitalfields home had been demolished to make way for an extension to the fruit and vegetable market.

△ *The top-lit synagogue interior at number 19.*

Victorian Spitalfields

By the 1840s Spitalfields was notorious as a highly depressed area, a home of thieves, prostitutes and 'resurrectionists' (body snatchers) and a place of appalling poverty. Spitalfields became known as the worst criminal rookery in London, the unacceptable face of Victorian London, and by the last decades of the century was a nest of robbers and pimps. It was near here that the serial killer Jack the Ripper started his murderous spree in 1888, while in 1903 the novelist Jack London famously profiled 'Itchy Park', the yard adjacent to

209

Hawksmoor's splendid and imposing Christ Church, as a down-at-heel rendezvous for homeless people.

Princelet Street, too, had come down in the world. As early as 1851– the year in which Henry Mayhew's explosive, three-volume *London Labour and the London Poor* lambasted Spitalfields as being 'in a dilapidated state' and an 'abnormally filthy' district where 'fever and other epidemics are rife' – number 19, formerly the Ogiers' luxurious townhouse, was being occupied by two households. In 1857 a wide new road, Commercial Street, cut a swathe through the slums just to the west of Princelet Street in order to clear some of the area's worst housing and to link Shoreditch and Spitalfields with the eastern edge of the City of London. Nevertheless, conditions in the area to the east of the new thoroughfare continued to deteriorate. On 24 October 1863 the *Illustrated London News* published a damning article on the 'disgusting details' and 'putrid sties' of this once-proud area. Dan Cruickshank ominously observes how the voyeuristic vogue for photographs of child poverty in Spitalfields became highly fashionable during the 1860s in perhaps the first example of what was later christened 'poverty porn'.

In 1862, however, things changed dramatically for number 19. The house found its purpose and its fortunes restored just as its neighbours slipped further into decay. In that year a synagogue was moved here from Fashion Street: as a result, a double-height, top-lit and galleried hall was inserted into the rear garden, below which was installed a large meeting room. At the same time the ground floor was remodelled and provided with a coat of rusticated stucco, a robustly proportioned door and window arches and recessed double doors.

The new facility actually anticipated, rather than met, demand. The earliest Jewish immigration from Russia, Ukraine and Russian Poland did not come until 1881, when the assassination of Tsar Alexander II triggered a wave of anti-Semitic pogroms across the Russian empire. This onslaught was encouraged by the reactionary new tsar, Alexander III, who blamed 'revolutionaries and Jews' for the murder of his father. Jewish immigration increased again after a new flood of government-sponsored pogroms, largely in present-day Ukraine, in 1903–6, and again after 1918, when the Russian Revolution had made life uncertain for so many. Altogether two million Jews fled the Russian empire between 1881 and 1920, the majority of whom emigrated to Britain and the US.

In London, the Princelet Street Synagogue was ready and waiting for them. The temple first appears in the Post Office Directory in 1871 as the 'United Friends' Synagogue'. Much work had already been done to the house to prepare it for its new function by a Mr Hudson for the Loyal United Friends Friendly Society. The ground floor was stuccoed externally to give it a more imposing aspect to the street and both the ground and first floors opened up to create a space for worshipping, complete with a 'ladies' gallery' supported on wrought-iron columns with fine Ionic capitals. (The weavers' attic with its seven-bay window, glazed with old-fashioned leaded lights, nevertheless survived.) The memorial inscriptions of the conversion's original donors, written in both English and Hebrew, still survives on the gallery fronts, albeit considerably faded. Above, three large, brass candelabra illuminated the prayer hall.

Enlarged in 1893, the hall was thereafter known as the Princes (later Princelet) Street Synagogue. Photographs of the interior in use show a joyful space, hung with brass chandeliers and lanterns, its galleries festooned with decorations. It was soon augmented by new housing built specifically for the growing Jewish community and funded by the Jewish banker Baron Nathan Rothschild, which began to open its doors in 1887 – a year before the series of local murders by the alleged serial killer brought Spitalfields's reputation tumbling into the gutter once more. Rothschild also helped to fund the Princelet Street Synagogue itself, as did the fabulously wealthy MP for Whitechapel, Samuel Montagu, whose tireless advocacy of Spitalfields's Jewish community and of a Jewish homeland in Palestine saw him raised to the peerage in 1907 as Baron Swaythling.

While the synagogue was well maintained during this time, however, the same could not be said for the rest of the street. When the social chronicler and reformer Charles Booth visited Princelet Street in the late 1890s he noted 'two common lodging houses [used by] thieves, prostitutes, bullies' at its east end, just before Brick Lane, and accordingly graded much of the street as black – the lowest possible category – in his Poverty Map of 1899. During his visit he observed that the former grand Huguenot family townhouse at what is now 21 Princelet Street was now occupied by eight families, totalling forty-eight people in all, most of whom he labelled as 'Lowest Class. Vicious, semi-criminal'. Even number 19 itself was occupied by three Jewish families living in the three or four rooms above the synagogue. In 1901 the *Daily Mail* labelled nearby Dorset Street 'The Worst Street in London'.

In the mid-1890s the evangelist Henry Walker visited Spitalfields for the first time and was astonished by what he found:

We suddenly see ourselves in a foreign land. The streets we enter might be streets in Warsaw or Cracow... an alien world [of] the thickly-herded, poorer immigrant Jews... In the heart of London, it is yet a foreign town, with its own liberties of trade, own segregated peoples, religions, customs and industries.

The twentieth century

Spitalfields's Jews had to cope with vicious and violent anti-Semitism from the moment they arrived in London. Yet by the 1930s Spitalfields's still-vibrant Jewish community had also become an unusual, off-the-beaten-track tourist attraction. Its Jewish population had already contributed so much to British life – the introduction of fish and chips to the nation may well have originated here, adapted in the 1860s from a Hispanic–Jewish culinary tradition – and now they became the object of national media attention. However, as Dan Cruickshank has observed, 'Writers and journalists who explored Spitalfields and the East End in the inter-war period constantly returned to the same clichés and lazy evocations of the exotic and the mysterious.'

At the same time, the community became the target for the emerging fascist movement led by Sir Oswald Mosley. On 4 October 1936 more than three thousand of Mosley's Blackshirts – escorted by around twice that number of policemen – were stopped from marching up Brick Lane and past Princelet Street by a huge anti-fascist crowd at a confrontation which was later dignified by the name of 'the Battle of Cable Street'. However, the damage was done. Equally worryingly for local Jewish residents was the fact that some of Mosley's recruits had been found in Spitalfields's own distressed streets. Accordingly, after the Second World War, and particularly following the establishment of the state of Israel in 1948, the Jewish community of Spitalfields began to disperse The demolition of much of western Spitalfields in 1961 for the extension of the fruit and vegetable market and for road widening hastened this exodus. (It was even suggested at the time that Hawksmoor's monumental masterpiece of Christ Church be demolished, a plan that was thankfully resisted.) By 1969 most of the Jewish community had moved north or east and the Princelet Street Synagogue fell into disuse. In that same year the Jewish scholar David Rodinsky,

▷ *West Spitalfields today. Some of the houses have been restored and gentrified; some still await intervention.*

who lived in number 19's attic, disappeared without trace, leaving his chaotic home as a record of his research and times. Eleven years later his front door was reopened, revealing notebooks in many languages, sets of Kabbalistic drawings, a mummified cat and his old boots, filled to the brim with dust.

From the 1950s the Jewish presence in Spitalfields was replaced by an influx of Bengali immigrants, fleeing the chaos of the 1947 partition of British India and the grinding poverty of what was then regarded even by the new Pakistani government as a backwater. In 1971, following a vicious war of independence, the new nation of Bangladesh rose out of the ashes of East Pakistan; but the brutality of this war encouraged yet more emigration. Many of these new arrivals, like the Huguenots and Jews before them, worked in the local textile industry. At the same time they made nearby Brick Lane, formerly a very Jewish thoroughfare, the curry capital of London and the symbol of the capital's vibrant ethnic mix. By 1981, at least 60 per cent of households in Spitalfields were of minority ethnic origin.

During this period 19 Princelet Street, like most of its neighbours, remained decaying and unloved. Its condition worsened even after media attention focused on the miraculous survival of its atmospheric Victorian synagogue. The house became a synecdoche of Britain in the 1970s: a new-found enthusiasm in the nation's past, galvanised not by government but by a host of private pressure groups, failed to be matched by any large-scale investment or vision. As with so many traditional British enterprises, size now mattered: the synagogue was considered for at least one major film shoot but was ultimately rejected for being too cramped and for the restrictions attendant on its precious listed status.

Resurrection

However, as the conservation movement gathered momentum, so there appeared a chink of light for number 19. In 1982 the building was bought by the Spitalfields Historic Buildings Trust, a campaigning group (now known simply as the Spitalfields Trust) which had been rescuing derelict or deteriorating Spitalfields homes since 1977. The Trust's committee sounds like a roll call of the great and the good of architectural conservation during this era: from Dan Cruickshank, Ian Bristow and Colin Amery to Mark Girouard, Neil Burton and Julian Harrap. It was led by the indefatigable Douglas Blain, who, like Cruickshank, put his principles on the line by actually taking on one of the area's imposing but degenerating silk-weavers' townhouses as a restoration challenge. In 1984 Blain recalled how, twenty-three years earlier, he had stood one morning at the junction of Elder Street and Spital Square and, 'staring across the glistening cobbles, all I could see in any direction was Georgian domestic architecture... the subtle glow of purple and rose-coloured brick, the glint of crown glass in every window, each house drab but dignified, untouched, virtually, in all its details'. By the early 1980s much of this historic townscape had been demolished – and more was to come. Worryingly, there were few to stop the onwards march of the developers. As Blain lamented:

The trouble with Spitalfields in 1977 was not so much that it was derelict as that it was empty. The area we call west Spitalfields... was by then a social desert, a wasteland blighted by bungled planning, poverty and greed. More than 20 of those wonderful early buildings I had wept over 15 years earlier had gone. The merchants' houses in the square were just a memory perpetuated by a series of fine photographic plates in the [Greater London Council's] Survey.

Raphael Samuel, another stalwart supporter of the Trust, noted how, in the early 1960s, Spitalfields's streets 'had been preserved by their poverty from improvement', and that 'when one went inside a house the panelling was intact, the original floorboards were still in place and the window-panes, often as not, filled with antique glass'. Now the very survival of all this was threatened. As Samuel continued:

Spitalfields has been under threat from the developers for as long as I have lived here. In the 1960s, it seemed, there was no-one to oppose them. Landlords and estate agents winkled out tenants and allowed properties to decay. Developers, acting without the law in some cases, and only just within the law in others, seized on empty sites and bullied and pressured Tower Hamlets Council into giving planning permission for new offices.

The Trust worked its magic by buying decaying local properties, restoring them sensitively and then selling them to sympathetic buyers, using the profits of the sale to invest in other endangered buildings. Their early triumphs – as well as their failures – were immortalised in the Trust's polemical classic of 1984, *The Saving of Spitalfields*. Inevitably, though, despite the Trust's avowed aim to create a 'balanced' community, 'with improved housing for the local population and better accommodation for its trades', their success precipitated a gentrification of the area. This was welcome to some, particularly those who were uneasy about the disappearance of much of the area's architectural character. Yet it was also unwelcome to others, notably those who were concerned about the consequent shift in the social demographic from Bangladeshi textile workers to bankers and lawyers. Already by 1984, as *The Saving of Spitalfields* observed, the area was home to middle-class heroes such as the interior designer Jocasta Innes, textile designer Polly Hope and music critic Edward Greenfield. House prices started to rise correspondingly, particularly after the old fruit and vegetable market left Spitalfields for good in 1991. In the face of vociferous opposition from the Spitalfields-based Georgian Group and from other conservation organisations, the western end of the old market buildings was demolished and the site redeveloped as a leisure area with new retail 'streets'. Only the eastern part of the old market, built to the designs of George Sherrin in 1885–93, survived. William Morris's splendid campaigning and advisory group, the Society for the Protection of Ancient Buildings, still occupies one of the few Georgian houses to survive in what is left of the square. To its east there now stands a bland new development, Bishops Square, where the Huguenots once wove and market traders stacked and sold fruit and vegetables.

Many Asian families could not afford to rent the newly fashionable properties now so painstakingly restored by the Spitalfields Trust. Accordingly, a 'Spitalfields divide' emerged between the revitalised terraces in west Spitalfields, which included Princelet Street at its western end, and the area to the east of Brick Lane, which remained a predominantly working-class neighbourhood. Brick Lane itself remained a haven of 'Indian' restaurants and cafés but by 1990 featured just one kosher bakery, in a street where years before there had been numerous Jewish cafés.

Not all of Princelet Street benefitted from late twentieth-century gentrification, however. Number 19 presented a particular problem: while its rare Rococo chimney surround and its fine Victorian synagogue were rightly deemed worthy of protection (it was awarded rare Grade II* listed status as early as 1969), this meant it was almost impossible to convert into modern housing. Audrey Sacher assembled the English Chamber Orchestra to perform a fundraising concert to enable emergency repairs to be effected to the synagogue. But after that, nothing. Since the 1990s the house has been earmarked as the location for a Museum of Immigration and Diversity, which has long bid for, but is still awaiting, substantial grant aid in order to fulfil its admirable mission. Owing to the site's fragility the house-museum is currently open to the public only for a day or two a year, and at the time of writing is still on the national Buildings at Risk Register.

While many of the finer houses of Spitalfields were reborn thanks to the ministrations of careful conservationists, and found themselves decked out once more in authentic Georgian paints and wallpapers, the rise in the area's fortunes – and particularly its proximity to the blank canyons of the City of London – brought developers flocking to streets which 150 years before had been no-go areas for respectable citizens. Anything that was not a Georgian terraced house was deemed fair game. Today the fringes of Spitalfields are constantly threatened by unsympathetic development. Even in the post-Covid era, with its changing patterns of workplace attendance, developers are still seeking to introduce profitable high-rise office blocks into what was once a dense urban cityscape, intrusions whose scale and form have nothing to do with historic Spitalfields (or indeed with any recognisable British building tradition) and everything to do with the commercial ambitions of the City. Seasoned campaigners such as Dan Cruickshank, the Spitalfields Trust, the Georgian Group and SPAB continue to resist ill-mannered and thoughtless erosion of the historic fabric which provided Georgian, Victorian and twentieth-century Spitalfields with its unique character and diversity. It seems that even today, when Britain is so often derided by critics as becoming a vast heritage park, managing the past in order to shape the future is so often a lost cause. While 'Bishops Square' flourishes, 19 Princelet Street – the Miss Havisham of east London, where 'everything had stopped... a long time ago' – gently decays.

12

COMPTON VERNEY, WARWICKSHIRE

REBUILT FROM 1711

The Rise and Fall of the Leisured Classes

The great house at Compton Verney has no especial claims to fame. At the height of the Georgian era it was remodelled by the most fashionable architect of the day, Robert Adam, and provided with perhaps the first 'minimalist' English park by the doyen of Georgian landscape architecture, Lancelot 'Capability' Brown. However, aside from those interventions the house never possessed a fine art collection; nor did its owners play a major part in national life.

What makes Compton Verney particularly interesting is that its history presents us with a typical example of the fate of so many English country houses in the nineteenth and twentieth centuries. And, unlike so many country houses, it actually managed to survive the twentieth century – almost entirely thanks to a single generous act of patronage from an individual wholly unconnected either with the house or with Warwickshire.

Journalist and broadcaster Andrew Marr certainly thought the house was of great symbolic importance, and accordingly featured Compton Verney prominently in his 2009 book and television series, *The Making of Modern Britain*. In both of these media he cited it as an archetype of the complex history

Compton Verney today, restored as a major museum and art gallery.

of English country houses in the modern era, a period when only the fortunate few, such as Blenheim Palace and Woburn Abbey, were able to maintain uninterrupted family ownership.

The Verneys

Compton Verney's owners, the Verney family (who enjoyed the hereditary title of Barons Willoughby de Broke), never diversified their revenue streams and remained almost entirely reliant on farm rentals for their income. The Willoughby de Brokes preferred the traditional pursuit of the country landowner – hunting, shooting and fishing – to dirtying their hands with trade. Indeed, it was in pursuit of these sporting goals that 'Capability' Brown had explicitly re-landscaped the park for the 14th Baron after 1768. As a result, in contrast to the more far-sighted members of the landed gentry such as their namesakes, the Verneys of Claydon, who invested heavily in Buckinghamshire railways in the 1850s and 1860s, the Warwickshire Verneys were caught out

220

by the agricultural depression of the 1870s. They assumed that renting out their house and park to wealthy tenants was a temporary expedient; but they were wrong. Their house and estate once defined the rural economy in their particular corner of Warwickshire; but for the past century there have been no Verneys at Compton Verney.

The first record of a settlement at Compton Verney mentions a late Saxon village called, simply, Compton, meaning a settlement in a valley. This village was probably sited to the east of the present house, on both sides of what was then a small river. (The ponding of the river for fishing may have occurred as early as the twelfth century.) It had good communications, as it was served by the Fosse Way, which ran north–south half a mile from the site and led to the major Roman settlements of Cirencester and Leicester. In 1086, at the time of the first appearance of the Domesday Book – a national survey carried out for the Norman king, William I, to record land ownership and values –the village was divided into two manors. The larger manor was then held by the Count of Meulan; this was in turn inherited by the earls of Warwick, who held it in the king's name. Shortly before 1150, the smaller manor was granted to Robert Murdak, and its village therefore became known as Compton Murdak, passing by inheritance to the heirs of the Murdak family. Murdak ownership survived the murder in 1316 of Sir Thomas Murdak – killed by his wife, Juliana de Gayton, with the help of Sir Thomas's squire and two chaplains. Thomas's body was hacked to pieces and left at his Northamptonshire estate, and Juliana was subsequently burned to death for her crime in 1321. Fifty years later, after two centuries of Murdak ownership, a later Sir Thomas Murdak was forced to surrender the estate to Edward III's unscrupulous mistress, Alice Ferrers. On Edward III's death in 1377, Ferrers was banished from London and later married Sir William de Wyndsore. Compton Verney passed to Wyndsore's daughter, Joan, and it was Joan and her husband who in 1435 sold the house and estate to the ruthless and ambitious Richard Verney, who had secured the financial assistance of his younger brother John Verney, Dean of Lichfield, and his local aristocratic patron, the powerful Richard Beauchamp, Earl of Warwick.

What we know of the Verney family takes us back to the thirteenth century, when Ralph de Verney (who died in 1223) bought land at Middle Claydon in Buckinghamshire, where this branch of the family still live. Sir Ralph Verney (c.1410–78), a successful merchant, made the family's fortune; he became Lord Mayor of London in 1465 and was elected MP for the City in 1472. A later Sir Ralph was closely implicated in the suspicious death of Amy Robsart, the wife of Robert Dudley, Earl of Leicester, in 1559: many suspected Amy had been poisoned by her husband, in order to leave him free to marry Queen Elizabeth I. Leicester and Verney were exonerated but the scandal put an end to Leicester's royal ambitions.

Sir Ralph's son Sir Edmund Verney (d. 1600) had two sons: Sir Francis (1584–1615), who became a mercenary and a pirate, converted to Islam and died in penury in Sicily; and Sir Edmund (1590–1642). It was the latter who was entrusted with the Royal Standard of King Charles I when civil war broke out in 1642 and who was slain at the war's first battle – Edgehill. The latter was fought only a few miles to the east of Compton Verney; indeed, the Earl of Essex's parliamentary army must have marched through the Compton Verney estate on their way to battle.

The Verney family had begun acquiring lands in the area of Compton Murdak and the surrounding villages in the early 1430s, before purchasing the entire estate in 1435. By about 1500 the manor had become so closely associated with them that it began to be known as Compton Verney. According to Sir William Dugdale's *The Antiquities of Warwickshire* of 1656, the Verneys also built a manor house here, in about 1442.

The early house

Very little is known about the Tudor house: a drawing by Wenceslaus Hollar of about 1655, published in Dugdale's county history, shows a great hall, a long south wing with gabled dormer windows looking down to the lake, and chimneys. It had octagonal turrets, kitchens to the left (the south-west corner) and a chapel by the ponds.

The house was extended in the late Tudor and early Stuart periods, following the advantageous marriage of another Richard Verney (d. 1630) to Margaret, daughter of Sir Fulke Greville, Lord Brooke, and 6th Baroness Willoughby de Broke. Richard inherited not only Margaret's family estates but also the Grevilles' claims to the barony of Willoughby de Broke. It is Richard and his wife Margaret whose fine double tomb by Nicholas Stone – eclipsed by Inigo Jones in his day but perhaps the greatest British sculptor-architect of his age – dominates the chapel at Compton Verney.

The hereditary title of Baron Willoughby de Broke had been created in 1491 for Sir Robert Willoughby, 9th Baron Latimer. But in 1668 Greville Verney's great-great-grandson, William Verney, 10th Baron Willoughby de Broke, died aged only fifteen, without an heir, and the title went into temporary abeyance. It was subsequently claimed by William's great-uncle, Richard Verney (1621–1711) in 1695, and the House of Lords duly ruled in his favour. On Richard's death, his son George (1659–1728) became the 12th Baron Willoughby de Broke.

Rebuilding the mansion

It was George who resolved to rebuild completely the house and re-landscape the gardens after 1711. The new design he commissioned – the basis of the house we see today – has been convincingly attributed to the Oxford master mason John Townesend and his son William, who had worked at Blenheim Palace and at many of the new college buildings then being built for Oxford University – including, as we have seen, Christ Church. A surviving map of the site from around 1736 shows that the house was now a square block, with stables to the north and formal gardens to the north and south. The impressive stable block had been added in 1735 to the design of the renowned Scottish architect James Gibbs (1682–1754). Gibbs was then markedly out of favour with the London elites, on account of his unfashionably Italianate Baroque style and his suspiciously Tory connections. Yet he *had* been employed by the Duke of Shrewsbury at Heythrop in Oxfordshire – not far from Compton Verney – shortly before he was commissioned to design these handsome stables. The building features the architect's characteristic 'Gibbs surrounds' of rusticated quoins, which he often used to punctuate his door and window surrounds.

In 1752 the Willoughby de Broke title passed to George's great-nephew, John Peyto Verney, who became 14th Baron. John also inherited the neighbouring estate of Chesterton, thus raising the family's income to a handsome £4,000 a year. This additional revenue, and John's marriage in 1761 to the sister of the local grandee (and future prime minister) Lord North, encouraged John to improve the estate and remodel the house. It was the 14th Baron and his family who were portrayed at Compton Verney by the celebrated society painter Johann Zoffany around 1766, a picture which today hangs in the J. Paul Getty Museum in Los Angeles.

Until 1760 Compton Verney had been just another great house in the country: an economic hub for surrounding villages but of little consequence to the wider world. The 14th Baron, however, brought it a wider audience by commissioning two of the most celebrated names of the day, Robert Adam and Lancelot 'Capability' Brown, to completely remodel both house and park. Adam's principal patron was then the powerful Lord Bute, confidant of young King George III and recently installed by the latter as prime minister. Verney's brother-in-law and near-neighbour Lord North, already an intimate of the royal circle and a junior member of Bute's ministry of 1761-3, had doubtless recommended Adam's talents; and it may have been either North or Adam who subsequently commended 'Capability' Brown to the baron as someone who would convert the family's traditional, geometrically disposed gardens into a leisure park.

Adam's proposed scheme involved demolishing much of the Baroque house of 1711. In the event, however, he had to content himself with opening up the house's formerly closed courtyard by demolishing its east range, modernising the internal walls and introducing a large portico to front a new, larger hall (with a saloon behind it). Adam also added a library and octagonal study to the south wing and adapted the brewhouse and bakery to the north of the house. Inside the new hall he provided a tessellated marble floor, using native British marbles where possible, and large plaster surrounds to frame Antonio Zucchi's specially commissioned neoclassical *capricci* of artfully combined ruins.

Adam's building work was supervised not by the architect himself – who was probably rarely on site – but by the Warwick architect-mason William Hiorne (*c*.1712–76), who had already been employed locally at Charlecote House and Stoneleigh Abbey. Adam was sufficiently proud of his work here, however, to provide floor plans of the house to be published in the fifth, 1771 volume of the ambitious survey of Britain's great houses, *Vitruvius Britannicus*. Yet while Adam was often responsible for the interior decoration as well as the architectural design of his buildings, at Compton Verney he designed the decoration of only a few rooms, including the hall and the saloon; the remainder were decorated by local craftsmen using their own pattern-book designs.

The park

It may have been Robert Adam who introduced Lancelot Brown to the Willoughby de Brokes. Or, alternatively, the 14th Baron might have seen Brown's recent work for himself at nearby Charlecote or Warwick Castle. Either way, in November 1768 Brown commenced work at Compton Verney. There he replaced the formal Bardens with grassland and trees, including cedars and more than 2,200 oak and ash saplings. A new south drive, which revealed the house to visitors from the bridge, was created by altering the early eighteenth-century formal avenue into a serpentine route. The nearby road was moved for a ha-ha to be created west of the house, and views from the house to the south and west were opened up. Brown also turned the existing ponds into a single expanse of water by removing the dam between the Upper Long Pool and the Middle Pool to make way for his new Upper Bridge.

Compton Verney was one of Brown's first minimalist landscapes. By the time he arrived at Compton Verney in 1768, he had become so successful that he was able to turn down jobs he believed unworthy of his talents, and now enjoyed a greater degree of autonomy than most of his rivals. When he turned his attention to Compton Verney, he had the freedom to do as he wished, which involved the introduction of fewer garden buildings and less tree and shrub cover. He swept away the formal gardens (*parterres*) and ornamental canal added to the rear of the house after 1711, together with the geometri-cally patterned shrubbery and the radiating avenues – all of which were so very old-fashioned and, more to the point, French. In its place he introduced some-thing very English: a park designed for sport and leisure rather than mathe-matical delight or neoclassical allegory.

Brown's landscapes were modern, activity-led parks, designed for leisure and pleasure rather than to showcase the owners' erudition through numerous classical allusions or Arcadian installations. His new, unfussy landscapes were designed both for viewing – from horseback, from a carriage or from a drift-ing boat – or for shooting and fishing: his lakes could be used for fishing and boating, while his carefully planted belts and copses provided useful cover for game birds. Guns had, in recent years, become lighter, shorter and more accu-rate, and could now be used to shoot running or flying targets – the annihila-tion of which was encouraged by the publication of the classic manual *The Art of Shooting Flying* in 1770 just as work was beginning on the Compton Verney park. Pheasants were now encouraged to roost within the copses and clumps of the new park and thus flew high, providing gentlemen with a moving target. Landowners such as the Verneys were soon releasing large numbers of such birds onto their estates with the express purpose of shooting them down again.

Aesthetics were not forgotten in this brave, new, leisured landscape,

▷ *The mansion at Compton Verney from the south-east, showing the original, Baroque south elevation to the left and Adam's remodelling of the courtyard.*

however. Brown planted dextrously at estates like Compton Verney, ensuring that dark evergreens would be used as a backdrop to highlight temples and other garden buildings. An alternate use of evergreens and deciduous planting allowed for changes of mood as a visitor rode or walked along paths that threaded through the woodland.

Compton Verney's revolutionary new landscape was also designed to be seen by carriage, putting Britain firmly in the vanguard of the leisure revolution. Brown's parks were devised as a sequence of pictures that darted into view from a speeding vehicle and were valued for their ability to impress guests and the growing band of garden visitors. Clumps of trees were introduced to frame buildings and lakes, replacing the more geometrically planned formal avenues of earlier periods.

Despite what is often alleged, the medieval village at Compton Verney was not swept away by 'Capability' Brown (as had been the case at some of his other parks), nor erased through the ruthless application of Georgian enclosures. By the time Brown arrived at Compton Verney in 1768, all trace of the settlement had long since disappeared. The ancient settlement of Compton Murdak appears to have become seriously depopulated in the fourteenth and fifteenth centuries, possibly as a result of the Black Death of 1348 and the plagues which subsequently ravaged the country, and the village was almost deserted by 1500. In 1491 a Warwick priest, John Rous, compared the number of villagers still living locally with those listed in the Hundred Rolls of 1279: at Compton Verney, the twenty-nine tenants and their families of 1279 had, by 1491, shrunk to just two.

Brown did, though, demolish the medieval chapel sited between the house and the lake. He replaced it with a new, plain, Palladian-style building located on the slope to the north of the house and built in 1776–9. His chapel was no simple neoclassical statement, however, but a typically English synthesis of old and new that was ahead of its time. Nicholas Stone's fine double tomb of Richard and Margaret Verney of c.1631, along with the historic brasses, the memorial floor slabs and two of the large wall monuments (whose sculptors remain tantalisingly unknown), were all brought by Brown from the old chapel and reinstalled in the new structure. Indeed, Brown deliberately placed Stone's tomb firmly centre stage, and appears to have built his new chapel around it. Much of the old chapel's English heraldic glass was also rescued and augmented in its new location by fine German sixteenth-century glass, obtained for Willougby de Broke by an art dealer – possibly the same one used by the baron's brother-in-law, Lord North, for a similar task recently undertaken at nearby Wroxton Abbey.

After 1945, however, the chapel was rarely visited, let alone used, and by 1990 was in a very poor condition. Its windows had been smashed and boarded up for years and its coffered ceiling habitually shed lumps of plaster. In the mid-1990s it was structurally secured and repaired by Rodney Melville and Partners (who also stabilised the crypt after flooding caused by the building of the new houses in the former Kitchen Garden), while grants secured by the Compton Verney House Trust in 2011 enabled it to repair and reopen one of the nation's most important Georgian chapels for public viewing.

The complacent nineteenth century

With the completion of Adam and Brown's work, and the death of the 14th Baron in 1816, Compton Verney effectively went to sleep. Subsequent heads of the Verney family were little more than amusing caricatures who changed little and thought less. Henry, 16th Baron Willoughby de Broke (1773–1852), for example, was an engaging though increasingly reclusive eccentric who delighted in new inventions. He had a scaled-down frigate built upon the lake at Compton Verney, and employed an old seaman to assist him in sailing it. In middle age Henry also became an Ultra Tory – a political path which most of his descendants were to follow – and strenuously opposed the Great Reform Act of 1832, the first measure to attempt to modernise Britain's archaic and corrupt franchise.

As he grew older, Henry became obsessed with his own funeral arrangements. He devised a winch for lowering coffins into the chapel's vault and, as the 19th Baron remembered, 'made his men practise lowering a coffin filled with stones equal to his own weight and swore roundly at them if they carried out the operation with jerks and bumps'.

The agricultural depression of the 1870s and 1880s had a disastrous impact on the Verneys, who continued to depend on rents from their local estates for the bulk of their income. Between 1875 and 1900 agricultural rents in south Warwickshire fell on average by around 40 per cent; indeed, as early as 1872 the Willoughby de Brokes were forced to mortgage their estates. By 1887 the family felt it had no other option but to move out of the main house and rent it to prosperous tenants.

The first of these temporary residents was just the sort of figure the ultra-conservative Verneys loathed as a louche, foreign, Jewish arriviste. German-born Sir Ernest Cassel had started life as a penniless immigrant but subsequently made a fortune in banking – the sort of profession the Verneys despised – and became an intimate of the disreputable Prince of Wales, the gambling womaniser who, as King Edward VII after 1901, astounded everyone by brokering the Entente Cordiale. The Verneys may have detested Sir Ernest Cassel, but they needed his money, and he remained at Compton Verney for eight years.

He was succeeded by Lord Connemara, a racy aristocrat who, although he had served as Governor of Madras for four years, was better known to the public for being sued by his wife for infecting her with syphilis and for committing adultery with her maid. (Although he had trained as a barrister, Connemara did not defend himself and accepted both the verdict and the costs.) In 1896 Connemara was visited by Cassel's great friend Edward, Prince of Wales, who was on his way to visit his mistress, the Countess of Warwick, and was accompanied by Winston Churchill's notoriously wayward mother, Lady Randolph Churchill. The prince was driving a car for the first time – enraging Lord Willoughby de Broke, who loathed the new fad for automobiles and whose last request to his son was that motor cars should not be used in the Warwickshire Hunt. The baron was consequently delighted when, as the royal car advanced up the drive, it broke down, and the prince and his female companions had to jump out and push. Compton Verney had, in the space of nine years, passed from sleepy rural backwater to epicentre of county scandal.

In 1890 the house's tenancy was taken over by Marshall Field, the Chicago department-store tycoon. The Verneys' reaction can only be imagined: an American retailer occupying their ancestral home. Field joined the Warwickshire Hunt and was elected President of the Stratford-on-Avon Polo Club in 1900 but mostly used the house as a base from which to travel to London and the Continent.

Meanwhile, seething with indignation in their nearby retreat in the village of Kineton, successive Willoughby de Brokes lamented the state of the nation and plotted to frustrate the Liberal government's reforms. Faced with the prospect of Home Rule for Ireland, the 19th Baron helped to form the British League for the Support of Ulster and the Union, becoming its chairman in 1913, and by 1911 was even advocating the creation of a 'sufficient fighting force' to ensure that Ireland remained under Westminster rule. Like his ancestors, Richard Verney, 19th Baron (1869–1923), combined a passion for hunting with intense political conservativism. One contemporary described his personality as being 'not more than two hundred years behind his time'. He campaigned against the financial and constitutional reforms of the Liberals' radical chancellor of the exchequer, David Lloyd George, after 1908 and led the opposition to Lloyd George's Parliament Act of 1911, which severely curbed the powers of the House of Lords. Richard was also, however, a keen supporter of women's suffrage, and enthusiastically hosted 'suffragette' meetings at Compton Verney. Indefatigable to the last, shortly before his death in 1923, while he was putting the finishing touches to his hunting memoir, *The Passing Years*, he was campaigning for the local Conservative candidate for the parliamentary seat of Warwick and Leamington, one Anthony Eden.

In 1912 the family's fiscal fortunes appeared to have improved to the extent that they were able to return to Compton Verney. To mark the 19th Baron's return, electric lighting was installed in the house, involving the installation of more than five miles of wire. However, with the outbreak of the First World War in August 1914, traditional events were cancelled as the men of the estate, including the 19th Baron's son, left to fight in France. Wartime taxation bit deep, servants were conscripted and, as a result, the family were pushed into occupying a single wing of their house. Wounded soldiers were occasionally hosted by Lady Willoughby de Broke, while her husband commanded the 2nd Line (reserve) regiment of the Warwickshire Yeomanry, which remained in England.

After 1918, straitened post-war economic conditions made the Verneys' ownership of Compton Verney even more challenging. Income tax had risen from 6 per cent in 1913 to 30 per cent in 1918, while death duties were raised to 40 per cent in 1919. As was the case for so many other aristocratic families, a buyer had to be found for the estate. In 1921 the family moved out of Compton Verney for the last time. The *Leamington Spa Courier* blamed 'Radicalism and Socialism and the Death Duties' for their departure.

Continued decline

Throughout the ensuing century, Compton Verney passed through a series of lamentably unsuitable owners before it found its white knight. In this it was no different from many of Britain's country houses – which, to borrow from Dean Acheson, had lost their traditional way of life yet failed to find a new role. Indeed, the house was lucky to have survived the century at all. So many of the nation's great aristocratic piles were left to moulder or were deliberately demolished – or, as the phrase had it, 'caught on fire' in order to claim on the insurance – in the years after both world wars. Only a lucky few could afford the necessary dowry to ascend to country house heaven by joining the National Trust. In 2012 the gallery's finance director calculated that the sum required in order to donate Compton Verney to the National Trust by the 'Chorley formula', i.e. to maintain its current operation, would amount to more than £98 million.

Compton Verney's shiny new owner in 1921 was Joseph Watson, a Yorkshire soap manufacturer and racehorse owner who had made a fortune during the late Victorian era as the legendary Lever Brothers' biggest rival. After selling his soap-making company to Levers in 1906 he concentrated on agricultural research and, during the First World War, helped the government to set up new munitions factories. In 1921 he bought Compton Verney from Lord Willoughby de Broke, and in January 1922 'obtained' (and presumably paid for) a peerage from Lloyd George's cash-strapped government, which was strewing titles-for-cash about like confetti. Now the Leeds industrialist became Baron Manton of Compton Verney. The new Lord Manton was so keen to launder his commercial past and be accepted as the true heir to the Willoughby de Brokes that he appropriated his new home by adding it to his title. He also joined the local Warwickshire Hunt, still led by the ageing but spirited 19th Baron. However, demonstrating the truth of the old adage to be careful what you wish for, two months later the new Lord Manton was killed in a hunting accident.

Manton's son George Watson, the 2nd Baron, both looked and behaved like a classic British villain straight out of Hollywood casting. As such, he perhaps approximated more to the foreign concept of the English country house owner than any proprietor we have yet met. He was, in the language of his time, an utter cad. In the 1950s he would have been played on screen by Terry-Thomas; today perhaps by Rufus Sewell or Hugh Grant.

Manton was largely uninterested in Compton Verney, except in so far as it could support his lavish expenditure, and preferred to concentrate on breeding racehorses in Wiltshire rather than live the life of a landed gent in Warwickshire. He rode as a jockey during the 1920s and, having been forced to sell the family stud near Marlborough in 1927, started to look for buyers for Compton Verney itself. His spending invariably continued to exceed his income: having run through his father's legacy, he was plagued by horses that never won, bets that were never paid off and mounting debts, which eventually took their toll. In 1929 – the year of the Wall Street Crash, which would depress land values still further – Manton resorted to slaughtering animals at the Compton Verney stables and hawking the meat round the county in his own car. He additionally sold some 1,500 ancient trees on the venerable Compton Verney estate to local timber dealers. Worse still, in 1931 Manton sold the outstanding stained glass in Compton Verney's 'Capability' Brown chapel at auction – the buyers included the American newspaper tycoon William Randolph Hearst – before selling the whole estate to wealthy Cheshire businessman Samuel Lamb. Two years later Manton was sued by his former accountant for unpaid debts while his second wife divorced him in 1936.

Astonishingly, in 1938 he somehow managed to steer down the aisle, as his second wife, the former wife of the heir to the John Player tobacco empire; this alliance briefly restored his fortunes, enabling him to build a sustainable horse-breeding business in Sussex and Newmarket.

Compton Verney's new purchasers were Samuel and Gita Lamb. He was a Cheshire cotton magnate who was quiet and unassuming; she an amateur opera singer from Germany who was a self-confessed Nazi and, in the words of one old retainer, 'very pleased with herself, a typical Hun [sic]'. She was universally loathed in the area. Rude and aggressive to her servants, Frau Lamb found a perverse pleasure in setting her dogs on the gardeners, calling them off only at the last minute. A former housemaid recalls an incident when Mrs Lamb, apparently dissatisfied with a flower arrangement in the saloon, threw the vase and its contents through a closed window. Another servant described her as 'not a very nice person' and as 'a most improbable blonde'.

Presumably encouraged by his German wife, Lamb joined the Anglo-German Fellowship, the pernicious and at best fatally naive pro-Nazi society famously explored by Kazuo Ishiguro in his celebrated novel *The Remains of the Day* of 1989. As a result, Hitler's notorious (and disastrous) ambassador to Britain, Joachim von Ribbentrop, may well have been welcomed to Compton Verney in the late 1930s.

The Lambs moved out of the house during the Second World War, when Compton Verney was requisitioned by the army. From 1940 the park was used as an experimental station for smokescreen camouflage in its new role as an outstation for the Leamington-based Camouflage Unit. Officers were billeted in the house, with NCOs in the attics and other ranks in huts in the park. Inevitably, though, things were broken and damaged. As early as October 1941, an official report concluded:

△ *The interior of the restored chapel at Compton Verney: a rare building by Lancelot 'Capability' Brown, begun in 1776.*

The damage already done in a short period of time is disquieting, and will present a serious problem unless prompt action is taken... Although Military occupation of the house has only begun recently, there is no doubt of its damaging effect on the walls, doors and interior decoration. Windows of the stable block were smashed and others missing.

Dirty water leaked into the tessellated floor of the hall, and a portion of plaster ceiling above, from a blocked lead gully on the roof, collapsed in 1944. 'Kicking and stumbling' had damaged the portico, and the north wing was 'used for sharpening knives'. The Upper Bridge was wrecked – a gardener reported that soldiers 'were responsible for deliberately pushing over a section of the balustrading on the west side' – though an official subsequently noted that 'it is quite obvious that the stone parapets of this bridge were not in a good state of repair when the property was requisitioned'. The small bridge over the nearby stream, meanwhile, lost its Georgian balustrade on the night of 8 May

1945 – VE ('Victory in Europe') Day – when Pioneer Corps troops celebrated the end of the war by lobbing grenades at the blameless historic structure. By this time an estimated 300 tons of barbed wire was also left surrounding the site, while numerous smoke bombs littered the area – one being discovered as recently as 1995.

The Lambs never returned after the army's departure in 1945. Living at Compton Verney was no longer an attractive prospect: in addition to the damage caused by its wartime occupation, thieves had stripped the roof of lead in 1948, while poor electricity supplies necessitated power cuts on Mondays and Thursdays. Moreover, Gita Lamb in particular apparently regarded the prospect of reoccupying the house with undisguised distaste. As no doubt did her former neighbours. Occasional events still took place in the park – the hall was twice used for hunt balls during the 1950s – but the life of the house itself largely ceased. Following the death of his wife, Lamb finally sold Compton Verney in 1958 to Harry Ellard. He was an eccentric, self-made engineering millionaire who had bought and occupied a nightclub in Solihull, which he dignified by the unlikely name of the Regency Club.

Ellard had no intention of occupying the house at Compton Verney. Instead, he left it to rot. He would visit the estate every Thursday, arriving in an elderly Austin and carrying scraps from the Regency Club to feed to the pigs he kept there. A groundsman took care of the pigs in his absence and also grew fruit and vegetables in the Kitchen Garden; both pigs and produce were subsequently served at the Regency Club. When Ellard occasionally hosted visitors on site he did so from his custom-made caravan, which was permanently moored in the park. The 21st Lord Willoughby de Broke recalled his visits to Ellard as 'deeply depressing', citing 'rusting barbed-wire fences, hungry Alsatians barking in the James Gibbs stables, and evidence of neglect everywhere; crumbling masonry, gaping holes in roofs, even a sapling growing from one of the dormer windows'.

Ellard did, though, occasionally permit television and film production companies to use the grounds for film shoots. Peter Hall's celebrated film of Shakespeare's *A Midsummer Night's Dream*, featuring a stellar cast which included Judi Dench, Diana Rigg, Helen Mirren, Ian Holm and Ian Richardson, was filmed here, entirely on location, in 1968.

By the time of Ellard's death in 1983, the house's ceilings had buckled and collapsed, the walls had rotted, the sky could be glimpsed from the ground floor, and Compton Verney was fast becoming a picturesque ruin. Both the house and the chapel were listed Grade I by English Heritage, but still the future for both park and mansion looked bleak.

On Ellard's death, the estate was bought by property developer Christopher Buxton, who aimed to convert the main house to hotel use, build two large homes in the Kitchen Garden (which he succeeded in doing), subdivide the stable block into ten apartments (which he also achieved), and, most crucially, build a large opera house in the Old Town Meadow. In the event, however, Buxton failed to secure detailed planning permission for the overall scheme, largely as the opera house was to be built on the site of both the ancient medieval village and the now Grade II* listed Brownian landscape. As a result, his ambitious plan ultimately collapsed. Consequently, having already disposed of many of the mansion's fixtures and fittings, in 1993 Buxton sold the house, and subsequently much of the remaining estate, to the Peter Moores Foundation.

Rescue

The Foundation's acquisition of the site provided Compton Verney with an exciting and viable new future. The brainchild of Littlewoods football pools heir Sir Peter Moores, the Peter Moores Foundation had been set up by Sir Peter in 1964 with a remit to assist opera, the visual arts and education. Sir Peter's aim was 'to get things done and open doors for people, but not to push them through', and he later observed that 'I feel passionately about demystifying the Arts and giving people the opportunity to make a choice. You cannot learn to like what you cannot easily come to know.' He subsequently channelled £45 million into the project in one of the most impressive acts of cultural patronage in post-war Britain, ensuring that the management of the site passed into the hands of an independent charitable trust, which still runs Compton Verney today.

Starting in 1994, architects Stanton Williams, working alongside conservation experts Rodney Melville and Partners, used Moores's money to restore the main house, converting it into a modern art gallery, and added a contemporary new wing to the north (on the site of a former service wing) to house exhibitions spaces, catering facilities and a shop. Following a trial opening of the lower floors in 1998, the attic (originally used as servants' accommodation, but subsequently empty and bare) was converted to house the gallery's new British Folk Art and Marx–Lambert collections. In 2004, the finished gallery finally opened to the public.

Without Sir Peter Moores's intervention and imagination, Compton Verney would today be a sad ruin, and its inspiring art gallery and much-admired park a mere pipe dream. His far-sighted patronage of the arts was subsequently followed by the government's Heritage Lottery Fund, an array of private charitable trusts and a slew of individual donors, who together funded the creation of a new Visitor Centre, built in 2015–16 to the designs of Purcell architects.

Today this bright new building welcomes visitors of all backgrounds and incomes to enjoy the leisure opportunities of Adam's house and Brown's park. Unusually for one of the nation's forgotten country houses, Compton Verney has survived years of neglect to reinvent itself for new audiences of the twenty-first century. It is a model which the rest of Britain would do well to note.

13

CROMFORD MILL, DERBYSHIRE

1771

And Was Jerusalem Builded Here?
The world's first modern factory

Built in 1771, Cromford Mill was a potent symbol of Britain, a wealthy and expanding empire built on the technological breakthroughs of the cotton revolution and on the ceaseless labour of a new industrial class. However, while viewed today as an engaging and educational emblem of the nation's industrial heritage, mills such as Cromford were often viewed with horror by their contemporaries. Cromford has rightly been called 'the birthplace of the modern factory system' for both Britain and the world. That double-edged accolade barely conceals the iniquity of a labour system that provided the world with cheap, durable cloth at the expense of human dignity.

King cotton

While traditional histories of the so-called industrial revolution understandably concentrate on the narratives of iron and coal, modern scholarship has come to see cotton as one of the foundations of modern society. By the end of the eighteenth century, cotton was being made available to millions across

△ *The Cromford Mill site today.*

the globe, largely thanks to spectacular advances made (mostly) by British inventor-entrepreneurs. The harnessing of water, and then coal, to power the new cotton mills transformed everyday life more than any other fixture, fitting, appliance or commodity of the Georgian era.

In the home and on the streets of late Georgian London, cotton was king. It was not just in everyday wear that cottons replaced heavier and more expensive traditional fabrics. Perhaps the most astonishing advances, however, had come in the areas of furnishing fabrics. The British upholstery- and curtain-making industries had been almost non-existent in 1750; fifty years later, their products could be seen on middle-class seating and windows all over the country. By the time of Waterloo, washable, light and inexpensive plain and printed cottons had flooded the market and displaced the majority of the heavy, dull and expensive fabrics prevalent at the time of the first George.

Of course, changing stylistic fashions and the niceties of classical (or even Gothic) architecture were important to the late Georgian middle-class home. But it was the rapid advance of technology which opened the door to 'taste' for the British middle classes and redefined aesthetics in terms of the possible, the aspirational and, most importantly, the practicable and cost-efficient.

Cotton had it all. It was cheaper and more versatile than silk and far easier to imprint than wool. It could be used for every task, from the manufacture of printed dresses for women to the mass-production of multi-coloured furnishing fabrics for the middle classes of Britain, America and Europe. Unlike many earlier clothing or furnishing fabrics, cottons were colour-fast: they could be easily washed (unlike their ponderous predecessors) and did not fade when exposed to light. They were lightweight, exploiting a trend that had begun late in the sixteenth century when thick woollens were replaced with 'worsted' textiles: finer, thinner and stronger than traditional woollens made of long combing wool. And, crucially, new British manufacturing techniques enabled them to be sold cheaply. At the same time, they also managed to be fashionable: the appeal of imported Indian cottons passed by osmosis to their less expensive British imitators, which were initially appreciated for their novelty and exotic motifs and later became a staple commodity.

Cotton goods from India – just like tea, china and chinoiserie from China – had captivated late seventeenth-century Europe. As local textile producers grew alarmed at their success, however, a wave of import controls and prohibitions had swept Europe. Following the example of her great rival France, which banned the importation of cottons in 1686, England had limited their use in 1702 (when Britain was once more at war with France) and, under pressure from the Spitalfields silk-weavers and their regional equivalents, proscribed them completely in 1721.

The challenge for budding entrepreneurs was to manufacture cottons in Britain at a lower price than, but at the same quality as, Indian imports. The prize was not just the home market: as we shall see, growing mercantile interest in the triangular trade between Britain, West Africa and the West Indies – where the defining commodity was human beings – offered tempting markets in Africa for durable British cloth, a product which could not only clothe the natives in suitably respectable western attire but could also be traded for their bodies, as slaves. As cultural historian Professor Giorgio Riello noted, however, these exports failed to secure the pan-African sales British cotton entrepreneurs had hoped for:

> As [British traders] learned about buying cotton and merchandising vari-
> eties in India, they also learned how to make cotton a global commod-
> ity by selling it on the African market in exchange for slaves. David Eltis
> [a historian of the transatlantic slave trade] is less optimistic when he
> claims that 'only a small proportion of Africans could have been wearing
> imported cloth'. The 9.5 million yards of cloth imported by Europeans
> into West Africa in the 1780s provided no more than 0.4 yards per person.

Cotton's impact on Britain and the western world, however, was extraordinary. The technology of the mill made mass-production possible, while cotton's economies of scale enabled its market to expand exponentially. Machine-
made woollens or linens were never able to rival cotton's success because the
processes by which the raw material was produced were so time-consuming
and labour-intensive.

Nineteenth-century British cottons were cheap, of course, because the
slave labour used to pick the raw material was cheap. Until supplies suddenly
dried up during the American Civil War of the 1860s, most of Britain's cotton
came from the slave states of the American South. As Riello observes, while in
1790 US cotton production was practically non-existent, 'ten years later... the
US exported as much cotton to England as the entire British West Indies'. By
1811 America provided 56 per cent of all cotton used by British mills – elbow-
ing the traditional Mediterranean producers out of the way. On the eve of the
American Civil War – when the Lancashire cotton masters were unsurprisingly rooting for the South – the southern states were sending more than four
million bales of cotton a year to Britain to supply the fastest-growing industry
in human history.

Between 1785 and 1830 British cotton textile production expanded
thirty times, and as early as 1806 could boast a workforce of 800,000. By 1841
Manchester had 128 cotton mills, twelve of which employed more than 500
workers each, while 70 per cent of the 1,105 cotton mills in Britain were located
in Lancashire, on account of the local coal deposits, the excellent canal system,
the proximity of Liverpool and other Atlantic ports, the availability of cheap
labour and the incessant rain, which created just the right damp conditions to
manipulate cotton fibres. As Riello notes, 'Cotton took over an entire local

economy, with more than a third of the Lancashire population finding work in the cotton industry between 1800 and 1840.'

Richard Arkwright

As is often told, it was British industrial technology which made this revolution possible. John Kay's flying shuttle of 1733, John Wyatt and Lewis Paul's roller-spinning machine of 1738, James Hargreaves's spinning jenny of 1765, Richard Arkwright's water frame of 1767, Samuel Crompton's spinning mule of 1779, Edmund Cartwright's power loom of 1785 – and, in the US, Eli Whitney's ginning machine of 1794, designed to remove the cotton seeds, all contributed to the coronation of 'King Cotton'. In 1793 a select committee of the British House of Commons reported that shops around the country offered 'British muslins for sale, equal in appearance, [and] of more elegant patterns, than those of India, for one-fourth or perhaps more than one-third less in price'. Yet in 1751 the House had judged that cotton 'was only a temporary Thing'.

Among this roll call of world-beating inventors it was Richard Arkwright (1732–92) who stood out, a man of astonishing vision and energy whose achievements, if not his originality, towered above even those of the entrepreneurial giants. Arkwright's new water-frame machine allowed yarn to be mechanically spun for warping, making it economical to produce pure cotton fabrics. His water came from a local sough, a tunnel constructed to drain water (originally sourced from the Bonsall Brook) from the nearby lead mines. Being located underground meant that the sough's water did not freeze in winter; thus Arkwright was able to harness the power of water all year round.

In 1774 Arkwright campaigned successfully for the repeal of the 1721 Calico Act banning cottons in Britain, claiming that his machine now allowed for 'Goods so made wholly of Cotton' that were 'superior in Quality to the present Species of Cotton Goods made with Linen Yarn Warps'. Thanks to Arkwright, British cotton conquered first its native land and then the world. In 1770 British export cottons stood at a mere 4 per cent of the wool textiles trade; by 1802, though, cotton exports overtook those of woollens – and never looked back. In Japan, Richard Arkwright was deemed worthy of inclusion among the four most important things to know about the west, while in India his machinery was soon being used in every town and city.

Arkwright not only developed the water frame to harness water power in order to drive his mills; he also patented a rotary carding engine to convert

△ *Richard Arkwright depicted in a print adapted from Joseph Wright's portrait of c.1789.*

raw cotton to 'cotton lap' prior to spinning, at a stroke mechanising both card-ing and spinning operations under one roof. Few of these new technologies were of his own devising, however. Arkwright was more of an entrepreneur who appropriated, perfected and popularised other people's inventions. As social historian Barbara Hahn of Texas Tech University has noted: 'His card-ing machines were the work of John Wyatt, patented by Lewis Paul, along with a crank and comb used to prepare the fibre. The roller that fed the fibre into the device was the work of John Lees.' Even Arkwright's celebrated water frame was not entirely novel: the Italians had been using a primitive form of water power since the fourteenth century. And the mechanised factory that Cromford Mill epitomised was not the first textile mill to be built in Britain:

244

that honour belongs to Thomas Lombe's Derby silk mill of 1719, which used Italian silk and continued to manufacture until 1890. What Arkwright did so well was to exploit the British patent system to affirm his personal rights to these innovative tools. On many occasions his own patents were either invalidated or, in turn, usurped – but not before he had made a fortune and expanded his empire of cotton.

The other key ingredient in Arkwright's success was labour. He created the modern factory by using semi-skilled labour both night and day to turn out his mass-produced cottons. And his template was Cromford Mill in Derbyshire, now preserved as part of the Derwent Valley Mills World Heritage Site.

Richard Arkwright was born in 1732, the son of a Lancashire tailor and the youngest of seven surviving children. Even as a barber's apprentice in Bolton he showed his talent for invention, devising a waterproof dye for use on the fashionable wigs of the time. In 1768 he moved back to his hometown of Preston, where he soon patented a mechanical spinning frame which used wooden and metal cylinders rather than human fingers to make the weft. This machine was initially powered by horses but, by using water, Arkwright found he could obtain more power to make the manufacturing process quicker and cheaper. With finance from the Midlands hosiery manufacturers Jedediah Strutt and Samuel Need, in 1771 he accordingly built the world's first water-powered mill at Cromford.

Cromford Mill

Effectively the world's first factory building, Cromford Mill housed both carding and spinning operations and originally employed 200 people, working day and night in two shifts. Arkwright's new factory was not, however, created to be pretty. Its façades, designed by millwrights Samuel and William Stretton, were simple and utilitarian. The main block was of three storeys, built of local stone and lit with plain sash windows. Behind it lay two blocks of two and three storeys built not in finely cut ashlar but using a cheaper, rustic, rubbled stone.

The mill's forbidding brick elevations were devised not just to house the machinery and its human operators but also to resist rioters: bands of local handloom weavers who had been put out of business by the modern mechanisation which Arkwright had pioneered. Such attacks were not uncommon by 1770. Indeed, one of the reasons why Lancashire-born Arkwright had chosen Cromford in next-door Derbyshire, rather than in his native county, was that the Derwent Valley was relatively little known, was sited nowhere near major centres of population and could thus be successfully defended from assailants. At a time when the pace of mechanisation threatened to put thousands out of work, the threat of attack was very real. In 1788 the Protection of Stocking Frames Act was drawn up specifically to criminalise this sort of behaviour. It came too late to save the mill which Arkwright had built at Birkacre in Lancashire, which was completely destroyed in anti-machinery riots in 1779. By the 1810s, particularly after most of Britain's servicemen had been thrown back onto the labour market in the wake of the Battle of Waterloo, anti-industrial protestors, now labelled 'Luddites' after the probably apocryphal Leicestershire weaver Ned Ludd, became a major headache for millowners.

Child labour

There were other reasons for Cromford Mill's location. As we have seen, the village boasted a year-round supply of warm water from the underground sough which fed the nearby lead mines. More ominous was the ready availability of child labour in and around Cromford, where the lead-mining industry offered little scope for the employment of young children. Arkwright also sought to be near the hosiery centres of Derby and Nottingham, where he expected to sell his finished yarn. The idea that his cotton fabrics would find vast markets overseas had not yet occurred to him.

However, even after the advent of the mill had transformed a Derbyshire lead-mining village into a thriving industrial community based round its three cotton mills, Cromford – by now a town, but still a small one – could not provide the labour force that Arkwright's twenty-four-hour operation demanded. Arkwright had to advertise for families to come and work in his mills; he also devised a scheme for employing orphans, who were brought from London and other large cities and were housed and educated in the very mill in which they worked. By the time of Arkwright's death in 1792 almost two-thirds of his 1,150 employees were children. While this sounds appalling, recent research has shown that Poor Law authorities did at least try to ensure tolerable conditions for the children. The late Professor Katrina Honeyman of Leeds University pointed out that factories such as Arkwright's mill, employing large numbers of children, were easier to monitor and better regulated than traditional child-labour trades such as farming and domestic service. Moreover, Arkwright did allow his workforce the novelty of a week's holiday a year – provided, that is, that they did not travel beyond the confines of the town.

To house all these incoming families and orphans Arkwright built an instant village near the mill, comprising not just homes for his workforce but also shops, chapels, a school and a pub, the Greyhound, for them to drink in. In doing so, he created the first factory-housing community in the world.

Arkwright's new industrial community was fortunate in its Pennine setting. As Jacqueline Yallop has written:

> At Cromford the topography of the landscape forces the cottages and the mill apart... When workers finished their shift and made their way to the cottages they turned into streets which had hid them from the gaze of mill managers... and the mill from their own view... They could perhaps step out of their role as factory hands and become something more... a mother or a father, a gardener, a craftsman, a musician, a raconteur.

Not that everyone chose to remain in Arkwright's new, close-knit terraced cottages. By 1800 many millworkers preferred to live slightly further away, in the tightly packed homes built on the steep escarpment known as Scarthin. As Carolyn Steedman notes, when Richard Arkwright's son (also Richard) gave evidence to the House of Commons Select Committee on child labour in 1816, he cited the fact that much of his workforce 'reside in different townships' as a means of frustrating proposed legislation allowing workers to return home for mealtimes: 'they had not time to get home and back in a dinner break, he said.'

Life in Arkwright's mill was not easy. While Cromford was, to the hugely gifted local painter Joseph Wright, an astonishing and almost picturesque vision of Britain's industrial future, to its workforce the mill was the only world they knew and offered a life of unremitting and repetitive toil.

Arkwright himself was known as a highly focused and difficult man who often fell out with his collaborators. His single-minded determination was reflected in the novel yet highly disciplined working arrangements he dictated at Cromford. Bells rang at 5 a.m. and 5 p.m. and the mill gates were shut precisely at 6 a.m. and 6 p.m. Latecomers were simply excluded from work for the rest of the day and lost that day's pay.

Cromford Mill heralded the age of the industrial society. Unusually, though, Arkwright's achievement was widely recognised even within his

▷ *A detail of Joseph Wright's evocative view of Arkwright's Cromford Mill of c.1795.*

own lifetime. The poor tailor's son from Preston served as High Sheriff for Derbyshire and was knighted by George III in 1786. By 1788 more than 200 'Arkwright' mills had been established in Britain – mostly in central Lancashire and north Derbyshire – while there were four similar mills built in France and five in Germany by the time of his death.

The Arkwright system created the global textile industry and made possible the production of cheap clothing and household textiles for a vast swathe of the world's population, improving their comfort and their personal hygiene. Many of Arkwright's inventions continued in use until the middle of the twentieth century; indeed, much modern machinery still carries recognisable elements descended from Cromford's technology.

Less positively, Arkwright's factory system also created a blueprint for child labour. By the time Queen Victoria came to the throne in 1837 thousands of children worked in Lancashire and Derbyshire's cotton mills. The legendary historian E. P. Thompson was far from alone when he wrote in 1963 that 'the exploitation of little children' was one of the most shameful aspects of British industrialisation.

Textile enterprises such as Cromford Mill remained profitable largely as a result of their child labour, since the children received no wages, only shelter and food, for their work. Katrina Honeyman cited a Shrewsbury factory which was held up as a model of benevolence, in which, 'if a child became sleepy, the overlooker touches the child on the shoulder and says "come here". In the corner of the room there is an iron cistern filled with water. He takes the boy by the legs and dips him in the cistern, and then sends him back to work.' Child workers were often beaten, were poorly fed and on occasion were sexually abused. Abuse was rarely mentioned in factory visitors' reports; either because it was not witnessed during inspections – and it almost certainly would not have been – or because it was implicitly condoned. At one cotton mill in Arkwright's hometown of Preston visitors were disconcerted to notice 'a large pair of stocks at end [of the eating room] for refractory children to be fastened to and whipped at'. One observer described the children he saw working there as 'Poor, Squalid, deformed beings, the most pitiful objects I think I ever saw'.

The impact of incessant labour on fragile young bodies and spirits was inevitably highly damaging. One boy who worked at a mill in Marsden, West Yorkshire, which employed children as young as five, was carried to the mill when he was too ill to walk and made to work the usual shift. Many others were carried to work by their parents while they were still sleeping.

Once at work, there was little time to eat, and what meals they could manage invariably gave their recipients little nourishment. The luxury of an hour's lunch at midday was unusual. At Toplis Mill in Cuckney, Nottinghamshire, for example, half an hour was allowed for dinner, but this included the time taken walking to and from the eating room – which was half a mile away. At the notorious textile mill at Litton in Derbyshire, the children's diet comprised water-porridge and oaten cakes which were piled up in heaps and, in the factory heat, were liable to ferment and grow mouldy. A report of a meal at George Merryweather's brand-new Manchester mill in 1810 noted that 'the potatoes for dinner were boiling with their skins on in a state of great dirtiness, and eight cow heads boiling in another pot for dinner' while 'a great portion of the food we were told was of a liquid nature'. Children occasionally used their 'overtime' allowances on extra food, but the effect of the latter on stomachs used only to the barest nutrition was often to make them ill.

Notwithstanding their poor diet, badly fed mill children were often forced to clean the mill machinery during their dinner hour, depriving them of much-needed breaks and essential nourishment. At Litton, children were also kept back after work and at weekends to clean and maintain the machines. Katrina Honeyman cites two further examples:

At Backbarrow [cotton mill, now in Cumbria] a large part of Sunday was dedicated to machinery maintenance and repair. John Moss, once superintendent of the apprentice house, claimed that every Sunday morning some children worked from 6 till 12 in cleaning the machinery; and at Lowdham [paper mill, in Nottinghamshire] 'once in ten days or a fortnight, the whole of the finer machinery used to be taken to pieces and cleaned and then they had to remain at the mill from morning to night'.

Where they were paid, child wages were often low: sometimes as little as 10 per cent of an adult male's wage.

Water-powered mills such as Cromford were subject to yet another imposition on their workers. Low river levels during summer droughts meant that the mill could not operate. As a result, when the river rose and power was restored, the management demanded that the workforce worked to clear the backlog of orders.

After the Napoleonic Wars, pressure grew to restrict or ban the use of child labour in Britain's factories, and particularly in the nation's cotton mills.

But action was slow in coming. The Cotton Mills and Factories Act of 1819 stipulated that no children under nine were to be employed in the cotton industry, that children aged nine to sixteen should be limited to twelve hours' work per day, and that a meal break of an hour should be taken between 11 a.m. and 2 p.m. Yet even this legislation was effectively unenforceable: its policing was left to local magistrates who could only inspect a mill if two witnesses had given sworn statements that the mill was breaking the Act's provisions. A subsequent amendment even allowed for the imposition of all-night working on the entire workforce to make the necessary repairs if one of them had deliberately sabotaged or even accidentally damaged the factory's machinery. Even then, one mill-owning MP preposterously claimed that the Act put mill-owners at the mercy of millhands and that 'it was now in the power of the workmen to ruin many individuals, by enforcing the penalties for children working beyond the hours limited by that act'. An Act of 1825 limited children's Saturdays to nine hours of work, rather than the usual twelve, but despite many attempts it was not until 1847 that the normal working day for women and children working in textile factories was reduced to ten hours by Lord John Russell's Whig government.

Campaigns to end child labour in Britain's factories, and particularly in the textile industry, gained momentum in the mid-nineteenth century. In 1835 the famously eccentric Letitia Elizabeth Landon denounced child labour in her polemical poem *The Factory*, part of which she pointedly included in her *18th Birthday Tribute* to Princess (and soon to be Queen) Victoria in 1837:

There rises on the morning wind
A low appealing cry,
A thousand children are resigned
To sicken and to die...

Alas! 'tis time, the mother's eyes
Turn mournfully away;
Alas! 'tis time, the child must rise,
And yet it is not day.

The lantern's lit – she hurries forth,
The spare cloak's scanty fold
Scarce screens her from the snowy north,

△ *A print of 1800 depicting Cromford Mill as a picturesque backdrop as well as a pioneering factory.*

The child is pale and cold.

And wearily the little hands
Their task accustom'd ply;
While daily, some mid those pale bands,
Droop, sicken, pine, and die.

More famously, in 1844 the wealthy German social reformer and future writing partner of Karl Marx, Friedrich Engels, was appalled by the conditions in which he saw children working in Manchester's cotton mills. In his subsequent account of *The Condition of the Working Class in England*, published in German in 1845 but not translated into English until 1885, he fulminated that:

253

The great mortality among children of the working class, and especially among those of the factory operatives, is proof enough of the unwholesome conditions under which they pass their first years... A nine-year-old child of a factory operative that has grown up in want, privation, and changing conditions, in cold and damp, with insufficient clothing and unwholesome dwellings, is far from having the working strength of a child brought up under healthier conditions. At nine years of age it is sent into the mill to work 6½ hours (formerly 8, earlier still, 12 to 14, even 16 hours) daily, until the thirteenth year; then twelve hours until the eighteenth year. The old enfeebling influences continue, while the work is added to them... but in no case can its [the child's] presence in the damp, heavy air of the factory, often at once warm and wet, contribute to good health.

Ironically, salvation for factory children came with the very technology which had initially enslaved them in Arkwright's time. As industrial technology improved and grew more complex, education of the workforce was needed so that they could operate the new machinery. Older, educated employees were now needed rather than illiterate children. This in turn provided a boost not just for the child labour campaigners but for the educationalists. The most immediate result was Forster's Education Act of 1870, which provided young Britons aged from five to twelve with the first national framework for universal state education. As for child labour, it was only in 1933 that legislation was passed restricting the use of children under fourteen in employment.

Child labour still remains a scourge worldwide. With the world's attention focused on the Covid epidemic and political upheavals, few noticed that 2021 was designated by the United Nations as the International Year for the Elimination of Child Labour, and little came of this admirable initiative. There is still much to be done.

Obsolescence

From the 1790s most British mills converted to coal-fired steam power; yet a few continued to use water as the means of energy capture. As a result, by 1840 Arkwright's mill had become too old-fashioned to turn a healthy profit, as its now-antiquated machinery could not be converted to steam operation and the old Meerbrook sough was producing less and less power. It was also a fire risk, being built before iron-framing had become the norm for large mill buildings whose combustible textiles and proliferation of candles and oil lamps made them obvious candidates for conflagration. (In 1785 Arkwright's small mill at Cessbrook had burned to the ground after only six years of operation.) Accordingly, Cromford Mill was converted by new owners into a paint mill (for grinding paint pigments) and dyeing plant, in which role it fed its toxic waste straight into the adjacent River Derwent. The original 1771 building was reduced by two storeys in 1929 and for many years access to the historic core of the site was forbidden due to the toxic residue which still lingered from the twentieth-century paint-making processes. (The most toxic tank was actually built upon the foundations of Arkwright's 1775 extension building.) Following the paint factory's closure in the 1960s the mill's future was uncertain and, like so much of Britain's historic legacy during the 1960s, it was threatened by wholesale demolition.

Thankfully, the growth of the conservationist lobby in the later 1970s came to the site's rescue. The Arkwright Society had been set up by local enthusiasts on the bicentenary of the mill in 1971; eight years later they had garnered sufficient financial backing – including £70,000 from the Historic Buildings Council – to buy the mill and its curtilage, making Cromford one of the country's (and indeed the world's) first major industrial sites to be restored and opened to the public. By 2019, £48 million had been spent on restoring the site and bringing its story to new audiences.

The partially restored Mill site now constitutes the epicentre of the Derwent Valley World Heritage Site and was recently declared by Historic England to be 'one of the country's 100 irreplaceable sites'. The birthplace of Richard Arkwright's industrial breakthroughs has also been recognised by a UN agency, UNESCO (The United Nations Educational, Scientific and Cultural Organization) as a World Heritage Site since 2001.

Cromford Mill survives as a testimony to Britain's global head-start in industrialisation. Whether it can be said to have been the birthplace of the industrial revolution is much contested, as is whether we can call such a disparate and complex narrative of technological evolution an 'industrial revolution' at all. Either way, Cromford still remains the place where, for good or ill, the modern factory system was born.

14

7 GREAT GEORGE STREET, BRISTOL

1790

The Backs of Others: slaving profits incarnated in a Georgian townhouse

For more than two centuries, this handsome, stone-built late Georgian town-house stood proud and untroubled on the western side of Bristol's Great George Street. Built a hundred yards away from the busy, steeply ascending arterial connector of Park Street, number 7's perfectly proportioned façade looked out at the city's commercial centre and floating harbour barely a mile below. Celebrated as an embodiment of Georgian taste and refinement, the house was regarded by generations of Bristolians as one of the jewels of the city and one of the most visible symbols of its mercantile wealth and historic significance. It is only in recent years that number 7's true and disturbing past has been uncovered. As a result, the house has been recast not as a cynosure of Georgian luxury but as an ominous incarnation of the greed, cruelty and inhumanity of the eighteenth-century slave trade. And at the dark heart of the slave trade was a commodity beloved of Britons for three centuries: sugar.

▷ *The handsome façade of William Paty's number 7.*

The sugar trade

In 1650 most Britons lived on a starch-based diet, one which reflected not a proactive lifestyle choice by individuals but the sheer poverty of the resources available to almost the whole population. Yet within a century, as the nation's mercantile strength grew, Britain's eating and drinking habits had been transformed by a handful of products imported by British ships from around the globe. These novel foods started life as expensive luxuries, but by the turn of the nineteenth century they had become essentials for Britons of all classes. Even the poorest labourers of London, Liverpool or Leith took sugar in their tea. Sugar was the most important of these revolutionary new foods: the carbohydrate which changed Britain, and indeed the world, for ever.

Sweetness seems always to have delighted humans, but until the early modern era the sensation of 'sweet' could largely be derived only from fruit or honey. The making of sugar from the sugarcane plant (*Saccharum officinarum*) has been traced back to the first century AD, but it only began to be manufactured in large quantities in Persia and the Arab world in the seventh century. By the tenth century it had arrived in Venice; but by then sugar had already reached Spain with the Moorish conquest of Iberia of the eighth century. Yet by the time the Spanish finally conquered the Moorish enclave of Granada in 1492, sugar manufacturing was in decline around the Mediterranean, from Cyprus to Portugal, and was still regarded as a luxurious and prohibitively expensive spice or medicine.

It was during the late fifteenth and early sixteenth centuries that the Portuguese and, later, the Spanish began to experiment with establishing sugar plantations in their Atlantic island colonies, which offered far better conditions in which to grow *Saccharum officinarum* than their possessions in coastal West Africa, with their poor, saline soils. It was the Spanish who first established sugar plantations in the West Indies, in Santo Domingo, during the 1510s. Sugar cultivation and processing was notoriously labour-intensive, so in order to people these plantations the Spanish colonial masters, having expunged much of the native population, began to import black slaves from West Africa. By 1530 both the Portuguese and the Spanish were importing large quantities of sugar into Europe from plantations in Brazil and the West Indies, respectively. A century later the British, French and Dutch had muscled into the West Indian colonies and into the sugar trade, and by the closing years of the seventeenth century their sugar exports had come to dwarf those of the Iberian nations.

By 1590 London had become Europe's largest centre for sugar refining and was soon being supplied with large quantities of raw Barbadian sugar – Barbados having been settled by the British after 1627. The Barbadian trade was in turn eclipsed by British sugar imports from the large Caribbean island of Jamaica, captured from the Spanish by Cromwell's navy in 1655. The European market continued to elude British sugar traders – protective French legislation kept British sugar out of France until 1740 – but they still made vast fortunes from the home market, which grew with astonishing rapidity during the eighteenth century as sugar moved from being the luxury of the few to the mass-produced necessity of the many.

As historian Sidney Mintz noted, 'like tea, sugar came to define English "character"'. Yet, as many observers then and since have noted, both of these nationally defining products were hauled from the other side of the globe at great expense and – especially in the case of sugar – were only possible thanks to the widespread use of slave labour. Campaigners called for the consumption of more patriotic British substitutes for tea; even beer was touted as a home-grown alternative drink. Yet there was no viable alternative to West Indian sugar, and seemingly no stopping the inexorable progress of the sugar jugger-naut. Slavery made sugar cheap, and sugar made naturally bitter yet fashionable drinks such as tea, chocolate and coffee palatable. In England alone, per capita sugar consumption rose from one pound in weight to 25 pounds between 1670 and 1770. By 1790 English working families spent around 10 per cent of their total food budget on treacle, sugar and tea.

One of the British cities which benefitted most from the sugar industry – and, by direct association, the slave trade – was the large and historic port of Bristol, which looked westwards to the Atlantic, the Americas and Britain's Caribbean colonies. By 1750 Bristol had twenty working sugar refineries, more than any other British port. Many Bristol sugar importers lived for spells in the Caribbean in order to gain an inside knowledge of the trade which would be invaluable when they returned home. One of the most successful of these sugar merchants during the city's 'golden age' of the late eighteenth century was one John Pinney.

Georgian Bristol

Pinney's Bristol was a place of bustling commercial activity in the early eight-eenth century, centring on the harbour and on John Wood's handsome, classical Exchange of 1741–3 in Corn Street. Historian Kenneth Morgan has colourfully described the thriving city during the second half of the eighteenth century:

> Merchants, shipowners, manufacturers, packers, hauliers, shipwrights, sailors and customs officers jostled one another in the centre of what was still largely a medieval walled city. Business vitality was most evident in the centre of Bristol where a spacious quay, about a mile in length, was surrounded by wooden ships, merchants' counting houses, shops and warehouses, sugar refineries and glasshouses, taverns and coffee houses, all clustered by the rivers Avon and Frome. Commercial affairs were also conducted by merchants at the Tolzey, a covered walkway in Corn Street, and, from 1745 onwards, at the Exchange in the same street... By the 1760s, many an hour was whiled away with talk of the Atlantic trading world at the Exchange coffee house and at the American and West Indian coffee houses. Trade and shipping were regularly discussed by the Bristol Corporation, which met at the Council House in a square at the intersection of Broad, Corn, High and Wine Streets. Politics and commerce were also intertwined in the lobbying activities of the Society of Merchant Venturers, founded in 1552 and based at Merchants' Hall, King Street, and in the work of Bristol's MPs.

From the late 1720s the fashionable new streets of the city were built not of timber or local brick, as in the past, but of honey-coloured Bath stone – although Horace Walpole, appalled at the priority Bristolians gave to business and industry, later called the city 'the dirtiest great shop I ever saw'. By the time the local architect William Paty was building a house for John Pinney, he had pared down the Bristolian classical style to a calm, refined and minimalist idiom which nicely suited the reserved businessmen of the city.

John Pinney was at the centre of all this commercial and architectural activity, and was one of the main reasons why the port was so successful. Yet his commercial success was founded, like the new residential terraces which were springing up across the city, on the backs of others. For Pinney's fortune emanated from the notorious triangle of trade by which goods from the southern colonies of America and the West Indies were carried to Britain. Sugar from the West Indies was refined and packaged in London or Bristol; raw cotton arrived in Liverpool to be woven and finished in the north Midlands and north-west. British-made cotton textiles were then shipped to the west coast of Africa to be sold to unsuspecting local populations, from whom they bought – or seized – slave labour. British ships then transported captured slaves to operate the sugar and cotton plantations of the Americas, in the final leg of the tragic triangle.

The fundamental basis of this trade was the exploitation of other peoples. To make this business economically viable for merchants such as John Pinney, human cargoes were central to its operation. Live beings were, as a result, treated as commodities, alongside sugar, cotton and spices, in order to make sizeable profits. As Mintz noted, 'The wealth [the merchants] created mostly returned to Britain; the products they made were consumed in Britain; and the products made by Britons – cloth. Tools, torture instruments – were consumed by slaves who were themselves consumed in the creation of wealth.'

John Pinney

John Pretor Pinney was born in Chard, Somerset, in 1740. At only twenty-two he inherited large tracts of land in Dorset and a number of sugar plantations on the West Indian island of Nevis, which had been worked by black African slaves since they were first created in 1682. Nevis had been won from Spain by the British in 1670 and was soon renowned as a major staging post for the British trade in African slaves as well as for the high quality of its sugar. It became for a time the richest of the British Leeward Islands and, by the time the American War of Independence erupted in 1775, 90 per cent of the population were black. Not all of its black inhabitants were slaves, however. Some escaped slaves, known as 'maroons', resisted the government forces from their hideouts in the interior. Ironically, it was the largely enslaved black population of Nevis which successfully resisted French incursions at the time of the American war. When the French were driven off, they took with them a number of black prisoners – six of whom became the first persons of African descent to arrive in the then French-owned territory of Louisiana.

Pinney went to inspect his new inheritance in person in 1764. Arriving at Nevis, he found the plantations rundown and in debt. Accordingly, he stayed on the island and spent the next nineteen years rebuilding the business. He did this so successfully that he returned to England in 1783 a very wealthy man, with a fortune which has been calculated at between eight and nine million pounds in today's values.

Soon after he moved into his Mountravers plantation, Pinney bought more than sixty African slaves at a local market. As he did so, he admitted to a twinge of guilt – a sentiment he was never again to exhibit publicly:

> Since my arrival I've purchased nine negroe slaves at St Kitts and can assure you I was shock'd at the first appearance of human flesh exposed to sale. But surely God ordain'd 'em for ye use & benefit of us: otherwise his Divine Will would have been made manifest by some particular sign or token.

In 1772 Pinney married a white Creole – a local resident of largely (but not always wholly) European descent – called Jane Weekes, with whom he had seven children.*

On his return to Britain, Pinney spent some of his time in his inherited Dorset mansion of Racedown, a handsome if plain brick villa near Bridport of the mid-eighteenth century, today more famous for having been sublet (at no cost) to William and Dorothy Wordsworth in 1795–7. Pinney subsequently declared: 'My greatest pride is to be considered as a private Country Gentleman therefore I am resolved to content myself with a little and shall avoid even the name of a West Indian.'

Pinney also built a substantial townhouse in Bristol in order to be close to the docks where his sugar cargoes landed and near to his business partner, the Bristol sugar merchant, notorious pro-slavery campaigner and stalwart of the Bristol West India Association, James Tobin. Tobin, whose advocacy helped to defeat the bill to abolish the slave trade of 1792, eventually fell out with Pinney and died a year before his erstwhile partner, in 1817.

Number 7

Pinney's new Bristol home reflected the fashions of the time and of the city. Its imposing, nicely proportioned façade was of three bays and three storeys and built of local, honey-coloured ashlar limestone. It was provided with a large, six-panelled front door framed by mannered Doric pilasters support-ing a broken triangular pediment; tall sash windows on the ground and first

---

* The American statesman Alexander Hamilton was also born of a Creole mother in Nevis, and was still living on the island when Pinney arrived.

floors; and rusticated stonework on the ground floor denoting the more utilitarian functions of this level – as opposed to the grand public rooms on the
floor above. Inside, a sweeping central stair led visitors from the Hall directly
up to the landing on the principal floor, from which six-panelled mahogany
doors led to the Drawing Room (invariably placed at the front of the first
floor) and the Dining Room, both of which were equipped with appropriately
sized chimneypieces in the still-fashionable Adam style. So far, so predictable.
In the basement, however, was something different from the late Georgian
norm. Pinney asked the builders to create a stone-lined plunge pool, approx-
imately 5 feet deep, 4 feet wide and 10 feet long, with panelled shutters. In
1760 he had written that he found a daily coldwater plunge bath to be 'of great
service', at a time when most Britons seldom bathed with any regularity.

Number 7 Great George Street was one of a number of five- and three-
bay detached houses built after 1788 by William Paty (1758–1800), son of a local
architect who had just returned to the city after training in London. Paty's father
had been responsible for building many of the Georgian buildings in Bristol and
both of his sons, John and William, joined the business, which William headed
on the death of his father in 1789. As Historic England has acknowledged, the
Patys have sometimes been accused of a lack of originality; but, thanks to them,
'Bristol was transformed from a medieval city of wooden houses to a modern
city with paved streets, stone buildings and suburbs'.

Great George Street's houses were all built according to the time-
honoured speculative system, ubiquitous in Britain since the Great Fire of
London of 1666. As we have seen in Chapter 11, the landowner would commission an architect or surveyor to devise a master plan for the site, and would
allocate leases for the planned houses to the architect's team of craftsmen at
a peppercorn rent during the period of construction. Paty would distribute
these plots to the key members of his team, thus spreading the financial risk;
Paty's team would then finish each house to the specifications set by the first
commercial leaseholder, for whose purchase they alone were responsible. In
Paty's case, he and his team of building craftsmen successfully completed the
street before the advent of war with France in 1793 prompted the housing
market to screech to an abrupt halt, bankrupting many speculative building
teams which had not yet completed their developments. As Andrew Foyle has
written, by 1793 many building speculators were hopelessly over-committed:
thus 'the financial collapse of 1793... had devastating consequences for Bristol
business'. Paty was fortunate to avoid ruin.

△ *The Pinney's dining room at 7 Great George Street.*

John Pinney ran his business from his ground-floor study at Great George Street, which was provided with built-in bookcases and a safe for this purpose. On the first floor he entertained a wide circle of friends, who were more than happy to mingle with the family of one of Bristol's most illustrious sugar tycoons. Not just the Wordsworths, but also fellow poets Samuel Taylor Coleridge and Robert Southey, not forgetting the neglected wife of Britain's latest naval hero, Frances, Lady Nelson, all dined here.

John Pinney was a methodical and cautious man who sought to gain healthy profits from moderate risks and believed that he had 'succeeded much better than such as have engaged in wild and unlimited schemes and speculations in hopes of larger profits'. He kept a hoard of gold conveniently hidden in a window seat, ready to fund a swift escape should the French ever invade Bristol, and his accounts were meticulous and obsessively detailed. His prudence, though, paid dividends: by the time he died in 1818 his fortune amounted to about £25 million in present-day values, about three times his worth on his return to England thirty-five years earlier.

Pinney's household reflected the origins of his fortune. He brought two principal servants with him from Nevis: Frances (Fanny) Coker, a freed servant of mixed race (then termed a 'mulatto') who served as maid to Pinney's wife, Jane, until her death in 1820, and his own manservant, Pero Jones, who was never freed. (Fanny's father is thought to have been Pinney's plantation manager in Nevis, which may be why she was freed in 1778.) Shortly before his death in 1818, Pinney wrote of Pero: 'He has waited upon my person upwards of thirty-two years, and I cannot help feeling much for him, notwithstanding he has not lately conducted himself as well as I could have wished.' In 1999 a new footbridge at Bristol's Harbourside was named 'Pero's Bridge', in recognition of those, like Pero, whose enslavement had effectively helped build the city of Bristol. The bridge was designed by the Irish sculptor Eilis O'Connell and built by Arups, and even in 1999 its naming was condemned by some as too tangential a gesture to atone for Bristol's central role in promoting and benefitting from the slave trade. Today the structure could be said to be the Bristol equivalent of the Pont Neuf in Paris: bedecked with 'love locks', padlocks attached to the bridge's superstructure as lasting tokens of love and remembrance, it is better known as the site for lovers' trysts than as a commemoration of Bristol's association with slavery.

Altogether at least five of the servants the Pinneys installed at 7 Great George Street came from Nevis. They were either enslaved, like Pero; had been freed, like Fanny Coker; or were the children of favoured slaves, like Christianna Jacques. Their cook, Mary Chaplin, was the highest paid of the female servants (though her remuneration was still substantially less than that of the footman, Charles Thomas). The day after she started, on 15 September 1791, a kitchen range was installed in the form of William Stark's newly invented 'steam apparatus', a radical design by the ironworker who was to transform the kitchen at Brighton Pavilion. David Small and Christine Eickelman suggest that Chaplin 'may have been taken on because she was familiar with this method of cooking' and note that:

> Her basic wage was 10 guineas a year (equivalent to about £1,200 in 2017), paid quarterly. She was also given an allowance of 1 guinea a year in place of the usual 'perk' of selling 'kitchen stuff': dripping, bones, globs of fat and suet. In addition she had 1 ½ guineas for washing. When staff were in Bristol they had an allowance to pay for having their own washing done. So, in total, Mary Chaplin was paid 12 ½ guineas a year. In the 12 years

she worked for the family her wages never increased.

Like other servants working for the Pinneys, Mary Chaplin had money invested for her by John Pinney. And she had an important role, since when the family travelled to their Dorset homes or to London the cook was left in charge of the house almost alone weeks on end. Nonetheless, Mary Chaplin was sacked on 15 May 1802. Mrs Pinney recorded simply that 'Mary Chaplin left my service after living with me near 12 years – she was discharged for highly improper conduct.' Small and Eickelman suggest that 'the fact that the very next day Elizabeth Morgan was hired as a cook suggests that Mary Chaplin's departure had been planned and she had been given notice beforehand'. The Pinneys were clearly not over-sentimental about their servants.

Fanny Coker was the Pinneys' longest-serving employee in the household. Born enslaved on Nevis in 1767 but freed by Pinney when she was eleven years old, she was a trained seamstress but also acted as a nursemaid to the Pinneys' young children, a personal maid to Mrs Pinney's lady's maid and, given that she could read the newspapers, a source of information for her illiterate fellow servants. Her mother, called 'Black Polly' by Pinney, was brought as a slave from Africa, and later alleged that Fanny's brother, Billey Jones, was actually Pinney's son. This claim Pinney, unsurprisingly, denied.

Pero himself was trained as a manservant and barber. David Small and Christine Eickelman give some indication of his daily life in Bristol:

> Pero, like other live-in staff, had free board and lodging plus some perquisites, such as a livery and tea and sugar, but he received no wages; only occasional sums of money. As Pinney's personal servant Pero would have been on hand at all hours: helping Pinney dress and undress, shaving him in the mornings, cutting his hair and on special occasions powdering and arranging his wig. He would have received visitors, waited at table and performed other duties around the house, such as cleaning and locking up silverware and at night locking up and securing all doors and windows. When Pinney was absent, Pero paid for items and services, such as money owed for hiring a coach. He ran private and business errands, carrying money, messages and letters... When he travelled with Pinney, he would have taken care of their horses and luggage and generally made sure his master had everything he needed.

Pero accompanied his master on trips to Paris in 1789 and Germany in 1790, and went back to Nevis at least twice with Pinney, where he appears to have fathered one or two children. He and Fanny Coker often shipped presents to Nevis, generally commodities which could be sold for cash to support their families back home.

Pero was far from happy, however – something Pinney seems to have completely failed to notice. Separated from his children who had remained in Nevis, Pero grew depressed and ill. He finally died in 1798 – 'after being almost useless, caused by drunkenness and dissipation', as Pinney coldly declared in a letter to a friend. Pinney's heartless reaction to the decline and death of a man who had been constantly at his side for so many years shows little in the way of Christian charity or humanitarian fellow-feeling.

The anti-slavery movement

Those like the Pinneys who benefitted from slavery never got their comeuppance. Even after slavery had finally been abolished by the British government in 1833, Pinney's sons subsequently received the highly generous recompense of £23,100 – roughly £2.3 million today – for the loss of their slave 'property' by the government's Slave Compensation Act of 1837. The family had actually claimed £36,396: roughly £3.5 million today.

Undoubtedly, though, the anti-slavery Acts of 1807 and 1833 did demonstrate that, notwithstanding the huge fortunes to be made in sugar or cotton, the slave trade was not without its vociferous opponents in late Georgian Britain. Nor did Britons fail to relate their own consumption of sugar with the perpetuation of its injustices. Public revulsion at the West Indian sugar trade's traditional dependence on slavery is not a modern phenomenon. Even before 1800, the British anti-slavery movement was linking the iniquities of slavery with the British public's love of sweet things and consequently attempting to encourage their fellow Britons to boycott Caribbean sugar. A research project run by Professor Kathryn Gleadle of the University of Oxford and Dr Ryan Hanley of the University of Exeter found many young people of the 1780s and 1790s who had enthusiastically taken up the cause of 'anti-saccharism'. They cite young Katherine Plymley, who in 1792 wrote that:

... her seven-year-old nephew Panton had been refusing to have his shoes shined because he had heard that the polish contained sugar. She also

recorded how Panton and his two sisters Jane and Josepha spent time chatting and putting together a jigsaw puzzle of Africa with her friend, the anti-slavery campaigner Thomas Clarkson. After discussing the issue with Clarkson, young Jane declared that she would only eat sugar grown in the new abolitionist colony of Sierra Leone.

They also cite the physician Elizabeth Blackwell – who, looking back on her childhood in Bristol in the 1820s, claimed that many of the city's children 'voluntarily gave up the use of sugar' because it was a 'slave product' – and scientist Mary Somerville, who recalled taking 'the anti-slavery cause so warmly to heart' as a girl that she 'would not take sugar in my tea, or indeed taste anything with sugar in it'.

How Bristolian sugar dynasties such as the Pinneys' regarded such sentiments being expressed on their very own doorsteps is not recorded. What is fascinating, though, was that anti-saccharinism was a movement led by the young. As Dr Hanley concluded, confident young Britons of the post-Napoleonic age sought to cast off old assumptions, prejudices and practices in order to make a better world for themselves and their contemporaries:

Children used the anti-slavery movement to negotiate their own place in the world. Sometimes they were the first members of their families to abstain from using sugar and they also encouraged their parents to do it. In other cases, children questioned their involvement to leverage authority over their own lives... children had a political voice and they used it.

Even more recently, Newcastle University historian Dr Garritt Van Dyk has looked more closely at the sugar boycotts of the Regency era. The first mass petition against slavery was signed by ten thousand men in Manchester in December 1787, a few months before work began on Pinney's Great George Street townhouse. Thereafter campaigners quickly fastened onto a highly visible product of slavery: sugar. As Van Dyk observes, coffee, tobacco and cotton were also slave goods, but tobacco and coffee consumption was largely a male preserve while an anti-cotton campaign 'would have been perceived as an attack

◁ *Royal York Crescent in Bristol's prestigious Clifton district, begun in 1791, the year after 7 Great George Street was designed by its architect (probably local man William Paty) as a reflection of Bristol's slave-fuelled mercantile wealth. However, its grand architectural ambitions were frustrated by the Revolutionary and Napoleonic Wars, and it was thirty years before the terrace was completed.*

△ This 1873 compendium of Bristol's architectural glories omits the medieval magnificence of the church of St Mary Redcliffe and anything to do with the Georgian city. Instead it prefers to emphasise Foster and Wood's recently-opened Colston Hall, which was part of late Victorian Bristol's preferment of the slave trader Edward Colston. In 2020 the Hall was renamed the Bristol Beacon.

on the manufacture of English textiles, jeopardizing support for the movement'. Sugar, on the other hand, was a cross-gender commodity consumed by everyone. It was also a temptingly big target: by 1800 sugar was, by price, easily Britain's largest import.

The anti-sugar campaign was not for the faint-hearted. One leading abolitionist argued that abstaining from sugar for twenty-one months 'would prevent the slavery or murder of one fellow creature' and that for every pound of sugar used 'we may be considered as consuming two ounces of human flesh'. Support for the anti-sugar movement did fade temporarily after Revolutionary France declared war on Britain in 1793 – a war that was to continue, with just one brief interruption in 1801–3, for the next twenty-two years. However, once war had become a familiar feature of everyday life, old passions returned. In 1807 William Wilberforce and his allies succeeded in getting Lord Grenville's government to finally enact the abolition of slavery. Grenville himself steered the bill through the House of Lords while the future Lord Grey, now best known as the father of the Great Reform Act of 1832, navigated it through the Commons. The termination of slavery across the British empire, though, had to wait another twenty-six years.

Modern Bristol

In the meantime, the new century had been less kind to Bristol than its predecessor. The tightening of credit after the French declared war in 1793 hit Bristol particularly badly, and more than sixty speculative builders went bankrupt in the city before the final peace of 1815. William Jessop's ingenious floating harbour of 1804–9 attempted to solve the problem of the tidal River Avon; but by the 1870s the city admitted defeat and was forced to build large new docks on the coast at Avonmouth and Portishead. Tempers boiled over in 1831 on the defeat of Grey's Reform Bill, although the savage Bristol Riots that followed actually spurred some MPs to vote *for* reform the following year, in the expectation that legislation would prevent such unrest ever happening again. Meanwhile, Bristol's traditional copper, brass and glass industries all went into decline. And despite the well-publicised launch of Brunel's astonishing SS *Great Britain* in 1844, railways replaced seagoing traffic as the mainspring of Bristol city's transportation network in the years after the Great Western Railway route to London opened in 1841 and rail links were established to Exeter in 1844 and Plymouth in 1848.

Nevertheless, Bristol's population continued to rise astronomically – from 68,800 in 1801 to 330,000 in 1901. And there were great Victorian achievements in the city, from Brunel's posthumous memorial the Clifton Suspension Bridge, opened in 1864, to M. D. Wyatt's Temple Meads Station of 1865 and the city-wide electric tram system of 1895. Tobacco and chocolate manufacture supplanted historic industries, as Bristol manufacturers Wills and Fry became household names – names far better known than those of the sugar merchants who had dominated the city at the end of the eighteenth century.

By the early twentieth century the city of Bristol began to be embarrassed by its former reliance on West Indian trade. Number 7 Great George Street remained in the Pinney family until 1861, and in 1938 it was given by the then owner, a canon of Bristol Cathedral, to the city of Bristol to be opened to the public as a historic house museum, showcasing the furniture and art of the eighteenth century in a domestic Georgian setting. Although the Pinney family made many loans to the museum from 1939, it was simply called 'the Georgian House' and the Pinney name was initially downplayed.

When, towards the end of the Victorian era, the city of Bristol sought to commemorate the great Bristolian merchants of the past, Pinney was an obvious candidate for memorialisation. Strangely, however, the conservative Society of Merchant Adventurers who then dominated the city's commercial life plumped instead for a far more remote, peripheral and tainted figure, the late Stuart merchant Edward Colston (1636–1721). Significantly, Colston had been a member of the Merchant Adventurers, whereas Pinney never was. The resulting statue, by Irish-born sculptor John Cassidy, was unveiled by the floating harbour in 1895. As early as 1920, however, Colston's tarnished origins as a leading slave trader and one of the mainstays of the Royal African Company, which had been awarded a monopoly on trading African slaves, were being advertised in print. It was not until the 1990s, though, that English Heritage began to organise a wide-ranging consultation on what should be done about Colston's legacy across the city.

When the list description of Pinney's Great George Street house was reviewed by English Heritage (EH) in 2007, EH admirably bit the bullet and included a substantial narrative detailing Pinney's unflattering history as a slave-owner. In recent years, too, the museum has done far more to advertise Pinney's past and the life of the house's servants, making this valuable resource a mirror to the Pinneys and their household rather than a generic reflection of fashionable Georgian life.

In the event, just as negotiations were being held to find a new home for Cassidy's statue of Colston, events overtook the well-meaning heritage professionals of Bristol. Following the worldwide Black Lives Matter protests precipitated by the murder of George Floyd in Minneapolis on 25 May 2020, protestors toppled the Colston memorial into the water. For four days in June 2020 it lay at the bottom of the harbour.

It was not just Colston who had been toppled. The Bristol protestors' dramatic action implicated Pinney, Tobin and all those British merchants who had made their historic fortunes at the expense of enslaved humans. Reigniting the memory of just how much of our nation was built on the backs of others encourages us to look anew at our architectural and civic heritage, and how much of our built environment is controversial or contested. All of this helps us to think more about not just *why* but *how* Britain's buildings were conceived and created. Which often brings us to some very sobering conclusions.

15

BRIGHTON PAVILION, SUSSEX

BEGUN 1783, REMODELLED FROM 1815

The Prince Regent's Bizarre Seaside Confection: making royal patronage fun

Brighton Pavilion, originally built on the Sussex coast as a modest, classical retreat in the years after 1783, was from 1815 remodelled by architect John Nash and an outstanding team of interior designers as a capricious orientalist fantasy, a retreat in which the heir to the throne and his mistresses could ignore the staunch, puritanical formality of the Court of St James's and indulge their passions for food, drink, companionship, sex – and fun.

Nash's Brighton Pavilion did not initiate a revivalist style; nor did its fairy-tale domes inspire a new generation of Indo-Chinese decorators. Its eclectic elevations and indulgent interiors lacked even the neo-Mogul rigour of S. P. Cockerell's Raj retirement home at Sezincote, Gloucestershire, of 1803–5. However, the Pavilion certainly helped to inaugurate the nineteenth-century fashion for mixing and matching objects and treatments from different periods

▷ *Even though its domes and minarets seem as insubstantial as a wedding cake, the bravura roofscape of Nash's post-1815 Brighton Pavilion was created through an innovative use of structural cast iron.*

and styles. Rejecting the classical straitjacket of the Georgians, the Pavilion showed Britons that entertainment and architecture were not incompatible. Moreover, the construction of Nash's building, supported as it was by a strong core of cast iron, looked not to Britain's imperial past but to a bright future of technological potential.

The Prince Regent

Prince George of Hanover, Prince of Wales from 1762, Prince Regent from 1811 and King George IV from 1820 to 1830, gave his name to an era and a style. Yet during his regency and reign, the British monarchy became irrelevant to most Britons, and George's personal exploits – from his affairs to his disastrous marriage to the construction of an exotic retreat at Brighton – a national joke.

It is often assumed that the monarchy has always been secure in its position at the top of the hierarchical pyramid that is British society. However, the early nineteenth century, a time of falling dynasties and royal assassinations, was an uncertain time for the royal families of Europe – not excepting the House of Hanover. The fact that Britain's monarchy survived these turbulent times at all was partly due to Britons' sense of humour, to the strength of the unwritten yet helpfully flexible British constitution, and ultimately to the talent shown by an obscure German princeling for making Britain's royalty relevant once more.

On paper, Prince George was one of the most gifted members of the royal family ever to have sat on the throne. The prince had a notable eye for paintings, sculpture and architecture; and, alas, also for women. He could be charming and considerate; he was a talented musician and had an ear for languages; and he was possessed of an innate fashion sense, helping during the 1790s and 1800s to make London *the* global centre for men's tailoring. His eclecticism in art, architecture and the decorative arts, as exemplified at his Brighton Pavilion, was in the van of taste, and he helped to make the Regency era the first truly eclectic age in architecture and the decorative arts – anticipating by several decades the Victorians' love of mix-and-match. He was the greatest ever royal builder, erecting a stunning set of royal buildings which today constitute the core of the royal family's official residences. At Brighton and elsewhere he tried, via his patronage of the arts, to manufacture an image to eclipse that of his father, George III. Yet he consistently failed to achieve the status of 'Patriot King' enjoyed in his middle years by George III – at least before the latter's final descent into madness after 1811. George IV liked to picture himself as a military hero; yet the nearest he ever got to a continental battlefield was Brighton Beach.

Lecturing in America on the subject of the Hanoverian monarchs in the mid-1850s, the celebrated English novelist William Makepeace Thackeray – born in Calcutta in 1811, the year Prince George of Wales had attained his regency – regaled his audiences with a description of the prince having dressed 'in every kind of uniform and every possible court-dress – in long fair hair, with powder, with and without a pig-tail – in every conceivable cocked-hat – in dragoon uniform – in Windsor uniform – in a field-marshal's clothes – in a Scotch kilt and tartans, with dirk and claymore (a stupendous figure) – in a frogged frock-coat with a fur collar and tight breeches and silk stockings – in wigs of every colour, fair, brown and black'. Thackeray's opinions were largely derived from the prints and pictures of thirty and forty years before; his derision of George's Scottish costume of 1822, for example, is clearly inspired by David Wilkie's decidedly uncomfortable full-length portrait of 1829. (Wilkie himself privately admitted that George merely looked 'like a great sausage stuffed into the covering'.) However, as early as 1782 George's friend Georgiana, Duchess of Devonshire, observed that the prince was 'fond of dress even to a tawdry degree [and that] his person, his dress and the admiration he has met... from women take up his thoughts chiefly'.

From his earliest years George's principal concern had been how he appeared, as communicated to his subjects by the media of paint, print and clothes. In this recognition of the importance of image and iconography, he can perhaps be regarded as the first truly 'modern' monarch. His self-image was influenced by his friends and advisers, shaped by his awareness of the crucial role fashion could play in updating and elevating the reputation of the royal family, and bolstered by the heroic portraits of himself that he commissioned from artists and sculptors. Art, architecture and the decorative arts were all enlisted to create a picture of an heir to the throne who was virile, martial and – in contrast to his parents – at the cutting edge of fashion and taste. Unfortunately, as George grew older, his subjects increasingly recognised that this carefully crafted image was becoming ever more distanced from reality.

As his friends were chosen in order to appal his frugal father, George III, so George's excessive expenditure on fashion was an implied rebuke to a king whose creation of the staid, red and blue court 'Windsor uniform' represented the high point of his foray into the world of fashion. George had already as a young man discovered the imposing and slimming effects that dark colours

281

and subtle cuts could achieve, as seen in Stubbs's fine equestrian portrait of 1791, in which the prince is depicted wearing a long, dark blue coat with buff breeches – the colours of the Foxite Whig opposition (which were themselves borrowed from the uniforms of George Washington's American revolutionaries). Indeed, George was still wearing the same figure-reducing combination a decade later.

Following his first meeting with George Brummell in 1794, however, the prince's enthusiasm for the cut and colour of his clothes became all-consuming. On Brummell's advice, George followed the lead of the 5th Duke of Bedford in 1795 and discarded his powdered wig for natural, cropped (though waxed) hair, in what was both a gesture of defiance towards the Pitt government his father backed so strongly – framed as a protest against Pitt's new tax on hair powder – and at the same time a rejection of the conventional dress of his father's staid and dull court. Despite his daring innovation, however, George was unfairly depicted by cartoonists as wearing an old-fashioned powdered wig until well into his regency.

With their deliberate austerity, understated cuts and sober, dark colours, Brummell's innovations – and George's patronage – had by 1820 made London the global epicentre of men's fashion. Brummellesque clothes defined a quintessential Englishness; they did not advertise wealth and privilege, but instead subtly implied taste and discretion. Not everything was left to nature, however. George's coats were often padded at the front to suggest a full musculature and a slim waist. And, while Brummell did not actually invent the neckcloth, his introduction of the clever combination of a very high, starched collar which almost touched the ears with a soft neckcloth below was soon being widely mimicked – not least by the prince himself, who used it to hide his multiplying chins.

Below the waist, George adopted Brummell's novel abandonment of traditional knee breeches. The prince's legs were thereafter slimmed by a bewildering variety of pantaloons (some of which included feet: the ancestor of today's tights) and their looser-fitting cousins, trousers. Trousers could vary considerably in width – from thigh-hugging to capacious 'Cossack' trousers, after the Russian specialist cavalry. Thus was the modern concept of trousers born, and the foundations laid for the ubiquitous modern suit.

Never in modern times has a sovereign died so unlamented as George IV. Robert Huish's venomous biography of 1830–31 declared of the late king, who had died in June 1830, that 'with a personal income exceeding the national revenue of a third-rate power, there appeared to be no limit to his desires, nor any restraint to his profusion'. Rejecting the argument that 'his example was too secluded to operate dangerously on the manners of the people', Huish claimed instead that George IV had contributed more 'to the demoralisation of society than any prince recorded in the pages of history'. George's palaces – principally Carlton House, Brighton Pavilion, Windsor Castle and Buckingham Palace – had, Huish insisted, been erected 'at the expense of a people already overwhelmed by a severe, unjust and unequal taxation'. To those who pointed to the architectural achievement represented by George's eclectic array of royal residences, Huish had a stinging rebuke:

> The reign of George IV has been called a splendid reign – and justly so, if the Pimlico Palace, the [castle] of Windsor, the nicknacks of the Pavilion, the fleet on Virginia Water, the elegant jumble of the royal cottage, and the soi-disant great public improvements, had either been promoted or encouraged by the King for the happiness of the people.

Having begun his account with the ominous statement that 'there is scarcely a monarch... whose private and public life abounds with more extraordinary and interesting incidents than that of George IV', Huish subsequently judged that George IV's regency and reign had been a tragically missed opportunity. While the prince could have 'exhibit[ed] himself at one time a Colossus of virtue, standing upon an eminence which few would essay to reach' and as 'sovereign of the greatest and most civilised nation of the world', he was more generally perceived to be a figure happy to 'sink into an abyss of profligacy characteristic of the most degenerate reprobate'. Equally dismaying for Huish was the elderly George IV's admiration for the absolutism of 'continental systems' – a trait which many Whigs were also to discern in his brother, King William IV, in 1834. Huish's grim conclusion was that the late king would never 'demand honour from mankind... neither as a public nor private individual', and that 'If posterity award approbation to his memory, the task of discovering the grounds on which it is to rest may be well left to their labour and ingenuity'.

Even *The Times* joined in. In its official obituary of 28 June 1830, the newspaper castigated not only George IV's 'most reckless, unceasing and unbounded prodigality' but in particular 'the tawdry childishness of Carlton House and the mountebank Pavilion'.

The Chinaman

After George's death it was invariably his 'Hindu-Chinese' Pavilion at Brighton which came in for most criticism. China was then seen popularly in Britain as a shorthand for corruption, excess, indolence and drug-taking, a habit the British were callously to exploit later in the nineteenth century. The British public were not to know that George himself actually grew increasingly dependent on laudanum, which he usually washed down with a glass of cherry brandy.

The drug-addled Chinaman was a trope which already had much popular currency by 1815. Samuel Taylor Coleridge wrote *Kubla Khan*, his opium-fuelled poem about Kublai Khan's summer palace Xanadu, in 1797 and published it in 1816, when Nash's Chinese makeover of the Pavilion had begun in earnest. As historian Kara Blakeley has observed:

> Coleridge describes the fantastical, edenic pleasure grounds of Kublai Khan, which find parallels to what was known of contemporary China; namely, Qianlong's (and then Jiaqing's) summer palace at Jehol. The conflation of opiates, pleasure grounds, and imperial grandiosity characterises George IV's rule and his architectural magnum opus much more closely than quaint Rococo willows could have.

As a result, the Chinese decoration of the Pavilion was used by printmakers and poets alike as an easily recognisable shorthand by which to express the popular view of an increasingly remote, reclusive and self-indulgent king. Associating George with the purported stupefaction and detachment of the typical Chinese mandarin was a common satirical image in the years after the reinvention of the Pavilion from 1815. Popular prints portrayed the regent as an obese Chinaman, an identity that referenced his Brighton Pavilion retreat to imply inordinate excess in food, fashion and sex, and the alcoholic stupor of a regent who was increasingly distant from his subjects and was kept amused by a succession of mistresses and court cronies.

Thankfully – at least for those devotees of the British constitutional

◁ *The Prince Regent portrayed in an unconvincingly martial guise by the incomparable Thomas Lawrence in 1815.*

285

monarchy – George's relevance to British society and British politics had by the time of his death become quite peripheral. The Prince Regent had clearly not, as J. B. Trotter had piously hoped in 1811, metamorphosed into 'a great king – the lover of his people – the protector of liberty and defender of the laws – as bright, if not brighter, than any of his predecessors'. Nor, on the other hand, was he popularly regarded as a menace to the nation's constitutional equanimity – as was, for example, his former friend Charles X of France, who was ejected from his throne two months after George's demise. Instead, George IV was, by the time of his death, generally viewed by his subjects as little more than an entertaining sideshow – if a somewhat expensive one.

As prince, regent and king, George IV had striven to fashion an idealised image of himself that increasingly bore little relation to reality. His glittering collections and over-ambitious building programmes, the colourful nationalist pageants he devised for his coronation and his visit to Edinburgh of 1822, his fascination with soldiering and with the trappings and symbols of military success – all testified to his seemingly inexhaustible desire to promote himself to a place in the nation's hearts which his conduct had signally failed to win. Depressed by his failure to reinvent himself, in his later years the ailing king simply withdrew into a fantasy world of laudanum and chinoiserie.

It is sad that one of the most gifted of British monarchs was, by the time of his death, also one of the most despised. George IV's undoubted charm, his evident wit, his innate aesthetic sense, his enthusiasm and his imagination ultimately left him insufficiently equipped to rise to the challenge of a nation daily growing in self-confidence and wealth. His self-indulgence and short attention span, together with his evident ability to abandon political principles and to forget friendships with barely a backward glance, won him few encomiums after his death.

One obituary in the *Westminster Review* attested, 'At an age when generous feelings are usually predominant, we find him absorbed by an all-engrossing selfishness; not merely careless of the feelings of others, but indulging in wanton cruelty.' The obituarist's subsequent comment that 'George IV was essentially a lover of personal ease', and that 'during the later years of his life, a quiet indulgence of certain sensual enjoyments seemed the sole object of his existence' is difficult to fault.

To George IV, everything revolved around his own whims and desires; if these altered, so the attitudes and actions of his friends, his household and his government were expected to follow suit. Notwithstanding the king's incontrovertible charm, this major failing was to exasperate even his political supporters. In 1829, by which time his former admiration for George had wilted in the light of what he saw as the king's feeble resistance to the passage of the Catholic Emancipation Bill, Charles Greville put his finger on it: 'He has a sort of capricious good-nature, arising however out of no good principle or good feeling, but which is of use to him, as it cancels in a moment.' Greville concluded that 'a more contemptible, cowardly, selfish, unfeeling dog does not exist'.

The artist Thomas Phillips also testified to George's tendency to forget or dismiss obligations and his inability, despite his obvious natural intelligence, to concentrate on any matter or person for a reasonable length of time:

> [The Prince of Wales] is influenced by caprice, and has no steadiness... He has the power of giving a proper answer to whoever addresses him upon any subject, but nothing fixes him. The person who last spoke to him makes an apparent impression, but it is gone when another person or subject comes before him, and his Taylor, or Bootmaker will occupy his mind to the doing away [with] any other consideration to which his attention might before have been drawn.

Revealingly, much of what George IV had striven to create was demolished or dispersed immediately after his death. In 1965 the royal historian Sir Owen Morshead observed that 'George IV had melted like a snowman: only the clothes remained – and their dispersal at public auction created a nine days' wonder'. The late king's cooks and his French servants were immediately dismissed by William IV, who would 'have none but English'. William, with scant regard for technological innovation and an innate suspicion of any of his brother's so-called 'improvements', also ripped out all the gaslights and gas pipes that had been so recently and laboriously installed at Windsor Castle at George's behest. One day in August 1830, Charles Greville and some of his friends drove their carriage along what had, only weeks before, been a private road bisecting Windsor Great Park, and gleefully imagined that the ghost of George IV 'must have been indignant at seeing us... scampering all about his most secret recesses'.

Huish's great contemporary William Cobbett was of much the same opinion. His biography of George IV warned future parliaments against sanctioning such self-centred and wanton excesses as George had been allowed to perpetrate:

When we behold such mighty and fatal effects, arising... from the mortifi-
cation, the caprice, or the antipathy, from the mere selfish passions, and,
almost, from the animal feelings and propensies of one single man...
must we not be senseless indeed, must we not be something approaching to brutes, if we do not seek for some means of protecting ourselves
against the like in future?

Cobbett's proto-republicanism climaxed in his magisterial conclusion:
'England never appeared little in the eyes of the world', he declaimed, 'till the
time of this Big sovereign.'

Although her conclusions were not as damning as Cobbett's, the diarist
Princess Lieven found George's character similarly wanting. 'Full of vanity' and
able to be 'flattered at will', the late king was, in her opinion, ultimately 'Weary
of all the joys of life, having only taste, and not one true sentiment'. The princess was by no means alone in her judgement. Junior minister (and future prime
minister) Lord Aberdeen acknowledged sadly in 1829 that his sovereign had
'no idea of what a King of England ought to do'. And Charles Greville was far
more vehement in his appraisal of the king's 'littleness of... character'. His vices
and weaknesses were, Greville adjudged after close inspection of the sovereign,
'of the lowest and most contemptible order'; his court was fuelled by 'every
base, low and unmanly propensity, with selfishness, avarice, and a life of petty
intrigue and mystery'.

Officialdom preferred to avoid the open criticism favoured by authors
such as Huish and Cobbett by taking refuge in modest praise of George's
achievements in the visual arts. Another future Tory prime minister, Robert
Peel, studiously avoiding any comment on the deceased monarch's character,
instead declared after George IV's death that the king was 'universally admitted to be the greatest patron the arts had ever had in this country'.

Creating the Pavilion

The royal project which inevitably caught the eye of the Regency satirists
most often was Brighton Pavilion. Ostensibly an exotic, wedding-cake fantasy
built for an increasingly out-of-touch prince, Brighton Pavilion was actually a
testimony to stylistic plurality and technological experimentation. Its revolutionary iron framing has enabled its domes and minarets to survive into
the modern era as a reflection of British technological advances as well as the

celebrated British sense of humour. This is not, however, how it was generally viewed in the nineteenth century.

The Pavilion began life as a cool, sophisticated seaside villa, built in a restrained neoclassical idiom by Henry Holland in 1783. In that year, in which the twenty-one-year-old prince came of age, George visited what was then the tiny fishing village of Brighthelmstone in the company of his uncle, the notoriously dissolute Duke of Cumberland. Both were seeking escape from the stultifyingly dull, straitjacketed and morally repressed court of George III. Cumberland suggested that the restless prince could create his own alternative court there, one where mistresses, gambling and drinking would all be permissible. At Brighton he could live with his then mistress, the divorced Catholic Maria Fitzherbert, far from the disapproving mutterings of court or government. From 1785 George hired the most fashionable neoclassical architect of the day, Henry Holland, to create a small, exquisite classical villa which would not have looked out of place in Paris or Rome. To ensure that His Majesty's Treasury could not interfere in the project, it was sublet to the prince's pastry-cook-cum-factotum, Louis Weltje, who only leased it back to the prince on its completion in 1793.

George had a notoriously short attention span when it came to buildings and pictures – and, indeed, women. Tiring of his chaste villa, he invited Holland to reclad his neoclassical pavilion in a 'Chinese' idiom, a request which must have appalled the architect and may have led to his subsequent break with the prince. After Holland had stormed out, work orientalising the villa continued under his nephew, P. R. Robinson. Meanwhile, architect William Porden was hired to assist with this work as well as to build a large new 'Hindu' riding school and stable block, which dwarfed and outshone the neighbouring villa. The landscape designer Humphry Repton thought Porden's structure resembled 'rather a Turkish mosque than the buildings of Hindustan', but most visitors were impressed that such a lavish facility had been built just for horses.

George wanted more, however. In 1815, and now able to access government funding as Prince Regent, he hired his new architectural protégé, John Nash, to recommence the transformation of the Pavilion. While the carcass of Holland's pavilion was retained, inside and outside the building was redecorated in an idiom loosely borrowed from Thomas and William Daniell's *Oriental Scenery*, a compendium of views of India published from 1795 and which Nash borrowed from the Carlton House library in 1815. Neither Nash's 'Hindu' motifs nor the materials he used were intended to be authentically 'oriental'. Holland's

glazed cream mathematical tiles were replaced by eccentric oriental fantasies executed in honey-coloured stucco or, in the case of the finial and surrounds, in Bath stone.

Beneath these playful features, however, lurked some remarkably advanced technology. Much of the building, including its bizarre onion domes, was, as Porden's stables had been, framed internally in cast iron. This was an innovation that was years ahead of its time, one which gave great structural strength to what was seemingly a frail jumble of oversized motifs. While it looked like a fragile confection, the Pavilion was actually one of the most advanced buildings of its era. Even the main staircase was made of cast iron, its balusters moulded by the resourceful local ironworker William Stark to resemble Chinese bamboo. And its kitchen, whose high clerestory was supported by ostensibly comical iron-and-copper 'palm trees', was the most innovative cooking cockpit of the day, incorporating all the latest technology, including Stark's novel 'steam table', designed to keep the prince's dishes warm.

Holland's pavilion interior was redecorated and refurnished by the firms of Frederick Crace and Robert Jones in a bizarre mix of Chinese, Indian and Gothic elements, all stuffed into Holland's classical shell. The entrance hall, for example, retained Holland's classical proportions but now featured a dado of 'Chinese' fretwork, a Gothic-Chinese cornice, pale green dragons expertly imagined by Crace's craftsmen and a classical chimneypiece with applied chinoiserie motifs. In the Saloon, Jones created an unorthodox but oddly successful synthesis of French empire and 'Indian', with added allusions to two of the prince's favourite motifs: the Garter star and the sunflower of Louis XIV. The dramatic Music Room, with its massive red and yellow panels of Chinese scenes, its huge, silvered flying dragons supporting the silk drapery and spectacular lotus-flower lamps and a domed ceiling encased in plaster cockleshells gilded in four subtly different shades of gold leaf, was designed to be seen at its best at night. The Banqueting Room was – appropriately, given George's love of food and drink – even more glitteringly ostentatious than the Music Room. The stupendous, one-ton central chandelier, with its six lotus-flower lamps issuing from the mouths of silvered dragons, was itself suspended from a single winged dragon, from whose jaws protruded an alarmingly realistic red

◁ *The sumptuous Banqueting Room at Brighton Pavilion: created by Robert Jones from John Nash's architectural shell after 1815, this was designed to be the epicentre of the Prince Regent's lavish seaside retreat.*

291

tongue and above which spread a copper-leaved plantain tree. The smaller lotus-lamps were carried by four 'F'eng' birds, lifted from Chinese mythology; below them stood sentinel four great torchères of Spode porcelain coloured in a deep blue which imitated that of the old Sèvres factory of *ancien régime* France. The result was one of the most breathtaking interiors of Europe, which alternately entranced and appalled visitors.

An essential counterpoint to the Banqueting Room was the nearby kitchen. Here George IV installed the greatest chef of the age, Marie-Antoine Carême, at the epicentre of a palace whose main function was the celebration of food and drink and which, George hoped, would become the envy of Europe. It was one of most advanced kitchens in the world: its tall, glazed clerestory aided dispersal of fumes and heat; its copper awnings drew smells from the ranges; its smoke-powered and clockwork jacks turned joints of meat (obviating the need for those traditional power sources, dogs and small boys).

Carême, recruited in 1816, had previously worked for Napoleon – a résumé which greatly appealed to the Prince Regent – and is now considered one of the first internationally renowned celebrity chefs. In the Pavilion's kitchen he created 100-dish dinners for George IV which hugely impressed the royal guests. Yet Carême found the English climate depressing, his English fellow cooks ignorant and the English preference for 'the roasts of beef, mutton and lamb [and] the various meats cooked in salt water' pitiable. He left Brighton abruptly in 1818 to work for Tsar Alexander I in St Petersburg and James Mayer Rothschild in Paris.

The Pavilion showed that, while Britons could laugh at themselves, even the most frivolous architectural statement was, in Regency Britain, underpinned by enviable technological strength. It also said much about Britain's complicated relationship with the Far East. Many decorative historians have suggested that George IV envied the absolutism of China. Kara Blakeley has noted that:

> Like the French king that George IV so admired – Louis XVI – the Chinese emperor would have had absolute power over his dominion. The British prince's Chinese interiors may signify the reverence that he craved in his own land, especially following the French Revolution. Indeed, George IV did not shy away from creating his seaside palace in the image of Versailles or Yuanmingyuan. Within his own realm, the Chinese emperor was permitted the grandiosity that George IV was denied in his. By bedecking

his interiors in a bombastic chinois style, George's persona is conflated with that of the emperor.

Local observers, however, were more impressed with the glitz and glitter of the Pavilion's interiors than with any putative political allegory. In 1823, the year that Nash's interiors were finally completed, local author Richard Sickelmore commented:

> Splendour of light and colour, with a natural and effective disposition of shade, appear to have been a grand and successful aim of this room; and art, guided by judgment, lively and polished taste, has availed itself of all sorts of materials to attain the end proposed. The splendid number of glossy jars of blue porcelain, well appropriated and judiciously placed, contribute magnificently to this effect; they excel, in richness and brilliancy, whatever the kind we have before seen, foreign or native.

Sickelmore was understandably impressed with the fabulous dragon chandelier in the Banqueting Room: 'The lilies, when illuminated, dart their copious and vivid rays through the multiplied and sparkling tints, and influence connected objects to the semblance of rubies, pearls, glittering brilliants, and shining gold – creating, if the figure may be allowed, in mid-air, a diamond blaze. Its effect is magical: it enchants the senses, and excites, as it were, a feeling of spell-bound admiration in all.' Most would agree with this judgement today. Far more recently, the Pavilion's historian David Beevers has observed, 'The sheer scale, the opulence of furnishings, the richness of colour, and the drama of plunging chandeliers and rearing dragons, evoke a "China" of imperial extravagance and self-indulgence – something quite different from the gently whimsical realm of mid-Georgian rococo.'

The Pavilion becomes an embarrassment

As his short reign progressed, George IV grew ever more reclusive, relying on his mistress and his inner circle of courtiers to provide him with his daily amusement. He failed to open parliament, one of the basic requirements of a British sovereign, on a number of occasions, and was rarely seen in public. When he did go to Brighton, he found that the locals could get far too close to his rooms for his liking. As a result, he did not return there after 1827.

△ *Jones's Banqueting Room pictured in John Nash's* Views of the Royal Pavilion *at Brighton of 1826, just as George IV was tiring of the building.*

After George IV's death, his brother, now King William IV, expressed his fondness for the Pavilion. But after her accession in 1837, George and William's niece, now crowned Queen Victoria, found both the Pavilion and the natives of Brighton far too vulgar for her taste. On her last visit there, in February 1845, she complained that 'the people here are very indiscreet and troublesome here really, which makes this place quite a prison'. From 1846 she and Prince Albert began systematically to strip the building of its contents. In 1847–8, 143 vanloads containing furniture, decorative woodwork, clocks, the Music Room organ, porcelain, chimneypieces and carpets were removed from the Pavilion to Buckingham Palace, Windsor Castle and Kensington Palace. The Pavilion's servants were dismissed and a sale of plants and garden implements was held. Even the building's copper bell-wire was pulled out, the Chinese wallpaper torn off and skirting boards brutally removed. Seemingly content with its vandalism, the crown now proposed that the bare building be pulled down and the site sold, the profit being used for 'improving and enlarging...

Buckingham Palace'. In the face of this high-handed provocation, Brighton Corporation bravely bought the site for £53,000 in June 1850.

Once in possession of the Pavilion's mutilated carcass, Brighton Council hired the leading sculptor John Thomas to carve reproductions of the stolen chimneypieces. A replacement organ for the Music Room, guiltily donated by the queen, was then installed in 1851. Over the following years the Nash interiors were recreated and the Banqueting Room and its attendant kitchen re-equipped. In the ensuing decades Victoria did return some fixtures and furniture. More was returned by George V and Queen Mary in the 1920s after the Pavilion had, rather fittingly, served during the First World War as a hospital for wounded Indian soldiers. The eight magnificent Spode lamps were returned by the royal family in 1920 while a decade later Queen Mary bought a grand piano for the Music Room of the same make and date as the one which had originally been placed there. A splendid set of copperware bearing the Duke of Wellington's crest was transferred to the kitchen from Apsley House, the duke's home in London, in the 1950s.

In place of the exotic fantasy of Brighton Pavilion, Victoria and Albert began to build themselves a private retreat on the far more secluded Isle of Wight. Osborne House, begun in 1845 and designed largely by Prince Albert himself, working with the builder Thomas Cubitt, was conceived as an exercise in a stark and restrained Italianate idiom that was far removed from the gaudy domes and dragons of Brighton Pavilion. It exemplified Victoria's and particularly Albert's reconfiguring of the British monarchy as a devoted family at the heart of Europe. Gone were the gaudiness, scandal and exoticism of George IV's notorious inner circle: mistresses were now superseded by an ostensibly loving royal couple with a growing brood of children, whose marriages were designed to populate the courts of Europe. Albert reinvented the British monarchy as a middle-class institution with the same morals, ambitions and work ethic as most of its subjects. As Albert's biographer Andrew Wilson has commented, Albert's goal at Osborne was to make 'an eclectic and distinctive statement of his domesticated European aesthetic'. In his example, Albert put the royal family back at the heart of the nation. As the subtitle of Wilson's life of Albert has it, he really was 'The Man Who Saved the Monarchy'.

The spirit reawakens

Almost a century after Victoria and Albert left Brighton for the last time, in

June 1944 a British army officer, Lieutenant Rex Whistler, painted a brilliant yet highly satirical picture on the wall of the officers' mess in Brighton where he was stationed before being shipped out to Normandy in the aftermath of D-Day. *HRH The Prince Regent Awakening the Spirit of Brighton* was not a composition which found favour with many Brightonians at the time. Whistler depicted a predatory, cartoonish Prince George about to ravish a naked maiden on Brighton beach. However, it neatly captured both the enduring cinematic appeal of George IV and the sexual and decorative licence epitomised by his Pavilion. In the grey post-war years of rationing and restraint the mural became increasingly popular. Brighton Council transferred it to the Pavilion in April 1946, and although for years it was hidden away in the tearoom, today it hangs in pride of place on the ground floor. Whistler himself, though, was never to enjoy its reception. Fighting with the Guards Armoured Division in Normandy after D-Day, he was killed by a mortar round on 18 July 1944 as he left his tank to help his comrades.

Unsurprisingly, many filmmakers of the twentieth century have turned to the Pavilion and to its colourful patron's life for inspiration, finding in the Prince Regent's flair and faults a fitting allegory for Britons' complicated relationship with their royal family. As a result, George IV has been used as a subject for film more than any other British sovereign – more than Henry VIII, Elizabeth I and Queen Victoria – having appeared as a central character in twenty-six English-language films since 1913. Historically, George's controversial and racy life has engaged the modern British public more than the courts of Elizabethan or Victorian England.

In 1948 Cecil Parker starred as the Prince Regent in the period drama *The First Gentleman*, a film adapted by director Alberto Cavalcanti from the 1945 play by Norman Ginsbury which was almost entirely shot inside and outside the Pavilion. *Time* magazine's visiting critic believed that it was incongruous that post-war Britain, which had just elected a Labour government by a landslide, was flocking to see a story about 'one of its most dissolute and luxury-loving monarchs, a bully, a wit and a sot'. Yet *Time* missed the point: it was exactly that distance and context which allowed the British public, who still vividly remembered the pre-war abdication of Edward VIII, to be cheerfully realistic about the royal family. Channelling the Regency cartoons of Robert Heath, Cecil Parker (who was to die in Brighton in 1971) played George IV dressed as a Chinese emperor.

The Pavilion itself also starred in the bizarre, Georgette Heyer-ish Hollywood fantasy *On a Clear Day You Can See Forever* of 1970, which brought together one of the most unlikely movie casts ever assembled. International stars Barbra Streisand, Yves Montand, Jack Nicholson and Bob Newhart rubbed shoulders with British film stalwarts such as Roy Kinnear (as the Prince Regent), John Le Mesurier and, as Streisand's mother, none other than the classic British character actor and comedian Irene Handl. The scene in which Streisand and Handl meet in the Pavilion is one of the most unlikely in cinema history. Its incongruity and sheer kitsch, though, would doubtless have appealed to George IV.

16

THE BRITON'S PROTECTION, MANCHESTER

C.1810

Beer, Protest and the British Pub

The Briton's Protection, crammed as it is into a hectically busy corner of post-industrial Manchester, appears to casual visitors to be a fine example of the nation's much-cherished legacy of historic public houses. Both the external elevations (modernised in the 1930s) and the ground-floor bars seem to support that theory. Built during the Regency period, at a time when the British brewing industry was expanding confidently and exponentially, the building was one of a new generation of public houses purpose-built to serve the burgeoning new industrial population.

However, if you venture upstairs you will see that the Briton's Protection is not just a living memorial to the success of the brewing industry and the triumph of British beer. For here you will find a set of twentieth-century murals commemorating the calamitous event which put not just the pub and the city of Manchester on the map, but which significantly advanced the causes of both parliamentary and, ultimately, army reform.

The British pub

Along with the railway station and the industrial mill, the pub is perhaps the most characteristically British building type of the nineteenth century. The term 'public house' denoted a building open to the public for refreshment. But the British pub did far more than serve spirits and ale (and, since the sixteenth century, beer: ale with hops added as a preservative). The pub defined communities and their built environments; it acted as a social hub and a centre for development and regeneration; it provided a sense of identity, of belonging and of continuity in an ever-changing and increasingly industrialised, automated and impersonal environment. The British pub was, and is, so much more than somewhere to have a pint: it was, and is, the beating heart of the city, town or neighbourhood, a place that defines British identity and a sense of place as well as providing a vehicle for relaxation, renewal and revitalisation.

The pub originated from Georgian coaching inns and hotels, as well as from private houses selling beer for consumption off the premises and from shops which acted as a combination of an 'on' and 'off-licence' – beer sales for drinking on or off the premises, which were subject to different rates of tax. Beer was not always the pub's drink of choice, however: by 1700 beer was taxed more heavily than gin, which was now being promoted as a patriotic drink at a time when, during the French wars, brandy imports were prohibited. But the peace of 1713 and the general desire to promote beer as a healthy alternative to insidious gin or imported tea prompted an immense expansion of the beer trade and the pub network in the mid-eighteenth century. This was the age in which Britain's great national breweries were founded: the Stag Brewery (later Watneys) in London's Victoria in 1715; Whitbread in the City of London in 1742; Worthington in Burton-on-Trent, brewing's capital, in 1760; Charrington in London's Stepney in 1766; Bass (also in Burton) in 1777; and Courage in London's Bermondsey in 1787.

Nineteenth-century Britain was the great age of beer. To combat the rising tide of 'gin palaces' – large, modern buildings characterised by large, etched plate-glass windows designed to attract punters to their well-lit and welcoming interiors – the pub was dramatically updated in the early decades of the

◁ *The Briton's Protection today, defended from the ravages of Inner Manchester's road system by some shockingly inappropriate railings.*

century. Many of these new pubs appropriated some of the innovations daringly introduced by the gin palaces such as large areas of window glass, bar-counter service (prior to this, pubs had enjoyed table service, a custom inherited from the traditional inn or hotel) and counter handpumps, which had originally been devised, believe it or not, to dispense gin and which clearly made bar service far more speedy. In 1830 the Duke of Wellington's government attempted to supplant the popular gin palaces with the Sale of Beer Act, which abolished beer duty and made beer licences available to any householder who could pay two guineas. Spirits licences, meanwhile, still remained the responsibility of licensing magistrates. As a result, in 1831 31,000 new beer licences were issued, and over the next few years 24,000 new pubs were created. This explains why so many old British pubs are named after the royal family and other notables of the 1830s, such as George IV, William IV and Queen Adelaide – not forgetting the Duke of Wellington himself.

These early nineteenth-century pubs were typically built in a classical idiom and inside were usually of a two-bar plan: one public bar for the working classes and a slightly more comfortably furnished saloon bar for the better-off. The two bars shared the same central counter and, thanks to the great advances made in Georgian glass manufacture, were copiously glazed to admit as much natural light as possible. Most of these smaller city pubs were decorated with simple panelling, grained or painted brown, although by the 1890s larger pubs featured sanitary wipeable materials both above and below the dado rail: tiles, faience and gloss-painted embossed or 'sanitary' wallpapers.* On the floor would have been just bare wooden boards or, later in the century, ceramic tiles; floorcloths were simply too fragile for the everyday wear and tear of the average pub bar, linoleum was only patented in 1861, while pub carpets are very much a post-1945 novelty.

The beers which the late Regency and early Victorian pubgoers would have drunk would have been porter and, from the 1820s onwards, bitter. Porter had dominated the British beer trade since the early years of the eighteenth century: Henry Jackson's *An Essay on Bread* of 1758 noted that 'Beer, commonly call'd Porter, is almost become the universal cordial of the populace'. Its name comes from its first consumers: not just market porters but also 'fellowship porters' (stevedores) and 'ticket porters' (couriers). There were many variants

---

* At the Briton's Protection, though, these hygienic and glittering innovations had to wait for a refurbishment in the 1930s.

of porter. 'Stout' in the eighteenth century merely meant 'strong' and was not a term necessarily associated just with porter; in 1810, though, Guinness invented a 'stouter' kind of porter, 'Superior Porter' (later renamed 'Extra Stout'), and the name stuck. 'Mild' was just a weaker version of porter – though not necessarily as weak as its modern-day image would suggest: James Herbert's *The Art of Brewing* of 1871 cited the strength of a typical mild at a formidable 7 per cent.

The beer revolution

In 1817 industrial entrepreneur Daniel Wheeler took the principle of the new iron coffee-roasting machine and used it to kiln malt. The result was dark brown or black malts with few fermentable sugars – what were called 'patent malts' which proved ideal for brewing porter and stout. However, while Wheeler was perfecting his malt kiln a beer revolution had already begun.

Brewing at the great beer centres of Burton and London was heavily hit by the Napoleonic Wars. The number of breweries in Burton alone had decreased from thirteen to five by 1815. Sales picked up again after British soldiers and sailors returned from service on the Continent or at sea after Waterloo. Nevertheless, nervous brewers now sought new markets – and believed they had found one in the growing military and administrative population of British India. It was, however, difficult for them to ensure that their beer tasted as good on its arrival in India as when it left the banks of the Trent or the Thames. The best defences against the great length of the journey and the heat of the Indian Ocean sun were twofold: a high alcohol content of at least 6 per cent alcohol-by-volume and the beneficial preserving effect of hops.

The first brewer to attempt to meet these criteria was Londoner George Hodgson, whose 'India Ale' was stronger than 6 per cent and contained twice the hops of conventional beers. Hodgson, however, had both outreached his resources and alienated his contacts, and subsequently went bankrupt. Instead it was an established Burton brewer, Sam Allsopp, who perfected a viable 'India Pale Ale' or IPA for the Indian market in 1821. Well-hopped IPA was first sold in India 1822 and at home from 1827, though from the 1830s weaker versions of IPA designed for domestic consumption were being branded as 'pale ales' and sold in casks or bottled.

By 1830 Allsopp and his Burton rival Bass were together sending 6,000 barrels of Burton IPA to India. When Barlow and Ordish's magnificent train shed at St Pancras Station in London was begun in 1865, provision was made

△ Whitbread Brewery in Chiswell Street, Islington, London, pictured in 1792 by George Garrard.

for hundreds of hogsheads of Burton IPA – brought by the Midland Railway's trains directly from the breweries of Burton – to be stored under the train shed's false concourse floor.

IPA was an invention whose time had come. Bright, sparkling, amber-coloured IPAs and their weaker pale ale siblings looked far better when seen behind glass than murky stouts and porters, whose dark colour was, notoriously, often used to conceal a multitude of slops or additives. With the new, clear IPAs, any adulteration would be swiftly detected. Such beers benefitted from new advances in glass technology, which meant that by 1830 glass tankards became the rule rather than the exception in the pub while glass bottles were increasingly being used by the burgeoning 'off' trade. By the end of the nineteenth century pale ales and 'bitter' (effectively the same thing) had largely replaced porter in cities such as London and Manchester. Although in 1863 porter still accounted for 75 per cent of beer sales in London – porter's birthplace and traditional stronghold – by 1900 its market share had diminished to only 25 per cent. London's last porter-only brewery, Meux in Tottenham Court Road, converted to pale ales in 1872.

By the time Hodgson and Allsopp fomented the IPA revolution, one recently built Manchester pub was already there to take advantage of the new tastes in ale. And by the time Wellington's Beer Act was passed in 1830, this same pub already boasted an illustrious history, based on not one but two modest yet far-reaching revolutions.

Regency Manchester

By the time of George IV's death in 1830 Manchester had grown from a small Georgian town to become the nation's centre of cotton manufacture. The population of the city and its dependent towns, which had stood at only 10,000 in 1717, had already surpassed 100,000 by 1800. By the end of the nineteenth century it had reached well over two million.

Inevitably, though, unfettered industry took its toll on the city's environment. In 1814 the visiting Swiss industrialist Hans Caspar Escher vom Glas observed, 'In Manchester there is no sun and no dust. Here there is always a dense cloud of smoke to cover the sun while the light rain – which seldom lasts all day – turns the dust into a fine paste which makes it unnecessary to polish one's shoes.' In such a setting a local pub, whose welcome beers could slake the thirst and wash away the dirty air, was more necessary than ever.

One such Manchester haven was a canalside pub which, by 1820, was known as the Briton's Protection, a jingoistic name which presumably derived originally from the Napoleonic Wars but which after 1819 acquired more radical connotations. The pub is said to have been used as a recruiting centre for soldiers to fight Napoleon's armies in Spain, France and, latterly, the Low Countries, but no proof survives of this function. Built on Great Bridgewater Street, close to the Rochdale Canal – part of the Duke of Bridgewater's huge, pioneering canal network – it was originally intended to serve the canal's traffic and was built some time after this end of the Rochdale Canal opened in 1800. A date of 1806 has been suggested for its completion, while the pub's bicentenary was confidently celebrated in 2011. We do know, at least, that the pub was well established by 1821, the year that it appeared prominently in the *New*

Directory of Manchester & Salford. Whatever the precise date, the pub's large sash windows with narrow margin lights certainly identify it as a building of the Regency era.

In 1819 the pub's principal elevation, which faced north, still looked out at fields: a long strip of undeveloped land known as St Peter's Fields. Only the western end of Great Bridgewater Street had by then been built on. The high railway embankment just a hundred yards away which now completely blocks the pub's view north was not constructed until sixty years later, when the Midland Railway employed the celebrated engineer Sir John Fowler to design a grand new terminus, Manchester Central Station, nearby.

Peterloo

Recent research has suggested that the violent episode for which Regency Manchester was to become infamous took place not just at what, since 1907, has been called St Peter's Square. The latter space is an Edwardian creation, built on the site of James Wyatt's church of St Peter's, which is today a short walk from the Briton's Protection up Lower Mosley Street. The square certainly occupies much of the area in which the large, peaceable crowd gathered on 16 August 1819 to hear the radical speaker Henry Hunt advocate the three prime goals of the reform movement: universal male suffrage, annual elections and a secret ballot. However, St Peter's Fields then extended some way south-west from the church, along Lower Mosley Street right down to where the Briton's Protection stood. The modern association of the events of 10 March 1817 with the square probably owes more to the ornately Italianate icon that was formerly the city's Free Trade Hall, built on this site by Edward Walters in 1853–6. (For all its radical history, it is now a Radisson hotel.)

In truth, the events of that terrible day, which involved tens of thousands of people, probably extended across the whole of St Peter's Fields, right down to the banks of the Rochdale Canal. Accordingly, many of the panicked, fleeing attendees would have passed, and perhaps even taken refuge in, the Briton's Protection. The events of that day were to show just how illusory and ironic the new pub's brave name was.

Manchester, like most towns and cities in Britain, had suffered in the years of depression which followed the nation's victory at Waterloo. Warwick University historian Alison Morgan has observed that, after 1815:

△ *George Cruikshank's print of September 1819 deriding both the perpetrators of Peterloo and the reactionary response (top left) of the Prince Regent.*

Poor harvests and the reduction in demand for cotton had resulted in wage cuts. When their wages fell from thirty shillings to fifteen shillings a week, the spinners went on strike, but the masters refused to concede. The weavers' plight was even worse; their earnings were as low as four shillings and sixpence a week.

On 10 March 1817 between 40,000 and 60,000 people assembled at St Peter's Fields with the aim of marching to London to present a petition to the Prince Regent, alerting him to the terrible conditions then prevalent in Lancashire. As Morgan relates:

Unfortunately for the Blanketeers, as they were known, government spies had infiltrated them, and the authorities were well prepared: the Riot Act was read, the leaders arrested and the marchers attacked by the cavalry, leaving one person dead. It was a foreshadowing of events two years later.

Two years later another popular assembly at the Fields aimed merely to voice popular concerns, rather than to march south. Nevertheless, on this occasion the authorities' response was even more intemperate.

The 16th August 1819 was a bright, sunny Monday. A large gathering of around 60,000 people – 'half of Manchester', it was said – was expecting to hear Henry 'Orator' Hunt (supposedly nicknamed by the poet Robert Southey). It was not anticipated that they would cause any problems. Nevertheless, this time the city authorities were taking no chances:

> Between three or four hundred special constables had volunteered to police the event, many recruited within the previous forty-eight hours... Some residents had closed and even boarded up their shops in anticipation of trouble breaking out. Jeremiah Smith, headmaster of Manchester Grammar School, considered it prudent, for the safety of his scholars, to close the school for the entire day.

When Hunt ascended the hustings, the authorities took fright after just twenty minutes and ordered his arrest as well as that of his fellow 'leaders'. However, the local police were worried that their hundreds of constables would not be enough to disperse the crowd, and demanded that the Manchester and Salford Yeomanry cavalry be summoned. The *Manchester Chronicle* later feebly justified their actions with the wholly erroneous claims that:

> The rebellious nature of the meeting, its numbers and threatening aspect, the warlike insignia displayed, the order of march and military arrangements, many of the Reformers having shouldered large sticks and bludgeons as representative of muskets, coupled with the depositions of very many respectable inhabitants as to the consequences that must in their opinions unavoidable flow to lives and property from such an immense meeting... rendered it imperative to interfere.

Every one of these allegations was untrue. Nevertheless, the military were brought in, with the regular soldiers of the 15th Hussars joining the part-time cavalrymen of the Cheshire Yeomanry and the Manchester and Salford Yeomanry cavalry. The Yeomanry comprised gentlemen who had been recruited from the well-fed ranks of the county gentry or the city's conservative merchant class, all of whom were fervently opposed to reform. E. P. Thompson, celebrated historian of the English working class, claimed that the Yeomanry's subsequent panic 'was not (as has been suggested) the panic of bad horsemen hemmed in by a crowd. It was the panic of class hatred.' Hunt himself, who had believed that 'the orderly conduct of the people would deprive their enemies of all pretence whatever to interrupt their proceedings', looked up to see 'the Manchester Troop of Yeomanry... galloping into the field'. The crowd shouted and hissed at the hundred or so mounted troops of the Yeomanry, who clumsily drew their sabres in response. One of the special constables was knocked down and killed by the cavalry as they awkwardly advanced, an aggressive act which in turn precipitated stone-throwing from some of the onlookers. Within seconds the ill-disciplined Yeomanry, in Hunt's words, 'Charged amongst the people, sabring right and left, in all directions. Sparing neither age, sex nor rank.' There were cries for the protesters to 'stand fast' as the Yeomanry indiscriminately attacked men, women and children. Eyewitness Samuel Bamford later recalled that the Yeomanry were 'in confusion... [their] sabres were plied to hew a way through naked up-held hands, and defenseless heads; and then chopped limbs, and wound-gaping skulls were seen; and groans and cries were mingled with the din of that horrid confusion.'

Seeing the amateur horsemen of the Manchester and Salford Yeomanry in great difficulty, clearly out of their depth and, as their colonel testified afterwards, 'in conflict with the people', the 15th Hussars rode into the field to support them and clear the area, using the flats and sometimes the edges of their swords. Many in the crowd were killed or seriously wounded as a result of this action. Yet another eyewitness, Nathan Broadhurst, saw a Hussar officer berating Yeomanry troops for 'cutting at the people', shouting, 'Damn you, what do you mean by such work? For shame! Gentlemen, what are you about? The people cannot get away.'

Altogether some eighteen people were killed and more than 650 injured by the Yeomanry cavalry and the Hussars. As Morgan remarks, 'The true scale of the injuries will never be known as many victims were too scared or too poor to seek medical help. The relatively small number of fatalities is due to luck rather than the actions of the troops.'

The aftermath

The immediate response to these horrific events was predictable. Government-funded and conservative-leaning media lauded the military's actions and condemned the 'revolutionary' protestors. The *Gentleman's Magazine* of August 1819 expressed 'our strongest approbation of the conduct of unprincipled individuals, whose only object, under the specious names of patriotism, is to effect a Revolution, and aggrandize themselves on the ruins of their country'. In London, the increasingly reactionary Prince Regent expressed 'his great satisfaction' at the soldiers' 'prompt, decisive and efficient measures to preserve the public Tranquillity'. However, journalist John Tyas, who had been at St Peter's Fields and had been arrested at the height of the massacre, provided an invaluable eyewitness account which was published in *The Times* on 19 August: 'Not a brick-bat was thrown at [the Yeomanry] – not a pistol was fired at them during this period – all was quiet and orderly.' Once arrests had been made, he added, the Yeomanry had begun 'cutting most indiscriminately to the right and the left'.

Tyas's article helped stoke popular indignation at the cavalry's literally heavy-handed response. Just five days later a local newspaper, the *Manchester Observer*, christened the tragedy as 'Peter Loo', a civil coda to Wellington's famous victory of four years before, but this time the sabres and swords of British troops were used not on the French but, shamefully, on their fellow countrymen. This label was doubly ironic, in that the 15th Hussars had actually fought at Waterloo.

On 28 August the same paper published a treatment of the story in the style of a ghastly children's tale:

This is the field of Peter Loo.

These are the poor reformers who met, on the state of affairs to debate; in the field of Peter Loo.

These are the butchers, blood thirsty and bold, who cut, slash'd and maim'd young, defenceless and old. Who met, on the state of affairs to debate; in the field of Peter Loo...

Within ten days of the massacre, radical poet Percy Bysshe Shelley, in *The Masque of Anarchy*, was lauding the Manchester protestors and exhorting their fellow Britons to rise against the government:

Rise like lions after slumber
In unvanquishable number
Shake your chains to earth like dew

Which in sleep had fallen on you
Ye are many – they are few.

These resonant lines can still be read in Salford today on the walls of Transport House, the former regional headquarters of the Transport and General Workers' Union. In turn they inspired the opening words of the universal socialist anthem, 'The International', written by French revolutionary Eugène Pottier after the crushing of the Paris Commune in 1871: 'Arise ye workers from your slumbers/Arise ye prisoners of want...'

Evaluation

In the short term, Peterloo achieved little. The government of Lord Liverpool – which, in the view of historian Robert Reid, was 'the most repressive regime in modern British history... closer in spirit to that of the early years of the Third Reich than at any other time in history' – arrested and imprisoned most of the rally's leaders, including Hunt, for sedition. The progressive *Manchester Observer* was forced to close in 1821, though the same year also witnessed the foundation of the less overtly radical but still determinedly liberal *Manchester Guardian*, a newspaper which ensured that the torch of liberty would continue to shine in the city for decades to come. Parliamentary reform was not achieved for another thirteen years, when the Great Reform Act was passed by Lord Grey's Whig administration – the first Whig government for almost twenty years. Only then was the city of Manchester appropriately represented in parliament. Lord Liverpool's oppressive Corn Laws of 1815 – a measure devised to keep the price of British grain artificially high, thus protecting landowners' profits while increasing the price of bread – were not repealed until 1846. And universal male suffrage, one of the cornerstones of the Manchester protestors' manifesto, was not achieved in Britain until 1918.[*] In the ensuing decades, as Alison Morgan has commented, 'Whilst the Chartists continued to champion Peterloo in the 1830s and 1840s, it was not until 1951, when a mural was commissioned in the newly rebuilt Free Trade Hall, that Manchester provided a memorial to those who had died, although the mural painted by A. Sherwood Edwards, now on an upstairs corridor in the Radisson Hotel, depicts only the

---

[*]   That for women was not secured until 1948.

aftermath of the event.' It was, astonishingly, only in 2007 that interpretative panels were installed in St Peter's Square to explain the massacre.

However, Peterloo is today recognised, in E. P. Thompson's stentorian words from his ground-breaking *The Making of the English Working Class* of 1963, as 'without question a formative experience in British political and social history'. Thompson observed, 'Since the moral consensus of the nation outlawed the riding down and sabreing of an unarmed crowd, the corollary followed – that the right of the public meeting had been gained.' In Alison Morgan's view, the twenty minutes during which the cavalry regiments violently dispersed 60,000 peaceable protestors calling for reform resulted in one of the most significant events in modern British history. Its momentous nature was underscored with the production of a large number of books and articles – together with a major feature film, Mike Leigh's well-observed *Peterloo* – timed to mark the massacre's bicentenary in 2019.

The pub today

The Briton's Protection stands as a monument to the terrible events of 1819 and to the city of Manchester's resilience as it fought for its people and its right to be heard. It is also a fortunate survivor of the twentieth-century's decimation of Britain's irreplaceable legacy of historic pubs. The heyday of the British pub was more than a century ago, in the 1890s. Then pubs such as the Briton's Protection served as essential community centres. Women were now entering pubs as saloon and even public bars became more salubrious, while larger urban pubs often had small music halls or theatres attached. Everyone was happy to drink their troubles away. In 1895 the average annual consumption of beer was 31.2 gallons – that's 250 pints for every man, woman and child. (Let's hope that the children were not drinking too much beer, although 'small beer' of around 0.5–2 per cent alcohol-by-volume, or abv, was then still given to children and servants. Having been made with boiled water, small beer and indeed its full-bodied cousin was generally healthier than drinking water obtained locally from a nearby pump.)

In 1900 beer was far stronger than it is today. While twenty-first-century beers generally weigh in at 3 to 5 per cent abv, in 1900 the *average* strength of beer was 7 to 8 per cent. This is not to say that Victorian Britain was habitually drunk. Most working-class jobs involved a high degree of heavy manual labour; this, combined with the long distances that many had to walk to get to work, meant that turn-of-the-century Britons shrugged off the effects of alcohol far more easily than their more sedate and cosseted descendants.

The golden age of the pub came to an abrupt end in 1899, when many pubs were shut and increasing numbers of breweries closed. The reasons for this sudden downturn are still debated. Were the publicans, then largely independent traders holding premises leases from non-brewing landlords, becoming too ambitious in their refurbishments? Was the pub market saturated? Did the outbreak of the Second Boer War in 1899, bringing with it a number of unexpected reverses sustained by over-confident British armies, put a brake on general enjoyment?

Most likely the downturn in brewing was initially prompted by the actions of the larger brewers, who from the 1880s began to realise that there was more money to be made in property than in beer. Increasing numbers of individually leased pubs were bought up by the breweries, who then converted them into 'tied' houses, in which only their products could be sold. Those that rejected the suffocating embrace of the big boys were called 'free houses'. The new licensing laws passed by Lloyd George's temperance-leaning government in 1916, at the height of the First World War, were allegedly aimed at stopping munitions workers getting drunk (not that there was any concrete evidence that they were). In the event the new legislation merely consigned yet more independent pubs either to the scrap heap or to the grateful maw of the big brewers.

Between the two world wars the British pub witnessed something of a revival, as the taste for alcohol – in Britain, if not in Prohibition America – became respectable again. Many new pubs were built either in a determinedly historicist (usually Tudorbethan) idiom or, from 1930 onwards, in a Modernist-cum-Art Deco synthesis categorised by architectural critics as 'Moderne'. Some existing pubs were also modernised in a manner that reflected Moderne Britain, adopting the latest fashions and equipment while ensuring that wipeable, hygienic materials were used wherever possible. The Briton's Protection was, thankfully, one of these. Around 1930 its interior was comprehensively remodelled: a long, classical wooden bar counter was installed, new fireplaces with copper insets were installed, the passageways hung with glazed tiles, the toilets rebuilt with fashionable glazed white bricks and the ceiling of the front bar was hung with an ornate yet robust Lincrusta paper, coloured red and gold so as to disguise the cigarette smoke that would yellow paler coverings. Lincrusta was a heavy, embossed, linseed-based wall or ceiling covering which was durable and easily cleaned. It was invented in 1877 by Frederick Walton – the man who had introduced linoleum to the world in 1861 – and by the 1930s was being manufactured north of Manchester in Darwen.

Today the Briton's Protection looks much the same as it did in 1939. It was given the statutory protection of a Grade II listing in 1990, and is registered on the National Inventory of Historic Pub Interiors maintained by the Campaign for Real Ale (CAMRA). Since 2014 it has been independently run and, even after the Covid pandemic, is still a flourishing venue for the city and its visitors. Looking out from its front windows does not give you a grandstand view of the Peterloo Massacre, as it would have done on 16 August 1819. However, both inside and out, the building reinforces the peculiarly British nature of the enduring institution of the pub.

Surely the one key omission from Danny Boyle's spectacular and insightful London Olympics opening ceremony of 2012 was a nod to traditional British pubs. Buildings such as the Briton's Protection are as fundamental a part of the national landscape as industrial chimneys, heritage railways or merry morris dancers. Britain's invaluable historic pub stock does so much to shape and define our environment and our character. Yet today the British pub is at risk as never before. A decade before the Covid pandemic CAMRA's Pub Design Awards panel declared that more than a hundred pubs a month were currently being shut by their owners, heedless of the social and economic ramifications of such wanton vandalism. By 2017 this figure had been updated by CAMRA to twenty-seven a week.

The effect of Covid has been to pronounce a death sentence on hundreds more of Britain's pubs. Many of those that survived the pandemic have been bought and sold just to make a quick profit on the real estate they represent, while others are being deliberately run down in order to circumvent planning restrictions and enable them to be converted to more profitable residential use. But closing a much-cherished local robs a community of its heart and soul, as well as its economic lifeblood. The pub has been at the hub of our way of life for five centuries, and can continue to do so for another five. Its distinctive architectural form and prominent site invariably make it one of the best-loved and most easily recognised of Britain's historic building types: one that serves to define our town centres and villages both aesthetically and socially. When so many things about our daily lives are changing, surely it is even more important than ever that we hang on to what we hold dear: to what has shaped our past, sculpted our identity and can help define our future.

17

THE ROYAL WILLIAM YARD, PLYMOUTH

1826–35

After the Navy: repurposing the nation's industrial heritage

Plymouth's Royal William Victualling Yard, as it was initially called, was built expressly to sustain the Royal Navy, which in the 1820s still represented the nation's principal bulwark against foreign aggression. Designed as the most advanced facility of its kind in the world, even by the time it was completed, a decade later, the astonishing pace of British technological advance at the height of the industrial revolution meant that it was now obsolescent. It lingered for a century and a half in government ownership but, for the last fifty years of its working life as a naval yard its future was constantly in doubt.

The site finally closed in 1992, its imposing group of buildings – largely hidden from public view – swiftly became derelict, and its prospects appeared grim. The yard's resurrection as a new focus of employment and leisure in the twenty-first century, however, proved to be a welcome and very timely ray of hope for the benighted port of Plymouth.

▷ *A hidden masterpiece reborn: Plymouth's Royal William Yard today.*

317

The City of Plymouth

Plymouth has often been described as a northern working-class city that has unaccountably found itself transported to Britain's south-west. It is the largest city on the south coast, yet is also the least known. It has little in common with its more genteel neighbours to the east and west, nor even with maritime rivals Southampton and Portsmouth. Its poorest wards boast one of the highest indices of deprivation in the country, while its beleaguered football team, Plymouth Argyle, wins the dubious accolade of being the nation's most under-achieving side per head of population.

Plymouth's gritty nature and working-class complexion derives from its many centuries as a base for the Royal Navy. Its outward aspect is hardly helped, either, by the dour granite from which many of its older buildings were constructed, which make the city seem almost Scottish on a rainy day (of which, given the city's location between sea and moorland, there are many). The city has always been dependent – overly so, it now seems – on the Royal Navy for its existence. It was a big town in the sixteenth century, with a population of around 3,500; that had doubled by the time of the Civil War, then in the nineteenth century it grew exponentially from 16,000 to 108,000. Today the city is home to 260,000 people – not counting some of its dependencies, which bring the total up to 300,000. Plymouth is, however, almost unique among large British cities in barely growing during the twentieth century: its population of 211,000 in 1900 grew by only around 50,000 during the past century. Moreover, the city's biggest employers today are the city council and Plymouth University. The navy now directly employs around only 2,500 civilians, although it does provide work for about 20,000 people in the Plymouth area and generates about 10 per cent of the city's income.

Plymouth has long realised that it needs to diversify its industrial base and rebuild its image. As planners David Mackay, Roger Zogolovich and Martin Harradine commented in 2004 in their inspirational (but sadly ignored) *A Vision for Plymouth*, 'The city often suffers from a perception of urban decay and stagnation associated with the rigid rebuilding of the post-war city centre, the overbearing nature of much of the road network, and the feeling that Plymouth simply isn't punching its weight.' They also noted that Plymouth is an ageing city: between 1991 and 2001 the number of twenty to twenty-four-year-olds living here declined by 31 per cent, and twenty-five to twenty-nine-year-olds by 35 per cent.

Distant from London and the industrial Midlands, the city has always relied on naval work and a constant influx of sailors into the city to sustain its economy. Yet today that navy is a fraction of the size it was in 1900 or 1945. At present the navy's nuclear submarine force is based in Scotland, but if one of its boats were to visit Plymouth an Astute-class submarine would disembark a complement of ninety-eight service personnel. This is a huge disparity from, say, the years just before the Second World War, when aircraft carriers such as HMS *Ark Royal* or battleships such as HMS *King George V* would discharge around 1,500 seamen at a time. Unsurprisingly, the massive reductions made in the size of the Royal Navy since 1945 have had a substantial effect on Plymouth's economy.

Plymouth harbour

A visit to Plymouth Hoe, the high, grassy outcrop on the Plymouth waterfront where Sir Francis Drake allegedly played a leisurely game of bowls before setting off after the Spanish Armada in 1588, shows why Plymouth offers such a good natural harbour. Plymouth Sound and its many estuaries off the rivers Plym and Tamar already make for an excellent maritime refuge; this advantage was further enhanced by the protection afforded by the massive Plymouth Breakwater, built after 1812 halfway down the Sound to the designs of the gifted engineer John Rennie. Even Napoleon admired the breakwater's construction when he left Plymouth as a captive aboard HMS *Bellerophon* in 1815.

The naval yard, and the city with it, subsequently grew at the places on the waterfront where there was access to deep water. As a result, the three coastal towns of Devonport (with its dockyard), Stonehouse (where the Royal William Yard was sited) and Plymouth (the civic centre) grew relatively independently until all three were united in the City of Plymouth in 1914.

Drake's celebrated departure from Plymouth in 1588 to intercept the Spanish, whose fleet he and his fellow captains successfully managed to keep away from the English coast, demonstrated the value of a westward-facing port that could cover the entrance to the English Channel. A century later, in 1691, work was begun on constructing a permanent naval base here – one which is, despite its hugely reduced operation, still the largest naval base by size in western Europe. After the Treaty of Utrecht of 1713 ended the long war with Spain, the historic naval port of Chatham, poorly placed geographically to send fleets to the Atlantic and the Mediterranean and (as the embarrassing Dutch raid of 1667 had shown) vulnerable to attack from the Continent, was increasingly neglected in favour of Portsmouth and Plymouth. As a result, the existing naval base at Devonport on the Tamar was significantly extended throughout the Georgian era.

By the end of the eighteenth century, as the navy came to rely increasingly on blockades, it was essential that Royal Navy vessels left British dockyards fully provisioned and made as few stops as possible on their extended tours. Plymouth had played a historic role by provisioning Wellington's Peninsular army between 1808 and 1814 and was well sited to supply victuals to the strategically important naval stations at Gibraltar and on Ascension Island. In addition, from the 1820s onwards innovations such as steam power, screw propulsion and iron construction created a need for the Royal Navy to be able to commission, build and maintain ever-larger warships. As a result, all three naval dockyards were massively extended into their adjacent coastal areas. At Plymouth, the needs of the growing navy led to the creation of an additional dockyard and naval base to the north of the current Devonport anchorage as well as the construction of a colossal Victualling Yard, built between 1824 and 1833 to the south-east of Devonport dockyard.

The Royal William Yard was named after the sailor-king William IV, a former naval officer, now promoted to Admiral of the Fleet, who was on the throne when the complex was completed in the 1830s. The Yard is one of Britain's most magnificent industrial monuments, yet it is also one of the least known. Plymouth is a city not often visited by tourists – if they do arrive in the city they are generally passing through to catch ferries to France or Spain – and the Yard's Cremyll Point site is a dead end at the southern tip of Stonehouse. In addition, the Royal William Yard site was only released by the Ministry of Defence in 1992 and became accessible to the public only from 2006.

Providing the growing navy with enough food and drink to sustain its sailors at sea was vital to Britain's defence in the eighteenth, nineteenth and twentieth centuries. As J. G. Coad and Nicholas Cooper have observed:

It is not often appreciated that the Victualling Board was the country's first really large-scale food manufacturing and catering organization and that any failure on its part could have had speedy and tragic consequences for naval crews. Until the advent of canning and then refrigeration in the nineteenth century, the science of food preservation was rudimentary: salt was the chief preservative and scurvy was one of the most feared effects of a lack of fresh food. However, the Victualling Board in the eighteenth and nineteenth centuries strove to provide provisions of good quality and ample quantity and sailors of the Royal Navy were on the whole far better fed than their peers in the merchant marine or ashore. Biscuits, beef, pork, peas, fish, butter, cheese, and beer were staple foods, to which were added in the eighteenth century oatmeal, sugar, soup-concentrate, and sauerkraut.

In 1821 it was decided to centralise Plymouth dockyard's victualling provision in a new location. Cremyll Point was chosen for its 'great depth of water' and its location between the city, the dockyard and the Sound. Historian Chris Miele has sagely observed:

> The new yard would require a sheltered position, and one that was easy to secure from the land side (to protect the goods from theft). The site needed, ideally, to be level, but also to enjoy access to deep water. Of course the owner had to be willing to part with it at a fair price; any new victualling factory and depot had to be economic to develop, avoiding unreasonable expense, complexity of construction and delay. No sites on the Hamoaze fit this bill exactly, but Cremyll Point presented certain obvious advantages. The Navy had an interest in the land here already and, by happy coincidence, the rest of the peninsula was owned by Lord Mount Edgcumbe, who was a member of the Victualling Board.

Three years later, the site was bought and the navy's Victualling Commissioners appointed John Rennie as the project's architect.

John Rennie's Yard

John Rennie (1794–1874) was the son of one of the greatest ever Britons, John Rennie the Elder, creator of London's Waterloo Bridge of 1811–17 as well as waterways, docks and harbours across Britain – including the Plymouth Breakwater, a project John the Younger inherited from his father on the latter's death in 1821.

The younger John had a tough act to follow. He did so with aplomb, designing a new London Bridge – for which he was knighted in 1831 – and the astonishing group of buildings which form his architectural masterpiece: Royal

William Yard, called by Coad and Cooper 'arguably the finest group of buildings by the Royal Navy and built by one man'.

The Yard's monumental classicism was a self-conscious statement of Britain's assumed role as the globe's greatest power and the crucial importance of the Royal Navy in securing this ascendancy. Even while the Royal William Yard was being built, the British admiral Edward Codrington annihilated the Turkish fleet at Navarino in 1827, thus making Greek independence possible, while thirteen years later the British navy's bombardment of Acre ended the expansionist dreams of the Egyptian nationalist Mohammed Ali. The British navy was the arbiter of the world, an awesome force which could intervene at any given point across the globe. At the same time, the Royal Navy took care to remain at the forefront of maritime technology. Its first steam-powered ship, the paddle-tug HMS *Comet*, was launched in 1822, while in 1849 it launched its first screw-driven steam battleship, HMS *Agamemnon* (a ship better known today for laying the first transatlantic telegraph cable in 1858).

In 1823 John Rennie acknowledged that the new Yard would be 'capable of embracing every requisite purpose', from brewing to baking and slaughtering to storage. The Royal William Yard was not, though, designed as a symmetrical whole, with each function subjugated to an overall design concept. Such an approach smacked of continental absolutism and was, at the same time, a barrier to efficiency. As a result, each of Rennie's buildings on the site was devised as a separate entity, according to its particular function, and each given a separate architectural character – an indirect allusion to the separate-but-equal emphasis of the British constitution and the professed social mobility of contemporary Britons.

By the time it was finished in 1833, the Royal William Yard was one of the largest and most arresting industrial sites in Britain. However, such was the pace of innovation in nineteenth-century Britain that within a few decades the complex was wholly obsolete.

To maintain security for the Yard, there was (and still is) just one entrance and exit to the site. This was through a grand triumphal arch with massive, rusticated pilasters at the end of Cremyll Street, atop which was placed a high podium carrying an oversized statue of William IV. (As First Lord of the Admiralty in the 1820s, William had presided over the dramatic expansion in dockyard facilities.) The memorial may have been designed by the great contemporary sculptor Sir Francis Chantrey, who had already designed statues

△ *Martin Archer Shee's coronation portrait of King William IV of 1833.*

of the king for the Royal Chapel at Greenwich Naval Hospital and another for Penshurst Place in Kent.

Beyond the gateway, Cremyll and Durnford streets led to the handsome Royal Marine Barracks, built in 1779–85 and expanded after 1805, at the height of the Napoleonic Wars, and again in 1860, to meet the imagined threat from the Second Empire of Napoleon's nephew, the Emperor Napoleon III. To the gate's east a long, high wall ran the length of the site, keeping prying eyes away from naval business.

The Yard was and is dominated by three vast, imposing buildings grouped round a central dock facing the Hamoaze, the estuarine continuation of the River Tamar. All three were built of limestone with local granite dressings. Their enormous size and unapologetic grandeur reflected the strength and pride of the post-Trafalgar navy, a formidable force which, by the time the buildings were completed in 1833, dominated the world's sea lanes as the arbiter of international politics.

To the north, nearest the entrance gateway, was the colossal Mills and Bakery; across the dock, its scale and bulk almost matching the Mills, was the gigantic Brewhouse. Both of these blocks were arranged around a projecting, five-storey pavilion, and both carried matching tall but slender chimneystacks. Between the two, on the eastern side of the central dock, was the equally substantial Melville Building, housing stores and administrative offices and named after Robert Dundas, the 2nd Baron Melville. Melville was Lord Liverpool's First Lord of the Admiralty for fifteen years until Liverpool's death in 1827, and then again under the Duke of Wellington's leadership in 1828–30. His protection of and concern for the navy were much appreciated at the Admiralty, who happily commemorated his name in the new block following his retirement in 1830.

To landward, the Brewhouse's immense, arched first-floor windows were supported by an emphatic rusticated basement to create courtyard elevations of Brobdingnagian scale. The building's size meant that it could brew 120 tuns of beer at a time, making it one of the biggest breweries in Britain. However, in the very year in which the Brewhouse was finished, 1831, the navy abolished the beer ration. The rationale for this decision was that new technology was now allowing ships to carry large quantities of fresh water at sea, thus eliminating the need for the beer rations – beer, with its boiled water, being considered a healthier alternative to stored water. A shed was later built to store ships' water tanks in the Brewhouse courtyard. As a result, despite the Brewhouse's vast notional capacity, beer was only ever brewed here in very small quantities, principally to supply the dockyard's Hospital and Infirmary. The main purpose of the building was switched to the distilling of rum, which was far easier to keep for long periods than beer. Rum was distributed daily to British naval ratings until 1970 in the form of neat spirit or, more usually, in the form of 'grog' – rum diluted with water and sometimes lemon or lime juice to combat scurvy on long sea voyages. The name 'grog' appears to have derived from the drink's first proponent, Admiral Edward Vernon, who in 1740 first distributed it to his crews. Vernon's nickname was 'Old Grog' on account of the stout overcoat he habitually wore, which was made of stiff, heavy 'grogram' fabric.*

Rum distilling necessitated far less manufacturing space than beer. Thus much of the Brewhouse was under-used from its earliest days. In 1885 the building's west wing was converted into a new slaughterhouse and a store for meat, vegetables and rum, while its central engine house was repurposed to provide hydraulic power to the Yard's many cranes. For much of the twentieth century the Brewhouse even housed a torpedo workshop. Today it is home to seventy-eight apartments, which sit above a ground floor of offices, exhibition spaces, cafés and restaurants.

The vast Cooperage and the long Clarence storage block sited behind the Brewhouse endured similar fates. In the first decades of the Yard's operation, the increasing use of tinned foods – canned beef was available in Britain as early as 1813, although it was only issued to naval ships in 1847 – and the arrival of the South Devon Railway in Plymouth in 1849 meant that the Yard came to be used less for manufacturing and increasingly for storage. The city's principal railway terminus, in Millbay, was usefully close to the Yard, and its trains[†] brought ready prepared food and supplies from all over Britain, thus obviating the need for much food processing at the Royal William Yard. In 1869 the navy also decided to concentrate the majority of its barrel manufacturing work at Deptford in London; as a result, by 1880 the Plymouth Cooperage was employing only twelve coopers. In 1891 the Brewhouse, Cooperage and Clarence blocks were all closed and converted to create a new Ordnance Depot. Despite the Yard's changing uses, though, it continued to fulfil a crucial role in provisioning the Royal Navy for another century.

---

*   Grogram or grosgrain was a fabric made from wool, silk and sometimes mohair stiffened with glue. It was tough, heavy and resistant but notoriously scratchy. Its durability made it ideal for wearing on a ship's highly exposed quarterdeck.

†   From 1876 run by the Great Western Railway.

.   Opposite the Brewhouse across the dock was the massive Mills and Bakery (now known simply as the Mills Bakery), possibly the most monumental and dramatic baking facility in the world. Its ambitions were prodigious. As Chris Miele notes, 'Rennie reviewed existing baking and milling facilities to ensure his own new facility would surpass these in every respect. His chief innovation was to combine milling and baking within a single building, producing a Flour Mill and drying kilns for Peas and Wheat and a Bakehouse capable of converting a thousand sacks of Flour into Bread per week.'

Rennie's mill was driven by steam engines, which the multi-talented engineer designed himself. His building was designed as an engine for empire: the central granary – served directly from the quayside, from which sacks of wheat and rye were brought through the long colonnade – was flanked by four mills, which were driven by no less than twenty-seven sets of steam-powered millstones, which together could produce 270,000 pounds of flour per week. The southern range contained the bakery, which was arranged around two sets of six giant ovens arranged on either side of the central spine wall, back-to-back. The central boiler house was itself powered by two steam engines, which additionally ran the equipment designed to make the dreaded ship's biscuits – hard crackers made from only flour, water and (if you were lucky) salt, and repeatedly baked and dried until they were hard enough to survive the changing weather conditions of long voyages. Sailors joked that the biscuits were resilient enough to stop a musket ball. Dr Miele describes how the raw dough was processed:

[T]he material was gravity fed into a shoot that led to one of two mills – East Mills and West Mills – each capable of working independently of the other. The coarse flour was sifted, and then passed to the ground floor for mixing into dough. Mechanical rollers formed a uniform sheet of raw biscuit which was then mechanically shaped, punched and trayed for passing through the ovens.

Reinventing the Yard

In the event, the Royal William's much-vaunted biscuit and bread factory lasted only five years before, in 1839, its equipment was removed and reinstalled in the Victualling Yard at Deptford. The Admiralty had underestimated the growth of the mid-Victorian navy, though, and by 1843 milling and baking recommenced at Stonehouse. Its production of bread and biscuits gradually diminished as ships developed the capability to accommodate on-board bakeries, but baking did not stop there until 1925 when, as a result of the naval economies dictated by the international Washington Naval Treaty of 1922, which limited heavy ship construction, it was finally closed and converted into a clothing and equipment store. The building was then damaged by a fire twice, in 1929 and again in 1960. Today, in its guise of the Mills Bakery, the building has been rescued and repurposed as eighty-six apartments and many offices and restaurants.

The Melville Building anchored the whole composition with its tall, domed cupola supported by a massive, rusticated tripartite triumphal arch. In its sheer confidence and dour majesty, the main elevation would not have looked out of place in an Edinburgh or Glasgow square. Yet for three decades after 1992 it was without a purpose. Earmarked as a large boutique hotel as far back as 1997, this optimistic project never got off the ground. At the time of writing Melville is occupied by offices, a restaurant, a small boutique hotel and a boutique cinema (there's that word again), all thanks to enlightened developers Urban Splash. But in these uncertain times much of the block still lies empty.

To the east of the gatehouse and guardhouse, a matching pair of very handsome, tall, detached houses were built for officers and their families. With their substantial basements, large sash windows and anchoring chimney-stacks at either end, their rusticated ground floors and ashlared elevations, the 'Residences', as they were logically called, added a touch of London, Edinburgh or Bath sophistication to this far corner of Devon. The Royal Navy had hoped to house a number of their Yard officers on site, and the blocks did indeed remain occupied by naval personnel until the Ministry of Defence handed the site over to the Plymouth Development Corporation in 1992. To most naval officers, though, the appeal of Plymouth was limited. By the later nineteenth century Plymouth's hills were increasingly covered by cheap terraced housing, built to accommodate naval ratings and their families as well as the many workers who depended on naval business. The Royal Navy's officers, though, tended to seek homes to the east of the city, particularly in the attractive area of south Devon known as the South Hams. As a result, Plymouth remains unusual among British cities of its size and age in having no obvious middle-class suburbs. It was and still is a working-class city disturbingly dependent on precious few sources of employment.

Today the two Residences look out over attractive lawns which stretch

△ *An engraving of 1878 showing the full extent of the Royal William Yard's site.*

southwards. This area was indeed always known as The Green, which conjures an image of naval officers' wives and their flaxen-haired children dancing round the maypole in the spring sunshine. In fact this area was, until 1992, used for open-air storage. Not one square yard of the Royal William Yard was without a specific purpose. Today the apartments of Residence 2 are currently used as office space while Residence 1 has now been converted for use as (you guessed it) a boutique hotel.

In all of his Yard buildings Rennie ensured that he used the latest cast-iron technology. The windows were pivoting metal casements rather than traditional Georgian timber sashes, which after 1920 were replaced by the classic, multi-paned metal windows made by the celebrated Essex firm of Crittall and Co. The Cooperage, with its large stocks of wood, was provided with a cast-iron fireproof floor, while the Melville Building was supplied with iron roof trusses.

Such sound construction served the Yard well when it found itself at the epicentre of German bombing in the Second World War. The Luftwaffe were aiming to obliterate the Devonport dockyards but, as was all too common at a time when bold predictions and disappointing results characterised bombing campaigns on all sides, the military dockyards continued to function even while the civilian city centre to the east was devastated. With air raids continuing from 6 July 1940 until May 1944, Plymouth earned the unenviable distinction of becoming, per square foot, the most heavily bombed British city during the whole war. Some 1,174 people were killed and 4,448 were injured in the city during the conflict, while 30,000 were left homeless. Virtually all the civic buildings, eight cinemas, twenty-six schools and forty-one churches were destroyed and by 1944 the central city hub of St Andrew's Cross – before the war said to be the busiest intersection in the country – was flattened beyond recognition. The Royal William Yard was hit, too, but its strong stone walls and liberal use of cast iron ensured it continued to operate throughout the war.

With the contraction of the Royal Navy after 1945, however, the future of the Royal William Yard began to be questioned. Britain entered the Second World War with the largest navy in the world, and although its size was rapidly overtaken by the Americans it could still dispatch more than 900 ships in support of the D-Day landings of 1944. Thirty years later, however, it was a much-reduced force. In 1981 Margaret Thatcher's Conservative government proposed the sale of the navy's new aircraft carrier to Australia and the axing of the entire Royal Marines amphibious resource, which would have made both the Royal Navy's assault ships and the Royal Marines' Stonehouse Barracks redundant. As a footnote, the government also proposed withdrawing the ice patrol ship *Endurance* from the South Atlantic, a proposal the Argentinian military junta interpreted as a sign of weakness, emboldening them to invade the British-held Falkland Islands. In the ensuing Falklands War of 1982, Britain was still able to muster a fleet of 115 ships to send to the South Atlantic. Yet in the ensuing years spend on the Royal Navy continued to decline, from 4.1 per cent of GDP in 1982 to 2.6 per cent in 2010. Today Britain's proud navy boasts only seventy-five commissioned ships.

In this context, the future not just of the Royal William Yard but of the entire Plymouth naval base is at risk. In 2016 it was again proposed to close the Royal Marines' Stonehouse Barracks – though this time not to axe the unit entirely, but to locate it somewhere cheaper. At the time of writing, however, this plan has been shelved, and the historic barracks have been reprieved until at least 2027. The axe still, however, hangs over the Royal Marines' two Plymouth-based assault ships, HMS *Albion* and HMS *Bulwark*, which have, one after the other, been on 'extended readiness' (a euphemism for mothballing) since 2011. It is also possible that the Type 23 frigates now based at

Plymouth will be decommissioned, while the principal base for the remaining Trafalgar-class submarines has already been moved from Plymouth to Faslane. At the time of writing Devonport serves as a refuelling base for Britain's nuclear submarine deterrent – and, as has often been pointed out in recent years, represents the only realistic alternative base for the nuclear deterrent and attack submarines in the event that Scotland wins its independence. More worryingly, there are also a number of decommissioned nuclear submarines lying in Devonport dockyard, implying that Plymouth could become a sort of nuclear graveyard.

Whatever the fate of Devonport dockyard, Plymouth has already tried hard to diversify its economy and change its traditional image as a coarse and downmarket metropolis, epitomised in the graphic canvases of famed Plymouth artist Beryl Cook (1926–2008). Sadly, though, the exciting new urban future envisaged by *A Vision for Plymouth* in 2004 has, like so many plans for the city before it, joined its predecessors on the shelf.

Thankfully, one area of the city which has seen successful redevelopment is the Royal William Yard. At first its prospects looked bleak. The Yard closed in 1990 and two years later was handed over to Plymouth Development Corporation. The Corporation's seven-year tenure of the site saw little real progress, however. For much of its time it was hamstrung by corruption charges aimed at its Chief Executive, while its support of developer MEPC's scheme to convert the site into a factory outlet centre was strongly opposed by English Heritage and other conservation bodies and was halted at a subsequent public inquiry. At the same time, a proposal by the University of Plymouth to convert the site into a university campus with on-site student housing was also unsuccessful. Meanwhile, the Yard was fast becoming a conservation scandal as well as an urban eyesore.

In 1999 the Corporation was wound up after only seven years and responsibility for the Yard passed to the South West of England Regional Development Agency (SWRDA). At a time when many of the University of Plymouth's constituent faculties were still spread across the county of Devon, in 2004 the university's then Dean of Arts, Humanities and Architecture spearheaded an initiative to install the arts faculties in a series of teaching studios and public exhibition spaces across the Brewhouse and Melville buildings. Sadly, this plan, too, was unsupported. Later that year, however, SWRDA gave the green light to Urban Splash to produce an overall site masterplan for the whole of the historic site.

Work on the Yard has proceeded slowly since 2004. While badly needed conservation and restoration work was swiftly carried out by architects Gilmore Hankey Kirke and Acanthus Ferguson Mann, repurposing came far more slowly. The Brewhouse and Mills were converted to largely residential and office use, with the ground floors earmarked for restaurants and cafés, but investors and operators were slow to respond to the opportunities for new commercial enterprises. The continuing conversion works, now mostly in the hands of local Devon firm Gillespie Yunnie Architects, won hatfuls of awards, but for years there was little to see. Today there is a healthy community of cafés, restaurants and bars of different shapes and sizes, but thirty-two years after the Royal Navy left the site Melville is still partly empty, the much-heralded boutique hotel having predictably failed to materialise.

Looking out across the bustling waters of the Hamoaze from the Royal William Yard, the view is as stunning as it ever was. If you then turn back towards the city, you find yourself standing in front of one of the most outstanding conglomerations of industrial architecture ever assembled in Britain, if not in Europe. The Royal William Yard is an eloquent testimony to the power, ambition and reach of the British nation at a time when Britannia really did rule the waves. It is to be hoped that, in its current incarnation as a mixed-use redevelopment which, over the past forty years, has lurched from hope to uncertainty and back again, this neglected seafront jewel will continue to remind us of what once was.

18

BIRMINGHAM TOWN HALL

1832–4

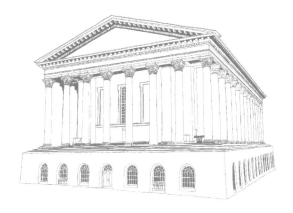

The Noblest Roman: lifting horizons in England's second city

The city of Birmingham has taken a few knocks over the last few decades. Until recent years Britain's second city had, in both physical and economic terms, not fared as well as some of its British rivals in the post-war era. Founded as the world's first manufacturing city, Birmingham's inventions and products transformed the world in the nineteenth century, while its extensive network of industrial canals earned it the affectionately ironic tag as Britain's Venice. However, the devastating effects of German bombing in the Second World War, the disintegration of its complex industrial base of small manufacturing trades after 1960 and the pernicious arrogance of the post-war planners, who inflicted perhaps more damage on Birmingham than on any other major British city, brought Birmingham to its economic and aesthetic knees by the time of the millennium. Its nadir came in the first decades of the twenty-first century, farcically symbolised in a series of mishaps which befell Victoria

▷ *Hansom's Town Hall, cleaned and restored.*

Square, the poorly pedestrianised focus of the city centre. First, the badly leaking giant fountain in the middle of the square by Dhruva Mistry, The River (popularly known as The Floozie in the Jacuzzi after its reclining incumbent), was turned off in 2013 – ostensibly to save money. Subsequently, its location was awkwardly re-landscaped. At the same time, Buro Happold's flamboyant and much-heralded Library of Birmingham building was, not long after its grand public opening, largely emptied of staff as a result of the city council's budgeting crisis. Then the library's Victoria Square neighbour, Birmingham Museums and Art Gallery – its extensive, world-class collections a hidden jewel at the heart of the second city – was closed for two years for urgent repairs caused by decades of inadequate council funding.

A few yards away from these city landmarks, however, proudly stands Birmingham Town Hall. This outstanding building survives reassuringly as an embodiment of the city's – and indeed the nation's – independent spirit and resilience. It has survived bombers and planners to represent perhaps the boldest civic statement ever made by any British city: a testimonial not just to the city's cultural diversity, wealth and ambition but also to its proud radical tradition of resistance and reform.

The workshop of the world

Birmingham and its satellites to the west of the city were, by 1800, well established as a centre of small-scale industry which focused mainly on metalware products, from nails and guns to toys and jewellery. (The industrial towns to the west were, in another example of the region's dark humour, christened 'the Black Country' in the 1840s on account of the coal beneath the ground and the soot in the air. Today Black Country towns such as Dudley and West Bromwich fiercely guard this identity and refuse to be considered as part of Birmingham.) Aside from Matthew Moulton's Soho Manufactory and a few other large factories, most of the city's industrial enterprises employed just a handful of workers.

Birmingham was also a proud centre of religious dissent: by 1800 the town featured seventeen places of nonconformist worship covering eight different denominations. And it was an enthusiastic cultural centre, too, boasting a fine Baroque parish church, St Philip's, by Thomas Archer of 1710–15, and, partly thanks to the support of the local entrepreneur-tycoon Matthew Boulton, a thriving programme of orchestral and choral performances.

338

The Town Hall was devised principally as a centre for these musical events. But it became far more than just a concert hall. Its origin lies with the Birmingham Triennial Music Festival, launched in 1768 with Boulton's support to help raise funds for the city's new General Hospital, which opened in 1779. A competition held in 1831 to build a permanent home for the Festival attracted sixty-nine entries featuring an enormous variety of architectural treatments, from John Fallows's giant neoclassical pile to the submissions from established London architect Charles Barry, who offered schemes in Tuscan, Corinthian and Italianate styles. Barry was well known in Birmingham and his new buildings for King Edward School were already under construction in New Street. It was assumed by many that his persuasively attractive perspective drawings and towering reputation would sway the judges. However, the competition was surprisingly won by the little-known architect Joseph Hansom, who subsequently enlisted fellow contestant and long-time friend Edward Welch to help him. After this signal success, the Welsh-born Welch spent most of his working life in Liverpool and the Isle of Man. Hansom, however, became an internationally renowned figure – and not just for his architecture.

Birmingham in 1831 was, like the other burgeoning industrial cities of Britain, full of confidence, ambition and wealth. As Anthony Peers has noted, at the time the Town Hall was being planned and built, 'Birmingham was an exciting place to be. The town was expanding quickly, its comparatively free-thinking and uncommonly unified inhabitants were to prove themselves, in some respects, more progressive than the people of the nation's larger and longer-established urban centres.' But, as with most of those cities, it lacked representation in parliament. As Professor Peter Marsh of Birmingham University has observed, 'The leaders of Birmingham in the 1830s wanted to stake out a twofold claim for their town: that it was a cultural centre of European distinction and was, at the same time, eager to set the pace of political reform in Britain.'

The pressure for reform

The radical move to give Britain's Catholic population full civil rights in 1829 – controversial legislation introduced and passed, to the astonishment of many, by a Tory government led by the highly conservative Duke of Wellington – had in turn increased pressure to transform the nation's antiquated and corrupt franchise. And nowhere was the pressure more keenly felt than in Birmingham.

In 1829, in response to the city's well-founded grievances, local banker Thomas Attwood founded the Birmingham Political Union, which held its first public meeting of more than 10,000 people on 25 January 1830. Attwood was interested not just in monetary reform but also in abolishing property qualifications and introducing salaries for MPs, steps which would ensure that not only the well-heeled could afford to become parliamentary representatives. He was also eager to extend (male) suffrage to the middle and working classes, men who, Attwood alleged, 'had been deceived into attacking and blaming each other for their sufferings'. In emulation of Birmingham's example more than one hundred Political Unions were set up in the following months, spurred on by Attwood's articulate leadership and by the election in November of the first wholly Whig government since 1783, led by the prime minister Earl Grey. Grey's Reform Bill of March 1831 was passed by the House of Commons largely as a result of the campaigning by Attwood and the other Political Unions, and particularly the national media coverage that the Political Unions were able to secure from the ever-increasing number of regional and national newspapers. Historian Nancy Lopatin cites a contemporary opinion that the Political Unions had 'taken vigorous hold of the public mind' during the agitation for the Reform Bill. In this context the new media outlets were essential. As Lopatin continues: 'The press made it possible for thousands of political outsiders to become part of the political debate on reform by making news and information concerning the Reform Bill and Political Unions readily available.'

Attwood's campaigns put Birmingham at the epicentre of the modern media revolution. Partly thanks to Attwood's Birmingham Political Union, the *Birmingham Journal* metamorphosed from a conservative governmental mouthpiece to a platform for reformist agitation, steered by its new editor, Jonathan Crowther – formerly of the *Manchester Advertiser* of Peterloo fame. In a similar vein, the *Manchester Guardian* helped to make the Manchester Political Union possible.

While the House of Lords prevaricated over the Reform Bill, more than 200,000 people met at the Birmingham Political Union rallies amid rumours that the Union would take up arms if the bill was not passed. In a revolutionary atmosphere – the French and Belgian revolutions were still fresh in the minds of many, while the Bristol Riots and other pro-reform disturbances of 1831 were an even more recent memory – the Lords capitulated and the 'Great' Reform Act passed into law. Inevitably, the new legislation did not go nearly far enough for many of the Unions, who felt betrayed and frustrated that the goal of universal male suffrage was still so remote. Yet with the passing of the Act the Political Unions dissolved, having lost their main reason for being. Nevertheless, two new MPs now represented the city of Birmingham; fittingly, one of whom was Thomas Attwood himself.

Joseph Hansom

Birmingham Town Hall's architect, Joseph Hansom, was well placed to take advantage both of Catholic Emancipation and of parliamentary reform. Of pronounced liberal tendencies and a friend of both Attwood and the social reformer Robert Owen, Hansom came from a Catholic dynasty of York joiners and builders. He was also – unlike his fellow Catholic architect, the messianic Augustus Welby Northmore Pugin – a clubbable diplomat who got on well with his clients. As his biographer Penelope Harris has noted, 'Hansom made full use of both his family background and the personal connections he developed within the local Roman Catholic community, to create a network of patronage upon which he became dependent.' He was also, a contemporary declared, a man whose 'character was one of much power, mingled with still greater gentleness'. Hansom's only major only failing was that he was not much of a businessman, as his subsequent business failures were to demonstrate.

Hansom and Welch conceived the Town Hall as a reflection of Birmingham's radical ambitions – and, from 1832, as a testimony to the city's growing political influence on the national stage. It was not planned to be designed in either of the architectural styles which had become so familiar by 1830: picturesque Gothic or solemn Greek Revival. Instead, it was based on a celebrated model from the early days of the Roman Republic: the Temple of Castor and Pollux, built in Rome after 495 BC in the early years of the new nation to celebrate a military victory over local Latin rivals. The architects' concept was to revisit this early Roman masterpiece, complete with a high, rusticated podium, at three-quarters of the size of the illustrious original. The Town Hall was not, though, constructed as the Roman original had been, of load-bearing stone; instead it was created from local brick from Selly Oak faced with Welsh Penmon limestone, popularly known as 'Anglesey Marble'.

Hansom's concept was something entirely new in British architecture. Its pure Roman classicism was politically far more charged than the familiar and comfortable Greek Revival of establishment figures such as Robert Smirke and William Wilkins. Its evocation of early Roman values ostentatiously compared Birmingham, and by implication Britain, to the lofty ideals and astonishing achievements of the Roman Republic which had famously died with Julius Caesar's successor, the Emperor Augustus. There was also a nod to revolutionary Paris – the city which had, in 1830, finally ejected the Bourbon dynasty from the French throne once and for all – in the building's resemblance to Pierre-Alexandre Vignon's Church of the Madeleine, which had been planned from 1806 but was only opened in 1842.

Birmingham Town Hall was a bold challenge to London government, and an appeal for representation from a growing populace which was contributing so much to the nation's rapidly expanding economy. The Town Hall's design also raised the standard of radicalism to implicitly challenge a monarchy which, in the 1830s, was under fire from all directions. To the more radical members of the Political Unions the British sovereign was at the apex of an antiquated system which maintained a corrupt franchise, the inequitable mechanisms and the outmoded class distinctions of Georgian Britain in a new age of industry, entrepreneurship and social mobility. When Hansom won the Town Hall competition in 1831 the throne was still occupied by George III's undistinguished progeny, and revolution and reform were much in the air across Europe. Even after George and William's niece Victoria acceded to the throne in 1837, the scandals surrounding her shabby treatment of her lady-in-waiting Lady Flora Hastings and the queen's own rumoured affair with Prime Minister Melbourne initially suggested that Victoria was cast from the same mould as her dispiriting uncles George IV and William IV. It took the guiding hand of Prince Albert of Saxe-Coburg-Gotha to restore the reputation of the British monarchy. In this context, for Hansom to design a building which was proudly based on one of the greatest monuments of pre-imperial Rome was a brave republican statement whose significance was not lost on the nation's capital – nor, indeed, the world. It was a gesture which put Birmingham and its ambitions firmly on the map and the London government on notice.

The design of Birmingham Town Hall also signalled the beginning of a rift between Hansom and his fellow Catholic and great architectural rival A. W. N. Pugin (1812–52). Pugin was the son of a French émigré who had been taken to a Scottish Presbyterian church in his early years. But in 1834, the year in which Birmingham Town Hall was opened, he formally and very publicly converted to Catholicism. Two years later Pugin published his crude polemic *Contrasts*, decrying the classicism prevalent in present-day Britain and appealing for a return to the forms and values of medieval England. This was an implicit

342

censure of his co-religionist Hansom for the unapologetically 'pagan' Roman classical style of the Town Hall. Hansom and Pugin had already locked horns regarding a church commission in York: Penelope Harris cites Pugin, having been undercut on price by Hansom, decrying the latter as a 'broom-stealer'. Now Hansom's evident eclecticism, which allowed him to design in either Gothic, Jacobean or neoclassical idioms, appeared as a betrayal of Gothic principles to both Pugin and, from 1841, the taste police of the influential architectural magazine *The Ecclesiologist*, who sought to recreate the beauties of fourteenth-century England in an increasingly industrialised Britain. To Pugin, classical styles were both un-Christian and un-British, and for that reason English Gothic was the only acceptable style of architecture. However, Britain's most famous Catholic convert of the period, John Henry Newman, refused to side with his fellow convert Pugin – whom Newman famously labelled 'rough tongue-free [and] unselfgoverned' – but instead took Hansom's part, believing that the Catholic Church, and indeed Britain as a whole, should not just seek its inspiration from the distant past but should also look to the future. This viewpoint seemed to strike a chord: Newman was, in his own lifetime, to become a cardinal and, in 2019, was canonised as a saint.

As Hansom does...

Hansom was a man in the Newman mould: someone who looked forwards to the new industrial age, not backwards like Pugin. In many senses he epitomised the confident, industrialising Britain of the 1830s and 1840s: always keen to try new things, to explore new avenues and to reflect political and technological change. Ironically, though, Hansom did find himself working briefly, and uncomfortably, with Pugin in Leicestershire and Lancashire before Pugin's total breakdown and premature death, aged only forty, in 1852.* Eleven years later Hansom formed a partnership with Pugin's son Edward Welby, but this too lasted only a few months.

Hansom's Birmingham Town Hall was both a civic and a national call to arms: a plea for reform executed in brick and stone and an exhortation to newly industrialised Britain to emulate the high principles of their early Roman predecessors. Unfortunately, it was a bold gesture which, for Hansom personally,

---

* Pugin's biographer Rosemary Hill has speculated that Pugin's symptoms in the last year of his life suggest he died of syphilis picked up from a Covent Garden toilet seat.

backfired spectacularly. In their excitement following their unexpected competition victory, Hansom and Welch had rashly agreed to a significantly undervalued budget and to stand as financial guarantors for their contractors. To make matters worse, they had also taken out a sizeable bank loan to facilitate this. Added to this, the kindly but radical Hanson refused to use machinery to speed up and simplify the building works, but continued to employ a large labour force of local workmen. As the imminent financial shortfall on the project loomed, Hansom attempted to save money on materials; but his use of Penmon limestone, for one, proved unavoidably expensive. Three guarantors donated money to enable the completion of the building in time for the delayed Triennial Music Festival on 7 October 1834. Thanks to their support, the Town Hall was finished; but Hansom was bankrupted.

Hansom's reaction to this major setback was typical. He now resolved to harness his talent for design to a completely different context: the horse-drawn carriage. While working on the Town Hall in Birmingham, Hansom had made friends with the wealthy lawyer Dempster Heming, whose turbulent personal life was to be fictionalised by local author George Eliot as the Radical candidate Harold Transome in her 1866 novel *Felix Holt.*[*] Heming had made a fortune in India and, on his return, spent it on acquiring the Caldecote estate in south-west Leicestershire. Like Hansom a keen reformer, Heming stood as Radical candidate for parliament under the 1832 franchise for the new seat of North-West Warwickshire. Despite the vast outlay on his campaign, though, Heming – unlike Attwood in Birmingham – failed to win the seat. Two years later, Heming invited Hansom to manage his estate at Caldecote and it was while staying at nearby Hinckley that Hansom reinvented himself as a carriage designer. Heming, meanwhile, was subsequently to follow Hansom into bankruptcy after some disastrous investments, and was forced to sell Caldecote.

On 23 December 1834 Joseph Hansom registered the design of a 'Patent Safety Cab' which was designed to combine speed and economy with safety. Its low centre of gravity and larger wheels made for a smoother ride, less wear and tear and safer cornering than was feasible with traditional hackney carriages.[†]

---

[*] Transome's name suggests that Eliot might have also had Hansom himself at least partly in mind.

[†] The name 'hackney', denoting a carriage available for instant hire on the street, first appears in the seventeenth century and seems to have derived either from the Norman-French *haquenée* (a medium-sized horse) or from the London borough of Hackney. Or both.

△ *Hansom is...: his hugely popular cab design of 1834.*

Most importantly, the carriage's single horsepower made for economical operation. Hansom himself drove his invention down Coventry Road in Hinckley, some 22 miles east of Birmingham, in 1835. The result was a huge success, and Hansom's name became a household word and a generic term. The 'hansom cab' – cab was a diminutive of cabriolet, a two-wheeled vehicle drawn by a single horse – was, in its many subsequent forms, exported worldwide and became a familiar feature of the nineteenth-century town.

In contrast to the practice in four-wheeled carriages, the hansom's driver sat behind the cab to balance the vehicle, in a sprung seat set in a raised position, and held long reins which were tethered at the front of the cab roof. Passengers could communicate with him through a hatch above their heads, in the rear wall of the carriage. While Hansom's original patent made provision for only one passenger, most cabs in service accommodated two comfortably and three at a squeeze. The driver could release the folding side and front doors to admit or let out his customers and could rebalance the cab axially by using a sliding

345

weight if there was only one occupant. Early models of the cab were open to the elements above chest height, but by the 1880s glass windows were fitted above the front doors to fully enclose the passengers and protect them from the weather.

Hansom cabs soon graced the streets not just of London and Birmingham but of every major city in the world. A Hansom Cab Company was set up in New York City in May 1869 and hansoms were ubiquitous in Britain until petrol-driven cabs (called 'taximeter cabs' after the mechanical devices they used to calculate fares by distance and time) were introduced in 1908.* In 1910 petrol-engined cabs outnumbered hansoms in London for the first time, and the last hansom ceased operation in the capital in 1947. The hansom still survives in literature, however, having earned prominent roles in Anna Sewell's *Black Beauty* of 1877, Arthur Conan Doyle's Sherlock Holmes stories of 1887–1927, G. K. Chesterton's *The Man Who Was Thursday* of 1908 and T. H. White's 1933 novel *Farewell Victoria*.

Once again, though, Hansom failed to take financial advantage of his achievement. Needing cash quickly, he sold the rights to his cab patent to a company for the relatively modest sum of £10,000. Even this undervalued amount was never paid: all Hansom ever received from his world-famous innovation was a mere £300.

Hansom now turned back to architecture to restore his fortunes. In 1843 he founded a new architectural magazine, *The Builder*, which, like Birmingham Town Hall and the hansom cab, was markedly different from anything that had previously appeared in Britain. His models were the first architectural title aimed at homeowners as well as building professionals: John Claudius Loudon's *An Encyclopaedia of Cottage, Farm and Villa Architecture and Furniture* of 1833, the nation's first-ever consumers' manual for both house and garden, and the same author's influential *Architectural* Magazine, and Journal, which had appeared in 1834, and closed nine years later on Loudon's death. Hansom had met Loudon in Birmingham and the two had got on well. In many ways Hansom intended *The Builder* to be a sequel to Loudon's own magazine, for as well as discussing architectural issues – notably Hansom's own *bête noire*, the conduct of architectural competitions – he also sustained Loudon's emphasis on the landscaping of domestic gardens.

---

*   The world's first taxicab was, inevitably, invented by the Germans: Gottlieb Daimler's 'Victoria' first appeared on the streets of Stuttgart in 1897.

Hansom was determined that his new periodical should not become a vehicle for prescriptive dogma like its main rival, the Cambridge Camden Society's polemical journal *The Ecclesiologist*, founded two years earlier. *The Ecclesiologist* was designed to urge architects and patrons to abandon modern classical revivals and turn back to the moral certainties of English 'Decorated' Gothic architecture at the time of King Edward III. Even A. W. N. Pugin at times fell foul of *The Ecclesiologist*'s inflexible and doctrinaire stance. Hansom's *The Builder*, on the other hand, was intended as a forum for debate and exchange rather than rigid rule-setting. It proved an invaluable source of reference for architects, builders and householders alike, carrying informed articles on antiquarian topics as well as on current architectural trends. Hansom assured his publishers that there was a potential readership of half a million for a title which would, in Penelope Harris's words, 'be a vehicle of trade knowledge to be kept, and a newspaper for the wife and family to read'. *The Builder* indeed advertised itself as 'an illustrated weekly magazine for the architect, engineer, constructor, sanitary reformer, and art lover'. It was something for everyone, in the manner of today's consumer magazines.

Once more, though, Hansom was let down by his endearing inability to play the role of the ruthless capitalist. As with Birmingham Town Hall, he attempted to support a large workforce to produce the magazine rather than introduce cost-saving new technology – in this case steam-powered presses, which *The Times* had pioneered as early as 1814. Within a year Hansom and his business partner, Alfred Bartholomew, were forced to sell the title to their printer, John Lewis Cox, who soon ejected Hansom and then Bartholomew from the editor's chair and ultimately installed the architect George Godwin in their place. Godwin grew the readership exponentially and remained as editor until 1883, ensuring that *The Builder* became required reading for anyone interested in the architectural profession. Renamed *Building* in 1966, the title continues to thrive today.

A catalyst for music

Hansom's great Town Hall continues to prosper, too, despite the vicissitudes of its immediate neighbours and of the city whose aspirations it embodies. The Town Hall swiftly became one of the nation's leading music venues and played host to many musical firsts. Indeed, its musical record throughout the next century seems to disprove the German Anglophobe Oskar Adolf Hermann

Schmitz's unkind taunt of 1904 that modern Britain was 'das Land ohne Musik' – the country without music. Hamburg-born composer Felix Mendelssohn, whose reputation dominated the German music scene of the 1830s and 1840s, was particularly fond of Britain and especially of Birmingham. In 1837 he conducted a performance of his oratorio *St Paul* in 1837 in the Town Hall and also played the piano for the world premiere of his Second Piano Concerto, a work which had been specially commissioned by the Triennial Music Festival. Mendelssohn was keen to impress both Birmingham and Britons. He was so impressed with the Town Hall and the reception he was awarded there that he returned in 1840 to play his First Piano Concerto and again in 1846. On this last visit he honoured Birmingham by conducting the world premiere of his oratorio *Elijah*, based on the Baroque masterpieces of Bach and Handel, at the Town Hall. The Festival responded by founding a Festival Choral Society to perform the commission. *Elijah* was hailed as an instant classic, *The Times* declaring: 'Never was there a more complete triumph – never a more thorough and speedy recognition of a great work of art.' Mendelssohn repeated this success in London in the spring of 1847, with one special performance of *Elijah* for Queen Victoria and Prince Albert. The oratorio became a staple of British choral societies for the next century and was repeated at every Triennial Festival until the last, in 1912. Its first German performance, though, had to wait until February 1848, by which time the spectre of revolution was once more haunting the courts of Europe. By then, tragically, Mendelssohn was dead following a breakdown and a series of strokes at the age of only thirty-eight. Birmingham's Festival Choral Society is, however, still in good health at the venerable age of 176.

During the subsequent decades Birmingham Town Hall's Triennial Music Festival maintained its national reputation for supporting new music. In 1873 Arthur Sullivan, who had won the first ever Mendelssohn Scholarship to the Royal Academy of Music as a fourteen-year-old, conducted a new oratorio especially commissioned by the Festival: *The Light of the World*, a piece which took as its inspiration William Holman Hunt's perennially popular if irredeemably cloying Pre-Raphaelite painting of 1853–4.

Birmingham Festival commissions for Mendelssohn and Gounod were followed in subsequent years by invitations to other leading European

◁ *A watercolour of 1845 showing Hansom's Town Hall packed for a concert. The Hall's fine interior is dominated by the William Hill organ of 1833–7.*

composers. In 1879 Max Bruch conducted the premiere of his cantata *Das Lied von der Glocke*, a controversial choice since it had been composed as an expression of German nationalism and triumphalism after the crushing defeat of the French and the declaration of the German empire in 1870–1. In 1885 Antonin ('the land without music'). In 1885, the Town Hall was the venue whereDvořák unveiled his cantata *The Spectre's Bride*, commissioned by the Birmingham Music Festival, and where, six years later, he returned with another commission, with his magisterial *Requiem*, a piece which has been recorded countless times in the twentieth and twenty-first centuries.

The Festival's most illustrious and consistent supporter in what, in retrospect, were its twilight years was the local British composer Edward Elgar, a man whose music has become such an integral element of the modern definition of 'Britishness' – even though, as an introspective and depressive Catholic from a poor Worcestershire family, he always viewed himself as an outsider. At the 1900 Festival, Elgar conducted the world premiere of his new oratorio (a term Elgar hated, incidentally) *The Dream of Gerontius*, which he had based on the poem of 1865 by John Henry Newman – a text and setting of which Joseph Hansom would undoubtedly have approved. Although the Festival Chorus was seriously under-rehearsed and made a number of mistakes, critics magnanimously forgave their poor first performance and hailed the work's genius – a verdict which still holds today. Elgar had written the piece to suit the venue; in particular, he exploited the availability of the fabulous 6,000-pipe organ which had been made for the building's opening in 1834 by Hills of London – the installation of which had made Birmingham Town Hall the first large civic assembly space in the world to include an organ. Elgar was so pleased with the reception afforded to *The Dream of Gerontius* that he returned with two more large-scale works for soloists, chorus and orchestra at successive Festivals: *The Apostles and The Kingdom*. Far less successful was his commission for the 1912, *The Music Makers*, an oratorio which quoted many of Elgar's earlier works and which was set to an 1874 poem by Arthur O'Shaughnessy, a now obscure zoologist-cum-poet.* The conductor at the premiere of *The Music Makers* was Henry

---

* O'Shaughnessy, it was said, owed his livelihood at the British Museum to being one of the many illegitimate children of the celebrity author-politician Edward Bulwer Lytton, a man who committed his wife to an asylum, who declined the throne of Greece and to whom we owe the origin of countless everyday phrases, from 'it was a dark and stormy night' to 'the great unwashed'.

Wood, the musician who had in 1895 created London's Promenade Concert festival (popularly known as the 'Proms'), which was to make a national icon out of Elgar's *Pomp and Circumstance* marches over the years. The 1912 Festival was, sadly, the last; it was never revived after the First World War – although, as a partial recompense, from 1918 until 1991 the Town Hall was the home of the illustrious City of Birmingham Symphony Orchestra.

An enduring symbol

Birmingham Town Hall also continued to be a focus of radicalism well into the new century. In April 1886, Birmingham MP and the city's former mayor, the radical Liberal Joseph Chamberlain, made one of his most significant speeches from the Town Hall's dais, condemning the plans of his own party leader and prime minister, William Gladstone, to give Ireland Home Rule. The subsequent rupture wrecked the Liberal Party but did not stop Chamberlain carving out a successful parliamentary career as the leading light of the 'National Liberals', who now sided with the Conservative Party. In 1906 Chamberlain, as acting leader of the opposition, had almost reached the top of the ladder when a severe stroke felled him and forced him to retire from politics.

A year after Joseph Chamberlain's death in 1914, his son by his second marriage, Neville, celebrated his election as Mayor of Birmingham at Joseph Hansom's Town Hall, just as his father and five of his uncles had done. Neville was never regarded as the high-flyer of the family, unlike his half-brother Austen, who rose to become chancellor of the exchequer and foreign secretary as well as leader of the Conservative Party. His abject failure as a Bahamian businessman in his early years certainly did him no favours. Nevertheless, Neville won the Ladywood division of Birmingham in the 'Khaki Election' of 1918, and from then on this seemingly unspectacular yet innately confident journeyman never looked back. His elevation to the premiership in 1937 was greeted rapturously in Birmingham, and his death in 1940, not long after his being ousted as prime minister and leader of the Conservative Party in favour of Winston Churchill, was sincerely mourned in the city. However, Chamberlain's reputation as the architect of pre-war appeasement meant that his national stock plummeted after his resignation, particularly after the publication of the anti-appeasement polemic *Guilty Men* in July 1940, four months before his death. Today there is no statue to Neville Chamberlain, Birmingham's only prime minister, in or near the Town Hall – or anywhere else in the city, for that matter.*

At the time of writing, Joseph Hansom's Birmingham Town Hall still stands assertively on its tall stone podium as a stately evocation of the city's autonomy and cultural independence. Inevitably, though, the massively insensitive redevelopment of Birmingham's city centre after 1945, led from 1966 by City Architect Alan Maudsley, had once envisaged demolishing Hansom's beating heart of Birmingham. Has this been allowed to happen it would have been an architectural disaster which could have been added to the lengthy tally of needlessly razed Victorian landmarks in Birmingham such as New Street and Snow Hill stations. Thankfully, the Town Hall was reprieved. The same could not be said of Maudsley himself, who in 1974 was jailed for thirty months on corruption charges arising from his dubious construction deals.

As Maudsley went to prison, he left the Town Hall in a sad state: filthy, crumbling and stranded on a shrinking perimeter behind the city's invasive new road scheme. Anthony Peers has noted, in his biography of the building, 'at this time the building competed with Thomas Brock and William Bloye's celebrated statue of Queen Victoria for the dubious honour of being the city's most benighted traffic island'. The Town Hall was cleaned after 1982 under the guidance of conservation expert John Ashurst; but its fate was once more left in the balance when, in 1991, the City of Birmingham Symphony Orchestra left the venue for the brand-new Symphony Hall which had been built at the International Convention Centre adjacent to Birmingham Airport. Yet again there were calls for the building's removal, or at least drastic alteration and conversion. Even the *Birmingham Post* proclaimed that the Town Hall was 'a bit past [its] shelf life'.

However, thankfully wiser heads prevailed and the building was closed for essential repairs in 1996. Three years later it was awarded Lottery funds to effect a sympathetic conservation programme under the direction of experienced conservation architects Rodney Melville and Partners. As part of Melville's lengthy, £35 million refurbishment, the Hall's upper gallery of 1926–7 was removed and the superb Hill organ restored.

In October 2007, at the grand concert held to mark its reopening, the Town Hall retook its rightful place at the heart of Birmingham. The rejuvenated

---

* The Chamberlain Memorial in (of course) Birmingham's Chamberlain Square was built in 1880 to commemorate the still very active career of Neville's father, Joseph. It was designed in a rather ponderous Gothic style by John Henry Chamberlain (no relation).

building acted as a primary focus for the activities surrounding the 2022 Commonwealth Games, which the city hosted, and as the hub for the future redevelopment of the much-abused architectural and cultural hub that is Victoria Square. As in 1834, the city of Birmingham now waits to take its cue from the noble building which was built to encapsulate its hopes and dreams.

19

NEWCASTLE CENTRAL STATION

1847–51

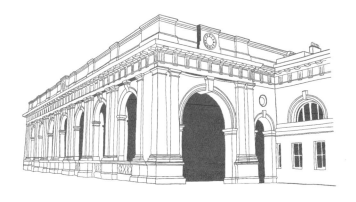

The Shock of the New:
the railways transform the nation

The first Norman castle built to guard the proud, north-eastern border city of Newcastle upon Tyne was a wooden affair. It was erected on the site of an ancient Roman fort by Prince Robert, the eldest son of William I, after 1080. Almost a century later, Henry II ordered the construction of an imposing stone keep, built in 1272–7; while during Henry III's reign, in 1247–50, the forbidding Black Gate was added.

As with most of Britain's medieval castles, as warfare grew more sophisticated during the sixteenth and seventeenth centuries, Newcastle's castle found itself without an obvious military role; but in 1643–4 it was given a new responsibility as the focus of royalist resistance in the north-east. When the royalist forces in Newcastle surrendered to the besieging parliamentary army on 19 October 1644, they did so in the castle's keep. By 1800 houses had begun to appear within the castle walls, but the castle itself was still considered the city's primary landmark. To that end, in 1809 the City Corporation bought the site and extensively restored the buildings, providing the key monuments with a roof and new battlements.

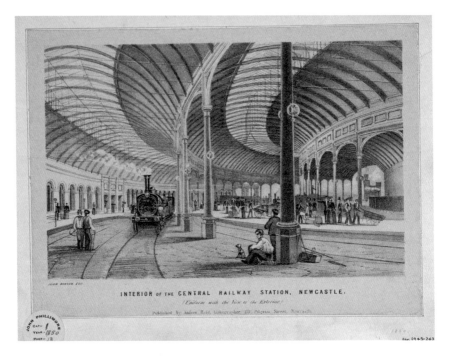

△ James Reid's 1850 print of John Dobson's revolutionary, curved trainshed.

In 1848, however, Newcastle's City Corporation happily demolished the vast majority of the castle, leaving only the keep and the Black Gate intact. Between these two medieval remnants was built a massive viaduct bringing the railway to the city. In order to create a major railway hub, Newcastle's ancient heritage was cheerfully sacrificed to make way for the modern era. Today, the best way to view the castle's restored keep is, predictably, from the platforms of John Dobson's Central Station.

Newcastle and the early railways

The High Victorian era was an age of industrial and political confidence. And nothing exemplified this more than the increasing size and daring of England's principal railway stations – and the vaulting ambition of the railway companies that built them. Communities were razed, old and even relatively recent buildings were demolished and churches and churchyards were ransacked and re-sited to make way for the new cathedrals of steam.

The city of Newcastle was by no means the only British metropolis to be caught up in railway mania. In the north-east, this enthusiasm and success were personified by the larger-than-life figure of George Hudson. By the 1830s Hudson (1800–71), the fifth son of a farmer from Yorkshire's East Riding, had progressed from running a drapery business in York to establishing a bank in the city and then promoting a railway line from York to Leeds. The latter soon evolved into the York and North Midland Railway, engineered by George Stephenson, and subsequently into a network of railways across Yorkshire, County Durham, Newcastle and Northumberland.

Elected MP for Sunderland in 1845 and vastly wealthy, he seemed the embodiment of the railway age, and was lauded in the press as the 'Railway King'. However, in 1849, just after work had begun on the new station of Newcastle Central, it was revealed that Hudson's railway empire was built on the quicksands of bribed MPs, shareholder dividends paid from capital and large-scale embezzlement. Those who had always regarded the expansion of the railways with mistrust were seemingly vindicated. (The historian Thomas Carlyle called Hudson a 'big swollen gambler' and Punch published a cartoon mocking him as 'off the rail'.) In the subsequent financial panic, hundreds of shareholders were ruined. Hudson, meanwhile, was forced to resign from all his numerous railway directorships, and he spent much of the rest of his life in self-imposed exile in France. He finally returned to York in 1865, only to find himself summarily imprisoned in York Castle for fraud.

Hudson's fall, however, proved to be only a brief interruption to the seemingly inexorable expansion of the railway network. The construction of Newcastle Central continued as if nothing had ever happened, albeit without the grand porte cochère – an imported French term, usually used for country houses, signifying a large, covered porch which could accommodate carriages of any size – that its architect had envisaged. Railway mania was more powerful, it seemed, than one ruined tycoon.

The late 1840s were boom time for the railway station. French poet and novelist Théophile Gautier famously hymned them as 'cathedrals of the new humanity' while the novelist and polemicist Émile Zola declared that 'our artists must find the poetry of stations as their fathers found that of forests and rivers'. In the year in which Newcastle Central opened, 1850, the Irish scientist Dr Dionysus Lardner wrote in his *Railway Economy*: 'It is impossible to

357

regard the vast buildings and their dependencies... without feelings of inexpressible astonishment at the magnitude of the capital and boldness of the enterprise.' Newcastle Central Station was just that: a revolutionary structure which, while it trampled on the old city, epitomised the ambition, the technological advance and the sheer boldness of the new railway age.

Most of the very early British railway stations had been, as historians Jeffrey Richards and John Mackenzie have noted, 'an assortment of sheds, huts and barns, invariably scruffy, draughty and uncomfortable', intended to serve both passenger and freight. Passengers were generally expected to climb up into trains from the line-side; indeed, the earliest railways were not actually very interested in passengers: goods traffic was, the railway companies assumed, always going to remain their principal business, while carrying people would be, they predicted, merely a minor sideline. Historian Christian Barman has remarked that:

> there [was] always a temporary look about these simple wooden shelters; it is as if those who built them knew they were dealing with an invention whose full development was certain to be so tremendous that it was useless for them to try to forecast what it would be like.

The first permanent stone- or brick-built railway stations were based on the stylistic precepts of domestic architecture. This was not just because this was a building type with which most architects were most familiar; it was also, to reassure the first passengers that the railway was safe and stable – just like home – and not dangerous or frightening. This was, after all, an important objective in the early years of the railways, a time when many passengers lost their lives in appalling and widely reported accidents. No matter that by 1850 the chance of a passenger being killed on the railways was in actuality just one in 420,000. The frequency with which newspaper reports gleefully recounted, in ghoulish detail, tales of demolished platforms, collapsing bridges, train fires and head-on collisions convinced many otherwise.

New railway stations had to impart reassurance, confidence and calmness. For example, at Newark Castle, an early station built by the Midland Railway in 1846, applied pilasters and a heavy stone entablature on a projecting, three-bay entrance gave this single-storey edifice the assurance of grandeur, longevity and stability. The same criteria were to apply to John Dobson's vast new railway station in Newcastle.

The coming of the railways

The grand, purpose-built railway stations of the 1840s and 1850s were regional attractions, drawing thousands of visitors and many admiring comments. They were intended to impress shareholders with the solidity and profitability of the company, and travellers with safety, reliability and commercial success. They also, it was quickly realised, provided exciting new markets for quick-witted retailers to plumb. Thus in 1848 the news-vending concern W. H. Smith was granted the exclusive right to sell books and newspapers on the London to Birmingham line of the London and North Western Railway (LNWR). Its first bookstall was erected at Euston in 1848; by 1851 it was operating news-stands across the LNWR's network; and by 1863 W. H. Smith was equipping all the principal railways with bookstalls – a monopoly they exercised until 1905. Not that the books sold by W. H. Smith and their smaller rivals were always very high-minded; critics coined the pejorative term 'railway novel' to typify the type of trashy, melodramatic book available at the station.

The railway station was also increasingly identified by local communities as the place at which time was defined and calibrated. The standardised time shown on the station clock underlined the national nature of the railways and the consequent shrinking of Britain. Local time, even if it had not differed substantially from that of the capital (the time at Barrow, for example, was in pre-railway days thirteen minutes behind that of London), now, thanks to the railway, rapidly became meaningless and unhelpful. The GWR was the first railway to standardise its timetable to London's Greenwich Mean Time (GMT) – which had become popularly known as 'Railway Time' – in November 1840. By 1847, the national Railway Clearing House – set up five years earlier to coordinate the distribution of revenue between the various railway companies – decreed that GMT should be adopted at all British stations. By 1855, 95 per cent of British towns and cities had transferred to GMT. Some station-masters stubbornly refused to alter their station clocks from traditional, local time, but in 1880 it became a legal requirement.

By 1850 locals were also using the station not just to check the correct time but to send messages. In 1839 the GWR opened the world's first railway telegraph line between Paddington and West Drayton, and by 1868 21,751 miles of line in the UK were covered by telegraph. In 1884 the Midland Railway alone sent five million telegrams on behalf of the public. Thus was the station made the centre of local communications.

△ *An aerial view of Dobson's station demonstrates just how much the arrival of the railway disrupted the historic centre of Newcastle upon Tyne.*

The railway station transformed Britain for ever. Thanks to the railways, what had been journeys of days were now mere hours while, thanks to government legislation, the poor as well as the rich could now travel. London was within easy reach: in 1850 *The Times* commented, 'Thirty years ago not one countryman in a hundred had seen the metropolis. There is now scarcely one in the same number who has not spent a day there'. The following year saw a huge surge in the popularity of railway travel thanks to the many thousands who took the train to London to see the Great Exhibition. The railway thus initiated massive geographical and social mobility – facilitated by the appearance in 1839 of the first national railway timetable available to the public, George Bradshaw's *Bradshaw's Railway Time Tables and Assistant to Railway Travelling*.

As the concept of railways became more familiar, so the architecture of stations, like that of banks, became ever more grandiose and ostentatious, as if to assure passengers as to the rock-like fiscal stability of this innovative enterprise. This trend was particularly necessary after the spectacular collapse of

Hudson's railway in the late 1840s, which made the whole railway industry seem suddenly vulnerable. As Michael Freeman has noted, 'It was the architect's task to counter the anxieties and terrors that characterized many of the first public reactions to the steam railway.' To that end, architects used familiar architectural styles for the public face of the station. Iron and glass would be used to create the internal train shed, but in the early years of the railways familiar motifs, materials and masses were employed in the principal offices so as to, sometimes quite literally, not frighten the horses. Thus at Newcastle Central its architect, John Dobson, built a revolutionary glazed train shed to house his platforms; yet, as the station's public face, he employed mighty stone walls phrased in a traditional neoclassical idiom which was derived from country house architecture – albeit devised on a far grander scale than anything yet seen in Britain.

Big city stations were not only designed as testimonies to the railways' permanence and resilience. They were also envisaged as city gates which advertised the economic vitality of the railway company, of the city and, indeed, of the nation as a whole. Dobson's vast new station at Newcastle certainly fitted that bill. While the castle had served as the focus and the main entrance point of the city until the eighteenth century, now Newcastle Central railway station – the symbol of Britain's economic might and her seemingly unassailable lead in this new industrial era – became the city's primary gateway.

Not everyone, though, welcomed the bright technological confidence of Britain's new railway architecture. The greatest architectural critic of the age, John Ruskin (1819–1900), dismissed many of the first stations as over-elaborate and tasteless. He wrote in *The Seven Lamps of Architecture* of 1849 – which became one of the most globally influential architectural books of the nineteenth century – that 'railroad architecture has, or would have, a dignity of its own if it were only left to its work. You would not put rings on the fingers of a smith at his anvil.' This judgement was rather unfair. Certainly many railway architects were seeking to lend decorum and grandeur to a means of transportation which was, in the eyes of many, fraught with danger and risk. Early station buildings were designed to be both novel and familiar; they needed to be simultaneously solid and spectacular, whether their model was Hardwick's giant portico at Euston, Brunel's imposing Tudor palace in Bristol, Cubitt's Brobdingnagian brick arches at King's Cross or Dobson's imposing neoclassical elevation at Newcastle. The collapse of George Hudson's house of cards in 1849 seemed to confirm to some observers that the whole railway business was merely a vehicle for irresponsible speculation and would prove a temporary fad. Stations such as Newcastle Central were designed to prove them wrong.

Dobson's station

John Dobson's grand neoclassical façade at Newcastle was by no means the first use of monumental domestic classicism in a railway context. Further south, in Yorkshire, J. P. Pritchett's Huddersfield station of 1847, built for the Huddersfield & Manchester and the Manchester & Leeds railways, boasted a giant pedimented Corinthian portico fronting a central block with Corinthian pilasters and pedimented side elevations (the sort of detail that Ruskin despised and later, more confident station designs would eschew), linked to pedimented pavilions by long, single-storey colonnades. The result resembled the colossal Georgian Yorkshire country house Wentworth Woodhouse – unsurprisingly, since Pritchett had been architect to the Earls Fitzwilliam, the owners of Wentworth Woodhouse, for some years. Pritchett's plan, as commissioned by the wealthy Ramsden family who owned much of Huddersfield, was to use the imposing classical station as the centrepiece for a new civic centre: St George's Square. Disappointingly, Pritchett's projected Town Hall was never built. (A Town Hall of much lesser architectural weight was eventually built on a different site in 1878–81.) But his magnificent station still dominates St George's Square and the town centre, terminating the vista up Northumberland Street in much the same way as Dobson's Central Station was to redefine Newcastle's city centre.

While being designed as a significant urban statement, the major railway station became an essential community hub and social centre for Britain's burgeoning industrial cities. This was certainly true of Newcastle Central, after Huddersfield the first station in the world to be explicitly designed as an urban focus for new development. Since 1824 the local developer Richard Grainger (1824–61) had, working with John Dobson, been rebuilding and extending the historic centre of Newcastle. By 1834 he had already created the soberly classical Eldon Square; now he sought to conjure a whole new city. His favoured architect, Dobson, had already tried to do this – and had been repeatedly rejected. Now Grainger harnessed Dobson's creative talents to submit a new plan for a 12-acre neoclassical suburb, predictably called Grainger Town, which would be anchored by a major railway station. The latter, Grainger insisted, should represent a 'concentration of termini', acting as the terminus for *all* the railway lines arriving in the city. The plan was accepted for everything save the station, which in these early years of railway expansion seemed too radical a step for the City Corporation, who feared that the railway might be a passing phase.

By the mid-1840s, however, Grainger's call for a large railway station to anchor the southern perimeter of his development was supported by new railway companies such as the Newcastle & Carlisle Railway, a pioneering company founded as early as 1825 and whose eastern terminus currently lay on the south bank of the Tyne, and George Hudson's York, Newcastle and Berwick Railway. This time the city accepted. Hudson nominated the architect of Grainger Town, John Dobson, to create a new station which would be served by a new line routed across the Tyne by the High Level Bridge, designed by the celebrated engineer Robert Stephenson. The city was happy for much of its medieval castle to be obliterated in order to ensure that it fully embraced the brave new railway age.

John Dobson (1787–1865), born in North Shields, could have been a national player. In architectural historian Christian Barman's view he was 'the greatest of all railway architects'. But he rarely left his beloved north-east, preferring to make his architectural mark in his hometown rather than spread his talents across the nation. Venturing to London in 1809, he studied for a while under the watercolour painter John Varley. But, while his friend Robert Smirke urged him to stay in the capital, Dobson decided to return to Northumberland, where he built an impressive number of churches, country houses and city terraces.

Dobson's Newcastle Central of 1845–50, built in a commanding Doric style with a street façade 600 feet long, was originally intended to include a huge portico, conceived as a vast, demonstrative elevation matched by a tall tower. Neither of these features was, however, actually built. Nevertheless, with the technical help of the Gateshead iron founders Hawks Crawshay, Dobson was able to design not just the station's architectural frontage but also, despite having no engineering training, the enormous train shed behind. The train shed comprised three arched glass roofs, each of a 60-foot span, and was built in a curve on an 800-foot radius. The end result was the first, true iron-and-glass vault on a giant scale: a structure in which, in Christian Barman's opinion, 'the English railway station reaches its highest moment of functional adventure and discovery'. It was the ancestor of all other great city station train sheds: a stand-alone structure which soared above both trains and passengers. (It was also the last major one-sided station, though island platforms were soon added to the south to facilitate passenger access.) And it was all Dobson's work:

he designed not only the station's remarkable neoclassical façade but, working closely with the ironwork contractors he had got to know well, created the magnificent, curving train shed, too. As architectural historian Simon Bradley has observed, this was an extraordinary leap for a man born in 1787 and whose first buildings were completed two decades before railway stations were even contemplated.

Dobson's revolutionary train shed boasted the first station roof to use round-arched, rolled-iron ribs, a form of construction hitherto reserved for garden glasshouses such as Paxton's 'Great Stove' at Chatsworth of 1836–40 or Burton and Turner's Palm House at Kew of 1844–8, and which predated the Great Exhibition's 'Crystal Palace' of 1851. Helpfully, the revolutionary curved iron ribs were manufactured locally, by two Gateshead firms: Hawks Crawshay and John Abbot & Co. They were supported by cast-iron columns adorned with simple leaf capitals. (William Bell's later train shed extension of 1892–4 used more florid capitals; Dobson's restrained lotus-leaf designs were more redolent of the quietly confident Britain of forty years before.) For these impressive technical achievements Dobson was rightly awarded a prize at the Paris *Exposition Universelle* of 1855. He and his train shed were now internationally celebrated.

Outside, along Neville Street, Dobson's long station elevation was curved so as to follow the alignment of the tracks and train shed behind. Two through platform lines were originally planned, with three bay platforms at the western end of the station and two at the east end. There was also to be a covered carriage drive on Neville Street side extending from the vast porte cochère – as noted, a term for a large, covered porch able to accommodate carriages.

Work began on the site in 1847 and continued even through the collapse of Hudson's railway empire. Sadly, though, the adjacent hotel Dobson had planned, along with the long, covered carriage drive, were both early victims of post-Hudson cost-cutting. On 29 August 1850, a day which the corporation had proudly announced as a local public holiday, Queen Victoria arrived at the newly completed building by train and formally opened the station. The queen's presence was most fitting, since it was she who – encouraged by her technologically minded consort, Prince Albert – had helped popularise the railway. The royal couple had successfully allayed many of their subjects' fears about the railway's potential dangers by travelling regularly on the rails as early as 1842, albeit at the frustratingly slow speed of 30mph.

John Dobson's building was not only an astonishing scientific achievement and a powerful symbol of the reach and wealth of the new railway companies. It also redefined a whole city, its neoclassical porte cochère providing a fittingly grandiose focus for Grainger Town.

However, in the event, Dobson's ambitious vision was never to be fully realised. The North Eastern Railway (NER), a large, composite conglomerate which rose from the ashes of Hudson's fallen empire, demanded that the size and cost of Dobson's original scheme be scaled down. Out went the vast portico, and out went the massive tower. Instead, hotel accommodation was squeezed into Dobson's east range while another local architect, Thomas Prosser, was employed to adapt a smaller, though still well-proportioned, Dobson design for a porch in a monumental Doric idiom. The latter was finally completed in 1863, in which year Dobson himself suffered a stroke from which he never fully recovered. (He died in New Bridge Street, Newcastle, two years later.) Gordon Biddle and O. S. Nock, in their invaluable guide *The Railway Heritage of Britain*, claimed that, had Dobson's original scheme been executed, it would have resulted in one of the finest nineteenth-century classical buildings in Europe. Even so, they concluded, 'Newcastle Central today is magnificent inside for its spectacular combination of curves and outside for its sheer size and length'.

Newcastle after 1850

Newcastle Central grew and prospered over the next century, as did the city it served. It survived the terrible conflagration of 1854, when an industrial fire in Gateshead prompted a massive explosion which spread across the river and caused devastation along the quayside and across the commercial district. Fifty-three people were killed and hundreds of buildings destroyed. Yet while the station miraculously survived, John Dobson's second son, twenty-six-year-old Alexander, was killed in the subsequent firestorm.

Having shrugged off this disaster, the burgeoning city of Newcastle continued to expand. The station grew to nine platforms in 1871, to twelve in 1877 and to fifteen in 1894, reflecting the economic growth of Newcastle as a linchpin of the economy not just of Britain but of the British empire. The 1894 work involved adding two new train sheds to the south of Dobson's original three to cope with the increased traffic.

As a reflection of its standing as one of the principal powerhouses of the industrial revolution, Newcastle was awarded city status in 1882, at which time its splendid, lantern-crowned medieval church of St Nicholas became a cathedral. By then Newcastle was one of the most illustrious engines of empire,

△ *A photograph of c.1900 showing Thomas Prosser's more sober – and cheaper – porte-cochère.*

with its great station a very public testimony to the city's wealth, success and confidence. Here Joseph Swan developed the world's first electric lightbulb in the 1860s and 1870s: both his electric lamp and that of America's Thomas Edison were patented in 1879, and Swan's Gateshead home was the first in the world to be illuminated by electric light. (Edison and Swan joined forces in Britain to form the company Ediswan in 1883.) Here lived Robert Stephenson, builder of numerous railways and bridges across the region and the nation, and since then rightly lauded as the greatest engineer the world has ever known. Here William Armstrong (subsequently the 1st Baron Armstrong and builder of the fabulous Norman Shaw house at Cragside) developed hydraulic power and effectively invented modern artillery. Here the great shipyards of the Tyne and the Wear turned out a bewildering succession of ships, great and small: by 1880 this region, together with the yards of the Clyde and the Tees, accounted for most of Britain's merchant tonnage, which itself represented around 75 per cent of the world's shipping. Here Charles Parsons invented the steam turbine, which transformed the industrial world and the global race

366

for naval supremacy. In 1897 Parsons's turbine-powered yacht *Turbinia* com-pellingly demonstrated the properties of the new powerplant when, wholly unauthorised, it circled the anchored ships of the Royal Navy at the Spithead Review and, reaching speeds up to 34 knots, simply could not be caught. Nine years later the Royal Navy launched the world's first Parsons turbine-powered big-gun battleship, HMS *Dreadnought*, at Barrow-in-Furness, rendering obsolete the world's navies at a stroke. The race was on. Tragically, though, the ensuing carnage of the First World War – in which Parsons-powered ships and Armstrong Whitworth field guns played a major part – also accounted for Parsons's only son, Algernon, in 1918.

The city's story after 1918 was not so high-powered. Lack of invest-ment in the local shipbuilding industry caused the great Victorian yards to fall behind their international competitors, particularly those in the US and Japan. Already by 1919 British-built ships only accounted for 32 per cent of the world's merchant tonnage. Naval shipbuilding, too, was drastically curtailed after the optimistic Washington Naval Treaty of 1921 naively attempted to impose a policy of multilateral disarmament across the globe. While foreign governments propped up their traditional industries, British governments of the interwar years mostly adopted a laissez-faire attitude to such enterprises, which on Tyneside employed hundreds of thousands of local residents. Long-established Tyneside companies now attempted to ameliorate their declining market share by diversifying – in Armstrong Whitworth's case, into automo-bile and aircraft manufacture and even paper production; but in most cases this led to disaster. Management resisted the modernisation of practices and production methods while the multiplicity of unions (in 1910 the shipbuilding industry accounted for eighteen separate trade unions) led to constant bicker-ing between sections of the workforce.

The writing was on the wall even before the Second World War gave the city a temporary artificial stimulus. By 1931 60 per cent of the city's shipyard workforce were unemployed. Two years later the famous Jarrow shipyard of Palmers went bankrupt; it was rescued by Armstrong Whitworth, but hundreds of its workers were made redundant in the process. It was these Palmers work-ers who formed the core of the 'Jarrow Crusade' of 1936: their long and ardu-ous march to London inspired a nation but Stanley Baldwin's government did nothing to remedy their plight. The demand for naval and merchant vessels during the war gave Newcastle industries a boost, but after 1945 many of these were revealed to be hopelessly uncompetitive. By 1956 Tyneside shipyards took an average of eighteen months to build a vessel while their Japanese rivals took only nine.

As heavy industry declined after 1945, so did the Newcastle cityscape, as civic leaders and their complicit developer and architect friends connived at the mutilation of this great imperial city. Large sections of the city centre were demolished in the early 1960s by the city council, led by their charismatic leader T. Dan Smith (1915–93). Smith preposterously suggested that the city should be transformed into 'the Brasilia of the North' and cheerfully backed the demolition of much of Grainger Town, including John Dobson's superb Royal Arcade of 1831–2. In place of Dobson's now-demolished Eldon Square of 1824, Smith planned the UK's largest shopping centre. His plan to employ the fashionable Danish architect Arne Jacobsen, though, came to nothing; instead, the city relied on the safe and sure hands of Taylor Chapman. Their design, finally opened in 1976, was no better and no worse than many city-centre shopping malls of the period; however, it was what it had replaced that raised national hackles. Writing in the *Spectator*, journalist Christopher Booker called Eldon Square's demolition 'perhaps the greatest single example of architectural vandalism in Britain since the war':

> Until ten years ago this most handsome piece of old Newcastle, with its blackened, post-classical frontages survived intact. Today only one side remains, the rest dominated by the astonishingly brutal shopping centre put up by Capital and Counties, turning its brick backside on the world in the most aggressive way, in order to lure Novocastrians into the softly-lit womb of the air-conditioned shopping malls within.

Its appetite whetted by the razing of Eldon Square, Smith's city council then turned its attention to Dobson's masterpiece. In 1970 and again in 1972 the replacement of Newcastle Central Station was seriously proposed by a council drunk on redevelopment. In their new plan, all Dobson's splendid work was to go, and the station was to be entirely rebuilt as a modern box behind Prosser's porte cochère. Mercifully, pressure from the Victorian Society convinced Newcastle City Council to reject this distressing proposal. However, the city council turned instead to the city's east end, much of which was bulldozed after 1972 to make way for the 'Central Motorway East' designed to carry the

A1.* This effectively severed the historic Quayside and Manors district both from Dobson's station and from the retail and social heart of the city. It is little consolation to learn that, by the time this atrocious piece of urban devastation was completed in 1975, one of its main proponents, the egregious T. Dan Smith, was in prison, having been brought down in 1973 by his close involvement with the corrupt Leeds architect John Paulson.

Newcastle's decline continued steadily through the 1970s and 1980s. The Labour government's nationalisation of the remaining British yards as British Shipbuilders in 1977 was too little, too late. By 1982 British Shipbuilders had sold off half of their yards, and the combine was finally put to sleep in 1989. Meanwhile, Armstrongs closed its last Tyneside yard in 1985 while in 2006 Swan Hunter, the city's last major shipyard, closed and its iconic cranes were sold to India. Britain now built less than 1 per cent of the world's merchant tonnage; Japan, on the other hand, accounted for 40 per cent.

In the early years of the twenty-first century, however, a new dawn beckoned for Newcastle upon Tyne. Relying on new, technologically oriented industries and on its excellent geographical position, close to the Scottish border and within easy reach of Scandinavia, the city reinvented itself as a major business centre. Formerly derelict properties on the quayside were renovated and reopened, returning the city's focus back to the Tyne. New offices, restaurants, bars and residential accommodation were created, the city's fine art galleries and museums restored and extended, and new arts venues – led by the Sage cultural centre and the Baltic Centre for Contemporary Art – added across the river. Dobson's Central Station, too, was renovated, with yet more platforms added to the south and the central concourse enlarged. And in 2001 a new bridge was added to the river's already inspiring cityscape: Wilkinson Eyre's 413-foot-long Gateshead Millennium Bridge, a curved roadway supported by a steel arch which can rotate to open for passing vessels. The subsequent revival of the city centre made Newcastle not just a vibrant commercial proposition once more but also, for the first time, a must-see tourist destination. With Dobson's imposing railway station still at its heart.

---

* Now demoted to the A167(M) and appropriately featured prominently on the 'Pathetic Motorways' website.

20

LIBERTY'S, REGENT STREET, LONDON

1922–5

Selling 'Merrie England' to the World

Liberty's, the luxury department store which sits at the corner of London's Regent Street and Great Marlborough Street, is famous the world over as a purveyor of high-end fabrics – and, in particular, for the Arts and Crafts and Art Nouveau designs of William Morris, E. W. Godwin, Archibald Knox and their contemporaries. Its brand is a household name, its patterns and products instantly visible across the globe.

However, Liberty's also deserves to be celebrated as one of the first commercial enterprises to harness British history and British identity to create a unique brand image which simultaneously looked both backwards and forwards. This approach was epitomised in its new, 'Tudor' flagship store of the 1920s, which audaciously rejected the dull, corporate Franco-Italian classicism of the time – an unimaginative trend epitomised by its humourless new neighbours

▷ *The triumph of Tudorism: the consciously historicist façade subverts the bland official classicism of the Crown Estate's remodelled Regent Street to the west.*

371

in Regent Street – in favour of something that was recognisably 'British'. The same synthesis of old and new was even applied by the firm's founder, Arthur Liberty, to the Buckinghamshire village in which he lived.

Liberty and Chesham

Chesham in Buckinghamshire is the most distant destination on the London Underground. It lies at the western end of the Metropolitan Line, 25 miles from Charing Cross and 12 miles from the nearest Metropolitan Line station in Greater London, Northwood. The Metropolitan Railway was the world's first underground railway: its first line was opened to great acclaim in 1863 between Paddington and Farringdon in the City of London. Thereafter the railway's directors – led from the 1870s by the ebullient Mancunian entrepreneur Sir Edward Watkin – indulged their taste for expansion. Thanks to Watkin, Chesham enjoyed a brief moment in the sunlight for three years after 1889 as the western terminus of the Metropolitan Railway. Watkin's original idea, his eyes always on his native Manchester, was to continue north from Chesham to link up with the London and North Western Railway (LNWR) at Tring in Hertfordshire, from where his trains could access Birmingham, Manchester and Liverpool.

Chesham had historically been a notorious centre of religious and political agitation, from the reformist Lollards of the fifteenth century through to the revolutionaries of the 1640s. The radical pamphlet *Light Shining in Buckinghamshire* of 1648 and its sequel, *More Light Shining in Buckinghamshire* of 1649, were produced locally by the Diggers, a spin-off from the more moderate Leveller movement which advocated the abolition of government and of private property. An equally left-field product of the Civil War was Chesham resident Roger Crab, a parliamentarian soldier who suffered a major head injury in battle and returned to Chesham to become a pioneer vegan and water-drinker and make a small fortune by selling hats, earning the name of the 'Mad Hatter'. Crab died in Bethnal Green in London in 1680; two centuries later he was immortalised in Lewis Carroll's *Alice in Wonderland* as the decidedly eccentric host of the celebrated tea-party.

Chesham's other world-famous resident was also in the textile trade. Arthur Lasenby Liberty (1843–1917) was the son of a local draper who ran a shop in Chesham's high street, next door to the George Inn (later renamed the George and Dragon in a fit of local republicanism). Young Arthur began work at sixteen

374

with uncles who worked in lace and wine and, three years later, secured a position at Farmer and Rogers' Oriental Warehouse in London's Regent Street. This shop had just opened to take advantage of the new interest in Japanese fashions and interiors prompted by the exhibits of the London International Exhibition at South Kensington which had just closed. Farmer and Rogers bought some of the Japanese exhibits – objects which had caught not just Liberty's eye but those of the architect and designer E. W. Godwin, the painter James McNeill Whistler and the designer and furnituremaker Christopher Dresser. Within two years Liberty was the shop's manager and, when he was refused a partnership in 1875, set up a small shop on his own nearby, at 218a Regent Street, which he grandiloquently called East India House.

Liberty's

Liberty's new store was an overnight success. In 1876, the year in which Liberty was able to buy the other half of 218 Regent Street, E. W. Godwin described Liberty's as, in Harriet Dover's words, 'the place to see and be seen'. Soon Liberty was importing goods from across the world, fabrics designed both for clothes and furnishings. The popularity of these bright, striking oriental fabrics, which Liberty reworked as British-made textiles as soon as was feasible, was considerable. By 1882 he had bought a second shop at 142–4 Regent Street, which he named Chesham House after his birthplace and which specialised in the sale of home furnishings, and had expanded the original East India House, where fabrics and dresses were sold, to occupy numbers 216, 218 and 222 Regent Street. This expanded store soon included an upholstery department (introduced in 1882) and furniture and design (1883) and costume (1884) departments.

Among the imported and Anglicised oriental textiles, Liberty made a point of featuring the latest handmade and traditionally dyed fabrics produced by Morris & Co.* at Merton Abbey. Like William Morris, Liberty believed that his market had the right to own hand-crafted furniture and fabrics rather than shoddy, mass-produced goods. Like Morris, too, he was a follower of the Ruskinian doctrine of honest construction and the elimination of unnecessary

---

* Morris & Co. – from 1861 to 1875 known as Morris, Marshall, Faulkner & Co. – pioneered the new Arts and Crafts approach to manufacture, using natural, organic pigments and medieval patterns and promoting handmade craftsmanship.

△ *Arthur Liberty, as portrayed by artist Arthur Hacker in 1913.*

decoration. 'Better a Windsor chair with comfort than a chaise à la Louis Quinze which makes one's back ache', he declared, adding the proto-Modernist sentiment: 'Utility which means fitness is in itself beauty if rightly understood.'

Liberty also helped to change Britons' attitudes to domestic colour. He worked closely with the Staffordshire dyer and printer Thomas Wardle – who also worked with Liberty supplier William Morris – to develop textile and colours which, as Alison Adburgham noted, 'had until then been supposed to be a closely guarded secret of the East... delicate pastel tints which they called "Art Colours" and that became described all over the world as "Liberty colours"'.

While business was expanding exponentially during the 1880s, Liberty was careful not to over-extend either his range or his expectations of his customers' taste. As design historian Sarah Nichols has noted, 'Liberty's entrepreneurial flair was sowing seeds for growth not dependent on *japonisme* or an import warehouse but on fabrics.' Indeed, 'Liberty Art Fabrics' were so successful that other manufacturers and retailers began copying them. In 1887 Liberty's resorted to law to restrain the Army and Navy Cooperative Society's shop in London's Victoria Street from selling fabrics using the 'Liberty' name. The same year, the peacock feather fabric, designed by Arthur Silver and manufactured for Liberty's by the Rossendale Printing Company, was exhibited at the Manchester Royal Jubilee Exhibition, and soon appeared in the store. The peacock design was an instant hit and has remained so ever since, becoming synonymous both with the Liberty name and the popular perception of British good taste.

Liberty made a big impression abroad, too. In France the term *soie Liberty* came to denote any softly draping silk, and to capitalise on his success Liberty established a shop in Paris in 1890. By the turn of the century Liberty's designers had accommodated the growing taste across the Continent for the sinuous forms of Art Nouveau, a style which became known in Italy simply as *stile Liberty*. In 1888 Arthur Liberty and his wife travelled to Japan to study Japanese arts and crafts at first hand and applied their new knowledge of Japanese manufacturing processes on their return. Meanwhile, Liberty fabrics were acquired for museum collections throughout the western world, from Trondheim to New York, while the very word 'Liberty' became an adjective, conveying a sense of British refinement and handmade elegance. Revealingly, though, while the Liberty brand became famous, the names of its designers did not, with the store only naming those who created their products if it had to.

By 1900 Liberty's was synonymous with British craftsmanship and with good, practical design – virtues which were, then as now, held to typify the artisanal tradition which allegedly underpinned British manufacturing and British history. Yet this was a narrative which, as William Morris discovered, was difficult to reconcile with Britain's evolution as the world's most industrialised nation, as well as with the unavoidably high prices that handmade goods would command. Nevertheless, in February 1900 *The Art Journal* wrote of Arthur Liberty:

He has built up an influence that has laid hold of almost every section of society, and has been responsible for a radical change in the general opinion on aesthetic questions. He has made a style different in many ways from anything previously existing and has cultivated it until it has gained an authority that is universally admired.

Arthur Liberty and The Lee

Liberty himself appears to have been a conservative but philanthropic figure. Following his move in 1880 to the country estate of Lee Manor in the village of The Lee, a few miles west of Chesham, he led the conventional life of a country squire. After renting the manor for eighteen years he bought the property in 1902 and set about transforming the village in which it sat. He still travelled up to London regularly from the nearby station of Great Missenden, and indeed had a marble seat made especially for him at the Great Central Railway's London terminus at Marylebone should he ever arrive early for his evening commute home. But at The Lee he and his wife Emma, née Blackmore, happily played the part of lord and lady of the manor, inviting all the shop staff up to The Lee annually and keeping busy the rest of the year with Good Works which benefitted local hospitals and children. (Many years before, Arthur had divorced his little-known first wife, Martha, citing her adultery. In 1875 he married again; but this marriage, too, remained childless.)

Interestingly, though, while he was certainly no socialist, Arthur Liberty was markedly more liberal than some of his contemporaries. For example, he refused to join the owners of Swan & Edgar and his other commercial West End rivals in prosecuting the suffragists' Women's Social and Political Union (WSPU) for their glass-breaking rampage along Regent and Oxford Streets of 1 March 1912. He did, though, wonder publicly in the letters' page of *The Times* at the WSPU's 'breaking of the very shrines at which they worship'.

At The Lee, Liberty imported his London business methods into the sleepy Buckinghamshire village. He greatly extended the Manor House (it was his descendants, not Arthur Liberty himself, who inexplicably pulled down the house's sixteenth-century wing in 1953) and created a new village green in 1901 by ruthlessly destroying a number of ancient cottages. By the time of his death in 1917, he had also rebuilt fifteen houses in The Lee. Considering the existing village pub unsightly, he demolished it and built a new one: the picturesque Cock and Rabbit of 1907. Liberty also erected a Guild Room behind the pub to serve as the village meeting place; created a football pitch for the village team; and had water pumped uphill to a new well in the village (but not, interestingly, to any of the surrounding communities) from the River Misbourne in the valley below. The village church was rebuilt and extended at his expense by the architect George Fellowes Prynne in 1911, the year in which Liberty also ensured the creation of The Lee Parish Council. (Formerly the village had been split between the parishes of Great Missenden and Wendover.) Indeed, today the quaint, artificially contrived village community of The Lee is much as Arthur Liberty left it: a picture-book, Hollywood idea of how an English village should look.

Liberty retired in 1914, aged seventy-one, a year after he was knighted by King George V. He died at The Lee three years later. At his funeral representatives from all the local societies which had benefitted from his patronage were there, along with 150 schoolchildren from Lee Common Church of England School, children from other nearby schools, 150 Liberty staff, the Earl of Buckinghamshire, the Bishop of Buckingham and a staff delegation from Great Missenden station. All were eager to attend, despite the exigencies of the First World War, then in its third year. In truth, the war had done little to dent Liberty & Co.'s profits, and the store emerged from the war in 1918 in good financial health.

Arthur's memorial in the churchyard at The Lee was devised, inevitably, by Liberty's chief designer, Archibald Knox. Manx-born Knox, a reserved, solitary man with almost monastic habits who preferred not to leave the Isle of Man, was one of the key proponents of the Celtic Revival style. His designs, synthesising Gaelic imagery with Art Nouveau rhythms and a Modernist discipline to produce a crisp, economical yet highly expressive idiom, ensured that Liberty products were still highly fashionable well into the 1930s. Knox's work later found favour with the Tolkien- and hippy-fuelled fervour of the 1960s and 1970s for Celtic imagery, although few had ever heard of Knox. Indeed, he deserves to be far better known today. It was only in 1996 that his work was the subject of a major touring exhibition, followed a decade later by the founding of the Archibald Knox Society.

Life after Liberty

After Arthur Liberty's death, his Lee Manor estate and his position as Chairman of Liberty's were inherited by his nephew, Ivor Stewart-Liberty,

379

who had served with distinction in the Oxfordshire and Buckinghamshire Light Infantry in the First World War, winning a Military Cross and losing a leg on the Somme in 1916. (The fine portrait of him by William Strang of 1917, now in the Old Gaol Museum in Buckingham, depicts him with his stick unapologetically featured at the very centre of the painting's composition.) Stewart-Liberty additionally inherited land in the nearby village of Chartridge, where Arthur's grandparents had owned a farm, and now added a small cottage in the idiom of Edwin Lutyens for his cousin Mary Lasenby-Liberty.

Stewart-Liberty already lived in the house in The Lee that his uncle had built for him and his wife. Pipers, a handsome if undistinguished gabled design, was built in 1913 by the local firm of John Liberty Kemp and How at the north end of the village. Pipers is best known for the painted timber figurehead of the celebrated Regency seaman Admiral Lord Howe, which has stood at its gate since 1924. Today, following essential conservation work carried out on the figurehead in 1994 (which was preceded by a threat to remove the piece to Liberty's store in London), it is protected from the Buckinghamshire weather by a small, tiled porch. The figurehead originally adorned the prow of the Victorian warship HMS *Howe*, whose timbers, as we shall see, helped to create Liberty's new store in London's Great Marlborough Street.

Liberty's and Regent Street

After the First World War, the Crown Estate decided to rebuild completely the John Nash masterpiece of Regent Street in order to exploit the street's air rights and thus maximise rental income. The result was the irreplaceable loss of one of the nation's finest Georgian thoroughfares. On the positive side, though, it also resulted in a brand-new building for Liberty's.

The idea of Regent Street was formed shortly after George, Prince of Wales, became Prince Regent in 1811 at the onset of the final and ultimately terminal illness of his father, George III, although the new street was not built until 1817–23. To the ambitious prince the project provided an opportunity to rebuild the West End of London in a manner which would eclipse that of Napoleonic Paris – a brave goal given that Britain then stood alone against Napoleon's continental empire. (Wellington's great victories in the Peninsular War were still to come, as was Napoleon's catastrophic invasion of Russia.) In a city not known for the theatricality of its built environment, George intended to inject a large slice of monarchical theatre.

John Nash's concept was to link the new royal park in north Marylebone – predictably called 'Regent's Park' and originally intended to host a new royal palace – via a grand triumphal route to George's London home of Carlton House and, beyond it, to the seat of government at Westminster. The route followed Robert Adam's Portland Place south of the park and then was expertly anchored by Nash by his new church of All Souls, Langham Place, as much a sculptural termination of a vista as a place of worship. Nash's grand new route then turned south-east once more towards Piccadilly Circus in a majestically sweeping, colonnaded quadrant which terminated on its north side with the imposing, arcaded façade of the County Fire Office.

Regent Street's curved, banana-like form was allegedly based on the hallowed precedent of Oxford's venerable high street. But in truth its bend was conceived for a far more pragmatic reason: to shrink from the poor neighbourhoods of Soho to the east and lean towards the streets of fashionable Mayfair to the west. This alignment guaranteed that Nash, allowed to act on behalf of the Crown Estate as a commercial speculator, could impose leaseholds for the street's properties at premium Mayfair levels. Nash himself admitted publicly that he wanted to avoid 'the narrow streets and meaner houses occupied by the mechanics and the trading parts of the community' and announced that Regent Street was designed *not* to unite east and west but actually to act as a boundary.

By the time it had been completed, Regent Street's ostensible ceremonial role had all but evaporated. By 1823 King George IV (as he now was) had become a recluse who rarely came to London. And soon there was no longer any royal residence to which to process: Carlton House was demolished in 1826 so that George IV could concentrate on his new, vastly expensive building projects at Buckingham Palace and Windsor Castle.

However, Nash's street was still lauded by contemporaries as a unique piece of British town planning. The king's artistic adviser Charles Long (Lord Farnborough after 1826) hailed it as 'the finest street in Europe' while the aristocratic Saxon visitor Prince Pückler-Muskau declared, 'Now, for the first time, [London] has the air of a seat of a government'. Some years later the Frenchman Francis Wey declared, 'Only here could you find the fashionable world so perfectly at home in the middle of the street', while a century later Sir John Summerson was to applaud it as an 'amazingly successful blend of formality and picturesque opportunism'. Not all joined in the chorus of approval, however. In 1858 the *Daily Telegraph*'s critic Augustus Sala lambasted it as 'an avenue of superfluities, a great trunk-road in Vanity Fair'. No shopaholic he.

By 1900 Regent Street was thriving, challenging the traditional West End shopping hub of Bond Street for retail pre-eminence. The arrival of the underground Central London Railway (now the Central Line) in 1900 substantially increased the market for the street's retail offer, as well as providing a welcome shot in the arm for Liberty's, which found itself only 200 yards from the new 'tube' station at Oxford Circus. The arrival of the thousands of underground railway passengers also, however, increased demands on the real estate of the street, prompting the urge to build higher and thus more profitably.

Nash's grandiose vision had already begun to be seriously eroded by the time war broke out in 1914. His colonnade was removed from the Regent Street Quadrant as early as 1848, while in 1880 the Metropolitan Board of Works demolished the east side of his Piccadilly Circus of 1819 to create an entrance to the new thoroughfare of Shaftesbury Avenue. The Circus's muddled vortex of streets was only redeemed by the arrival of Alfred Gilbert's celebrated statue Eros (properly the Shaftesbury Memorial) of 1886–93.

More importantly, by the early years of the twentieth century Nash's original eighty- and ninety-nine-year Regent Street leases were coming to an end. Encouraged by this deadline, the Crown Estate resolved to ruthlessly demolish all of Nash's Regent Street and, in order to maximise rental income from this lucrative real estate, to substitute taller blocks master-planned by the stolid and reliable architect Reginald Blomfield (1856–1942) in a Francophile Beaux Arts style that had little to do with Nash's Regent Street – or indeed with London. The Crown Estate's financially driven plan was bitterly fought over but was finally approved in 1913. The outbreak of the First World War postponed its implementation, but work began in earnest in 1917 with the creation of the new Swan & Edgar department store on the west side of Piccadilly Circus, built to the designs of J. J. Joass.

The Liberty board now had no choice. As Regent Street leaseholders, they were forced to abide by the demands of the Crown Estate and rebuild their Regent Street shop in a style approximating to Blomfield's charmless classical idiom. However, during the previous decade one of the Liberty board directors, Arthur Liberty's nephew Harold Blackmore, had craftily begun acquiring parcels of land behind Liberty's premises in Regent Street. Encouraged by booming sales in the years immediately after the First World War, the board then resolved on a bold step. They would, as mandated by the Crown Estate, rebuild their Regent Street shop in the approved Blomfieldian manner.

But they would also erect a new building along Great Marlborough Street to the rear, which would be linked to the Regent Street site by a bridge over Kingly Street. Freed from the stylistic straitjacket of the Crown Estate, this new building could be designed in a style of their own choosing. And the style they chose was English Tudor.

The Tudor building

The board's choice was a deliberately nationalistic gesture – and, for the times, a daringly audacious one. The stolid Beaux Arts idiom in which the rest of Regent Street was being rebuilt recalled the monotonous façades of Haussmann's Second Empire Paris or the giant railway termini of Gilded Age New York. Liberty's Tudor building, on the other hand, evoked the mercantile glories of Elizabethan England. The stylistic dichotomy of the new Liberty's site did not represent a failure of nerve, as some critics claimed after 1945. Rather, it was a daring and thoroughly modern strategy which both placated the Crown Estate and echoed the recent renaissance of the 'country house' style, which in the hands of expert architects such as Edwin Lutyens and Ernest George grounded unmistakeably contemporary form and function in a picturesque historic narrative of fantasy and allusion.

The guiding hand behind the decision to create two entirely different shops was Liberty board member John Llewellyn, a devotee of the architecture of the fifteenth and sixteenth centuries. Llewellyn lived in Little Kingshill, Buckinghamshire, two miles away from Arthur Liberty and Ivor Stewart-Liberty, in a grand neo-Tudor concoction created in 1906 from the timber-framed elements of a genuine French manor house, supposedly 'rescued' from the ancient, ruined French abbey at Blois by a Canadian millionaire. In 1924 Llewellyn told the *Architects' Journal* that he had chosen the Tudor style for Liberty's new building because it was 'quintessentially English' and because a Tudor-style shop would evoke 'the great days of guilds of craftsmen and the intrepid merchant adventurers who displayed their wares in the beautiful buildings of Old London, the productions of their handicrafts

▷ *Liberty's Tudor building today. The stone façade of the Beaux-Arts block facing onto Regent Street can be seen at the right. Dating from 1922 to 1925, both were by the same architects, Edwin Thomas Hall and Edwin Stanley Hall.*

and the treasures for which they had sailed so far and endured so much'. Llewellyn's concept, happily executed by the architects, was to give the long Great Marlborough Street elevation a complex roofscape, equipped with elaborate brick chimneystacks, varying gable and window levels and strong vertical emphases in order to make the façade resemble a row of traditional English shops. The result was a dramatic contrast to the neighbouring monoliths along Regent Street or the recently completed retail giant of Oxford Street, Selfridges, which had been built to the designs of the American railway terminus specialist Daniel Burnham and, while a fine and imposing building, was entirely alien to its British context. In marked contrast to Burnham's Selfridges, the Tudor building's external frame was authentically assembled with mortise-and-tenon joints and pegging – structural steel was used as sparingly as possible – and the resulting frame infilled with brick panels.

Internally, Liberty's new 'Elizabethan' shop was arranged around three light wells, top-lit and with open timber roofs. These vertical spaces were, as Historic England's list description states, 'evocative of old English inns, and were surrounded by new galleries, fitted with fireplaces and wall panelling, emitting an aura of intimate domesticity'. The surrounding rooms, arranged around seven staircases, were at the same time both spacious and intimate, a fitting environment in which to display William Morris's richly coloured fabrics from his workshops at Merton Abbey and the vivacious textiles Liberty's imported from the Near and Far East. They were decorated by the store's own trained shopfitters: the craftsmen, carpenters, carvers and metalworkers based at the company workshops in Highgate happily adapted to the Tudoresque idiom while ensuring that their work was also very much of their own time. The shop's roofs were provided with Tudor-style carved trusses and pendant hammerbeams, the fireplaces were all carved in a Tudor manner, while the main staircase at the western end of the building was made of English oak and endowed with carved balusters. The windows were casements and were glazed with leaded lights featuring a central composition of ships and merchants in the style of Albrecht Dürer. In the basement there was even a tea-room fitted out to look like a castle dungeon, with thick stone walls, massive round pillars and circular canopied fireplaces – all of which, sadly, is no more.

The Tudor theme even extended to the roof of the east central gallery, in which were hung six shields representing the great figures of Elizabethan England: Ben Jonson, Sir Thomas More, Sir Philip Sidney, Francis Bacon, George Herbert and William Shakespeare. Their inclusion accentuated the national character of the project and underscored the building's celebration of one of Britain's golden ages: a time to which many, in the aftermath of the carnage of the First World War, understandably preferred to return. For a while customers could imagine they were in a merchant's emporium from the days of Merrie England,* even though many of them had arrived there by an underground train or London General omnibus.

Most of the Tudor building's spaces were originally devoted to exhibiting Liberty's goods, while those for dress fabrics were provided with a dozen fitting rooms. Today, however, many of the original galleries and fitting rooms serve as offices. In 1925, though, all of the offices and workrooms, the four dining halls and kitchens, the toilets and cloakroom were located on the top floors, serving over a thousand staff. Below, on the third floor, were the banking offices and telephone exchange.

In an emphatic nod to supposed tradition, as well as to the national nature of the undertaking, the Tudor building's internal spaces were framed not with steel, as at Selfridges, but with ships' timbers repurposed from paid-off vessels of the Royal Navy. (The custom of using ships' timbers to create architectural frames clearly caught the British public's imagination during the twentieth century. If all the internal beams ascribed to naval origins were authentic, the wooden-walled Royal Navy must have comprised of hundreds of thousands of ships.)

The two wooden vessels bought by Liberty's specially for this purpose were HMS *Howe*, a 121-gun first-rate battleship launched in 1860, and HMS *Hindustan*, an 80-gun second-rate ship of the line launched in 1841. *Howe*'s lineage must have greatly appealed to Llewellyn, Stewart-Liberty and their fellow board members. The last of the line of British wooden three-decker warships, an illustrious tradition stretching back to Nelson's celebrated *Victory*, she was also the first – and only – three-decked wooden-hulled warship to be provided with screw propulsion. *Howe* was named after one of the most renowned of the navy's late Georgian admirals. Its figurehead of Admiral Lord Howe, the victor of the great naval Battle of the Glorious First of June of 1794, was, as we have seen, spirited away to serve as the gate guardian for Stewart-Liberty's

---

*   The term 'Merry England' had been popularised by the writer and critic William Hazlitt in an essay of 1819. Respelled, the phrase was disinterred by two highly successful West End productions from the turn of the century: Arthur Sullivan's 1897 ballet *Victoria and Merrie England*, which began in Elizabethan England, and Edward German's 1902 opera *Merrie England*, set at the court of Elizabeth I.

new home at The Lee. *Howe*'s subsequent career, though, failed to live up to her distinguished name. Made almost instantly obsolete by the new, ironclad battleships descended from HMS *Warrior* (launched in the same year as *Howe* and today berthed at Portsmouth alongside Nelson's illustrious flagship) after 1885, *Howe* – renamed *Bulwark* and then *Impregnable* – served as a training vessel until confusingly reverting to *Bulwark* in 1919. In 1921 she was sold to the breakers, which is where Liberty's discovered her.

Hindustan had, by 1860, became equally as obsolete as *Howe*, and spent most of her life as a training ship at Dartmouth and Portsmouth before being sold. Evocative footage of *Hindustan* being towed to the breakers' yard in 1921 can be found online.

Astonishingly, one little-known firm completed both of Liberty's building commissions with great aplomb. The architect Edwin Thomas Hall (1851–1923) had specialised in factories and hospitals, and has rarely been mentioned in the same breath as the likes of Blomfield and Burnham. On his death his firm passed to his son, Edwin Stanley Hall. Yet, between them, father and son made a great success of a seemingly impossible task. They kept determinedly to the Liberty brief. At the Tudor building, oak boards salvaged from *Howe* and *Hindustan* provided the flooring for the new shop spaces while the blocks of Portland stone used for the two towers flanking the Great Marlborough Street entrance were chisel-worked rather than sawn to produce a pleasingly hand-crafted texture. To underline the English Tudor theme, the Halls' building had Queen Elizabeth I's coat of arms carved onto the gable facing Regent Street and those of King Henry VIII and his wives were placed atop the entrance doors. And in a gesture to its many American customers, a gilded model of the *Mayflower* served as a rooftop weathervane. Yet at the nine-bay Regent Street store to the west – still called East India House, after Arthur Liberty's first shop – all was very much in the Beaux Arts vein. The main elevation was properly symmetrical, in contrast to that of its Tudor neighbour, and the rear façades clad in fashionable white tiles. As Kathryn Morrison has observed: 'Liberty's East India House looked like an imposing financial institution. Its concave classical façade was topped by an imperialist frieze celebrating the wealth of distant countries being borne by camel, elephant and ship to Great Britain.' The shop windows and lamps were of bronze, not of wood, and the shopfronts were framed not in naval timbers but with Swedish granite. Ventilation was provided by the novel 'Ozonair' system of ventilation: fresh air brought from above the roof was carried to an ozonising plant which 'washed' the air, passed it through a heating battery, cooled it (in summer) and ionised it; from here steel ducts transported it throughout the building while stale air was removed by suction. All was modern and up-to-the-minute. Only the images of the four Japanese *Iohan*, the disciples of Buddha, placed above the entrance recalled the original shop. Today, sadly, little survives of the Halls' 1920s interiors, as the building's ground floor has been subdivided and leased to other retailers.

Between the two buildings an arched bridge was created at third-storey level over Kingly Street. At its centre was a large clock designed by Hope Jones, Chairman of the British Horological Institution, which recalls John Douglas's Eastgate Clock of 1897 at another temple to English Tudor Revival, the reimagined city of Chester. The four winds form the spandrels of Jones's clockface while a crowing cock and rising sun symbolise morning, and an owl and the moon the night. (Originally, at the chiming of the hour, St George would emerge from the recess to fight the dragon.) On the keystone of the arch, beside a carved figure of Father Time, is the inscription: 'No minute gone comes ever back again, Take heed and see ye do nothing in vain.'

While the Halls' work at East India House was largely overlooked by critics, their new Tudor building was singled out for special praise. In 1924 the *Architects' Journal* reported: 'From the architects' point of view, and from the builders' and craftsmen's, the building must have been one of the most interesting and edifying that has been erected in the last fifty years.' The magazine went on to note how the Liberty craftsmen had taken their families around the building when it was finished, such was their pride in their work. Critics mostly applauded the Tudor allusions and found the high-quality and good-humoured craftsmanship a blessed relief after the sober corporate templates now used by most new commercial building projects.

Tudorism in hindsight

Twenty years later, however, the pendulum of taste had swung the other way. The architectural critics of Modernist Britain were less kind to the Halls' spectacular synthesis of old and new, which was now condemned as a retrospective pastiche of the sort which had no place in brave new Britain. The unapologetically Modernist historian Nikolaus Pevsner (1902–83), a German émigré who had already begun work on his magisterial architectural county-by-county survey *The Buildings of England* and was to become the first

President of the Victorian Society in 1957,* clearly hated the building:

> At the west end of Great Marlborough Street the thoughtful traveller will stop and consider which of two evils of our present civilisation he may be readier to put up with. On the left is Palladium House, an architectural parallel to the Wurlitzer in music-black sheer granite and rich gilt with the lush floral motifs of the Paris exhibition of 1925. On the right is Liberty's Tudor store, 1924... half-timber and all. The timbers are the real article; they come from genuine men o' war; they are not just stuck on. So technically there is nothing wrong, but functionally and intellectually everything. The scale is wrong, the symmetry is wrong, the proximity to a classical façade put up by the same firm about the same time is wrong, and the goings on of a store behind such a façade are wrongest of all.

The ineradicably Teutonic and judgemental Pevsner was evidently not the target market for Liberty's consciously historicist celebration of a bygone Britain. The average British shopper – or at least the middle-class consumer who could afford to shop at Liberty's – was. His description of the store's Tudoresque interiors as 'goings on' not only echo Sir John Summerson's dismissal of Tudor craftsmanship as a stylistic dead end – a claim Liberty's magnificent new building boldly refutes – but suggests that Pevsner was unaccustomed to spending much time inside the average store. As Pevsner mellowed in middle age, finding merit in Victorian buildings he had condemned in the 1950s, hopefully he came to see the Halls' Tudor creation in a more favourable light, as an invaluable expression of the British character and of the helpful British trait of being able to look simultaneously backwards and forwards.

Pevsner was by no means alone in wishing Britain's past away in the years after 1945. Even the Liberty's board began to lose their faith in the relevance of history, and for a time the store's fortunes waned as the directors' understandable eagerness to embrace contemporary design diluted Liberty's traditional image as a purveyor of Arts and Crafts, Art Nouveau and *japonisme*. However, the timely revival of Art Nouveau and of the designs (and the utopian politics) of William Morris in the late 1960s and early 1970s suited Liberty & Co. very well. Much was made of the centenary of the firm in 1975, the celebrations of which included a major exhibition on Liberty's held at London's Victoria

---

*   Pevsner was also knighted in 1969.

and Albert Museum at the urging of the museum's iconoclastic new director, Roy Strong. And by the 1990s the store was successfully combining its familiar late-Victorian patterns with a renewed enthusiasm for contemporary design.

Today the Liberty name is a global brand, exporting a vision of hand-made, late-Victorian Britain to the world. The fact that its products reflect a past that never really existed, and indeed was always to some extent commercially unviable, is to miss the point and to underrate the power of the construct that was Merrie England.

▷ *The finelyworked 'Elizabethan' galleries of the Halls' splendid new store.*

21

THE ELECTRIC CINEMA, NOTTING HILL, LONDON

1910

The Heyday of British Film

Portobello Road in west London was, until the mid-nineteenth century, a delightful, winding lane in the midst of the Middlesex countryside, connecting Notting Hill with the charming village of Kensal Green. In 1740 a farm had been built here, named after the famous naval victory won by Admiral Edward Vernon (of grog fame) at Spanish-held Portobello, in what is now Panama. However, the rural idyll of farm and fields was abruptly shattered when the Metropolitan Railway arrived here in 1864, opening Ladbroke Grove station and developing the surrounding fields with terrace after terrace of stucco-fronted brick homes. Soon a weekly market appeared, licensed in 1927 and later celebrated for its Saturday morning antiques stalls, and the last green spaces disappeared. In 1910, as the 'Edwardian summer' of entertainment, innovation and fun reached its apogee, one of Britain's first cinemas, the Electric, was added to Portobello Road's increasingly diverse streetscape.

The early British film industry

In 1910 the British film industry was still in its infancy. The moving picture process had only been patented by Bristol-born William Friese-Greene in 1889, although Friese-Greene never profited from his invention and died penniless. Thousands were now flocking to the new 'cinemas', a term derived from cinematograph, or kinematograph, the machine used to show celluloid motion pictures. Britons' leisure hours were never to be the same again.

The Electric in Portobello Road was not Britain's first cinema. That honour belongs to the Polytechnic in Regent Street (now known simply as the Regent Street cinema), which opened its doors in 1896. Thirteen years later, the Electric's sister cinema in Birmingham was opened two months before its Notting Hill sibling, at the end of 1909.

These picture houses were not just the first buildings in Britain to be built for the express purpose of showing motion pictures; they were also some of the first buildings to be entirely run by electricity. The Birmingham Electric was built by the theatre specialist William 'Bertie' Crewe, while the architect of the similarly sized cinema in Portobello Road was Gerald Valentin. Little is known about Valentin other than that he lived in Ealing, the self-proclaimed 'Queen of the Suburbs' (a phrase coined by Ealing's Borough Surveyor in 1902); was churchwarden at the medieval church of St Mary's in Perivale, in which capacity he authored a booklet on the building's architecture; and was also commissioned to design the Electric Cinema in Merthyr Tydfil and the Empire in London's Holloway.

Valentin's design for Notting Hill was more flamboyant than that of its early cinematic rivals. The building's façade was dominated by a large segmental arch, below which the cream-tiled ground floor featured two heavy swags placed between two fluted Ionic pilasters; these in turn flanked blind, semicircular arched recesses with rusticated voussoirs above what were originally the building's entrance and exit. Inside, the 600-seat auditorium was even more lavishly Edwardian Baroque in style, with ornate plasterwork and woodwork and a segmental barrel-vaulted ceiling with heavily moulded decoration. The unapologetically exuberant ornamentation signalled the main purpose of the building: to provide entertainment and fun.

◁ *The Electric reborn.*

Valentin's cinemas were rare in that they were specially built for the purpose of showing moving pictures. Thus they created a major new building type almost overnight. The majority of new cinemas of the early twentieth century, however, were converted from existing premises. The theatre critic W. R. Titterton lamented the sudden appearance of 'brand-new stucco and gold in the broad streets' and the fact that 'tottering dwelling-houses in the back alleys, slapped over with newness and disembowelled, old drill halls, chapels, public houses, assembly rooms, anything with a roof cover and space for a curtain and a crowd, hung out its sign and hung up its magic screen'.

The Electric's first offer was Will Barker's short (forty-minute) yet ultimately highly successful film *Henry VIII*, screened on 23 February 1911 and starring the legendary actor-manager Sir Herbert Beerbohm Tree as Cardinal Wolsey. Thereafter the Electric offered a mixed menu of British and American short – and, of course, silent – films, from Cecil Hepworth's *Mr Poorluck Buys Some China* of 1912 to D. W. Griffith's *A Burglar's Mistake* of 1909. Griffith, the American movie pioneer best known for directing the hugely successful but intolerably racist *The Birth of a Nation* of 1915, died in 1948 wealthy and widely celebrated. His British opposite number, Hepworth, was bankrupted in 1924 and died forgotten in 1953.

By 1911 cinemas like the Electric were a permanent feature on Britain's high streets and the cinema-going habit firmly established in the minds of average Britons. In the previous year, cinema entrepreneur Montagu Pyke – in Luke McKernan's words 'a larger-than-life figure, formerly a commercial traveller, gold miner and bankrupted stock market gambler who was inspired by the success of some of the first cinema exhibitions in London to make a quick fortune' – extolled the virtues of the escape from reality which the cinema offered:

> The Cinematograph provides innocent amusement, evokes wholesome laughter, tends to take people out of themselves, if only for a moment, and to forget those wearisome worries which frequently appal so many people faced with the continual struggle for existence. It forms in fact – I like the word – a diversion. It is in some respects what old Izaak Walton claimed angling to be: an employment for idle time which is then not idly spent, a rest to the mind, a cheerer of the spirits, a diverter of sadness, a calmer of unquiet thoughts, a moderator of passions, a procurer of contentedness.

In London alone by 1911 there were already 261 cinemas, a number which had grown to 383 at the onset of the First World War. British cinema audiences had grown astronomically, too: from a mere 3,750 cinema-goers in London in 1906 to 216,750 in 1911 and 287,250 in 1914. Even during the First World War cinema audiences remained steady. The 'total war' of the mass bombing of civilian populations was two decades in the future, and although the Germans' Zeppelin airships did bomb the capital from 1915, causing some loss of life and property damage, their effects were relatively negligible. One of these raids hit Notting Hill, and although the Zeppelin bombs missed the Electric Cinema some fell on nearby Arundel Gardens and Blechynden Street. The principal effect of the Zeppelin bombings was to whip up the already widespread anti-German sentiment to a mass hysteria. In Notting Hill a local mob even attacked the cinema in the belief that its German-born manager was signalling to the Zeppelins from the roof. Such incidents were far from uncommon in wartime Britain, where even 'German' dachshunds were attacked in the street and anyone with a Teutonic name was ostracised. It took three years for the royal family to acknowledge such irrational prejudices, however: it was not until June 1917 that George V of Saxe-Coburg-Gotha changed the name of the British royal house to 'Windsor'.

British cinema between the wars

Cinemas flourished after the First World War, as ordinary Britons sought a means of escape from their daily lives in the 'poor man's theatre'. Cinemas were accessible, cheap, open late and their customers did not have to dress up – unlike in the theatre.

Cinema-going was particularly popular in Notting Hill, where the respectable, middle-class terraces of the 1840s and 1850s had by 1900 become notoriously run-down and housed some of the capital's poorest communities. In 1925 a 'Notting Dale hunger queue' was featured in the *Daily Graphic* outside the newspaper's free food kitchen on Latimer Road, a powerful image which ultimately encouraged the Kensington Housing Association to launch a campaign to improve conditions in Notting Hill, fronted by the retired former Tory prime minister Arthur Balfour. Two years later the area was associated with its first grisly murder when the body of Vera Webb of Blenheim Crescent was found in the street. This would not be the last time that Notting Hill was to be nationally notorious for graphic homicides.

Thoug cinema audiences were burgeoning, the nascent British film industry was slow to exploit the commercial opportunity. After 1918, 'feature films' of well over an hour, rather than the twenty- or forty-minute shorts ubiquitous in the pre-war cinema, were becoming the rule. But these were generally American. British film companies were slow to react to the changing medium and feebly relied on the government's 1927 legislation stipulating that at least 7.5 per cent (later 20 per cent) of any cinema's output had to be British-made. The result was a flood of much-derided 'Quota Quickies', short films made as cheaply as possible, often by American companies using British actors, and designed to fulfil the British legal minimum.

By the late 1920s, many British film companies were reeling from the intense competition from Hollywood, while existing cinemas found they had to enlarge and modernise to cope with the new audiences now demanding a diet of American feature-length films. Old cinemas such as the Electric were deemed too small for these mass audiences and, like much of British industry in this era, received little or nothing in the way of future investment.

As Notting Hill sank deeper into poverty and decay, the Electric sank with it. By the late 1920s it was locally known simply as 'the Bug Hole'. In 1932 the cinema's management tried desperately to restore its upmarket image by rebranding it as the Imperial Playhouse, a name it retained until the 1960s. Similarly, Birmingham's Electric – whose opening roster of films had featured shorts such as *To Save Her Soul*, *Piedmont*, *The Shell*, *A Box of Chocolates*, *The Cabbage*, *Making Plate Glass*, *A Workman's Revenge* and *That Skating Carnival* ('with a complete change on Thursday') – was similarly renamed the Select. However, both cinemas were judged to be too small to accommodate motion pictures' new mass audiences. In 1937 the Birmingham cinema reopened as the Tatler News Theatre, showing newsreels from Pathé and British Movietone along with short films and cartoons. The Notting Hill Imperial, however, soldiered on with mainstream movies, even though it was eclipsed by the giant new Art Deco cinemas being built by cinema specialist Harry Weedon for unlikely Birmingham movie mogul Oscar Deutsch. By 1933 Deutsch's impressive, streamlined Odeon cinemas had sprung up all over Britain. (The name 'Odeon' came from the Greek word for amphitheatre, but Deutsch's publicity machine engagingly claimed it was an acronym for 'Oscar Deutsch Entertains Our Nation'.) The owners of the Imperial could only stand and watch.

Across the nation, cinema audiences climbed rapidly during the interwar years, and reached their peak in the 1940s. Thousands of Britons sought escapism in the dark, anonymous space of the cinema, hoping that the brightest stars of Hollywood and London's West End would usher them into new worlds. In 1938 Cecil Day-Lewis nicely captured the mood of the times, as well as the comforting refuge that the cinema afforded, in his ominous poem 'Newsreel': 'Enter the dream-house, brothers and sisters...'

Across Britain 912 million people attended the cinema each year in 1935, with admissions reaching their peak in 1946, when, the UK Cinema Association reports, 1.635 million Britons went to the movies.

The post-war film in Britain

The year 1946 was a grim one for Britain in many ways. The war may have been won but the country had been bankrupted – an admission Clement Attlee's Labour government effectively made the following year. Wartime rationing was not only continued, but even extended: on 27 June, barely three weeks after the government's Victory Parade, bread was rationed, limiting the supply of a staple commodity which had remained available even in the darkest days of the war. The brave new world which the electorate of 1945 had been promised had yet to materialise, although the government did nationalise the Bank of England and the coal industry. The winters of 1946 and 1947 were some of the bitterest on record, as a nation short of power and clothing struggled through the 'Little Ice Age'. In September 1946 the Victoria and Albert Museum in London bravely staged a jaunty and confident exhibition, backed by the Board of Trade and the Council of Industrial Design (later renamed the Design Council), to showcase the best of British. However, cynical exhibition-goers swiftly added a postscript to the exhibition's defiant title, *Britain Can Make It*: '...But You Can't Have It'. Most of the designs on display were destined to create valuable export earnings abroad, and few Britons could even begin to afford them.

Small wonder that millions flocked to cinemas such as the Imperial in 1946. Here they were able to see an astonishing range of British and American movies. Indeed, 1946 may arguably be said to have been film's finest hour. In Hollywood, William Wyler's superlative *The Best Years of Our Lives*, a magisterial study of the effect of war on three returning servicemen and their families, and starring Frederic March, Myrna Loy, Teresa Wright, Dana Andrews and rehabilitated war veteran Harold Russell, deservedly won Best Picture, Best Director, Best Actor (for March) and Best Supporting Actor (for Russell) at the subsequent Oscars. The year also saw the release of Charles Vidor's *Gilda*, with a mesmerising performance in the title role by Rita Hayworth; the epic Western *Duel in the Sun*, which starred Gregory Peck; Alfred Hitchcock's agonisingly tense *Notorious*, in which the veteran British director elicited outstanding performances from his three leads, Cary Grant, Ingrid Bergman and Claude Rains; *Blue Skies*, a vehicle for Fred Astaire and Bing Crosby stuffed with classic songs by Irving Berlin; Howard Hughes's racy *The Outlaw*, which introduced Hughes's well-supported protégée Jane Russell to the screen;* the tear-jerking *The Yearling*, a family film (again starring Gregory Peck) which proved an enormous worldwide success; and Edmund Goulding's compelling adaptation of the Somerset Maugham story *The Razor's Edge*, with award-winning performances from Clifton Webb and the young Anne Baxter. Perhaps uniquely in the history of cinema, all these films proved massive box-office successes, and all featured in the top ten in cinema admissions for the year. Less successful was another 1946 release, Frank Capra's *It's a Wonderful Life*, a Christmas fantasy which originally bombed at the box office but which found new popularity with a second coming on television – so much so that by the end of the twentieth century it was regularly being hailed as one the ten best films in the history of cinema.

The same year, 1946, was an *annus mirabilis* for the British cinema industry, too. Director David Lean (1908–91) capitalised on his quintessentially British successes of the previous year, *Blithe Spirit* and *Brief Encounter*, with a powerful version of Dickens's *Great Expectations*, starring Jean Simmons, Alec Guinness and the ubiquitous John Mills, who seems to have appeared in almost every British film of the 1940s. The multi-talented Peter Ustinov wrote and directed *School for Secrets*, a highly fictionalised account of the development of wartime radar which starred Ralph Richardson and featured a trio of actors who also seem to have acted in almost every British film of the post-war period: Raymond Huntley, John Laurie and Richard Attenborough. Frank Launder and Sidney Gilliat unveiled a spy thriller, the much-acclaimed *I See a Dark Stranger*, starring Trevor Howard and Deborah Kerr (and, of course, Raymond Huntley). Gilliat also directed the murder mystery *Green for Danger*, starring the inimitable Alistair Sim; while Basil Dearden's wartime romance *The Captive Heart*,

---

* *The Outlaw* was actually made in 1941 but was not released for five years owing to protracted disputes over the prominence of Jane Russell's breasts.

starring Michael Redgrave and his wife Rachel Kempson, was an even bigger box-office hit.

That year also saw the release of one of the best British films ever made: a fantasy-romance which, like so many films of the time, referenced the recent war but which also appealed to a public keen to escape from the hardships of the cold, rationed reality of post-war Britain. The Jewish-Hungarian émigré Emeric Pressburger (1902–88) had met the British film director Michael Powell (1905–90) in 1939, and together they formed a production company which they called The Archers. Their subsequent collaboration resulted in some of the best British pictures of the 1940s and 1950s – indeed, of all time. Possibly their masterpiece was 1946's *A Matter of Life and Death*, a film which alternated between a Technicolor present day and a black and white heaven, cleverly blurring the distinction between what is real and what is not and deconstructing the anguish and lasting pain of those who had lost loved ones during the war. Powell and Pressburger's Archers' Manifesto of 1942 had denounced 'escapism', yet 1946's *A Matter of Life and Death* cunningly wove fact and fantasy into one seamless narrative anchored by a towering escalator built expressly for the set by London Transport's engineers. The film cemented Powell and Pressburger's status and reinforced the reputations of its stars. Canadian supporting actor Raymond Massey, when first approached to appear in the film, had instantly cabled back: 'For The Archers anytime, this world or the next.' It certainly did no harm to the post-war standing of the film's recently demobbed lead, David Niven* (1910–83), for whom Squadron Leader Carter proved one of his most successful and enduring roles. In 2017 *The Times* declared *A Matter of Life and Death* to be the 'definitive fantasy classic' and 'essential viewing'. For the exhausted British public of 1946, desperate to escape for an hour or two from ration queues and their freezing living rooms to the dark, warm embrace of the cinema, it was just the job.

In the event, the vast cinema audiences of 1946 proved a false dawn for the British film industry. Indeed, the decline of British movie-making exactly paralleled the decline of the nation after the Second World War, when the high hopes of 1945 and the great expectations of the 1950s – a time when European industry was rebuilding and America was having trouble keeping pace with its own domestic demand – gave way to economic realities and unpalatable

---

*   Born in the year that the Electric was built.

truths. With the advent of a large national television audience by 1955, the year in which the nation's second, commercial television channel was introduced,* the future prospects for Britain's movie theatres, and especially for small, historic sites such as Notting Hill's Imperial, suddenly appeared less than rosy. British cinema audiences plunged from 1.181 million in 1955 to just over half a million in 1960.

The deterioration of Notting Hill

At the Imperial, decline continued inexorably. Even during British film's golden age of the late 1940s and early 1950s there was something nasty lurking in the Notting Hill woodshed. For it was during this period that Notting Hill clerk and convicted criminal John 'Reg' Christie (1899–1953) worked as a projectionist at the Imperial. Christie was, in fact, no harmless clerk, nor even just a habitual petty criminal; he was in reality a sadistic serial killer. It was probably during his time at the cinema that he murdered his lodger Beryl Evans and her baby daughter Geraldine, for which crimes Beryl's simple husband Timothy was tried, convicted and hanged in 1950. (Timothy Evans was posthumously pardoned after Christie's death, the victim of an appalling miscarriage of justice which helped to have the death penalty abolished in Britain in 1965.) After Christie was caught in 1954, he admitted to the murders of eight women, including his wife. All his victims were found buried in the walls or the garden of his tiny house after he left; but there may have been more. Notting Hill's reputation as a sink of vice and depravity had been gruesomely highlighted by these discoveries.

Worse was to come for the district. The Notting Hill race riots of September 1958, which saw a mob of more than three hundred white men attack local black households, showed just how desperate the streets of Notting Hill had become. The Victorian terraces were in an advanced state of decay and the local authority

◁ *Queueing at the Electric Cinema Club in 1970.*

* The BBC famously attempted to sabotage the launch of ITV on 12 September 1955 by introducing a dramatic plot twist into their already well-established radio serial *The Archers*, in which Jill Archer was killed in a stable fire. The new channel's viewing figures were healthy from the very start, however, while *The Archers'* audience began an inexorable decline as televisions became ever more common in British households.

was seemingly doing nothing, other than simply agreeing to the demolition of some of the most troubled areas in the north of the borough. These were razed after 1962 to make way for the Westway urban motorway, designed to be a key part of Inner London's new 'motorway box'. Despite local protests, the elevated expressway brutally bulldozed its way through a swathe of Notting Hill streets just to the north of the Metropolitan Line. Five thousand local families lost their homes during the decade of its construction. There was one reassuring outcome, though: thanks in part to the spirited public opposition to the Westway, in 1973 the rest of the Greater London Council's motorway box plan was shelved.

To try and raise the spirits of the local community, in 1966 the traditional Notting Hill Carnival was reinvented as a Caribbean festival to promote cultural and interracial unity. Within a decade, however, that long-standing event had fallen prey to violent clashes, with the sheer popularity of the carnival prompting ill-judged governmental calls for its closure. Thankfully, such pressures were resisted: today the carnival attracts hundreds and thousands of international visitors to Notting Hill and, it is estimated, contributes £93 million to the British economy.

The slow, mouldering decay of Notting Hill did at least attract filmmakers to the area. The producers who came here in the 1960s and 1970s, however, inevitably sought to use the area as a metaphor for decline and degeneration. They took their cue from the classic 1950 thriller *The Blue Lamp*, which had been shot in and around Portobello Road and which was celebrated for the scene in which Dirk Bogarde's panicked gangster shoots trusted local bobby Jack Warner. Bryan Forbes's *The L-Shaped Room* of 1962, an early pioneer of the 'kitchen sink' school which featured the unlikely pairing of the glamorous French film star Leslie Caron and the Lancashire hellraiser Tom Bell, was set in a dismal Notting Hill bedsit. Four years later, the bittersweet national allegory *Alfie*, Lewis Gilbert's brilliant, moralistic tale of a Cockney wide boy – played dazzlingly by Michael Caine in one of his best-ever roles – also sought to exploit Notting Hill's soiled notoriety. In a similar vein, Nicolas Roeg's *Performance*, actually shot in 1968 but not released by a nervous Warner Bros. until 1970, also did little to enhance the area's reputation as a desirable destination in its story of a reclusive rock star (Mick Jagger, in an early film role) holed up in his squalid Notting Hill retreat.

Another British film release of the era, *10 Rillington Place* of 1971, did even less to promote the Imperial's neighbourhood. Screenwriter Clive Exton adapted journalist Ludovic Kennedy's 1961 account of the infamous serial-killing case as the basis for an absorbing but unremittingly depressing account of John Christie's murderous career. It was only made watchable by a stellar cast led by Richard Attenborough, whose haunting performance as Christie created one of the most unforgettable and chilling villains in film history. At the time of filming, Christie's house in Notting Hill was actually still standing. Rillington Place had been renamed Ruston Close, but the London Borough of Kensington and Chelsea had done little else and number 10, where Christie had committed most of his grisly murders, was still occupied – although by then, according to a later occupant, haunted. As a result, much of the shoot was staged at the scene of the crimes. Only after filming had been completed did the council wake up and demolish both the house and the whole street. The creation of Westway just to the north of what had been Rillington Place then provided a handy excuse to redevelop the site beyond all recognition.

In 1972, the year in which Westway was finally finished,* the former Electric was in a sorry state – as indeed was Britain itself. The cinema's incoming general manager, Dave Hucker, later recalled, 'Nobody had spent any money on it in fifty years. It was a complete dump with no heating and no proper cinema seats, just rows of wooden bench seats. A 78rpm record player provided the sound for the interval music and the projectors were completely old and wrecked.' Under the leadership of Hucker and his inventive programmer, Peter Howden, the cinema enjoyed a new lease of life, pioneering the art-house cinema concept in Britain. Film critic Derek Malcolm later wrote that the venue had 'done more to widen the cinematic horizons in London... than practically any other cinema'. The projectors Hucker sourced to replace the old, life-expired ones were, incidentally, Winston Churchill's old machines from his former home at Chartwell in Kent. Howden and Hucker were both great fans of Powell and Pressburger's films and took great pleasure in showing timeless classics such as *A Matter of Life and Death* and *The Life and Death of Colonel Blimp*. (The pair took great pleasure from showing *Blimp* on the projectors previously owned by the man who, in 1943, had sought to ban the film without seeing it. Winston Churchill had wrongly assumed that the film, which starred Roger Livesey and Anton Walbrook, would be a caricature of the British officer corps. In fact, it was an

---

* Bizarrely, though, the expressway was already open. In 1970 Edward Heath's incoming Conservative government had been keen to open the as-yet-unfinished road as soon as possible, as a symbol of their 'progressive' credentials.

affectionate celebration of British resilience, persistence and good humour that exactly suited the mood of the times.) However, on Howden and Hucker's departure in 1980, the cinema's programming deteriorated, much of its audience left and the building once more became a target for developers.

Britain's film industry – and, some may argue, Britain, too – reached its nadir in 1982, a year which saw only sixty-four million cinema admissions, compared to 193 million in 1970.[*] The previous year there had been riots in inner city areas of high unemployment across England, from London to Manchester and Leeds. As Margaret Thatcher's government dismantled what remained of British manufacturing industry, while British troops distracted the nation's attention by fighting a brave and oddly old-fashioned colonial war in the Falkland Islands, the British film industry collapsed abjectly, leaving countless empty cinemas in its wake. By 1982 many former cinemas had either been converted into bingo halls or, like Birmingham's former Electric cinema, were now showing soft porn films. In 1983 Notting Hill's Imperial cinema, too, finally closed, ending seventy-two years of uninterrupted entertainment with a Powell and Pressburger double bill of *The Red Shoes* (partly shot in Notting Hill) and the powerful, nightmarish *Black Narcissus*.

British cinema remained in intensive care for the rest of the 1980s. Initially rescued from demolition in 1982 by Lew Grade's 'Classic' chain, by 1988 the Birmingham Electric was only surviving by screening a mixture of mainstream, art-house and exploitation films. Meanwhile, in March 1984 its Notting Hill sibling reopened in its original guise as the Electric with a repeat screening of Powell and Pressburger's *The Life and Death of Colonel Blimp*. Nevertheless, despite the support of local acting luminaries such as Julie Christie, Alan Bates and Anthony Hopkins, the Electric closed again three years later.

Resurgence

In keeping with the party spirit of the eighties, in 1988 a developer proposed to convert Valentin's exuberant cinema into a bar and restaurant with a rising dance floor. This proposal having been finally frustrated in 1992, for a while afterwards the venue was Britain's only black-owned cinema, in which guise it was prepared for a central role in the Notting Hill Carnival in 1993. Dispiritingly,

---

[*]   Fortunately, the subsequent revival of the movie industry saw numbers rise again: prepandemic national movie admissions stood at 176 million a year.

the cinema's doors closed once more in 1998; but on 21 February 2001 they reopened to reveal the Electric Cinema House and Brasserie, part of the Soho House chain of upmarket destinations. The building's 240 cinema seats had been replaced by ninety-eight leather armchairs, sofas (or 'daybeds') and a bar – all of which was a far cry from the 600 closely packed seats of the original 1910 cinema. The developers, European Estates, used the west London architects Gebler Tooth, who were able to ensure the viability of what was by now a Grade II* listed building by acquiring the shop next door; this provided invaluable space for essential upgrading, including toilets and air conditioning as well as a revenue-earning restaurant. This purchase was only made possible by the fact that the owner of the neighbouring premises was the founder of the international clothing giant Monsoon, Peter Simon, who had begun his career selling Afghan coats outside the old cinema. Simon subsequently bought out European Estates but retained Gebler Tooth as architects and personally funded the scheme to restore the Electric. The reinvigorated cinema was now provided with an ingenious expanding screen developed by audio-visual specialists Unusual Rigging, and both cinema and restaurant were leased to Soho House.

By the time the Electric's new future was being planned by Peter Simon and Gebler Tooth, its surroundings had metamorphosed from dodgy, down-at-heel backwater to one of London's most fashionable areas. The decaying Victorian terraces were restored, the Portobello Road Market tarted up, the local retail offer massively expanded and restaurants, cafés and bars, lured by the prospect of the proximity of tube stations and of the upmarket neighbourhoods of Holland Park and Campden Hill, began to multiply.

Epitomising both Notting Hill's astonishing transformation and the multinational appeal of Tony Blair's supposedly classless 'Cool Britannia' was the eponymous film which appeared just as work was beginning on the new Electric. *Notting Hill* was instantly hailed as an iconic classic and proved a massive success at the box office. This romantic comedy starred two highly bankable actors, Julia Roberts and Hugh Grant, and its fantasy theme – everyday chap gets together with a famous film star – was not entirely dissimilar to the plot device employed by *A Matter of Life and Death*. The film's writer, Richard Curtis, actually lived in Notting Hill; indeed, Hugh Grant's house in the film, 280 Westbourne Park Road, was owned by Curtis, who later auctioned the celebrated blue front door for charity. Curtis announced he had chosen the area as 'Notting Hill is a melting pot and the perfect place to set a film'. Interestingly,

△ *A long way from the fleapit days: the comfortable seating provided for today's Electric Cinema patrons.*

though, Curtis's 'melting pot' was a very white receptacle: hardly a black face was to be seen in the entire film, in contrast to the multicultural complexion of the real W11 and its renown as the home of the Notting Hill Carnival.

Most of *Notting Hill*'s exteriors were filmed almost entirely in the streets around the Electric, despite director Roger Michell's justifiable fear that 'Hugh and Julia were going to turn up on the first day of shooting on Portobello Road and there would be gridlock and we would be surrounded by thousands of people and paparazzi photographers who would prevent us from shooting'. Getting permissions from the inhabitants of this very dense urban area took a long time and was only secured by Sue Quinn, the doyenne of British film location managers, writing to thousands of local households and promising to make donations to their nominated charities.

Quinn's efforts were ultimately worth it: *Notting Hill* has continued to attract large television and streaming audiences long after its release. Notting Hill, too, has never been so fashionable; even the area's first homes of the 1830s were never as desirable as some of the terraced properties are today. The Electric cinema also prospers, in a manner which its original promoters could not have envisaged but would surely have applauded. Today it is officially known as the 'Electric Portobello' since, in 2022, it spawned a sibling in White City, sited at the old BBC Television Centre. Like its Notting Hill model, the White City cinema also offers 'mohair armchairs, cashmere blankets and footstools, not to mention a full bar and pick 'n' mix'. The dream-house has come an awful long way since its days as an Edwardian fleapit.

22

THE DE LA WARR PAVILION, BEXHILL, SUSSEX

1935

Transforming the Sedate Sussex Coast: modernism among the dahlias

For much of the later twentieth century, the story of Britain's seaside towns was a sorry tale of neglect and decay. Countless attempts were made from the 1960s to the 1990s to inject new life and new purpose into resorts whose former audiences now basked on the beaches of Spain or France. Some of these grafts worked; the majority, however, failed.

One seaside destination, though, had already discovered the art of re-invention as early as the 1930s. Bexhill-on-Sea is a quiet, reserved Sussex community to the west of Hastings. It would be entirely unknown* outside the county were it not for the landmark building erected here in 1935: a pioneering beacon of Modernist design that showed how Britain was, in the thirties, trying to come to terms with the new order of things both at home and abroad.

---

*   Indeed, Bexhill did not earn a single mention in the House of Lords' 2019 report into the plight of Britain's seaside towns.

The strange death of the British seaside town

The much-loved yet frequently derided English seaside resort, so long the butt of British comedy yet even today the default destination for many British families, was essentially a product of the railway. Sea bathing had been fashionable during the eighteenth century but was the preserve of only the privileged few. The Prince Regent many have been lampooned by the satirists heaving his bloated body into the sea at Brighton, but it was the arrival of the London and Brighton Railway in the town in 1840 which created the modern seaside resort of Brighton we know today and the blueprint for seashore destinations up and down Britain's extensive coastline.

As the nineteenth century progressed, working-class campaigns for more holiday entitlement, which would allow families looking for a break to venture beyond their own town or city, led to the increasing popularity of the seaside, which by the 1850s was served by special trains linking industrial cities with rapidly growing coastal towns. (British railways still offer a seasonal summer timetable to cater for this trade, even after the supposed ascendancy of the car.) By the time of Queen Victoria's death in 1901, there were well over a hundred seaside resorts catering for working-class families on holiday. Each town had its own unwritten place in the hierarchy of holidaymaking, with genteel venues such as Bournemouth and Scarborough considering themselves a cut above more rumbustious resorts such as Brighton and Blackpool. Entire towns in the North of England shut for 'Wakes Week' (a term derived from ancient religious feasts) to allow their working-class employees to race for the coast, a practice which was soon exported to Wales as 'Miners' Fortnight' and Scotland as 'Trade Weeks'. Resorts began to compete with each other to offer more in the way of live entertainment. Piers were extended, promenades built, amusement arcades introduced, concert halls created and Winter Gardens erected to lure visitors outside the summer months, creating an 'architecture of pleasure' which holidaying families now specifically associated with the British seaside.

The heyday of the British seaside town came during the four decades after 1918. In these tumultuous years the seaside holiday became a national institution, intimately intertwined with the social life of the average family, and one of modern Britain's most famous international exports. The new emphasis

◁ *A view of the De La Warr Pavilion of 1935.*

on the value of fresh air and outdoor exercise in the 1920s helped to encourage yet more families to holiday by the sea, however cold the water might be in the middle of a British summer. A suntan was now deemed chic and fashionable rather than, as it had been for centuries, associated with demeaning outdoor work. As a result, sunbathing on the beach became popular up and down the British coast. Looking back from the vantage point of 1941 in her celebrated detective story *Evil Under the Sun*, the novelist Agatha Christie identified 1922 as the year 'when the great cult of the Seaside for Holidays was finally established'. (In the novel, her hero Hercule Poirot laments the popularity and classlessness of the sunbathing beach: 'Regard them there, lying out in rows. What are they? They are not men and women. There is nothing personal about them. They are just bodies... everything is standardized.') The introduction of paid leave for employees by the Holiday Pay Act of 1938 – a major breakthrough that was, owing to the outbreak of war the following year, not really able to be enjoyed by families until after 1945 – further helped to cement the seaside holiday in the British consciousness.

By the 1960s, however, holidaymakers were faced with a broader range of choices. As a consequence, the British seaside resorts – mostly starved of investment since 1939 – began to decline. The car enabled holidaying families to visit remote rural or heritage destinations, and not just the rail-served seaside (1959 was the first year in which more Britons travelled to their holiday destination by car than by train). In 1949 Russian émigré Vladimir Raitz's new company, Horizon Holidays, inaugurated the first package holiday by chartering a plane to take holidaymakers not to Clacton or Cleethorpes but to Corsica. By the mid-1960s package holidays abroad were guaranteeing the British holidaymaker something the traditional seaside could not: sun. At the traditional British resorts decay set in, and seaside towns became associated more with social deprivation rather than happy families in hankie-hats and water wings jostling for space on the beach. The availability of increasingly empty holiday accommodation in many seaside towns led to them being used to resettle socially excluded families, leading to a perception that these towns were being used as social dumping grounds. A House of Lords Select Committee Report of 2019 into 'the economic and social deprivation of many seaside communities' cited Professor Rhiannon Corcoran of the University of Liverpool, who noted that 'Coastal towns tend to be characterised by an ageing population of long-term residents or incoming retirees and a transient younger, marginalised group', which in turn led to 'profound health and wellbeing challenges' as well as 'social drift and transience, insecure, low paid seasonal employment [and] skills gaps'.

By the end of the twentieth century it was clear something needed to change. In 1999 the Labour government made the regeneration of British seaside resorts one of the keystones of its new tourism policy. The British Urban Regeneration Association's 'Seaside Network' was subsequently set up to disseminate best practice in resort regeneration while the Department for Culture Media and Sport (DCMS) launched its Sea Change Programme, which by 2010 had awarded £38 million to coastal areas for culture and heritage projects. After its election victory in 2010, the Conservative–Liberal coalition government launched a £23.7 million Coastal Communities Fund, a further £36 million of investment to boost growth in coastal areas. and a £3 million Coastal Revival Fund to provide small capital grants for community assets in coastal areas.

The results in some seaside towns have been marked. Victorian resort towns such as Brighton, Whitstable and Margate have reinvented themselves as hip destinations for the twenty-first century. Brighton has always been helped by its reputation for diversity and its proximity to London, while Margate has benefitted from the knock-on effects of the new seafront art gallery, Turner Contemporary, built to the design of David Chipperfield in 2008–11. Other coastal towns still continue to search for a new role. Yet one East Sussex town appears to have successfully remade its traditional image as early as the mid-1930s.

Bexhill-on-Sea

Bexhill has a long and venerable history. It was founded by King Offa in 772, a year after the Mercian king's Bexhill forces 'defeated the men of Hastings', a feat the locals are still delighted to relate. The fledgling port was largely destroyed by William the Conqueror after his famous victory of 1066; thereafter the Normans reinvented the site as a retreat for royalty and the bishops of Chichester. Bexhill remained an obscure village until the 1880s, when the local landowner Earl De La Warr, a title which goes back to 1299, decided to rival the nearby coastal towns of Eastbourne and Hastings by creating a more upmarket seaside destination than either.

Reginald Sackville, 7th Earl De La Warr – pronounced as in the American state of Delaware, which had derived its name from the 3rd Baron De La Warr – was a quiet, thoughtful clergyman who had inherited the earldom unexpectedly when his older brother had died at the age of thirty-six. There were four main components of the earl's new Bexhill: a grandiose, multi-gabled seafront hotel, the Sackville; a 'Bicycle Boulevard' on De La Warr Parade, created in 1896 to exploit the new craze for bicycle riding; the Kursaal entertainment complex, also opened in 1896 – the year of the 7th Earl's death – which included a concert hall-cum-theatre and was intended to lead to a pier which was never built; and the ancient Manor House, which the 7th Earl rebuilt from 1891 for his son and heir Lord Cantelupe – as Wodehouseian a title as any in Britain. De La Warr had astutely arranged for Cantelupe to marry a scion of one of the richest families in Britain, Muriel Brassey, granddaughter of the famous and vastly wealthy railway contractor Thomas Brassey. However, their marriage was short-lived. By Christmas 1901 the 8th Earl was widely known about the town to be having an affair with an actress from the Kursaal, and in the New Year he left his wife and family at the Manor House and rented an apartment at Marina Court on the seafront. As the *Bexhill Observer* related in 1902, on the occasion of the Sackvilles' divorce:

> Lord De La Warr left England for South Africa in October, 1899, returning in the following July. Since his return the relations between him and his wife had entirely changed owing to the conduct of the husband, and the family circle became very unhappy. In June 1901, the Earl withdrew from the family home and has never been back since.

Muriel was granted a divorce on the grounds of adultery and abandonment and awarded custody of their three children. Her former husband lurched from one financial disaster to another; today he is best known merely for organising the first-ever car race in Britain, run along De La Warr Parade in May 1902. Thirteen years later he died of pneumonia while serving in the Royal Navy during the ill-fated Dardanelles campaign. In a fitting postscript, the 8th Earl was cited posthumously in a divorce case in which the assistant manager of the local Bexhill theatre sued his American wife for divorce on the grounds of her adultery with the earl. The lady had been visiting the earl so often at his rooms in Belgrave Mansions (a block which sadly disappeared in the 1960s) that, as the *Bexhill-on-Sea Observer* laconically reported, 'eventually he had been asked to leave'.

The Brassey marriage was not the only one of the 7th Earl's creations to meet a premature end. After 1945 more demanding visitors abandoned sedate

Bexhill for the racier delights of Eastbourne or Hastings. At the same time, the numerous independent boarding schools which had thrived in the town before 1939, catering for the children of armed forces personnel serving abroad, found their market dwindling with the decline of Empire. As a result, local businesses found it increasingly difficult to make ends meet. In 1956 the grand Sackville Hotel closed and seven years later it was converted into residential apartments.

The fifteen-year-old boy who inherited the De La Warr earldom from his father in 1915 grew up to become a very different character from his ne'er-do-well father. Herbrand Edward Dundonald Brassey Sackville (1900–76) appears to have inherited a strong socialist streak from his mother – an active suffragist and, after 1918, a staunch supporter of the young Labour Party* – and became the first hereditary peer to take a seat in the House of Lords under the Labour whip. In 1923 he became one of the youngest ever government ministers when he was appointed Lord in Waiting in the nation's first Labour government of 1924, led by Prime Minister Ramsay MacDonald (1866–1937). Labour's first taste of power was short: the government fell less than a year later due to an imaginary communist scare which hinged on the forged 'Zinoviev letter', supposedly advocating a British revolution. But when Labour returned five years later, De La Warr was offered a variety of posts by Ramsay MacDonald, starting as the government's chief whip in the Lords. In the midst of the Great Depression he followed MacDonald into the new National Government of 1931, earning the lasting enmity of many former Labour colleagues, and thereafter drifted increasingly rightwards, serving under the Conservative prime ministers Stanley Baldwin and Neville Chamberlain – while opposing their policy of Nazi appeasement – and ending his political career as Postmaster General in Winston Churchill's sclerotic last ministry of 1951–5.

The Bexhill to which Herbrand Sackville returned after the First World War was still a stolidly successful resort aimed at the middle-class market rather than the massed working classes, who were expected to remain on the South Eastern and Chatham Railway (SECR) train until it reached Hastings. The town now had an architectural feature to eclipse the De La Warrs' Sackville Hotel: the new Bexhill West Station of 1902, perhaps the most continental of all Britain's turn-of-the-century railway stations. Two large gabled pavilions,

---

*   Muriel's friend, Labour leader George Lansbury, later acknowledged that her money helped to support many campaigns of the time such as the fights for women's suffrage, trade union rights and self-determination.

△ *The swooping, Moderne lines of Mendelsohn and Chermayeff's stylish staircase.*

a steeply pitched roof, a large clock tower, segmental pediments *and* a dome gave visitors the impression they were in Saxony rather than Sussex.* The rest of the town, however, remained rooted to its Victorian past, despite the county council's attempt to market this area after 1930 as 'The Conqueror's Coast'. In 1933 the acerbic poet Keith Douglas visited the town, where his mother now lived, and in a subsequent poem slightingly dismissed the 'Small streets and posters which the lamplight shews', contrasting them with Europe's 'white-dusted avenues... where... the barbers chatter, the sky is clean'.

By the time Douglas's poem 'Bexhill' was published in 1935, however, the town boasted not only an up-to-date electric train service to London, inaugurated by the Southern Railway on 7 July, but also its own continental-style, white-dusted architectural icon. Bexhill's new seafront pavilion was an astoundingly

---

* This surprising station was closed in 1964 thanks to the Beeching cuts. However, thankfully it survives as offices and was finally listed Grade II in 2013.

bold architectural statement which rivalled the most avant-garde structures of contemporary Europe and demonstrated that even a staid Victorian seaside town could move with the times. Its architects were European in origin, too: the German-Jewish émigré Erich Mendelsohn (1887–1953) and Russian-born Serge Chermayeff (1900–96). But the driving force behind this startling new commission was as British as they came: Herbrand Sackville, 9th Earl De La Warr and Mayor of Bexhill from 1932 to 1934.

Earl De La Warr and the Bexhill Pavilion

In 1933 Hitler became Chancellor of Germany, unleashing the National Socialists (Nazis) in a wave of officially sanctioned violence against the country's Jews and limiting them from participation in public life. These developments persuaded Erich Mendelsohn, among many other German Jews, liberals and socialists, to leave Germany for Britain. It was also in 1933 that De La Warr, in the second year of his mayoral term following an uncontested election, conceived the idea of a large entertainment hall that would enable Bexhill to leapfrog its coastal rivals and attract the sort of cultured visitor that he and the town now sought. Such a building would also, he hoped, encourage other seaside reports to be more daring in their reception of modern architecture and modern times.

At every step of the planning and construction process it was the 9th Earl who got things done. It was he who reassured the locals that the new building would not ruin the town's relaxed and refined image: 'We all of us want to maintain the existing character of the town, but we believe that we can make more of our existing resources.' It was his idea to stage an open competition for the scheme which would be run by the Royal Institute of British Architects, no less. It was also De La Warr's vision that this building should not be built in a traditional idiom but should embrace the Modernist style which had already swept the Continent. In 1933 Modernist buildings were still rare in Britain; Amyas Connell's Amersham house, High and Over, of 1931 and the Tecton Group's buildings for London Zoo from 1932 were unusual commissions for a nation still in the grip of traditionalism. De La Warr, though, was determined that the new pavilion should be stylistically innovative:

It is the intention of the promoters that the building should be simple in design, and suitable for a Holiday Resort in the South of England. Character

421

in design can be obtained by the use of large window spaces, terraces and canopies. No restrictions as to style of architecture will be imposed but buildings must be simple, light in appearance and attractive, suitable for a Holiday Resort. Heavy stonework is not desirable.

Avoiding any prescription of style, the competition brief merely stipulated that the design must provide for:

An ENTERTAINMENTS HALL to seat 1500 persons, to be used for concerts, theatrical performances, lectures, etc.; An ENTRANCE HALL giving access to all public rooms (long corridors to be avoided); A RESTAURANT (available for dancing if necessary) to seat 200 persons, designed as a parlour with sliding or opening French windows leading on to a terrace facing the sea; A CONFERENCE HALL to seat 200 persons which could also be used as a lecture hall; A READING ROOM for news-papers and magazines, again in the form of a sun parlour; A LOUNGE adjacent to the READING ROOM.

The architectural competition for the Bexhill Pavilion was announced in the *Architects' Journal* in February 1934. The design potential and high visi-bility of the seafront location attracted over 230 entrants and a wide range of architectural styles, from Victorian Gothic to Modernist. Much to everyone's surprise, the winners were Mendelsohn and Chermayeff.

The architects

Mendelsohn and Chermayeff were an odd pair. Mendelsohn was from East Prussia and by 1933 was committed to a severe, monochrome Modernism, even though he had originally made his name in 1921 with his cheerfully eclec-tic Einstein Tower in Potsdam. Serge Chermayeff was born in what is now Chechnya, had lived in London for many years and was a larger-than-life figure who first worked for Waring and Gillow as an interior designer while simul-taneously winning the national tango-dancing championships and whose designs prioritised colour and light. At Bexhill it appears that the general design was Mendelsohn's while the interiors were largely Chermayeff's, which proved a winning combination. Mendelsohn, with characteristic immodesty, likened the building to 'a horizontal skyscraper' and described its interior as 'truly music'. It was De La Warr and the emollient Chermayeff, rather than the arrogant East Prussian, who made themselves the building's public advocates and who sold the design both to the architectural world and to the burghers of Bexhill. And it was, inevitably, De La Warr who led the measured response to the predictable misgivings about the architects' foreign origins and the 'alien' nature of Modernism. As Mark Cannata has noted: 'The fact that the competition was awarded to a German émigré and a Russian-born socialite was not welcomed in some circles.' It was De La Warr who reminded his audiences of Britain's long and honourable tradition of welcoming political refugees of all hues and of the unsullied credentials of the scheme's architects. It was important, he stressed, that Bexhill should be seen to lead the nation, rather than follow in others' footsteps.

It was De La Warr, too, who secured a visit during construction works from King George V and Queen Mary – hardly Modernism's most passionate advocates – and who booked the Duke and Duchess of York (subsequently King George VI and Queen Elizabeth) to open the building on 12 December 1935, a month after De La Warr had stepped down as mayor.

The completed Pavilion's main elevation sensibly faced the sea, ingeniously masking the ungainly bulk of the Metropole Hotel to its rear.* The most striking features of Mendelsohn and Chermayeff's building were the rows of Crittall steel windows and the cantilevered terraces of the restaurant and cafeteria, linked to the theatre by an astonishing, three-storey glazed staircase which projected out towards the English Channel and to France. Mark Cannata has remarked:

> Internally, the Pavilion fully demonstrated the tenets of the new architecture, with flowing spaces, clean, crisp detailing, its ivory-cream-painted walls, cork or cream terrazzo floors and extensive sea views. The contrasting colours, perhaps inspired by the colours of pebbles on the adjacent beach, were balanced by the bright vermilion Alvar Alto chairs in the restaurant and blue PLAN chairs in the reading room, on a backdrop of brown carpets and curtains. The main areas reflected instead, with the

---

*   The Metropole was later wholly demolished, allegedly due to severe wartime damage. This ungainly, six-storey block had inexplicably been built at right angles to, and not facing, the sea.

cork and terrazzo floor, the creams of the main elevations and exterior palette. The whole was delicately poised.

The effect was a human-scaled design which, in a very British way, did not take itself too seriously, refuting at a stroke most of the criticisms made of Modernism both then and since. There was to be no finer example built in the country of the fusion of continental design with the idioms and demands of the British seaside town and the peculiarities of the British people.

Selling the Pavilion

In 1940 J. M. Richards, the editor of the *Architectural Review*, was to pronounce that 'Englishness [was] not incompatible with modern architecture'. The De La Warr Pavilion proved he was right. With this building, the nation had, it seemed, fully embraced Europe. Four years later, however, this very same coastline braced itself once more to resist Europe: by 1940 the Pavilion looked out onto a nightmarish seascape of barbed wire, metal posts, tank traps and concrete pillboxes.

Critics loved the unassumingly graceful and dazzlingly white Pavilion, extolling its sense of openness and exquisite finishes. In 1937 the American critic and historian Henry-Russell Hitchcock unambiguously called it 'probably the most notable and most successful modern building in England'. Some locals were not so sure, however. The editor of the *Bexhill-on-Sea Observer* was worried that the winning design did not initially give 'the impression which they hoped and expected', while the Town Clerk of Bexhill was accused by one resident of a lack of patriotism by 'employing an alien architect to design the building'. Shamefully, two of the competition's unsuccessful architects also joined the ranks of the disgruntled. James Burford and Marshall Sisson had both been members of Oswald Mosley's British Union of Fascists and now weighed into the epistolary war against the 'alien' winners. Burford declared that there had been a 'strong public protest at the result of this competition' and suggested disingenuously that the winning design would hamper the cause of Modernism in Britain as 'the public generally will not discriminate between the design and its author'.

Earl De La Warr's response was magisterial, advertising the much-vaunted traditional British values of fair play and even-handedness. His letters to the

Architects' Journal and the *Bexhill-on-Sea Observer* calmly noted that the design had been won in an open competition judged by an impeccably regarded and emphatically neutral assessor (the architect Thomas Tait), in which the entries had all been anonymised. He pointedly added, 'The winning firm is a British firm and Mr Chermayeff is... a British member of the RIBA'; he also added that, while 'It is true that the firm has lately taken in Mendelsohn who was one of the greatest architects on the continent', the Home Office certificate required before a foreign member of a profession could be allowed to work in Britain was 'not issued without consultation with the profession in this country'. Moreover, De La Warr recorded that:

> he was given to understand that the reply of the RIBA to the Home Office when consulted about Mr Erich Mendelsohn was that he was so distinguished an artist that they welcomed his admission... and further that if he stayed and applied for naturalization they would be pleased and proud to consider him for the bestowal of the highest honour that the profession could give.

De La Warr concluded by expressing his delight that the prize had been awarded 'to a set of plans of which I hope that not only our small town, but all those interested in architecture in this country may be proud', which would 'fully satisfy the requirements of Bexhill, and will embellish the seafront with a striking feature that will be talked of far and wide'.

There was, nevertheless, a public inquiry into the design of the building. Mendelsohn attended but left it to the suave and persuasive Chermayeff to outline the proposals. Russell Stevens and Peter Willis have noted how he skilfully brought the audience round:

> The pavilion, [Chermayeff] said, was designed to obtain the utmost flexibility and was unorthodox and quite unlike any other building in the country. He announced that a steel frame not a concrete frame would be used (and welded rather than riveted) which would be cheaper and lighter... Many other witnesses, including De La Warr, were called by both counsels, and it became apparent that the overriding concern of the inspector... was that the project would not cause an increase in the rates over 4d., the maximum allowed under the Local Government Act of 1929.

Cost-cutting exercises were then conducted on the scheme to ensure that the inspector's anxieties were dispelled, and the Pavilion would keep within its budget. This was later used by objectors as an excuse to oppose the planned construction of a two-storey walkway to link the Pavilion with a beach-side circular swimming pool and a sea jetty, which would have proved a fine addition to the site.

Once the building was opened, though, only the most intractable Bexhillian found it difficult to admire. Even the nervous *Bexhill-on-Sea Observer* agreed that, while 'the unaccustomed horizontal lines and austerity of the walls were somewhat disturbing to conventional ideas of entertainment halls' during its construction, fears that 'Bexhill was making too bold an experiment in modern architecture' were now allayed, since 'the pavilion more than realises the public... expectation' and that consequently 'Bexhill is very proud of the building'. The London *Evening Standard* published a letter from caustic playwright George Bernard Shaw stating with his customary astringency that he was 'Delighted to hear that Bexhill had emerged from barbarism', while *The Times* opined that the Pavilion was 'by far the most civilised thing that has been done on the coast since the days of the Regency'.

As ever, Earl De La Warr emerged from the whole affair as the quintessential Englishman: altruistically proactive yet at the same time modestly fair-minded. Offered the Freedom of Bexhill once the building had been opened, he replied to his successor as mayor that 'I feel that it would be wiser for the matter to be deferred' given that there were still elements in the town who opposed the pavilion.

Dad's army

At the outbreak of the Second World War, the new De La Warr Pavilion was immediately requisitioned by the military because of its excellent location and fine seaward views. One of the units initially allocated to the building in 1940 to oppose a notional German invasion was the 56th Heavy Regiment of the Royal Artillery. One of the regimental gunners, Spike Milligan, later recalled that during training the gun crews had to shout 'bang!' in unison as they had no shells, either live or blank, with which to practise. This surreal episode must surely have helped to influence Milligan's virtuoso scripts for the post-war BBC radio comedy *The Goon Show*. Broadcast from 1951, *The Goon Show* became one of the most influential comedy series in British history, inspiring generations of comic ensembles from the Monty Python team of 1969 to the alternative comedy scene of the 1990s. Bexhill thus deserves at least a footnote in the annals of British comedy. The town also merits consideration as a model for the cosy fictional wartime community of Walmington-on-Sea conjured from 1968 by the writers of the classic television comedy series *Dad's Army*.

The Pavilion was fortunate to escape severe damage during the war. Although Bexhill possessed no military targets of value, its coastal location made it a favourite of German bombers looking to jettison their remaining bombs before returning across the Channel. However, while the Metropole Hotel behind the western end of the Pavilion was badly hit, the Pavilion itself suffered only minor damage to its foundations and emerged surprisingly unscathed.

After 1945, some of the concerns voiced by the inquiry's objectors actually came to pass. Thanks largely to post-war austerity and the dispersal of Bexhill's expatriate community, the redevelopment of the Bexhill seafront which De La Warr and others had assumed that the Pavilion would generate never took place. Instead, Bexhill sank back into its late Victorian torpor.

Trying times

By 1947 Britain was broke, and the $4 billion loan it had negotiated from its American allies at the end of the war was already nearly exhausted. As historian Corelli Barnett has remarked:

> Britain was literally bankrupt, and faced the prospect of unbridgeable balance-of-payments deficits for years to come. [The] victor's psychology... deluded both Labour and Conservative politicians into believing that Britain – at the centre of the Commonwealth and the Sterling area – could have a future that was similar to her past. British politicians saw the United Kingdom as a first-class power in the same league as the United States.

The new welfare state envisaged by the Beveridge Report of 1942 and the landslide-winning Labour government of 1945 had to be created using what the government could scrape together from its own resources – or borrow from the pot of Marshall Aid when the Americans weren't looking. John Maynard Keynes, chief economic adviser to the new Labour government, warned ministers in August 1945 that Britain's world role was a burden which 'there is no reasonable expectation of our being able to carry' and that the nation faced 'a financial Dunkirk'. When Marshall Aid was used as emergency support for the British economy after 1948, its strategic value was, in the view of commentators such as Barnett, largely wasted:

> The plain truth is that the Labour Government in the late 1940s sought to use Marshall Aid much as the Conservatives used the rake-off from North Sea oil in the 1980s – as a general subsidy for whatever they wished to do, like clinging on to the dream of a world power role.

The proportion of Marshall Aid which Britain allocated to industry and infrastructure was barely a third of that similarly allocated by the new West German government after 1949. By 1950 Britain was investing only 9 per cent of its Gross National Product (GNP) in its ageing and increasingly uncompetitive industries and its creaking, investment-starved infrastructure, while West Germany was spending 19 per cent of GNP. The prospects were not good.

With infrastructure so far down the post-war government's list of priorities, there was little hope that beleaguered seaside towns such as Bexhill would see much, if any, new government investment. Bexhill accordingly became a retirement destination of the sort which successive administrations of both parties simply preferred to ignore. In 1951, 28 per cent of the town's population were of pensionable age, yet by 1971 this had grown to 44 per cent, giving Bexhill the dubious accolade of being Britain's most elderly town. The pensioners of Bexhill were left to face the deleterious effects of the motor car, of television and of the continental package holiday alone.

When the redevelopment of Bexhill's seafront did finally take place in the 1960s, it was not the sort of imaginative, civic-focused masterplan that had been envisaged by De La Warr and his supporters in 1935. Rather, it was a ruthless and piecemeal surgery of the Victorian seafront which sought to exploit air rights and maximise profits rather than attract more holidaymakers or to make the town a more pleasant place for its residents. Like so many of Britain's seaside towns at the time, historic character was senselessly sacrificed to the goal of erecting as many characterless tower blocks as possible – each of whose developers demanded a sea view to ease sales. In 1968 even the De La Warrs' old Manor House was largely demolished to make way for road widening, its remaining fragments being used to decorate the newly christened 'Manor Gardens'.

△ *A 1939 postcard of the Pavilion, showing a sedate Bexhill just before war broke out.*

The 1970s were difficult times for Bexhill, as for most of Britain's seaside towns. The Local Government Act passed by Edward Heath's Conservative government in 1972, and enacted on, fittingly, April Fool's Day in 1974, callously swept away Britain's traditional county and borough authorities and replaced them with anonymous District Councils and instantly reviled new Metropolitan Counties. One of the many victims of this legislation – which, like the savage and unnecessary Beeching cuts to the railway system of a decade earlier, belied the Conservatives' ill-earned reputation as the champion of tradition and convention – was Bexhill, which lost its town council and found itself annexed by its long-despised rival, Hastings, in the blandly anonymous combine of Rother District Council.*

By the late 1970s the Pavilion was in a sad condition. The town's repertory company, the Penguin Players, had folded in 1975, and the Pavilion's once-lofty programme of upmarket entertainment had been replaced by a series of bingo sessions, social clubs, Christmas pantos and appearances by fading TV

---

* The town only won back a degree of genuine representative independence as recently as 2021.

celebrities. The same scenario was being enacted up and down Britain's coasts, as the nation itself increasingly resembled a cheap and impoverished end-of-the-pier assembly of out-of-date acts and worn-out routines.

Things got no better for Bexhill in the early years of Thatcher's Britain. As Stevens and Willis have noted, 'By the early 1980s the Pavilion had become neglected and decayed, its render crumbling, its metal corroded by the salty sea air and the exterior covered in scaffolding [and] the much-altered interiors were decorated with flock wallpaper and floral carpets':

> Years of exposure to the strong winds and salty air, combined with lack of maintenance and failing services, had reduced the building to a pale shadow of its former self. In 1991, when the first phase of the work commenced, Rother District Council, the owners, considered that the Pavilion had become economically unsustainable. Although the theatre in the Pavilion remained popular, its future was uncertain and its closure and sale remained a strong possibility... Most of the exterior render was crumbling due to water infiltration and the lack of expansion joints; the innovative welded steel structure was badly corroded; several original elements had been lost, including most of the windows; and the replacement windows were defective, as well as many of the 1930s fixtures and fittings. What remained was in a very poor state.

New horizons

In 1986, however, at the height of Britain's conservation revolution, the tide began to turn. In that year the Pavilion was awarded Grade I listed status, the highest level of protection available and a status only bestowed on the top 6 per cent of the nation's historic building stock. Three years later a trust was formed to protect and conserve the building.

There was still widespread concern, nevertheless, that the building might be saved physically only to pass into the private realm as offices or residential units. The playwright David Hare was not alone in demanding that the building remain in public use as an art gallery; even Queen Elizabeth the Queen Mother wrote to the local council asking what its intentions were for a building she herself had opened in 1935. In September 2000 architectural historian Marcus Binney wrote in *The Times*, 'Half the towns of Europe now dream of

△ *Mendelsohn and Chermayeff's design brought continental glamour to this quiet stretch of the Sussex coast. But their bold design was not without its critics.*

building a modern masterpiece like the Bilbao Guggenheim. Amazingly, sedate Bexhill achieved this 65 years ago.'

Thanks to pressure from the conservationists, a wholly new charitable trust was, in 2002, granted £6 million to turn the building into a contemporary arts centre, which opened in 2005 boasting one of the largest art galleries on the south coast and with sensitive new additions by the prestigious architect John McAslan. Today you can once more sit behind the Pavilion's glazed façade and raise a glass towards the European coast.

23

CASTLE BROMWICH FACTORY, WARWICKSHIRE

1936

From Spitfires to Jaguars: one factory produces some of the greatest British marques of the twentieth century

Castle Bromwich Factory – or 'Assembly', as it is generally known today – is no Lincoln Cathedral or Birmingham Town Hall. It is the only one of the twenty-five structures selected for this book which is not an outstanding or typical example of architectural design. Indeed, over the years it has lost some of the interesting architectural features it could boast when it was first built. Nor does its present location, bordered by the busy M6 motorway on the unremarkable eastern fringes of Greater Birmingham, inspire much interest. However, it has an emblematic worth out of all proportion to its undistinguished aesthetics: as a symbol both of Britain's success in the air war of 1939–45 and of the nation's post-war struggle to realign its failing manufacturing industries with new markets and new horizons.

▷ *Lancaster bombers being built at Castle Bromwich in 1944.*

433

The shadow factories

Castle Bromwich Factory started life as one of the 'shadow factories' planned to produce British armaments as early as 1935. While much has been written about the appeasement policies of the Chamberlain government of 1937–40, less is known about the steps that its predecessors took to counter German rearmament after 1935. In February of that year Hitler's National Socialist government publicly revealed the existence of the Luftwaffe and the following month introduced conscription and began rearming in earnest. In response, in May 1935 Britain's new prime minister, Stanley Baldwin (prodded from the backbenches by an insistent Winston Churchill), invited munitions expert Sir William Weir* (1877–1959) to examine what could be done to mobilise industry for arms production. Weir was given the title of Adviser to the Air Ministry and asked to help the visionary new Secretary of State for Air, Viscount Swinton, develop a new programme to manufacture parts and finished aircraft for the Royal Air Force. Weir, agreeing with Churchill that very little had been done to date, acknowledged that democratic Britain would not be able to command the same resources as totalitarian Germany, and told Baldwin that 'we must quietly but very rapidly find an effective British compromise solution as opposed to merely copying the centralised dictator system'. (Earlier in 1935 the War Office itself had admitted, 'The political and economic organisation of the German state is more favourable than our own to the adaption by industry to the production of war equipment of every variety.') Instead, Weir devised a very British compromise by which 'shadow' munitions factories would be paid for by the state but built and operated by the private sector. He also advised the Air Ministry that 'The best expansion channel for this, if needed, should come from the automobile industry', since Britain's large car factories already possessed the skilled labour necessary to turn out precision armaments. As Neil Forbes has explained:

> The layout and plant of the shadow factories were designed for quantity production rather than experimental or development work. The most important were the factories that were to produce aero engines; the No. 1 group (as it came to be called) was laid down in 1937–8 and the No. 2 group in 1939–40. Swinton initiated this aspect of the scheme when, on

---

*   Created the 1st Viscount Weir by Neville Chamberlain's government in 1938.

24 March 1936, he wrote to the motor manufacturers – Austin (based at Longbridge in Birmingham), Morris (based in Cowley, Oxford) and Coventry-based Daimler, Rover, Rootes (in the form of its subsidiary, Hillman Motors), and Standard.

As the scheme developed, the shadow factories were, following the German practice, built outside urban areas in order to minimise the risk of serious damage from potential enemy bombing.

The car factories of the Midlands thus became essential weapons in Britain's impending fight for survival. One of the most successful of these shadow factories, and one which produced the legendary Supermarine Spitfire fighter and Avro Lancaster four-engined bomber that played such a major part in spearheading Britain's war effort, was the vast new Castle Bromwich plant. This facility was built, somewhat unpropitiously, on the site of an old sewage works adjacent to an existing airfield to the east of Birmingham. More than 20,000 Spitfires were eventually made here, making Castle Bromwich the largest producer of this outstanding aircraft in the country.

William Morris, Lord Nuffield

Although the principal enthusiast for the shadow factory scheme in the automotive sector was Birmingham-based Herbert Austin, it was Austin's great rival, the Oxford-based carmaker William Morris (1877–1963),[*] who readily agreed to operate the new Castle Bromwich plant. Yet by the time the tools for the first aircraft had begun to appear in the factory, Morris's involvement in the site had been terminated. His shortcomings as an industrial dynamo having been vividly exposed, he had been swiftly ushered out of the door by the wartime government.

Morris was a strange man, a character simultaneously compelling and unappealing. Born in Worcester in 1877, six years before Daimler perfected the first successful petrol engine and eight years before Benz made the first car, Morris was the son of a shop manager from Witney, Oxfordshire, and was

---

[*]   Morris was awarded an OBE in 1918 and a baronetcy in 1929 by King George V, and created 1st Baron Nuffield, after the Oxfordshire village, in 1934. He chose the title of 'Nuffield' as both 'Morris' and 'Cowley' were already in use; and in 1938 he was promoted to a viscountcy by Neville Chamberlain's Conservative government.

brought up in a humble, brick-built terraced house in Oxford's James Street. In later years Morris tended to reinvent his past; a central element of this was his tendency to exaggerate his father Frederick's achievements and qualities while omitting any mention of his mother. In 1937 he described his father (whose school William had already converted into a primitive car factory) as 'a great accountant [and] a financial brain' who had sought his fortune in Canada, where he had lived for a time with a Native American tribe. In truth, Frederick Morris had been a mercurial lost soul, who moved rapidly from job to job and who migrated around the South Midlands. Morris's curious insistence on reimagining his background was, as his biographer Martin Adeney subsequently suggested, part of an attempt to 'cut deliberately away from his origins'.

William Morris was the archetypal self-made man. By the age of sixteen he was repairing bicycles for a living and was attempting to use his income to support his family. He started a cycle business at his workshop in Oxford's Holywell Street and developed a new motorcycle, selling the company in 1908 and using the profits to build a handsome new workshop-cum-showroom just around the corner in Longwall Street. With the success of his car factory in the Oxford suburb of Cowley after 1918, the humbly born mechanic swiftly ascended the social ladder.

Morris always believed he knew best and, like so many other self-made industrial magnates of the time, brooked no dissent. He was also ruthless in his personal relationships, suddenly dropping supposed friends and allies for the most trivial of reasons. Even Lord Macclesfield, whose initial financial investment had been integral to Morris's success, suddenly found himself *persona non grata* at Morris Motors in 1922 when Morris believed he was interfering too much in the business. Morris bought Macclesfield's shareholding and brusquely severed his link with the company which the blameless earl had done so much to rescue.

While he became immensely rich, Morris was also oddly parsimonious, frequently denouncing what he saw as 'extravagance' in others. Morris's publicity chief, Miles Thomas, later recounted how his boss had reacted to finding a piece of soap left in a full basin in a plant washroom (without asking what Morris was doing checking the factory toilets in the first place): 'That bright-eyed little man fumed and swore and became tremendously hot under the collar.' Morris noted down all his personal expenditure to the last penny until his death, while his eating and drinking habits were notoriously abstemious. (As, indeed, were those of his wife, who allegedly gathered scraps from

438

the Cowley canteen for her chickens at Nuffield Place and then sold their eggs back to the Morris workforce at the plant gates at market rates.) Morris was also socially clumsy and a poor communicator. Thomas later noted that 'Bill Morris was at his unhappy worst at a meeting... He lost his temper easily, wriggled in his chair and on numerous occasions simply had to leave the boardroom. Of these shortcomings he was acutely aware and avoided both calling and attending round-table discussions.' A shy workaholic – 'a self-centred withdrawn introvert' according to Miles Thomas – he was always moving and full of nervous energy. Yet at the same time he paid above the statutory union wage rate, attracting agricultural labourers from all over Oxfordshire to his Cowley factory with his munificent salaries, and at least until 1939 prided himself on knowing most of his workforce by name.

Morris was also an extremely generous benefactor to hospitals and health charities: his Nuffield Foundation gave generously to the local Oxford hospitals and, an inveterate smoker, he provided a fund in October 1939 to buy cigarettes for troops based overseas. By the time of his death Morris had given much of his fortune – over £25 million, a vast sum in those days – to charitable causes, particularly those which sought to alleviate the conditions of the 'deserving poor'.

Morris at Castle Bromwich

Morris's approach to car manufacture differed considerably from that of his rivals Henry Ford or Herbert Austin, and laid the seeds of his downfall at Castle Bromwich. He did not to seek to build cars from scratch but aimed to become an assembler of other companies' products, relying on his own mechanical skill to source and combine the best components currently on the market. While this policy of assembling other people's parts served him very well up until the Second World War, however, the absence of any real vertical integration within his company meant that after 1939 his systems were dangerously vulnerable and antiquated. Nor did he help himself by his lackadaisical attitude to war production. Having been made Director-General of Maintenance of the RAF at the beginning of the war, Morris stubbornly refused to come to London, and instead stayed in his Morris offices at the Cowley works in Oxford. By the time the Germans invaded Holland, Belgium and France in May 1940, it was clear that, in his intransigence and obsession with the assembly line, Lord Nuffield was unable to encompass factors such as the constant alterations that

△ *Clipped-wing Supermarine Spitfires Mark Vb in production at Castle Bromwich in 1943.*

had to be made to machine tools for such complex aircraft as the Spitfire and Lancaster, of which many disparate marques were made. The government had spent £7 million creating Castle Bromwich but, while Nuffield had claimed he could produce sixty Spitfires a week, by the time Winston Churchill came to power in May 1940 not one had been built. As Leo McKinstry has written: 'The government was in despair at the fiasco of Castle Bromwich, especially because Nuffield refused to recognise the scale of the disaster and constantly bleated about lack of technical support from Supermarine.' Nuffield's poorly managed labour force was also markedly un-cooperative and combative, with communist shop stewards encouraging grievances (at a time when Soviet Russia and Nazi Germany were notional allies and the British Communist Party was denouncing the war as a capitalist construct) and constantly halting production for go-slows and strikes in pursuit of higher pay.

The autocratic Morris had, though, met his match in Churchill's new

Minister of Aircraft Production, Lord Beaverbrook, who could be just as ruthless and demanding as the automobile tycoon. When Morris rang Beaverbrook to complain about the RAF's constant requests for modifications, the carmaker finally erupted with the threat, 'Maybe you would like me to give up control of the Spitfire factory?' Beaverbrook instantly seized his chance. Replying, 'Nuffield, that's very generous of you. I accept' and slamming the phone down. Morris, seething, stormed up to London and confronted Prime Minister Winston Churchill over the issue, tactlessly reminding the premier how much money Morris had in the past donated to Churchill's Conservative Party. But Churchill stood by his pugnacious minister, and Morris retreated to Oxford with his tail between his legs. The running of Castle Bromwich was handed by Beaverbrook to Vickers, since 1936 the owners of the makers of the Spitfire, Supermarine. Vickers ironed out the production difficulties at Castle Bromwich and produced twenty-two different types of Spitfire during the war years at a rate of more than 300 a month.

The aircraft factory

The architecture of the Castle Bromwich plant was understandably reticent. The first assembly line buildings, 'A' and 'B' blocks, being provided with simple brick walls punctuated by two rows of steel windows from Crittall of Braintree, some of which still remain today. More thought was given to the offices, which were provided with a tripartite entrance projection incorporating some vaguely Art Deco detailing. This feature suggests the involvement of cinema specialist Harry Weedon, an architect previously best known for his large, demonstrative Moderne cinemas for the Odeon chain but who, from 1940, spent much of his time working on Birmingham's new, dispersed factories.

The site of the Castle Bromwich plant was largely chosen for its proximity to an existing airfield, originally built in 1915. During the First World War it hosted a number of fighter and bomber aircraft types, including what was probably the best fighter Britain produced in the First World War, the Royal Aircraft factory SE5, which was mostly built at Longbridge by Austin Motors. In 1926 one of the first RAF Auxiliary Squadrons was formed here: 60 'County of Warwick' Squadron, whose Hawker Hurricanes played a major role in the Battle of Britain of 1940 but whose entire complement was captured by the Japanese in Java early in 1942, shortly before the swift and shocking fall of Britain's principal Far East base at Singapore.*

The wisdom of building shadow factories such as Castle Bromwich was soon evident. Industrial cities like Coventry and Birmingham were heavily bombed from July 1940, but the outlying shadow plants emerged largely unscathed, and were able to continue manufacturing. In 1940–1 the centre of Coventry was subject to forty air raids, the most serious of which, on the night of 14–15 November 1940, killed 554 people and wrecked the medieval city centre – including the magnificent church of St Michael, since 1918 designated a cathedral. Alvis's car plant was completely destroyed; its wartime production was, as a result, dispersed all over England, from Hinckley in Leicestershire to Ealing in west London. But while the city of Coventry lay devastated, the new shadow factory sites seemed to offer prospects of a miraculous, phoenix-like industrial rebirth.

At the Castle Bromwich Factory, finished aircraft were wheeled from the factory across Chester Road to the adjacent airfield. Here they were prepared for flight testing under the watchful eye of Vickers' test pilot Alex Henshaw (1912–2007), who had won the King's Cup air race in 1933 and who in 1938 had flown to Cape Town and back in his Percival Mew Gull in four and a half days, a record that stood until 2009.

The aircraft that Castle Bromwich produced helped to win the war for Britain. Along with its invaluable but more traditionally designed contemporary, the Hawker Hurricane, the sleek, fast and highly manoeuvrable Supermarine Spitfire was a worthy opponent to the German's Messerschmitt Me 109Es which accompanied the Heinkel, Junkers and Dornier bombers over England during the Battle of Britain. The Spitfires were often directed against the fighter cover of Me 109s and the twin-engined Me 110 *Zestörer* (a model which failed to justify the high hopes invested in it by Luftwaffe chief Hermann Göring) while the Hurricanes, which offered a more stable gun platform, engaged the bombers. Their astounding success against far larger forces led to Hitler abandoning the plan to invade Britain on 18 December 1940 in order to concentrate on attacking his notional ally, Russia.

---

*   605 Squadron was re-formed in Britain in June 1942 under the command of Wing Commander Peter Townsend, who was to earn post-war celebrity status as the partner of Princess Margaret. By 1948 it was flying early jet fighters such as the de Havilland Vampire, but it was disbanded in 1957. In 2014 the squadron name was revived for the RAF Reserve Logistics Support Squadron at RAF Cosford in Staffordshire.

The Spitfire and the Lancaster

The Supermarine Spitfire has often been depicted as the ultimate symbol of the best of British: a reflection of the inventiveness, style and perseverance of a proud nation. Spitfire biographer and journalist Jonathan Glancey has suggested: 'The spirit of the Spitfire is deeply embedded in our culture, a machine that somehow speaks of cricket, the sonnets of Keats, freedom from entrapment and, most of all, a desire to do things our own way.' Almost eighty years since the Second World War ended it still carries a powerful punch in Britain, having been appropriated to brand cars, beer, aluminium doors and audio products.

The first Spitfire the Castle Bromwich factory produced was the Mk II, a version of the original Mk I which had been provided with an uprated Rolls-Royce Merlin XII engine and a larger propeller, which gave the plane a higher speed and a better climb rate than its predecessor. The first Mk II flew on 24 September 1939 and by April 1941 all of Britain's Mk I models had been replaced with this improved model. However, owing to its teething problems, Castle Bromwich only reached full production of the Mk II in June 1940 and only supplied its first battle-ready Spitfire to 611 Squadron in August 1940, after the Battle of Britain had been in full spate for over two months. The eight-gun Mk II Spitfire now operated by the Battle of Britain Memorial Flight was built at Castle Bromwich.

Castle Bromwich's importance as a source of Spitfires was underlined when the original Supermarine factory at Southampton was heavily bombed twice in two days in September 1940 and production there was stopped. The Warwickshire factory was also repeatedly hit during the war, as test pilot Alex Henshaw later testified:

> The Germans seemed to find the factory at Castle Bromwich almost every time and one got hardened to the sight of a direct hit on, say, the machine shop before all the employees had gone to the shelters; as day slowly dawned it was common to find bits of bodies mingled with valuable equipment blasted to small pieces and hanging gruesomely from what had been the roof.

However, Castle Bromwich actually suffered far less than those plants, like Supermarine at Southampton, which were sited in the midst of large industrial cities. By 1945 Castle Bromwich had produced 12,129 Spitfires – well over half of the total built during the war – from the Mk IIs to the Mk XVIs, low-altitude versions of the Mk IX which had been introduced to match the new and formidable Focke-Wulf 190 German fighter. The Mk XVI carried cannon as well as machine guns and was powered by an American-made Merlin 266 engine.

Prime Minister Winston Churchill himself visited the Castle Bromwich factory in September 1941, during which he was treated to a typically ambitious aerobatic display in a Spitfire Mark V by Vickers' dauntless test pilot Alex Henshaw. As Henshaw later recalled, he almost lost his life on this occasion, glancing at his watch during a critical manoeuvre and losing thousands of feet in altitude as a result.

The Spitfire was not the only war-winning aircraft produced at Castle Bromwich. On 22 October 1943 Alex Henshaw test-flew the first example of the new Avro Lancaster heavy bomber made by the factory. That particular aircraft, HK535, was sent to 463 Squadron, a Royal Australian Air Force unit, and was lost over Lille on 11 May 1944.

The Lancaster was arguably the Second World War's finest bomber, boasting double the bomb capacity of, and a longer range than, the Americans' admittedly more robust and better-armed Boeing B-17. However, the Lancaster has not always enjoyed the reputation of its Castle Bromwich stablemate. As Leo McKinstry has noted:

> The Spitfire is remembered with near universal affection, but the Lancaster has been enveloped in controversy ever since 1945, because of its central role in the strategic bombing of Germany. The Spitfire was the hero of Biggin Hill and Malta. The name of the Lancaster is associated with the horrors of Hamburg in 1943 and Dresden in 1945. No one has ever accused Spitfire airmen of complicity in war crimes, but Bomber Command was facing that charge even before the conflict had finished.

The Lancaster originated from the disastrous Manchester twin-engined bomber, whose unreliable Rolls-Royce Vulture engines made it notoriously unpredictable and even dangerous in the air. Avro's designer substituted four tried-and-trusted Merlin engines for the Vultures, lengthened the wings and came up with the hugely successful Lancaster, which by 1943 had become the RAF's principal heavy bomber and which served with tireless distinction until the war's end.

△ *The vast Castle Bromwich site at the end of the Second World War.*

Castle Bromwich produced 305 of these magnificent machines by the end of production in early 1945. Spitfire production at the factory ended in January 1946 with the last Mk 22s, powered by Rolls-Royce Griffon 61 engines and with new teardrop canopies affording better all-round vision. Mk 22s continued in RAF service until 1955 and in other global air forces until the early 1970s.

From fighters to kitchens

When the Spitfire production lines were halted in 1946, many airframes were still on the factory's assembly lines. Those that were nearing completion were taken to Supermarine's newly purchased shadow factory at South Marston, outside Swindon. The factory was still full of unused parts, however, for which no obvious use could be found. That was until a Warwick engineering firm came up with a novel idea for a product which, in its own way, was as quintessentially British as the Spitfire and the Lancaster.

Constant Speed Aircrews of Warwick had made propellers and nosecones for Spitfire and Lancasters throughout the war. Like many wartime suppliers,

445

they realised that, as the end of the war approached, they might go out of business if they did not diversify their product base. Accordingly, in 1946 they reinvented themselves as CSA Industries and started making some of the first modular kitchens out of the parts at Castle Bromwich and using some of the labour originally allocated to making warplanes. Their classic 'English Rose' kitchen range was as stylish and streamlined as the Spitfire to which it was distantly related. Brightly coloured in pink, cream, red, pale green or pale blue – colours which had been often applied to wartime Spitfires* – and provided with equally colourful Formica worktops, the English Rose range was fittingly advertised, given its distant association with the legendary Rolls-Royce Merlin engine which had powered both the Spitfire and the Lancaster, as the 'Rolls-Royce of kitchens'. They were not designed to be retro products, however. English Rose kitchens incorporated American innovations such as a double drainer and sink and a pull-out cocktail cabinet, features hitherto unknown to middle-class Britons, as well as plenty of space for built-in appliances.

In 1952 CSA was acquired by the Birmingham luggage and steel furniture manufacturer J. B. Brooks, famous for their Antler brand of travel goods. Demand for English Rose kitchens fell appreciably in the later 1950s as cheaper alternatives made from MDF fibreboard were introduced. However, since the late 1990s vintage examples of original, Warwick-made English Rose kitchens now fetch high prices in the retro marketplace. Meanwhile the English Rose brand still survives as part of the portfolio of a firm of American venture capitalists.

Modernising the British kitchen played a part in the adaptation of Castle Bromwich Factory, too. In 1946 the plant was acquired by Fisher and Ludlow, which made bodies for car manufacturers such as Morris Motors and during the 1950s and 1960s also assembled washing machines under licence for the famous American firm Bendix. In 1953 Fisher and Ludlow were acquired by the new British Motor Corporation (BMC), which had been formed the previous year from the Austin and Morris car-making empires. (In truth BMC was a takeover of the antiquated Morris operation by Austin, which seized every opportunity to denigrate its former rival.) In 1968, the year in which BMC was absorbed into the maw of the ill-fated national car giant British Leyland, Fisher and Ludlow was forcibly merged with its principal rival to become Pressed Steel Fisher.

---

* Some reconnaissance Spitfires were painted pink (which the RAF called 'camoutint') or light blue to give them more invisibility in the air.

The arrival of Jaguar

By 1968 every trace of the adjacent airfield at Castle Bromwich had gone, save for a lone memorial unveiled by Alex Henshaw in 1965. The last squadron left in 1958 and two years later the Ministry of Defence sold the land to Birmingham City Council, which built its vast Castle Vale housing estate on the site.

Castle Bromwich Factory, however, was still in demand. In 1977 another famous British manufacturing marque joined Fisher and Ludlow there. To many it was fitting that Jaguar Cars should inherit the building which once made the Supermarine Spitfire. Jonathan Glancey has explicitly linked the two legendary marques:

> The closest thing to a Spitfire... is some makes of Jaguar. The Jaguar competes with BMW and Mercedes-Benz. Much of the character of that commercial battle can be divined from the earlier contest between the Spitfire and its deadliest rivals, the Messerschmitt 109 and the Focke-Wulf Fw190.

Jaguar had started life in 1922 as the Swallow Sidecar Company, making motorcycle sidecars. The driving force behind Swallow was William Lyons (1901–85), who in 1928–1929 moved the operation from Blackpool in Lancashire to the heart of Britain's Motor City, Coventry, in order to be closer to his suppliers, and in 1934 changed the company name to 'SS Cars.'

Lyons was a rare animal in the British motor industry: an automotive entrepreneur who could not only run a company but also design cars. His wide-ranging talents put most of his industry rivals in the shade – and were to prove crucial to Jaguar's post-war success. Born in Blackpool in 1901, he was set to join the Barrow shipyards after the First World War when a friend recommended the motor business. By 1922 he was making motorcycles and motorcycle side-cars and in 1931 Lyons unveiled their first cars: sleek, low-slung, two-door coupés which he named the SS1 and SS2. Their immediate success, even at the height of the Depression, was due to Lyons's unique qualities: as his own designer, he ensured that the cars looked good, giving them long bonnets and sinuous, curving lines, while the salesman in Lyons ensured that the cars were all fully road-tested before their launch and, crucially, were heavily marketed.

The Jaguar name first surfaced in 1935, when it was applied to the four-door variant of the SS1 model. The SS1 carried a distinctive, lozenge-like radiator that Lyons subsequently applied to all his 'Jaguars'. In February 1945 the

△ *A Jaguar factory today. But for how long?*

'Jaguar' brand was applied to the company's entire product range, since 'SS Cars' now seemed a somewhat inappropriate label given the infamy of Hitler's SS stormtroopers. Four years later Jaguar's big breakthrough came with the XK120 sports car. Available as an open roadster or a closed coupé, the model took America by storm, helped by a spectacular series of motor racing victories. With Britain still immersed in a world of rationing and currency controls, few of its own citizens could afford an XK120; but the wealthy denizens of Eisenhower's America certainly could. At a time when most British motor executives were opting for safety over innovation, Lyons cleverly built on the XK120's success by venturing into a different market segment while taking care that the XK120's core brand values of looks, performance and luxury – or, as

448

the Jaguar sales slogan of the time had it, 'Grace, Space, Pace' – were just as relevant to this new sector.

In 1961 Sir William Lyons (as he became in 1956) launched the E-Type: a beautiful, two-seater touring car that looked like a racing car but wasn't. The E-Type's classic curves, devised partly by Lyons himself, instantly won over motoring critics and customers on both sides of the Atlantic. Five years later, however, Lyons made a misstep when he agreed to merge the Jaguar Group with BMC, which in 1968 (and much against Lyons' wishes) helped to form the giant conglomerate British Leyland. Chained to a patient on life-support – a flailing combine principally geared to high-volume small-car production which had to be bailed out by Harold Wilson's new Labour government in 1974 – Jaguar's reputation and standards plummeted and took years to recover. The firm had no chief executive at all between 1975 and 1980, but as a sop was in 1977 offered the Castle Bromwich site in which to produce new models.

John Egan

With its arrival at Castle Bromwich and the appointment in 1980 of a new managing director, John Egan, Jaguar began to turn the corner. Coventry-born Egan was steeped in engineering and familiar with the shop floor. The son of a garage owner, he had studied petroleum engineering at Imperial College London and then worked for Shell, General Motors' ACDelco and Canadian tractor-maker Massey Ferguson. His arrival at Jaguar ended a long strike, with Egan giving workers his personal commitment to the company and its workforce in Coventry and Castle Bromwich.

Egan hired racing guru Tom Walkinshaw to guide Jaguar back into the racing world for the first time in over twenty years and began testing cars thoroughly before launch as the Germans and Japanese had always done but as the British, perennially focused on short-term sales and dealers' demands, had rarely achieved. He was also appalled by the poor quality of many of the cars Jaguar were then building, as well as by the abysmal productivity of the Jaguar workforce. He was particularly dismayed by the rock-bottom standards exhibited by many of his suppliers: 'There were tyres that weren't round; radio aerials which wouldn't go up and down; switches that failed.' He also created a black museum of badly made car parts to show visiting suppliers.

In 1984, to Egan's delight, Jaguar was privatised by the Thatcher government, now seemingly invulnerable after victory in the 1982 Falklands War

449

and its great success in 1983's general election. Jaguar was back to impressive profits and Egan was knighted in 1986. Ford bought the company in 1990 – just in time for the recession of the early 1990s, which saw luxury car sales decimated. Egan, who had turned Jaguar's fortunes around so spectacularly in the 1980s, sensibly decided to bow out.

By 2000 Jaguar had emerged from its malaise and had recovered some of the jaunty confidence of the Lyons years. In 2008 Jaguar was unloaded by Ford onto the Indian conglomerate Tata, which began by axing the models based on Ford platforms (the X-Type and the S-Type, derived from the Ford Mondeo and Lincoln LS, respectively) and launched a new executive car, the XF, which sought to revive the classic British style of the Jaguars of the forties and fifties. The XF won plaudits and honours across the globe and in 2010 the firm added both the XKR high-performance sports car and the top-of-the-range XJ to its growing portfolio. The XJ, designed as the heir to Lyons's classic XJs of 1968, was styled by Jaguar's Ian Callum in a manner which looked both to its contemporary competitors as well as its illustrious predecessors. By the beginning of 2010 Jaguar was back in the black, albeit now under Indian ownership.

Facing the future

Confronted with a declining market for luxury saloons, in 2008 and again in 2010 Jaguar's new owners, Tata Motors, announced that it would close either the Castle Bromwich Factory or the newer Land Rover plant in Solihull. (Jaguar's old factory at Brown's Lane in Coventry had already closed in 2005, its production transferred to Castle Bromwich.) Thankfully, an agreement with the unions saved both facilities for the time being. Moreover, in 2019 Jaguar Land Rover announced it was to build its new electric version of its flagship XJ at Castle Bromwich, safeguarding 2,500 jobs there.

Yet barely three years after this accord, on 15 February 2021 the firm's new CEO, Thierry Bolloré, announced that the nearly complete, all-electric XJ would after all be scrapped, since global consumers were evidently moving away from traditional saloons. He also announced that the entire Jaguar range would become all-electric and yet more upmarket by 2025. Current models would be produced at Castle Bromwich until at least 2024, but the company gave no assurances for their continuation beyond then. As the *Guardian* commented on the day of the announcement:

The Castle Bromwich plant had a paint shop and metal pressings facility that could be used for Jaguar's special vehicle operations, a lucrative sideline in limited edition, high-performance cars. But its days as one of Britain's great mass production car plants appear to be over.

Not long after dropping this bombshell, in November 2022 Bolloré declared that he was stepping down as CEO. As Jaguar Land Rover rushed around trying to restore market confidence and to consolidate the more realistic elements of Bolloré's radical strategy, the future of Castle Bromwich was plunged into doubt once again.

In the midst of these tribulations, it is worth remembering that Castle Bromwich Factory still remains an evocative reminder of Britain's wartime and automotive past. The original factory walls are still there. Even some faded green wartime camouflage paint can be glimpsed, while the cast-iron hoppers above the drainpipes still proudly carry the winged RAF roundel motif.

Today, in the context of the uncertainties surrounding the future of the Jaguar marque, these memories appear to evoke past glories rather than future aspirations. Britain emerged victorious from the Second World War, but at a price that bankrupted the nation. And as Britain's car-making industry – once the second largest in the world – contracts further every year, with every one of the nation's prestigious historic automotive marques now in foreign hands, one has to ask exactly what is the definition of the label 'British' in the over-globalised twenty-first century.

24

20 FORTHLIN ROAD, LIVERPOOL

1949

When I Get Home: from welfare state and mass housing to global cultural phenomenon

Built just four years after the end of the Second World War, Liverpool's Forthlin Road is a product of the post-war welfare state and of the social ambitions which lay behind it: a solid, brick-built promise to the working classes of brave new Britain that better times were on their way. It was also, for nine years, home to an individual who helped redefine Britain for the whole world.

Post-war housing

After the Second World War the new Labour government led by Clement Attlee, elected by a landslide in July 1945, was determined to avoid the empty promises which had been made to 1918's returning servicemen of countless new 'Homes for Heroes', so many of which failed to materialise. Attlee and his ministers were determined to provide appropriate housing for working families as soon as possible. Not only was there a need for new homes with modern amenities to house the growing population. More than 400,000 homes had

453

also been razed or severely damaged by wartime bombing, and large areas of cities such as London and Liverpool lay in ruins.

Forthlin Road in Allerton, a south Liverpool suburb, was one of count-less urban terraces erected by local authorities after 1946 to house Britain's urban population, many of whom had been decanted from the Victorian back-to-backs which had been notorious for their appallingly insanitary conditions and lack of access to light and basic facilities. These new council houses were plain but solid, and offered modern amenities at an affordable, controlled rent.

As with health, public transport and the coal, steel and shipbuilding indus-tries, Attlee's government was adamant that they were not going to leave the state's hugely ambitious house-building programme to the private sector and risk the highly embarrassing shortfalls that had occurred after 1918. As Peter Malpass has noted:

> Between the wars local authorities built only 28% of all new houses, but in the same period after 1945 they were responsible for 60% of new building. This was the only sustained period in the whole of the twentieth century when the local authorities out-built the private sector, and more than half of all council houses ever built in Britain were constructed in the twenty-five years after the war.

During the war there were lively discussions across all sections of society about what the post-war nation should look like, and housing was at the top of this agenda. What dominated these debates was a widely held belief that the squandered opportunities of 1918 should not be repeated, that real change was now within the nation's grasp and that this change should not be left to the pre-war Conservative government. Even Major David Niven, serving with the 'Phantom' GHQ Reconnaissance Regiment in Normandy in the summer of 1944, observed that, having encouraged his soldiers to discuss what post-war Britain might look like:v

◁ *Detail of the restored sitting room at 20 Forthlin Road. Television sales had soared as a result of the 1953 coronation.*

One thing stuck out a mile during these debates – the vast majority of men who had been called up to fight for their country held the Conservative party entirely responsible for the disruption of their lives and in no circumstances would they vote for it next time there was an election – Churchill or no Churchill.

The wartime mood of much of the population was graphically evoked by Abram Games's compelling contribution to the 1942–3 propaganda poster series on the theme of 'Your Britain – Fight For It Now', in which Frank Newbould's lyrical evocations of the British countryside were substituted by a trenchant contrast between the dilapidated ruins and sickly children of wartime Britain and the bright, promising post-war Modernism of Berthold Lubetkin's Finsbury Health Centre of 1938 and clean, white flats in the mould of Lubetkin's Highpoint of 1935–8. Churchill demanded that Games's posters be removed from the Harrods exhibition of wartime graphic art of 1943, denouncing the artist's vision of a tottering pre-war nation, but in truth many Britons agreed with Games's viewpoint. This was dramatically affirmed by the enormous sales of William Beveridge's 1942 report outlining potential post-war welfare reforms, which, despite its irredeemably dull title *Social Insurance and Allied Services* and its great length, became an instant sales phenomenon, with long queues at the bookshops forming on publication day and eventual sales of half a million.

Churchill attempted to dampen public enthusiasm for the Beveridge Report and to limit post-war expectations, warning the public 'not to impose great new expenditure on the State without any relation to the circumstances which might prevail at the time'. But he was seriously out of step with the mood of the nation, as the Conservatives' unexpectedly catastrophic defeat in the 1945 general election was to demonstrate. Despite Churchill's misgivings, an abridged version of Beveridge's report was distributed by the Ministry of Information to British troops after the victory at the Battle of El Alamein in 1942 conjured the prospect of Allied success, while Beveridge himself – a pre-war economist who was best known for having been Director of the London School of Economics and Master of University College, Oxford – became a most unlikely national celebrity.* Beveridge's report identified the five 'giants' who needed to be eliminated in post-war Britain: Want, Idleness, Disease, Squalor and Ignorance. His report laid the basis for the Labour government's welfare state after 1945 and influenced post-war debates on social reform across the globe.

In order to banish Beveridge's five giants, a cross-party consensus developed after 1942 that appropriate modern housing should be a key prerequisite of any post-war society. As a result, well before the end of the European war in May 1945, there was a detailed housing policy in place, covering issues ranging from an emergency programme of prefabricated temporary homes, to be instituted immediately the war ended, to a cross-party commitment to a massive public house-building programme over the next decade. By 1944 it was estimated that between three and four million new homes would be needed in England and Wales alone in the decade after the war, while the wartime coalition declared that: 'The Government's first objective is to afford a separate dwelling for every family which desires to have one.' In September 1944 even Churchill weighed into the dispute on the slow progress of the prefabricated homes programme, demanding immediate action and announcing: 'I have made up my mind about it because of my own personal commitment to the troops, which I regard as sacred as far as I am concerned.'

In the port city of Liverpool, which had been heavily hit by German bombing after 1940, post-war reconstruction was given the highest priority. New council estates were created in the outlying suburbs both to provide shelter for bombed-out families and, as the City Council's City Architect and Director of Housing from 1948 to 1970, Ronald Bradbury, later stated, to house 'those families from [city-centre slum] Clearance Areas who could be persuaded to move out into the peripheral estates'. These new estates were not to be updated versions of the Victorian terraces that made up so much of Liverpool's existing building stock. The council had, as Bradbury remarked, 'not been slow in appreciating the many advantages of four-storey maisonettes, and considerable numbers of dwellings of this type have been or are being built on both suburban estates and in the central area'. Bradbury went on to describe a bold new

---

* Ironically, the notoriously difficult Beveridge was only commissioned to write the celebrated report because the Labour cabinet member Ernest Bevin wanted him out of his Ministry of Labour. Beveridge himself was apparently tearful with disappointment when asked to take on the job.

Liverpool 'embracing not only a number of two-storey cottage-type dwell-ings, a few blocks of three-storey flats and a considerable number of four-storey maisonettes, but also a proportion of multi-storey tower and slab blocks of ten or eleven storeys in height'.

Not every new Liverpool council home, however, was built in this high-rise format. Forthlin Road in the new Mather Estate in Allerton, built between 1949 and 1952, was of a traditional housing type: two-storey terraces with brick walls and strangely old-fashioned tripartite wooden sash windows. The street had been built by contractors Costain (for £1,369 1s 6d) and designed by the traditionalist City Architect, Sir Lancelot Keay, in 1947. As a result, it was unapologetically backward-looking in both its materials and its detailing. Externally, the street's only nod to modernity was its glazed front doors. In a way, that dichotomy was to reflect the music of its most famous resident: looking forwards to a new, classless Britain while firmly grounded in the idioms of the past.

Inside, however, the Forthlin Road houses were a far cry from the cramped, dark and insanitary back-to-backs of the old inner city. They boasted indoor toilets, well-equipped bathrooms and small but modern kitchens complete with freestanding cooker and washing machine.

The McCartneys at No. 20

In 1955 the property's second occupants, the McCartneys, moved into number 20 Forthlin Road, halfway down the street. Jim and Mary McCartney's 1941 wedding had daringly crossed the city's sectarian divide which then dominated city life – even defining the identities of the city's two great football teams, Liverpool and Everton – and which still divides Liverpool communities today. Jim was a Protestant, Mary was Catholic; but both were of Irish ancestry. Their sons, James Paul and Peter Michael (both later known just by their middle names), were born in 1942 and 1944 respectively, and in 1947 the McCartney family had moved to a terraced house in Western Road, Speke, which Mary McCartney had been given rent-free on account of her job as a local midwife. They later moved to a similar terraced home in nearby Ardwick Road. Both homes were of stout, brick-walled interwar construction; both, though, had still been provided only with outside toilets.

In 1955, 20 Forthlin Road had a living room with a sofa and two armchairs, a standard lamp and a television. Television set sales had burgeoned after

Queen Elizabeth II's coronation of 1953, a landmark event – the first-ever televised coronation – which had prompted the McCartneys to buy theirs. The walls at number 20 were hung with test strips of wallpaper: Mary could never decide which she preferred, so her sons chose different samples to go on different walls. When the National Trust was conducting conservation work on the living room walls in the 1990s, they discovered fragments of a silvery chinoiserie willow pattern paper, a familiar design which dates back to the 1780s. Similarly, the living-room carpet was covered in narrow samples or runners which were usually reserved for staircases.

The living room also featured a telephone. This rare and valuable resource had been provided courtesy of Britain's newly inaugurated National Health Service on account of Mary's job. In 1955 it was the only private telephone in the street, and was the cause of many unexpected visits from neighbours. There was also an upright piano, which had been bought from the North End Road Music Stores, the record offshoot of the Epstein family's local chain of furniture stores that was run by the Epsteins' son, Brian. It was on this instrument that Paul McCartney learned to play from his father and on which he trialled and accompanied some of the Beatles' earliest songs. The original piano is now in Paul's possession, but a similarly sized one has been installed in the house by the Trust, who have also hung a framed photograph on the wall showing teenaged Paul and John Lennon sitting in the room's two facing armchairs, cradling their right-hand and left-hand guitars.

The kitchen originally possessed a wooden draining board to go with the freestanding porcelain sink; the stainless-steel sink unit was added by a later council tenant and the original drainer only rediscovered in the attic by the National Trust in the 1990s. By that time the original Belfast sink had been in use for many years as a plant pot in the back garden. The original garden was small, but was still a huge improvement on the old Liverpool back-to-backs which many rehoused Forthlin Road tenants had once occupied, as those lacked any private outdoor space whatsoever. Above the garden, the house's rear windows looked out at the handsome, brick-faced Police Training College in Mather Avenue, a large building which still fills the view at the back of number 20.

In 1953 Paul passed the 11-plus exam and started at the Liverpool Institute grammar school, or 'the Inny', as it was locally known. Grammar schools, elite but generally free secondary institutions, had been in existence for centuries, but had recently been appropriated as one of the three pillars of the new secondary education system set up during the war by the 1944 Education Act, whose author had not been a future member of Attlee's welfare-oriented Labour government but the Tory pre-war appeaser Rab Butler (1902–82). By Butler's Act, an examination was set at the age of eleven which defined which of the three secondary-level avenues boys and girls would then follow. It was a momentous choice for children as it could colour the rest of their lives. In the 1960s an impetus grew on both sides of the political divide* to tear down the allegedly unfair selective system, which made little allowance for children who developed after the age of eleven, and impose an internally streamed 'comprehensive' alternative. However, in 1953 a grammar school place was seen as a rung up on Britain's ladder of opportunity – a ladder which relied not on wealth, as at Britain's independent sector, but on ability.

Liverpool Institute High School for Boys (there was also a nearby girls' equivalent) was just east of the city centre. It was sited just off the appropriately named Hope Street, which in 1953 linked the towering Gothic mass of Giles Gilbert Scott's Anglican cathedral with the foundations of a vast classical Catholic cathedral, half a mile away and originally designed by Sir Edwin Lutyens but which had never progressed beyond its crypt. The journey to school from Mather Avenue, from which Paul would catch the 86 bus from Garston, would necessitate a change of green Liverpool Corporation buses at the Penny Lane bus interchange.

By the mid-1960s a grammar school education appeared to underscore the new, classless Britain of Harold Wilson's Labour government. Grammar school boys and girls studded the artistic and political landscape of the nation, from Paul McCartney and George Harrison (a year below Paul at the Liverpool Institute) and Mick Jagger (who had attended Dartford Grammar School) to Roger Moore (Dr Challoner's Grammar School, Amersham), Alan Bennett (Leeds Modern School), Honor Blackman (Ealing County Grammar School) and David Attenborough (Wyggeston Grammar School, Leicester) to opposition leader Edward Heath (Chatham House Grammar School, Ramsgate) and future Tory prime minister Margaret Thatcher (Kesteven and Grantham Girls' School).

With the election in 1983 of a Labour Liverpool City Council dominated

---

* The minister who closed most grammar schools during this period was Edward Heath's Secretary of State for Education, Margaret Thatcher.

by members of the Trotskyite, entryist Militant Tendency, however, the writing was on the toilet wall for Liverpool Institute. The new council leader, John Hamilton, was not a Militant member, but the power behind his throne, councillor Derek Hatton, was a staunch supporter. Hatton and his Militant cronies gleefully destroyed the city's top-tier state schools – and much of the city's remaining prosperity. Both the girls' and boys' Liverpool Institutes, which had an illustrious history dating back to the Mechanics Institute of 1825, were closed in 1985 at the instigation of Hatton, a former Inny boy himself who had hated his days there, and council education chair Dominic Brady, a former school caretaker. Hatton and the rest of Liverpool's Militant cadre were expelled from the Labour Party the following year, but this came too late to save the Inny. The historic school buildings were familiar landmarks for this part of Liverpool. The site, which had been listed a decade earlier, was fronted by A. H. Holme's imposing classical block of 1835 and its striking giant-order Ionic portico. But, listed or not, the school was left to rot until rescued by Paul McCartney, with the assistance of the Heritage Lottery Fund and other donors, to become a 'fame' academy for the arts. This opened its doors in 1996 and is now an affiliate of Liverpool John Moores University. Hatton, meanwhile, reinvented himself as a radio talk show host, a game show panellist* and property developer in Cyprus, and in 2020 was arrested for corruption in connection with shady Liverpool construction deals.

In the late 1950s and early 1960s life at 20 Forthlin Road was busy, hectic and unpredictable. It was at Forthlin Road that Paul's mother, Mary, died tragically early of breast cancer in 1956, barely eighteen months after the move to their new home. It was to this house in 1958 that Paul invited the stylish, sassy lead singer of the fledgling Liverpool skiffle band the Quarrymen, John Winston Lennon† – who had just failed all his O levels and was about to begin at Liverpool College of Art – and helped him to play the guitar properly. And it was here that the quiet young guitarist from the Inny, George Harrison, was inducted into the embryonic band. Most of the Quarrymen's rehearsals took place in the living room at 20 Forthlin Road, with Paul's genial father Jim banished to the kitchen – even though Lennon's semi-detached 1930s home

---

* In 1993 Hatton appeared in an episode of the TV show *Have I Got News For You* alongside former Conservative MP Edwina Currie, who had been a pupil at the Liverpool Institute High School for Girls.

† Born in October 1940, at the height of the Blitz, Lennon was indeed named after Britain's new prime minister.

at 251 Menlove Avenue (which had been pretentiously retitled Mendips) in the nearby Liverpool suburb of Woolton, had far more room. Mendips was, however, ruled with a rod of iron by Lennon's upwardly mobile Aunt Mimi, to whom John's glamorous but doomed mother Julia had given John when he was only five years old. It was here that the Quarrymen practised their first single, a cover of Buddy Holly's 'That'll Be The Day' on the A-side and the Paul McCartney-penned 'In Spite All the Danger' on the B-side. (They recorded this single on 14 July 1958 in their friend Percy Phillips's house in nearby Kensington, just a day before John's mother was run over and killed outside her sister's house.) And it was here where the Quarrymen metamorphosed into the Silver Beatles and then the Beatles in 1960.

Decades later, at the National Trust's behest, Paul McCartney wrote that Forthlin Road had been 'a pleasure to live in':

> I was living at 20 Forthlin Road when I first met John Lennon, and it was here that he and I rehearsed with the Beatles. From this house I would walk through the golf course up to Woolton where John lived with his Aunt Mimi. As she would usually be home during the day but my Dad was at work, John and I would sometimes sag off school and go back to my house to write many of our early songs. We wrote 'Love Me Do' and 'I Saw Her Standing There' in the parlour of 20 Forthlin Road. I was still living in the house when the Beatles found worldwide fame, so my memories of the house are closely connected with those times.

The advent of the Beatles

The subsequent story of the Beatles is well known. In 1962, their breakout year, Brian Epstein of the North End Road Music Stores (NEMS) offered to be the group's manager. It was thanks to Epstein that in June 1962 the band were given an audition at EMI's recording facility in the leafy, north-west London suburb of St John's Wood. Here at Abbey Road Studios they met producer George Martin, who orchestrated the replacement of drummer Pete Best by Richard Starkey (long known by his stage name of Ringo Starr) and helped them to issue a single, 'Love Me Do'. (The single's B-side was 'P.S. I Love You' – which, Martin later admitted, 'was probably a better song... But it wasn't a hit.') 'Love Me Do' reached number 17 in the British Top 40. However, the group's second single, 'Please, Please Me', reached number 1 in the UK and stayed at

△ *The Beatles playing at the Cavern Club, Liverpool, in 1962. Pete Best, seen here playing the drums, was dismissed in August of that year and replaced with Ringo Starr.*

the top for thirty weeks. The subsequent album of the same name followed suit, in an unprecedented development for the British pop charts; it was only replaced at the album chart summit by the group's second pressing, *With the Beatles*. From that point onward, every Beatles appearance was greeted with mass hysteria, and almost every Beatles single went straight to the top of the charts. When the Beatles toured the United States in January–February 1964, Beatlemania (a word first coined the previous October) gripped America, too; having previously regarded the British phenomenon with amused detachment, the Americans fell hook, line and sinker for the Beatles, and thereafter for all things British.

The album cover for *Please, Please Me* was an iconic image of sixties Britain. The photograph's backdrop was a building which incarnated the cool International Modernism of the new nation: EMI House in London's Manchester Square. Designed by curtain-walling pioneers Gollins Melvin Ward and opened in 1960, EMI House, like so many of its Modernist siblings, offered a promise of a brave new Britain of clean, sleek, functional architecture and class-blind opportunity. In the foreground of the shot were four cheery, working-class men whose accents, humour and songs were (under a veneer of Americanised vowels) unmistakeably British.

Since the 1930s British popular culture had been dominated by its former colony across the Atlantic. With the advent of rock and roll in the mid-1950s that influence became even more pronounced. In the fifties, home-grown British pop talent had acquired American-sounding names (Billy Fury, Cliff Richard, Marty Wilde) and sung American-sounding songs, or simply cover versions of established US hits. The Beatles reversed that cultural exchange, almost single-handedly creating an image of 'Swinging Britain' and a culture in which Britain now influenced America.

British music and fashion created the Swinging Sixties and gave the nation a new focus and a new image at a time when serious international competition was gradually eroding Britain's traditional industrial base. At the dawn of the Beatles era, in 1962, ex-president Harry Truman's former secretary of state, Dean Acheson, famously claimed that 'Great Britain has lost an empire and has not yet found a role'. In geopolitical terms this judgement was certainly correct: while the British empire of 1945 had been replaced in 1949 by a more outward relationship of equals in the British Commonwealth of Nations, the 1960s were marked by a constant procession to the imperial exit as former colonies sought – and, for the most part, were readily granted – independence: from Cyprus in 1960 and Tanganyika in 1961 to Barbados and Lesotho in 1966 and Bahrain, Qatar and the United Arab Emirates in 1971.* However, in Swinging Britain the nation had found a vivacious, appealing and unmistakeably 'modern' new identity, one which helpfully distracted Britons from the grim headlines demonstrating Britain's seemingly inexorable industrial and international decline.

The incoming Labour prime minister of 1964, Harold Wilson (1916–95), astutely exploited the Beatles' appeal to create a voter-friendly image of a fashion-conscious, unashamedly modern, technology-focused and post-imperial Britain of opportunity and innovation. Although a Yorkshireman, Wilson

---

* Granting the Gulf States' independence was part of Harold Wilson's momentous and pain-fully symbolic yet economically imperative decision of 1968 to withdraw a British presence from east of the Suez Canal.

sat for the Liverpool constituency of Huyton and ensured that he was photographed alongside the Fab Four – a term coined by NEMS press officer Tony Barrow in 1962 – as much as possible during his 1964 election campaign.

Wilson, another grammar school boy (from Royds Hall Secondary School, Huddersfield) who had won a place at Jesus College, Oxford, and was later a research fellow at University College, Oxford, was one of the brightest minds of his generation. He did not miss a trick, harnessing the Beatles' appeal and ensuring that his bourgeois preferences for cigars and whisky were concealed, at least in public: on camera his cigars were replaced by a working-class pipe and his glasses of whisky by pints of beer. Wilson later admitted that, while the pipe lent him an image of working-class gravitas and sagacity, puffing slowly on his pipe also gave him invaluable time in which to frame answers to interviewers' difficult questions.

Appropriating 1964's Beatlemania helped Wilson to a narrow victory at the polls and six years of uninterrupted government. Two years later, Wilson similarly exploited national euphoria over England's excellent prospects in the forthcoming football World Cup during his election campaign. His reward was a vastly increased electoral majority; the England team's reward was the World Cup itself. However, the same ploy failed to work for Wilson four years later, when England's undeserved exit from the quarter-finals of the World Cup at the hands of West Germany may well have helped precipitate Labour's unexpected defeat at the hands of Edward Heath's Conservatives.

The fact that British prime minister Harold Wilson astutely kept Britain out of the highly unpopular Vietnam War during the sixties only added to the cultural allure of Beatles Britain for the young of America. In April 1966 *Time* magazine christened London 'The Swinging City' in a cover story: 'In a decade dominated by youth, London has burst into bloom. It swings; it is the scene.' London's King's Road became a mecca for avant-garde fashion hunters, while the West End's Carnaby Street won an ill-deserved reputation as a global hub for alternative fashion, an image the street is still milking sixty years on when the majority of its retailers are multinational brands. Hundreds of thousands of American tourists, alongside other international visitors, flocked to Britain to participate in the 'scene' and hopefully to get a glimpse of the Beatles, who had now replaced the royal family as Britain's biggest tourist draw. Towns and cities across the nation became destinations for overseas tourists, lured by the Beatles, by Britain's built heritage and by the cheap air fares made possible by that new transatlantic workhorse, the Boeing 707. For the first time even the grimy old city of Liverpool became a tourist mecca, as visitors came to see where the Fab Four had been born and raised.

Memories of Forthlin Road

The Beatles effect was not apparent solely in the worlds of music, politics and tourism. It also permeated British culture. As Olivier Sykes and his fellow social historians have written:

> The Beatles and beat poets were just the most prominent representatives of the city's cast of 'war babies' and 'baby boomers' who energised and revolutionised the nascent popular culture of the 1960s. The phenomenon of 'Merseybeat' in music, poetry and other diverse art forms was influential and recognised far beyond the city and region's boundaries. Allen Ginsberg's statement that Liverpool in the 1960s was 'at the present moment, the centre of consciousness of the human universe'... captures this confident spirit.

Even while touring Britain, Europe and America in the early 1960s, Paul McCartney had continued to return to his family home at Forthlin Road. After his return from America in 1964, though, Paul's new-found wealth enabled him to buy his now retired father a house in Heswall on the Wirral, which he shared with his new wife, Angie. Paul, meanwhile, moved in with his new girl-friend, the actress Jane Asher, in London's upmarket Wimpole Street – a street whose architecture and historical associations were light years away from those of Forthlin Road.

Memories of Forthlin Road and its environs infused many of Lennon and McCartney's subsequent songs. The bus terminus of Penny Lane (a street actually named not after the traditional British coin but after eighteenth-century slave trader James Penny) was, as noted, where Paul, George and John had changed buses on the way to and from school. However, until he returned with actor and chat-show host James Corden in 2018, Paul had not revisited the interior of his former Forthlin Road home since 1964.

The demise of the Beatles at the end of the Swinging Sixties was also paralleled by the collapse of British self-confidence. In September 1969 John Lennon announced he was leaving the band but agreed to keep the news secret for fear of harming impending album sales. The following April, following producer

Phil Spector's ham-fisted butchery of his tender song 'The Long And Winding Road' for what turned out to be the band's last album, *Let It Be*, Paul McCartney resolved to walk out, too – this time, publicly. At McCartney's instigation, the band's legal partnership was formally wound up in December 1970. However, the next four years were to be punctuated by the unedifying spectacle of the ex-Beatles suing and vilifying each other. At the same time, throughout the 1970s band after band was tagged by the media with the burdensome label of 'the new Beatles'. But none of them were.

Into the seventies

Things just seemed to get worse after the Beatles broke up. The new Heath government inherited a deteriorating economic situation and responded with the disastrous Industrial Relations Act of 1971, whose first public result was the ill-advised imprisonment of striking dockworkers. Unemployment reached a post-war high while the totemic British car and aircraft engine manufacturer Rolls-Royce went into bankruptcy. It seemed as if Britain was following the Beatles into an irascible twilight.

The end of the Beatles and the dawn of the 1970s reconfigured both the political and the cultural relationship between Britain and America. After 1970 British prime minister Edward Heath (1916–2005) steered Britain towards its European neighbours and away from America. Accordingly, in 1973, the year in which Britain joined what was then known as the European Economic Community, Heath's government refused American access to British bases or British intelligence harvested in Cyprus during the Arab–Israeli War. In the event, Britain was to suffer as badly as anywhere else in the west after the Arab nations cut the supply and raised the price of oil in retaliation for the US's support of Israel.

As memories of Britain's Swinging Sixties faded, it was America – and particularly the sun-drenched state of California, home of Hollywood, the Beach Boys and bell-bottoms (and, increasingly, Britain's émigré rock and film stars) – which dominated British music, fashion and art in the early and middle 1970s. America offered Britons a promise of colour, sun and exuberance, a vision which served as a perfect antidote to the Three-Day Week and the bomb outrages of early seventies Britain. It also offered a prospect of colour.

In contrast to Britain's black and white sixties, the seventies was the age of colour, in which the spread of television – and in particular American-made colour television programmes – was a crucial factor. Colour television had first been introduced to the UK by BBC2 in 1967, sixteen years after the US had first introduced colour broadcasts. By the mid-seventies it had become widespread: 1976 was the year in which colour TV sets first outnumbered black and white ones. In 1957 only 44 per cent of UK households had owned a television; by 1970 that had soared to 92 per cent, and by the end of the decade it was nearing 100 per cent. However, despite the advent of colour TV in Britain in the early 1970s, neither the BBC nor ITV had many ready-made colour TV series to show. As a result, US imports soared: from family dramas such as *The Waltons* and *Little House on the Prairie*, sitcoms such as ABC's *The Partridge Family* of 1970–4, police dramas such as *Kojak* of 1973 and children's programmes such as NBC's *The Banana Splits* to Westerns such as NBC's *The Virginian* and *The High Chaparral*.

British popular culture – the Beatles, the model Twiggy, 'Swinging London' – had helped to define the sixties in America. Now the pendulum had swung the other way, and it was American popular culture that had become the arbiter of British taste and aspiration. While the American success of the Beatles had made young Britons a model for aspiring American artists, now the lure of America encouraged a new, post-Beatles generation of rock stars – Elton John, David Bowie, Cat Stevens, Rod Stewart, Phil Lynott – to join perennial Beatles rivals the Rolling Stones in America in searching for new inspiration and new audiences. In many ways, they never left.

As British rock stars fled to California during the 1970s, the city of Liverpool suffered more than most of Britain's former industrial centres. A decade after the Beatles had made the city into one of the beacons of Britain's swinging sixties, Liverpool had, thanks to the dramatic contraction in traditional maritime trade, become an industrial basket case. The city's unemployment rate was already high in 1971, at 10.6 per cent; twenty years later it stood at 21.6 per cent. As Sykes *et al.* have noted, 'Citing significant under-reporting, Liverpool City Council estimated that the true number of unemployed persons by the late 1970s was over 150,000 (20–30 per cent of the working aged population), treble the official figures':

> Between 1966 and 1977 no less than 350 factories in Liverpool closed or moved elsewhere, 40,000 jobs were lost and between 1971 and 1985 employment in the city fell by 33 per cent... Between 1979 and 1981 the rate of job losses accelerated to a frightening level, employment in the city falling by

△ *20 Forthlin Road today, looking immaculate in National Trust ownership.*

a further 18 per cent. By early 1981, 20 per cent of the city's labour force were unemployed and it was reported that there were just 49 jobs on offer for the 13,505 youngsters registered unemployed.

The result was increasing poverty, dereliction and social polarisation – and, in 1981, major rioting.

In the care of the National Trust

Only in recent years has the city of Liverpool realised that it has a seemingly inexhaustible economic resource in the form of the worldwide appeal of the Beatles' timeless legacy. It was only in 1990 that the Beatles Story Museum was opened in the newly restored Royal Albert Dock of 1846, and not until 1996 that 20 Forthlin Road was, thanks to the care and the patience of the National Trust, opened to the public. Seven years later the home John Lennon shared with his Aunt Mimi, Mendips (a house which, unlike 20 Forthlin Road, had been considerably altered since the 1960s), was also opened to the public, again under the aegis of the National Trust.*

The Beatles could yet save the city of Liverpool. In 2001, twenty-one years after his assassination, John Lennon's name was arrogated by Liverpool Airport, to the surprise of many who had expected that all the Fab Four would be commemorated. And while the Cavern Club where the Beatles had played in their earliest years was inexplicably demolished in 1973, to facilitate work on the local underground railway, in 1984 a New Cavern Club was created covering 70 per cent of the old site. It is, predictably, now a major tourist destination.

Today the city's waterfront has a palpable air of optimism, while Liverpool's cultural offer now ranks alongside that of any of the nation's major cities. The city now boasts two Beatles museums, not counting the displays at the splendid Museum of Liverpool of 2011. The global appeal of the Beatles and their timeless music certainly shows no signs of waning.

---

*   251 Menlove Avenue was always a cut above the council-owned terraced homes of Forthlin Road. A solid, semi-detached property of 1933, it was posh enough to be afforded a name: Mendips. John Lennon lived here with his aunt, Mimi Smith, from the late 1950s until 1963. Two years later Mimi sold the house, taking some of the pieces of furniture and giving others away. The house passed through a number of unsympathetic hands until Lennon's widow, Yoko Ono, bought it in 2002 and generously donated it to the National Trust.

25

30 ST MARY AXE ('THE GHERKIN')

2000–4

Shape of the Future or Relic of the Past?

The densely packed square mile of the City of London had been Britain's financial heart well before the foundation of the Bank of England, established in Edward Jerman and John Oliver's fine Mercers' Hall in 1694 in order to help fund William III's war against the French. Thomas Gresham's establishment of the Royal Exchange in the heart of the City in 1570 may be taken as a more helpful starting point for Britain's rise to global financial and commercial pre-eminence through the agency of City financiers. Gresham intended the Exchange to be a meeting place for London's merchants and brokers, creating what was in effect Britain's first purpose-built commercial building. The creation of the Bank of England across the road over a century later merely set the seal on London's dominance of British finances, in which regulatory role the British capital far exceeded the power, authority and size of other European capitals such as Paris and Madrid.

△ Foster's well-mannered tower adds a new dimension to this corner of the City.

The City of London

In 1694 the City of London dominated the commerce of the nation in a manner not seen anywhere else in Europe. As the City's biographer David Kynaston has noted, 'by the end of the seventeenth century London towered over the rest of the country in almost all types of trade' while 'its population of half a million was meekly followed by Norwich with 30,000'. In the ensuing century the vast explosion in British trade with the American colonies and the Caribbean, with the Far East and with the African coast, made London in particular, and Britain in general, spectacularly wealthy. As banker Henry Thornton commented in 1802: 'London is become, especially of late, the trading metropolis of Europe, and, indeed, of the whole world.' All this was underpinned by the dominance of the seas which the Royal Navy had firmly established by 1800, which in turn enabled the marine insurers Lloyd's to make their Lombard Street coffee house into one of the trading nuclei of the Square Mile.

However, it was Nathan Mayer Rothschild's opening of an office in the square mile's Great St Helen's Street in 1808 which was to set the City on the path to the international commercial pre-eminence it was to enjoy from the fall of Napoleon in 1815 to the Brexit vote two centuries later. Rothschild's aggressive banking methods, reinforced by his network of trusted brothers based in a string of strategically located continental financial centres, had by 1815 made Britain into the banker of Europe, if not the world. In the year of Waterloo, Rothschild earned £1 million (about £100 million today) as paymaster for the British army and its European allies. And in the decades that followed, no one now challenged sterling's claim to be the accepted currency of international finance and commerce.

The City of 1815 was almost as dense as it is today, with every square yard being earmarked for the purposes of formal or informal transaction. At its centre in Threadneedle Street was the grandiose palace that was John Soane's Bank of England, the 'Old Lady of Threadneedle Street' – its much-delayed expansion, started way back in 1788, now almost complete. All around the Bank's roofscape rose Christopher Wren's City of London churches, whose towers still soared clear over the City rooftops as late as 1918, jostling for ground space and air rights with livery halls, banks, coffee houses, shops and pubs – and, from 1865, great railway termini. Many of Wren's own churches were now forced to make way for new commercial premises or road widening; the victims included Wren's splendid Gothick essay of St Mary Somerset, demolished in 1867, and his masterly church of St Antholin, Watling Street, whose soaring spire was sold for scrap for just a fiver in 1875.

Over the following decades the City's merchants moved out to more spacious homes in the West End or in the villages of Middlesex or Surrey, and more commercial premises took their place. Those people who stayed in the City were generally of the poorer sort: clerks and shopworkers, Dickens' Cratchits or Dorrits. The furious parsimony of *Little Dorrit*'s Mrs Clennam was underlined by her refusal, despite her vast fortune, to move from her ruinous old townhouse near the north end of London Bridge.

All this was taken as the price of progress. Historians Barnes, Newton and Scott have observed that:

> The second half of the nineteenth century witnessed a huge building wave that transformed the City from a mainly residential area to a purpose-built business district – reflected in a fall in its residential population from 129,000 in 1851 to only 26,000 in 1901, with some 80 per cent of the City's physical fabric being rebuilt between 1855 and 1901. This included six new City railway stations and the remodelling of Lombard Street, at the heart of the City, as a throughfare for banks and insurance companies. The older residential buildings that were torn down to make room for the new office and warehouse premises were generally not then regarded as distinctive or endangered (being broadly similar to those in other parts of central London). The process thus generated very little controversy.

The new commercial buildings of the later Victorian era were large stone-built piles which radiated confidence, wealth and ambition. A bombastic classical idiom was established as the appropriate style for such grandiloquent architectural expressions as John Gibson's magnificent banking hall of 1865, built on the corner of Bishopsgate and Threadneedle Street for the National Provincial Bank. Gibson's masterpiece was wrapped in a giant Corinthian order and its parapet was topped by immense sculptural allegories of 'regional commerce and industry'. Twenty years later the walls of J. J. Cole's extension to the Stock Exchange were so laden with expensive blue-veined marble that it was quickly dubbed 'Gorgonzola Hall'.

Demolition and bombing

By the last decades of the nineteenth century, the old City was being demolished with barely a backward glance. In 1888 one of the square mile's oldest surviving buildings, 21 Austin Friars, was razed in order, as *The Statist* joyfully announced, to create 'a passage from Austin Friars to Throgmorton-avenue'. Two years later the famous Tudor inn in Bishopsgate, the Sir Paul Pindar, was hastily razed to make way for modern, electrically lit offices.

The nadir for the City's architectural heritage came in 1926–7. In 1926 Lloyds Bank destroyed many ancient houses in Cornhill and Lombard Street in order to build a new, eight-storey head office. The Midland Bank's vast new pile at 27 Poultry,* which was begun in 1924, opened in 1930 and extended yet further in 1935–7, also required extensive demolition of the City's historic heritage. The new building, though, was designed by Sir Edwin Lutyens (1869–1944), the author of countless masterly country houses and the master planner of New Delhi, whom the Midland had effectively engaged as their in-house architect in 1921. Designing the new head office for the National Provincial Bank next door to Lutyens's vast wedding cake, Sir Edwin Cooper remained inescapably in the master's shadow, both literally and metaphorically. When his building was completed in 1932 it earned but faint praise. As David Kynaston relates, the influential critic H. S. Goodhart-Rendel declared publicly: 'If the purpose of external walls in a city building were to display figure-sculpture and to keep out of the light, those of the National Provincial Bank would be hard to better.'

The smaller merchant banks, too, jumped on the bandwagon, sacrificing their modest Georgian and Victorian premises for chic, well-appointed and ostentatious neo-Georgian piles. Morgan Grenfell's new home at 23 Great Winchester Street, replacing a picturesque Victorian structure, was designed by the masters of corporate neo-Georgian, Mewès and Davis, in a bland 'Palladian' idiom which won the plaudits of the traditionalist architect Sir Albert Richardson (1880–1964) and even, in 1957, the approbation of Modernist historian Nikolaus Pevsner. Richardson, though, identified the main challenge for the City architects of the 1920s:

---

* 27 Poultry was abandoned by the Midland (now HSBC) in 1992 and is today an upmarket hotel.

English architects, when called upon to deal with awkward sites in congested streets, are faced with difficulties which would confuse those [in the US] accustomed to fewer restrictions.

Perhaps the most unnecessary and grievous City loss of the time, however, was that of John Soane's elegant and sophisticated banking halls at the Bank of England, which were destroyed in 1926 in one of the twentieth century's worst acts of architectural vandalism. The Bank had been determined to rebuild their crowded offices as a far taller edifice since 1920 and to that end had hired Lutyens's assistant at New Delhi, the unappealing Herbert Baker, to rebuild the site as a pompous and self-important seven-storey pile stuffed into Soane's original outer wall.

The influential head of Liverpool University's School of Architecture, Professor C. H. Reilly, was distinctly unimpressed, bemoaning the loss of Soane's 'majestic' halls and their replacement by an 'overgrown private residence of some plutocrat of more than Rockefeller proportions'. His punchline was unambiguous: 'I see nevertheless after all this, the Bank has erected a statue to Soane. When one had destroyed a man's best work, I suppose it is the gentlemanly thing to do.'

In 1957 Pevsner was even more unequivocal, lamenting the demolition of 'Soane's interiors with their infinite variety of domes… and several of a very high and exacting beauty' and also condemning Baker's buildings as 'oppressive and lacking grandeur'. He concluded that the razing of Soane's Bank of England was 'the worst individual loss suffered by London architecture', even allowing for the immense damage inflicted on the City by German bombing from September 1940.

Notwithstanding Pevsner's post-war judgement, Baker's despoliation of Soane's legacy was dwarfed by the effect on the City of London of wartime bombing. Countless City buildings burned to the ground; tragically, some of the smaller buildings could have been saved had they been provided with rooftop firewatchers, as the government had advised. On 11 January 1941 Bank underground station, sited underneath Baker's Bank of England and the Royal Exchange, suffered a direct hit, and 117 people taking shelter there were killed. Nor did the onslaught end with Hitler's attack on Russia in June 1941. As late as March 1945 London was still being targeted by the Germans' frighteningly advanced guided ballistic missile, the V2.

The post-war City

By the end of the war a third of the City lay in ruins. In August 1945 *The Times* brightly announced that 'the City has a magnificent new opportunity for comprehensive rebuilding', but for an exhausted and impoverished Britain, and a shaken City, the initial pace of reconstruction was understandably slow. A report of 1946 authored by the architect Charles Holden and the planner William Holford warned that 'The City cannot afford mediocre architecture', but for many years that was exactly what it did get. The large new Modernist blocks erected near Wren's magnificent church of St Stephen Walbrook by the developer Rudolph Palumbo after 1948, St Swithin's House and Bucklersbury House, were remarkable only for their pedestrian banality. Bucklersbury House, designed by Owen Campbell-Jones and built in 1953–8, was the first building in the City to deliberately breach the accepted rule that no buildings should exceed the 30-metre height of the base of St Paul's Cathedral's dome, soaring upwards to 164 metres. In 1964 the preceptive architectural critic Ian Nairn declared: 'It has no virtues and no vices; it is the null point of architecture.' In 2010 it was demolished to make way for Foster + Partners' Walbrook Square.

With the abolition of government building licence controls in November 1954, the pace of redevelopment in the City accelerated, with a growing proportion of projects involving the demolition of existing buildings. Between 1948 and 1956 planning permissions for offices in central London averaged 3,544,000 square feet; this rose to 4,753,000 in 1957 and 4,796,000 in 1961. By 1964 the new City thoroughfare of London Wall – or 'Route 11' as the Americanised planners were gratingly calling it – was lined with five wholly anonymous office blocks. One of the last of these, Royex House, was designed by Richard Seifert (1910–2001), an architect who had served as a colonel of the Royal Engineers during the war and who was now beloved of British developers owing to his ability to design quickly and cheaply and to interpret planning regulations as flexibly as possible.

By the 1960s the City's great banking halls were widely considered by their owners to be obstructing growth, since far taller structures could properly exploit the air rights above. In 1963 the National Provincial, for example, proposed demolishing Gibson's outstanding Victorian banking hall on Bishopsgate and replacing it with a modern tower. Barnes, Newton and Scott have recounted how:

National Provincial's Victorian head office symbolized an identity the bank no longer wished to embody... The ancient monuments suggested that National Provincial was stuck in the past – classical and opulent, yet obsolete. The bank looked to distance itself from this symbolism and develop a replacement head office, which reflected how it wanted to be seen. The new tower would communicate its progress and ability to keep pace with change and competition, symbolizing the future rather than the past... [and] a more democratic, corporate culture, housed in open, glass covered buildings.

Fortunately, the bank's plans were successfully halted by the London County Council, supported by the Victorian Society and, ultimately, by both the outgoing Conservative government *and* the incoming Labour housing minister, Richard Crossman. Gibson Hall at 13 Bishopsgate was saved. As Barnes *et al.* have noted, this was a landmark decision for the architectural conservation movement, setting 'an important precedent for the prioritisation of conservation over maximizing the functionality and economic value of building plots'. Following this ground-breaking judgement, the new Labour government of 1964 announced a complete ban on new office building in the City of London. Two years later, however, they were to bow to City pressure and rescind this.

Instead of replacing Gibson's splendid hall, the National Provincial inserted a new tower behind it on a site which opened onto Old Broad Street. The architect had already been chosen: inevitably, it was the corporate architect *par excellence*, Richard Seifert. In Seifert's defence, he did produce a far more imaginative and aesthetically pleasing composition than his original scheme for a dull, corporate-modernist tower in the idiom of Mies van der Rohe for the Gibson Hall site.

Work began on Seifert's thrusting tower in 1970, the year in which the National Provincial formally became the National Westminster Bank, or NatWest, having merged with the Westminster Bank two years before. When it was finally completed in 1980. Seifert's NatWest Tower was for a decade the tallest building in Britain and the second-tallest occupied building in Europe. It was a symbol of the power and ambition of the City of London intended to act as the City's 'crown' and which could be seen from all over the capital. Severely damaged by the Provisional IRA's Bishopsgate bombing of 24 April 1993, though, the building simply proved too expensive to demolish and was instead repaired, following which NatWest sold the block as general offices, in the process of which it was renamed Tower 42 after its forty-two floors. By 2006 the organ of Britain's financial community, the *Financial Times*, was disparaging Seifert's proud tower as merely one of the 'drab pinnacles stuck up a generation ago'.

The NatWest Tower at least has a purpose to it. Further west, above Tottenham Court Road tube station, another Seifert office block had already earned international notoriety as a typical example of what Prime Minister Edward Heath was subsequently to brand 'the unpleasant and unacceptable face of capitalism'. Designed largely by the Seifert office architect George Marsh, Centre Point of 1961–6 was an example of Corbusian Modernism come to London, while its principal tower was distinguished by its modulated, sculptural pre-cast panels, attached without the need for scaffolding. The Modernist pioneer Ernö Goldfinger (the inspiration for the famous Bond villain) called it 'London's first pop art skyscraper' while *Building* magazine enthused that, 'like the Beatles and Mary Quant, this building expresses the supreme confidence of sheer professionalism... more than any other building Centre Point made London swing, it backed Britain, a product of real team work which must figure as an invisible export'. However, its composition, which none other than the *Buildings of England* sage and Modernist advocate, Nikolaus Pevsner, had termed 'coarse in the extreme', signally failed to engage with the street. (The half-hearted fountains installed there were later removed to make way for the Crossrail tube extension.) Worse still, after it was finished, its owner, the property developer Harry Hyams, kept the entire tower empty for nine years while he waited for a better price. The resulting scandal caused national outrage and tarnished the image of the commercial office block irreparably. When activists from the charity Direct Action, campaigning to alleviate homelessness, occupied the building in 1974 they won considerable public support and widespread media attention. These days, although now a listed building and in constant use, it is better known as an extra in film or television production whenever fury or indignation is called for.

The City as conservation battleground

During the premiership of Margaret Thatcher in the 1980s it seemed as if the City of London's post-war malaise was finally over. The City had successfully resisted the attempts of other financial centres to wrest off the crown of global market supremacy from its lofty head. Following the financial deregulation of

Thatcher's 'Big Bang' of 1986, it looked as if the resulting expansion of City office space would result in many more Tower 42s being erected. Richard Rogers's new, hi-tech tower on Leadenhall Street for Lloyd's of London, opened in the year of Big Bang, had already set an enviably high design bar. However, the experienced City of London Corporation planning department has already set down a marker in the form of their 1984 Draft Plan, which limited the height of tall towers and sought to protect both the City's remaining historic building stock and those City firms and industries which were not connected with financial services, and which consequently did need great big, macho tower blocks to assert their economic power, prestige and ambition.

Disappointingly, two years later the City bowed to pressure from the financial big guns, made a major U-turn and agreed to an increase of around 20 per cent in the provision of City office space. However, large City firms had already been looking eastwards to the large, brownfield sites becoming available in the Docklands area of the Isle of Dogs, which had lain abandoned since the docks were closed to big ships in 1969 and the last London dock had shut in 1982. Canary Wharf was developed in the heart of Docklands as a direct alternative to the City.* With the City's planning officers still justifiably striving to protect the surviving historic buildings of the Square Mile from demolition, many banks and insurers preferred to move to Docklands.

Not all the battles went the conservationists' way. In 1982 the developer Peter Palumbo, who owned the splendid Victorian-Gothic block at No. 1 Poultry of 1870 by John Belcher, which housed the venerable jewellers Mappin and Webb, proposed that Belcher's block and most of its neighbours be demolished in order to erect a vast, rectangular tower by Mies van der Rohe who had died in 1969. The Mies skyscraper had been commissioned twenty years before and was now well past its sell-by date, as well as demonstrably inappropriate for this complex City site. Even the great American architect and friend of Mies, Philip Johnson, said of the proposal, 'I consider it a bad idea for one of the greatest architects of the 20th century to be represented in what may be the greatest city in the 20th century by a posthumous and unimportant piece of architecture' and boldly concluded that 'Mies and London deserve better monuments'.

Palumbo's scheme was duly rejected at a public inquiry but, in the year

---

* Nevertheless, until London Underground's Jubilee Line arrived at Canary Wharf in 1999, disgorging its passengers into a vast new station by Foster + Partners, public transport links connecting the new hub with London's West End and its main line stations were very poor.

of Big Bang, Palumbo returned with a new application for a lower but massier building on the site designed by the living architect James Stirling. Despite the opposition of the City and English Heritage, the inspector at the second public inquiry, swayed by the Thatcher government's strong hint that this application should be looked on favourably, gave way and the scheme was allowed. SAVE Britain's Heritage took this emotive dispute all the way to the House of Lords but lost and, moreover, were spitefully saddled with costs. Belcher's jaunty Gothic building was demolished in 1994 and Stirling's vast, impractical ocean liner of a building was completed in 1997, by which time both architect and patron were dead. Once again, it seemed as if history had no place in Thatcher's Britain. As an ironic coda, only eighteen years after its opening, major alterations were needed to make Stirling's building actually work.

The bombing campaign

Developers were not the only villains. On 10 April 1992, a one-ton bomb planted by the Provisional IRA* detonated in the heart of the City, killing three people – including a fifteen-year-old girl – and injuring ninety-one. The bomb also severely damaged the Grade II*-listed Baltic Exchange. The Exchange's owners sold the building in the expectation that it would be rebuilt, but the City subsequently agreed to demolish the remains† and build anew on the site. Following the IRA bombing a year later which badly damaged the NatWest Tower, however, conservationists mercifully frustrated developers' demands that the ancient, half-destroyed church of St Ethelburga be similarly razed.

After the Baltic Exchange bombing of 1992 more large devices were detonated in Warrington, killing two children, and London's Bishopsgate, killing one man, in 1993; three years later, massive bombs destroyed large areas of

---

* The Provisional IRA had spun off from the traditional Irish Republican Army (IRA) in December 1969, four months after British soldiers had first been sent to Northern Ireland to safeguard Catholic communities from Protestant Ulster loyalists, including the strongly Unionist members of the Royal Ulster Constabulary. Well-armed thanks to the money and weapons provided by Irish-Americans in the US and by Libya's maverick president, Colonel Gaddafi, the Provisionals swiftly turned what was originally meant to be a defensive campaign against the Protestant majority in Ulster into a bombing campaign across the whole of the United Kingdom aimed at military, political and 'economic' targets.

† The surviving remains were snapped up by an architectural salvage dealer and subsequently bought by the Estonian government in the hope that they would form the centrepiece of a new building in the Estonian capital, Tallinn. At the time of writing this has not transpired.

△ *30 St Mary Axe today: a nicely-proportioned addition to the Square Mile, sitting amid a cityscape of unsettlingly variable architectural quality.*

London's Docklands, Manchester's Arndale retail centre, a British army base outside Osnabrück, Germany, and numerous targets across Northern Ireland.

Phoenix from the ruins

By the time the IRA's gruesome terror crusade had finally ended, a new building had arisen at 30 St Mary Axe from the ruins of the bombed landmark. Once the decision had been taken to clear the site of the Baltic Exchange, the question was what to put in its place. With the saga of No. 1 Poultry fresh in everyone's minds, it seemed anything was possible in the City now. Simon Jenkins insisted in *The Times* that anything less than a complete restoration of Smith and Wimble's Edwardian Baltic Exchange would effectively be seen as a surrender to the IRA. Unfortunately for Jenkins and the conservation lobby, no funder came forwards to support this admirable proposal, on which both the City Corporation and English Heritage (EH) were lukewarm. EH did initially demand that the façade of the ruined Baltic Exchange be incorporated as the entrance to any new scheme. However, the government agency then

484

shifted its position after 'discovering' that the ruined Exchange was in a worse condition than they had originally thought – and after Trafalgar House had made a commitment to funding the conservation of other historic buildings in the City.

Despite the vociferous objections of conservation pressure groups led by the Victorian Society and SAVE Britain's Heritage, EH agreed that the remains of the Exchange could, after all, be demolished; this in turn encouraged the City, which was worried about losing yet more business to Docklands, to bow to commercial pressure. The City's planners consequently invited applications for yet another tall tower. The Exchange's fine stained-glass windows by J. Dudley Forsyth, which had miraculously survived the bombing, were painstakingly conserved and installed at the National Maritime Museum in Greenwich in 2005.

Armed with this new brief, the site's new owners, Trafalgar House,* hired one of the world's leading and largest corporate architectural firms, Foster + Partners, to design a replacement building for the suite. Disappointingly, the immediate result was yet another macho corporate gesture, to add to the many already disfiguring the City of London. Foster's proposed ninety-two-storey, 380-metre tower would, if it had been built, have been the tallest building in Europe and the sixth-tallest in the world.

What the owners were now brazenly calling the 'Millennium Tower' was no beauty. An ungainly, transparent, tripartite structure with two pointed 'ears' rising from the top, which Peter Rees of the City's planning department declared made the building look like 'a surprised rabbit', the *raison d'être* of the Millennium Tower was obviously to be bigger and taller than its playground rivals. The design maintained its full width almost to the top, rather than tapering at it rose – as Renzo Piano's graceful Shard, built across the river in Southwark in 2009–12, was subsequently to do. As a result, the design's testosterone-fuelled hubris won few supporters even within the architectural establishment.

English Heritage's response to the Millennium Tower was equivocal. EH merely stated that 'building would dominate not only the city but the whole of London, becoming the symbol of the capital and pushing St Paul's to one side', a comment that was interpreted as support by both sides. Thankfully, the London Planning Advisory Committee was more forthright, declaring

---

*   Themselves bought by Norwegian developers Kvaerner in 1996.

that 'In a curious way this proposal is backward looking and derivative rather than a forward looking and innovative indication of what London and Londoners are looking forward to for our next Millennium.' It was Palumbo's Miesian tower all over again. The casting vote was proffered, unexpectedly, by Heathrow Airport, which declared that the height of the tower might prove a menace to aircraft. As a result, Trafalgar House, having tried again by submitting a scaled-down version of the Millennium Tower in 1996, stomped off in a sulk and sold the site to the insurance group Swiss Re. The new owners called Foster's back, but this time briefed them to produce something more in keeping with the times. What they wanted was a stylish, well-mannered reflection of Tony Blair's caring, sharing Cool Britannia rather than a bid for the stars.

In their new building at 30 St Mary Axe of 2001–4, Foster's achieved just that. The architects succeeded where Richard Seifert and James Stirling had failed at the NatWest Tower* and No. 1 Poultry. They created a new commercial building for the City of London that was both fit for purpose and, at the same time, respectful of its context and aesthetically pleasing.

Foster's Gherkin

Unusually for the time, 30 St Mary Axe instantly became one of the City of London's best-loved landmarks. Finding itself within a few years surrounded by skyscrapers which preferred to gain attention and overpower their neighbours by adopting ever-more tiresomely ostentatious forms,† Foster's sophisticated and decorously tapered tower, quickly dubbed 'The Gherkin' by Londoners, appeared as an oasis of calm and decency. The architectural critic Farshid Mousavi has rightly observed:

> The Square Mile in the City of London is dominated by dry repetitions of the conventional office block – vertically extruded, horizontally striated – mingled with the weighty presence of its historical institutions. The 'Gherkin,' as 30 St Mary Axe is popularly known, has a distinctive shape

---

*   Which was actually three metres taller than Foster's new building.

†   Probably the worst offender was Rafael Viñoly's awkward, Dali-esque 20 Fenchurch Street, built in 2012–14 for Land Securities, and popularly nicknamed the 'Walkie-Talkie' Building' (although there have been more unkind names).

△ *The marvellous glazed Lens at the Gherkin's summit.*

and circular plan that immediately set it apart from the orthogonal towers around it.

Even architectural historian Marcus Binney, whose organisation SAVE Britain's Heritage had campaigned in vain to stop the erection of any new building in order to rebuild the old Exchange, reluctantly admitted that the Gherkin would 'bring much-needed interest to the dull cluster of existing blocks'.

Largely designed by legendary Foster + Partners' architect Ken Shuttleworth, 30 St Mary Axe was greeted with widespread acclaim from both architectural critics and City workers alike. On the firm's winning of the UK's prestigious Stirling Prize six months after its opening, the *Observer* declared that 'the Gherkin [was] everyone's cup of tea' and that 'The tower has won over Londoners – and now the judges of architecture's top prize'. Norman Foster* himself, when grilled by journalists hoping for an intemperate denunciation of the building's irreverent nickname, disarmed them by professing that he

---

*   Lord Foster of Thames Bank since 1999.

was delighted with the label: 'after all', he said, 'it's a term of affection.'

One hundred and eighty metres high and with only forty-one floors – a marked contrast to the ninety-two floors of the oversized Millennium Tower originally earmarked for the site – the pleasingly proportioned Gherkin became a recognisable and cherished landmark of London almost overnight. As the building's biographer, Ken Powell, has noted:

> Far from representing a surrender to the IRA, the new tower was a bold symbol of the confidence of the City. For the City's planning supremo, Peter Rees, this is a structure that has 'single-handedly changed the perception of tall buildings in London.' Swiss Re, he says, 'didn't set out to build an icon, but it's become a symbol of London.'

In keeping with the times, the Gherkin was as green as it could be. Foster's boasted that it was London's 'first ecological tall building', while its circular plan reduced wind shearing around the building and thus improved its immediate environment for both tower residents and passers-by. The building used energy-saving methods which allowed it to employ only half the power that a similarly sized tower would typically consume, while gaps in each floor created six shafts which served as a natural ventilation system for the entire building.

The building also quietly nodded to its predecessor on the site. The Gherkin featured a panoramic dome, 'the Lens', which recalled Smith and Wimble's glazed dome at the old Baltic Exchange of 1903. At the same time, the building also exploited the latest technology, its diagonally braced structure enabling the provision of an expansive, column-free interior and a fully glazed façade comprising 500 flat triangular and diamond-shaped glass panels – which, in turn, maximised natural light and cut the occupants' lighting bills. As the architects themselves bragged: 'The 180 metre, forty-storey tower breaks with the conventions of traditional box-like office buildings. Its circular plan is tapered at the base and the crown to improve connections to the surrounding streets and allow the maximum amount of sunlight to the plaza level.' Farshid Mousavi, meanwhile, was more lyrical in his judgement:

> Each floor is rotated five degrees from the floor below, generating six atria in the form of triangular prisms that spiral around the building, admitting daylight and allowing for air circulation in the offices... The twisting reminds us of roller coasters or the slides in water parks, or even Carsten

Höller's giant slide installations. The latticing reminds us of baskets or fishnet tights. The conicality reminds us of rockets or gherkins. The argyle pattern recalls Scotland, socks, Pringle, knitting patterns, intarsia, harlequin-patterned floors or furniture. It is no wonder that the Gherkin is only one of many nicknames that have been attached to this polysemic building.

Other commentators were a little more cynical. The Spanish critic Alejandro Zaera-Polo, who asked if 'London's "Erotic Gherkin" [was] the most direct embodiment and final proof of the high-rise building's psychological association with the phallus'. He suggested somewhat unconvincingly that a hidden influence on the concept had been Lady Foster, 'who just happens to be a sex therapist and television celebrity in Spain, and whose relationship with Lord Foster blossomed more or less simultaneously with the beginning of the Gherkin's design phase'. Zaera-Polo concluded that 'the sensual curves of the Gherkin make it actually the first female skyscraper, more akin to a siren's sensual shape than to the classical phallic metaphor'.

Notwithstanding its popularity as a London landmark, however, not even the Gherkin was immune from the financial, political and social crises of the early twenty-first century. The global banking crisis of 2008–9 and Britain's Brexit vote of 2016 jeopardised the future of the City as a global banking centre while simultaneously undermining the Gherkin's own future. In September 2006, only two years after it first opened, the building was put up for sale. It was bought by an Anglo-German consortium in a deal which gave original owners Swiss Re an obscene profit of more than £300 million on a £620 million deal – for a structure with a build cost of only £200 million. Less than eight years later, as the new owners defaulted on their loan repayments, the Gherkin was bought by the Brazilian billionaire Joseph Safra. The Gherkin's story now began to resemble a grotesque game of pass-the-parcel.

Fathoming the future

The Covid-19 pandemic which spread like wildfire across the globe at the beginning of 2020 not only killed million across the globe but also redefined the world's working habits, perhaps for ever. Even the most draconian employers were now forced to encourage more employees to work at least part of the week from home. As a result, the perception of tall office blocks such as 30 St Mary Axe transformed almost overnight from shining beacons of corporate success to costly dinosaurs. The future, it seemed in 2020–1, was in home-working, and perhaps in hot-desking in shared office spaces. Barely twenty years after its much-applauded unveiling, the Gherkin, together with its many siblings across the City of London and all of the nation's other commercial centre, suddenly seemed to belong more to Britain's past than to its future.

At the time of writing, as many (but by no means all) of the City's workers have returned to their office desks, waiting for the next strain of Covid to surface and banish them back to their homes, and as City traders continue to desert Brexit Britain for more business-friendly environments in Germany and other EU havens, the future of bold, brash commercial towers such as 30 St Mary Axe hangs in the balance. It is a cruel irony that one of the best-loved monuments of modern London has become a casualty of the financial hubris it once epitomised. As, in many ways, has Britain itself.

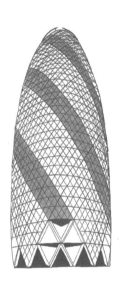

Sources and Further Reading

What follows includes some of the principal sources I have used in researching this book, with some suggestions of follow-on general reading if that is what you are looking for. Some of the articles may be hard to locate, although most should be available online. Increasingly, too, newer books are available online through university or institutional libraries.

As with any work involving individual historic buildings in Britain, the first stops are inevitably two prime sources of architectural and historical information, which I have generally not cited under the chapter headings: Historic England's list descriptions, which are all available online, and Yale University Press's 'Pevsner' guides to *The Buildings of England, Wales and Scotland*. List descriptions, which reinforce the statutory protection or 'listing' afforded to the entire historic building – comprising levels at Grades I, II* or II – vary in length and quality but are always helpful starting points for any architectural investigation.

The 'Pevsner' series of county-by-county architectural guides, which Nikolaus Pevsner inaugurated in 1951 and which is still alive and well today in the hands of his successors, provides invaluable and reassuringly detailed accounts of the historic buildings of each city, town and village – a priceless asset no other nation can boast.

CHAPTER 1: MAIDEN CASTLE, DORSET

Armit, Ian, 'Hillforts at War: From Maiden Castle to Taniwaha Pā', in *Proceedings of the Prehistoric Society*, vol. 73, 18 February 2014.

Cavaliero, Glen, 'Maiden Castle Revisited', in *The Powys Journal*, vol. 9 (London, 1999).

Cunliffe, Barry, in *Antiquity*, vol. 53, no. 207, 1979.

— *Danebury Hillfort* (Stroud, 2003).

— *Bretons and Britons: The Fight for Identity* (Oxford, 2021).

Hardy, Thomas, 'Ancient Earthworks and What Two Enthusiastic Scientists Found Therein', in *Detroit Post*, 15 March 1885.

— 'Ancient Earthworks at Casterbridge', in *The English Illustrated Magazine*, vol. 123, December 1893; reworked as 'A Tryst at an Ancient Earthwork', in *Complete Uniform Edition of the Wessex Novels* (London, 1913).

Hawkes, Jacquetta, *Mortimer Wheeler: Adventurer in Archaeology* (London, 1982).

McCarthy, James, 'John Ireland', in *Gramophone*, 11 June 2012.

Powys, John Cowper, *Maiden Castle* (London, 1936).

Redfern, Rebecca and Chamberlain, Andrew, 'A demographic analysis of Maiden Castle hillfort: Evidence for conflict in the late Iron Age and early Roman period', in *International Journal of Paleopathology*, vol. 1, no. 1, March 2011.

Russell, Miles, 'Mythmakers of Maiden Castle: Breaking the Siege Mentality of an Iron Age Hillfort', in *Oxford Archaeological Journal*, vol. 38, no. 3, 2019.

Sharples, Niall and Ambers, J., *Maiden Castle: excavations and field survey 1985–6* (London, 1991).

Wainwright G. J. and Cunliffe, B[arry] W., 'Maiden Castle: excavation, education, entertainment?', in *Antiquity*, vol. 59, no. 226, 1985.

Wheeler, Mortimer, *Maiden Castle, Dorset* (London, 1943).

CHAPTER 2: THE ROMAN BATHS, BATH

Davis, Graham and Bonsall, Penny, *A History of Bath: Image and Reality* (Lancaster, 2006).

Fergusson, Adam, *The Sack of Bath* (Compton Russell, 1976).

— and Mowl, Timothy, *The Sack of Bath – and After* (London, 1989).

Forsyth, Michael, *Bath* (London and New Haven, 2003).

Ison, Walter, *The Georgian Buildings of Bath* (London, 1948).

McNeill-Ritchie, Simon, *Historic England: Bath* (Stroud, 2017).

Mattingly, David J., *An Imperial Possession: Britain in the Roman Empire* (London, 2006).

— *Imperialism, Power, and Identity: Experiencing the Roman Empire* (Princeton, 2013).

Mowl, Timothy and Earnshaw, Brian, *John Wood* (Bradford-on-Avon, 2nd edn, 2022).

Spence, Cathryn (ed.), *Obsession: John Wood and the Creation of Georgian Bath* (Bath, 2004).

Wither, George, *A collection of emblems, ancient and moderne* (London, 1635).

Wood, John, *An essay towards a description of Bath* (London, 1742).

Wright, Neil and Crick, Julia C. (eds), *The Historia regum Britannie of Geoffrey of Monmouth* (Cambridge, from 1985).

CHAPTER 3: MUCKING VILLAGE, ESSEX

Adams, Max, *The First Kingdom* (London, 2021).

Carlyle, Thomas, *Past and Present* (London, 1843).

Colgrave, Bertram and Mynors, R. A. B. (eds), *Bede's Ecclesiastical History of the English People* (Oxford, 2022).

Cox, Oliver, 'An Oxford college and the eighteenth-century Gothic Revival', in *Oxoniensia*, vol. 212, 2012.

— 'The Cult of King Alfred', in Steven Parissien (ed.), *Celebrating Britain: Canaletto, Hogarth and Patriotism* (London, 2015).

Giles, John Allen, *The Works of Gildas and Nennius* (London, 1841).

Härke, Heinrich *et al.*, 'Evidence for an apartheid-like social structure in early Anglo-Saxon England', in *Proceedings of the Royal Society B: Biological Sciences*, vol. 273, no. 1601, 2006.

— 'Historical narrative as cultural politics', in N. J. Higham (ed.), *Britons in Anglo-Saxon England* (Woodbridge, 2007).

Hunter Blair, Peter, *Anglo-Saxon England* (London: revised edn, 1997).

Jones, Margaret et al., 'Crop Sites at Mucking', in *Antiquaries Journal*, vol. 48, no. 2, 1968

— 'An ancient landscape palimpsest at Mucking', in *Transactions of the Essex Archaeological Society*, vol. 5, 1973.

Keynes, Simon, *The Cult of King Alfred the Great* (Cambridge, 1999).

Kingsley, Charles, *Hereward the Wake* (London, 1866).

Melman, Billie, 'Claiming the Nation's Past; The Invention of an Anglo-Saxon Tradition', in *Journal of Contemporary History*, vol. 26, nos 3–4, September 1991.

Parker, Joanne, *'England's Darling': The Victorian Cult of Alfred the Great* (Manchester, 2007).

Pitts, Mike, 'Obituary: Margaret Jones', in *Guardian*, 2 May 2001.

Scott, Walter, *Ivanhoe* (Edinburgh, 1819).

Stenton, Frank, *Anglo-Saxon England* (Oxford, 3rd edn, 1971).

Tipper, Jess, *The Grubenhaus in Anglo-Saxon England* (Malton, 2004).

Worth, Chris, 'Ivanhoe and the Making of Britain', in *Links & Letters*, no. 2, 1995.

CHAPTER 4: CHEPSTOW CASTLE, GWENT

Gilpin, William, *Observations on the River Wye and several parts of South Wales, etc. relative chiefly to Picturesque Beauty; made in the summer of the year 1770* (London, 1782).

Heath, Charles, *Monmouthshire* (Monmouth, 1793).

Hope, William St John, 'Chepstow Castle', in *Archaeological Journal*, vol. 61, July 1904.

Hussey, Christopher, *The Picturesque: studies in a point of view* (London, 1927).

Johnes, Martin, 'History and the Making and Remaking of Wales', in *History*, vol. 100, no. 5 (London, 2015).

Owen, Orville Ward, *Sir Francis Bacon's Cipher Story* (London, 1894).

Perks, John Clifford, *Chepstow Castle, Monmouthshire* (London, 1971).

Turner, Rick and Johnson, Andy, *Chepstow Castle: Its History and Buildings* (Eardisley, 2006).

Turner, R. C. *et al.*, 'The Great Tower, Chepstow Castle, Wales', in *Antiquaries Journal*, vol. 84, September 2004 (Cambridge, 2011).

Walford Davies, Damian and Fulford, Tim, *Romanticism's Wye* (Edinburgh, 2013).

CHAPTER 5: LINCOLN CATHEDRAL

Antram, Nicholas, Pevsner, Nikolaus and Harris, John, *The Buildings of England: Lincolnshire* (London, 1989).

Fernie, Eric, 'Lincoln Cathedral, The Façade', in *Annual Conference Notes* (London: SAHGB, 1999).

Foyle, Jonathan, *Lincoln Cathedral* (London, 2015).

Gem, Richard, 'Lincoln Minster', in *British Archaeological Association Conference Transactions for 1982* (Leeds, 1986).

Gurnham, Richard, *A History of Lincoln* (Chichester, 2009).

Harrison, Stuart, 'The Original Plan of the East End of St Hugh's Choir at Lincoln Cathedral Reconsidered in the Light of New Evidence', in *Journal of the British Archaeological Association*, vol. 169, no. 1, January 2016.

Hendrix, John, *Architecture as Cosmology: Lincoln Cathedral and English Gothic Architecture* (New York, 2011).

Lubbock, Tom, 'Lincoln Cathedral, South Rose Window', in *Independent*, 22 December 2006.

Owen, Dorothy (ed.), *A History of Lincoln Minster* (Cambridge, 1994).

Quiney, Antony, 'In Hoc Signo: The West Front of Lincoln Cathedral', in *Architectural History*, vol. 44, 2001.

Ruskin, John, *The Seven Lamps of Architecture* (London, 2nd edn, 1855).

Theodossopoulos, Dimitris and Gonzalez-Longo, Cristina, *Development of Gothic vaulted space and perception of technology in The Cultural Role of Architecture* (Lincoln, 2010).

Warren, W. L., *King John* (London – New Haven, revised edn, 1997).

CHAPTER 6: GREAT COXWELL BARN, OXFORDSHIRE

Bernard, G. W., *The Dissolution of the Monasteries* (Oxford, 2011).

Colvin, Howard, *Architecture and the After-Life* (London – New Haven, 1992).

— 'The Origin of Chantries', in *Journal of Medieval History*, vol. 26, no. 2, 2000.

Hampton, D. W., *The Barn of Great Coxwell* (Letchworth, 1964).

Horn, Walter and Born, Ernest, *Barns of the Abbey of Beaulieu at Its Granges of Great Coxwell and Beaulieu-St Leonards* (Berkeley, CA, 1965).

Lawrence, C. H., *Medieval Monasticism: Forms of Religious Life in Western Europe in the Middle Ages* (New York, 3rd edn, 2001).

MacCarthy, Fiona, *William Morris: A Life for Our Time* (London, 1994).

Morris, William, *Manifesto of the Society for the Protection of Ancient Buildings* (London, 1877).

Noton, Nicholas, *Farm Buildings* (Reading, 1982).

Pickles, David and Lake, Jeremy, *Adapting Traditional Farm Buildings* (Swindon, 2017).

Vernon, R. W., McDonnell G. and Schmidt, A., 'An integrated geophysical and analytical appraisal of early iron-working: three case studies', in *Historical Metallurgy*, vol. 31, no. 2, 1998.

Wainwright, Martin, 'How a king capped a furnace of industry', in *Guardian*, 14 August 1998.

CHAPTER 7: LITTLE MORETON HALL, CHESHIRE

Clark, C. J., *The Glass Industry in the Woodland Economy of the Weald* (unpublished PhD thesis, University of Sheffield, 2006).

Davies, C. S. L., 'Tudor: What's in a Name?', in *History*, vol. 97, no. 325, 2012.

Figuereido, Peter de and Treuherz, Julian, *Cheshire Country Houses* (Chichester, 1988).

Girouard, Mark, 'Elizabethan Architecture and the Gothic Tradition', in *Architectural History*, vol. 6, 1963.

— *Elizabethan Architecture* (London – New Haven, 2009).

Gulley, J. L. M., *The Wealden landscape in the early seventeenth century and its antecedents* (unpublished PhD thesis, University of London, 1960).

Jenkins, Simon, *England's Thousand Best Houses* (New York, 2004).

Mowl, Timothy, *Elizabethan and Jacobean Style* (London, 1993).

Summerson, John, *Architecture in Britain 1530–1830* (London – New Haven, 9th edn, 1993).

Stubbs, Susie, *Little Moreton Hall, Cheshire* (Swindon, 2015).

CHAPTER 8: THE QUEEN'S CHAPEL, ST JAMES'S PALACE, LONDON

Baldwin, David, *The Politico-Religious Usage of the Queen's Chapel, 1623–1688* (unpublished MLitt thesis, Durham University, 1999).

Bradley, Simon, 'The Queen's Chapel in the Twentieth Century', in *Architectural History*, vol. 44, 2001.

Harris John and Higgott, Gordon, *Inigo Jones: Complete Architectural Drawings* (London, 1989).

Hart, Vaughan, *Inigo Jones: The Architect of Kings* (London – New Haven, 2011).

Leyden, Kyle, 'Vitruvius Hibernicus' *Consorting with the Enemy: The Queen's Chapel at St James's Palace*, 25 January 2015: kyleleyden.wordpress.com/2015/01/24/consorting-with-the-enemy-the-queens-chapel-at-st-jamess-palace

Sharpe, Kevin, *The Personal Rule of Charles I* (London – New Haven, 1996).

CHAPTER 9: HERIOT'S HOSPITAL, EDINBURGH

Bonner, Elizabeth, 'Scotland's "Auld Alliance" with France 1295–1560', in *History*, vol. 84, no. 273, January 1999.

Brownlow, John, *The History and Objects of the Foundling Hospital* (London, 1847).

Dziennik, Matthew, '*Armailt làidir de mhilisidh*: Hanoverian Gaels and the Jacobite Rebellion of 1745', in *Scottish Historical Review*, vol. C2, no. 253, August 2021.

Elliott, J. H., *Scots and Catalans* (London and New Haven, 2018).

Guidicini, Giovanna, 'A Scottish Triumphal Path of Learning at George Heriot's Hospital', in *International Review of Scottish Studies*, vol. 35, 15 July 2010.

Hutton, Ronald, 'The Making of the Secret Treaty of Dover', in *Historical Journal*, vol. 29, no. 2, 1986.

Parissien, Steven, 'The Architecture of the Foundling Hospital', in Robin Simon (ed.), *Enlightened Self-Interest: The Foundling Hospital and Hogarth* (London, 1997).

Riding, Jacqueline, *Jacobites* (London, 2016).

Rowan, Alistair, 'George Heriot's Hospital, Edinburgh', in *Country Life*, vol. 157, nos 4053–4, 6 and 20 March 1975.

Talbott, Siobhan, 'Beyond "the antiseptic realm of theoretical economic models": New perspectives on Franco-Scottish commerce and the Auld Alliance in the long seventeenth century', in *Journal of Scottish Historical Studies*, vol. 31, no. 2, 1 November 2011.

CHAPTER 10: PECKWATER QUAD, CHRIST CHURCH, OXFORD

Campell, Colen, *Vitruvius Britannicus*, vol. 1 (London, 1715).

Echlin, Alexander and Kelly, William, 'A "Shaftesburian Agenda"? Lord Burlington, Lord Shaftesbury and the Intellectual Origins of English Palladianism', in *Architectural History*, vol. 59, 2016.

Mowl, Timothy, 'Directions from the Grave: The Problem with Lord Shaftesbury', in *Architectural History*, vol. 32, 2004.

Parissien, Steven, Harris, John and Colvin, Howard, 'Narford Hall, Norfolk', in *The Georgian Group Report and Journal 1987* (London, 1987).

Parissien, Steven, *The Careers of Roger and Robert Morris* (unpublished DPhil thesis, Oxford University, 1989).

Shay, Robert, 'Henry Aldrich: selected anthems and motet recompositions', in *Early Music*, vol. 27, no. 4, 1999.

Tyack, Geoffrey, *The Historic Heart of the University of Oxford* (Oxford, 2022).

— *Oxford: An Architectural Guide* (Oxford, 1998).

CHAPTER 11: 19 PRINCELET STREET, SPITALFIELDS, LONDON

Blain Douglas *et al.*, *The Saving of Spitalfields* (London, 1989).

Cruickshank, Dan, *Spitalfields* (London, 2017).

Kershen, Anne J., *Strangers, Aliens and Asians: Huguenots, Jews and Bangladeshis in Spitalfields 1660–2000* (New York – Abingdon, 2005).

London, Jack, *People of the Abyss* (London, 1903).

Prestwich, Menna, 'The Revocation of the Edict of Nantes', in *History*, vol. 73, no. 237, February 1988.

Samuel, Raphael, 'The Pathos of Spitalfields', in *Spectator*, vol. 262, no. 8393, 1989.

Sheppard, F.H.W. (ed.), *The Survey of London, vol. 27: Spitalfields and Mile End New Town* (London, 1957).

Walker, Henry, *East London: Sketches of Christian Work and Workers* (London, 1896).

CHAPTER 12: COMPTON VERNEY, WARWICKSHIRE

Bearman, Robert, *Compton Verney: A History of the House and its Owners* (Stratford-upon-Avon, 2000).

Marr, Andrew, *The Making of Modern Britain* (London, 2009).

Parissien, Steven, *Compton Verney Park* (Reading, 2015).

Pickford, Chris, *The Buildings of England: Warwickshire* (London and New Haven, 2016).

Tyack, Geoffrey, *Warwickshire Country Houses* (Chichester, 1994).

CHAPTER 13: CROMFORD MILL, DERBYSHIRE

Bayles, Freda and Ede, Janet, *The Cromford Guide* (Cromford, 1994).

Beckert, Sven, *Cromford Mill* (Matlock, 1980)

— *Empire of Cotton* (London, 2015).

Engels, Friedrich, *The Condition of the Working Class in England* (German original 1845; this translation New York, 1887).

Honeyman, Katrina, *Child Workers in England 1780–1820* (Aldershot, 2007).

L. E. L. [Letitia Elizabeth Landon], *Poetical Works* (London, 1850).

Parissien, Steven, *Regency Style* (London, 1992).

Riello, Giorgio, *Cotton: The Fabric That Made the Modern World* (Cambridge, 2013).

Wrigley, Chris (ed.), *Industrialisation and Society in Britain: Cromford and Beyond in the Era of the Industrial Revolution* (Matlock, 2016).

CHAPTER 14: 7 GREAT GEORGE STREET, BRISTOL

Dyk, Garritt van, 'A Tale of Two Boycotts: Riot, Reform, and Sugar Consumption in Late Eighteenth-Century Britain and France', in *Eighteenth-Century Life*, vol. 45, no. 3, 2015.

Eickelman, Christine, *Pero, The Life of a Slave in Eighteenth-century Bristol* (Bristol, 2004).

Evans, Bergen and Pinney, Hester, 'Racedown and the Wordsworths'. in *The Review of English Studies*, vol. 8, no. 29, January 1932.

Foyle, Andrew, *Bristol* (London – New Haven, 2004).

Gleadle, Kathryn and Hanley, Ryan, 'Children Against Slavery: Juvenile Agency and the Sugar Boycotts in Britain', in *Transactions of the Royal Historical Society*, vol. 30, 2020.

Ison, Walter, *The Georgian Buildings of Bristol* (London, 1952).

Mintz, Sidney, *Sweetness and Power: The Place of Sugar in Modern History* (Harmondsworth, 1986).

Morgan, Kenneth, *Bristol and the Atlantic Trade in the Eighteenth Century* (Cambridge, 1993).

Pares, Richard, *A West-India Fortune* (London, 1950).

Small, David and Eickelman, Christine, *The Pinney Family Servants* (Bristol, 2019).

CHAPTER 15: BRIGHTON PAVILION, SUSSEX

Blakeley, Kara, 'Domesticating Orientalism: Chinoiserie and the Pagodas of the Royal Pavilion, Brighton', in *Australian and New Zealand Journal of Art*, vol. 18, no. 2, 2018.

Dinkel, John, *The Royal Pavilion, Brighton* (London, 1983).

Loske, Alexandra, *The Decorative Scheme of the Brighton Pavilion* (unpublished PhD thesis, University of Sussex, Brighton, 2014).

Musgrave, Clifford, *Royal Pavilion* (London, 1959).

Parissien, Steven, *Regency Style* (London, 1992).

— *The Grand Entertainment* (London, 2001).

Sickelmore, Richard, *History of Brighton and its Environs* (Brighton, 1827).

Thackeray, W. M., *The Four Georges* (London, 1861).

— *Thackeray's Lectures* (New York, 1867).

Wilson, A. N., *Prince Albert* (London, 2019).

CHAPTER 16: THE BRITON'S PROTECTION, MANCHESTER

Samuel Bamford, *Early Days* (London, 1849).

Hartwell, Clare, Hyde, Matthew and Pevsner, Nikolaus, *The Buildings of England: Lancashire: Manchester and the South-East* (London – New Haven, 2005).

Herbert, James, *The Art of Brewing* (London, 1871).

Morgan, Alison, *Ballads and Songs of Peterloo* (Manchester, 2017).

The National Inventory of Historic Pubs: pubheritage.camra.org.uk; accessed 11 February 2022.

Parissien, Steven (ed.), *Trouble Brewing* (Lavenham, 1991).

Poole, Robert, 'The March to Peterloo', in *Past & Present*, vol. 192, August 2006.

Prasch, Thomas, 'Peterloo', in *Film & History: An Interdisciplinary Journal*, vol. 49, no. 2, 2019.

Reid, Robert, *The Peterloo Massacre* (London, 1989).

Riding, Jacqueline, *Peterloo* (London, 2019).

Sander, Christensen Carsten, 'Civil rights, workers, women, financial figures and the orator, land-lord Henry Hunt: The Peterloo Massacre in Manchester on August 16, 1819', in *Studia Humanitatis*, vol. 1, 2020.

Shelley, Percy Bysshe, *The Masque of Anarchy* (London, 1832).

Strittmatter, David, 'The Evolving Rhetoric of Peterloo 1819–1919', in *Labour History Review*, vol. 83, no. 3, December 2018.

Thompson, E. P., *The Making of the English Working Class* (London, 1963).

CHAPTER 17: THE ROYAL WILLIAM YARD, PLYMOUTH

Coad, J. G. and Cooper, Nicholas, 'The Royal William Victualling Yard, Stonehouse', in *Archaeological Journal*, vol. 147, supplement 1, 1990.

Hoyle, Brian and Wright, Philip, 'Towards the evaluation of naval waterfront revitalisation: comparative experiences in Chatham, Plymouth and Portsmouth, UK', in *Ocean & Coastal Management*, vol. 42, 1999.

Knights, Antony M. *et al.*, 'Plymouth, A World Harbor through the Ages', in *Regional Studies in Marine Science*, vol. 8, no. 2, November 2016.

Mackay, David, Zogolovich, Roger and Harradine, Martin, *A Vision for Plymouth* (Plymouth, 2004).

Miele, Chris, 'Bold, Well-Defined Masses: Sir John Rennie and the Royal William Yard', in *Architectural History*, vol. 49, 2006.

Ware, Christopher, 'The Growth of Plymouth Naval Base and European Tensions 1717–32', in *The Mariner's Mirror*, vol. 99, no. 3, 2013.

CHAPTER 18: BIRMINGHAM TOWN HALL

Briggs, Asa, 'Thomas Attwood and the Economic Background of the Birmingham Political Union', in *Cambridge Historical Journal*, vol. 9, no. 2, 1948.

Eliot, George, *Felix Holt, the Radical* (Edinburgh, 1866).

Evinson, Denis, *Joseph Hansom* (unpublished MA dissertation, Courtauld Institute, London University, 1966).

Harris, Penelope, *The Architectural Achievement of Joseph Aloysius Hansom* (Lewiston, NY: *c*.2010).

— 'Joseph Aloysius Hansom (1803–82): His Yorkshire Works, Patronage and Contribution to the Catholic Revival', in *Yorkshire Archaeological Journal*, vol. 85, no. 1, 2013.

— *Joseph Aloysius Hansom and the Changing Practice of Architecture 1820–1860* (unpublished PhD thesis, University of Bangor, 2018).

Hill, Rosemary, *God's Architect: Pugin and the Building of Romantic Britain* (London – New Haven, 2009).

Lopatin, Nancy P., 'Refining the Limits of Political Reporting: The Provincial Press, Political Unions, and The Great Reform Act', in *Victorian Periodicals Review*, vol. 31, no. 4, 1998.

Peers, Anthony, *Birmingham Town Hall* (London, 2006).

CHAPTER 19: NEWCASTLE CENTRAL STATION

Barman, Christian, *Early British Railways* (London, 1950).

Booker, Christopher, 'Urban Rides', in *Spectator*, 5 May 1978.

Bradley, Simon, *The Railways: Nation, Network and People* (London, 2015).

Grainger, Richard, *A Proposal for Concentrating the Termini of the Newcastle & Carlisle, Great North of England and Proposed Edinburgh Railways* (Newcastle, 1836).

Hoole, Ken, *Railway Stations of the North East* (Newton Abbot, 1985).

Lardner, Dionysus, *Railway Economy* (London, 1850).

McCombie, Grace, *Newcastle and Gateshead* (London – New Haven, 2009).

Parissien, Steven, *The English Railway Station* (Swindon, 2014).

Paxton, Bill, *An examination of the decline of shipbuilding on the North-east coast of England and the west of Scotland during the interwar periods* (unpublished PhD thesis, Newcastle University, 2017).

Ruskin, John, *The Seven Lamps of Architecture* (London, 1849).

CHAPTER 20: LIBERTY'S, REGENT STREET, LONDON

Adburgham, Alison, *Liberty's: The Biography of a Shop* (London, 1975).

Barson, Susie, *The Liberty Shops* (English Heritage Report, London, 1999).

Dover, Harriet, 'Liberty & Co', in Joanna Banham (ed.), *The Encyclopaedia of Interior Design* (London, 1997).

Morrison, Kathryn, *English Shops and Shopping* (London – New Haven, 2003).

Nichols, Sarah, 'Arthur Lasenby Liberty: A Mere Adjective?', in *Journal of Decorative and Propaganda Arts*, vol. 13, summer 1989.

Pevsner, Nikolaus and Williamson, Elizabeth, *The Buildings of England: Buckinghamshire* (London, 1994).

Rieber, Marie-Therese, *Liberty: The History* (London, 2019).

Strong, Roy, *Liberty's 1875–1975* (London, 1975).

CHAPTER 21: THE ELECTRIC CINEMA, NOTTING HILL, LONDON

Eyles, Allen, *Odeon Cinemas: Oscar Deutsch Entertains Our Nation* (London, 2002).

Gray, Richard, *Cinemas in Britain* (London, 1996).

Holmes, Chris, *The Other Notting Hill* (Studley, 2005).

Kennedy, Ludovic, *10 Rillington Place* (London, 1961).

Kynaston, David, *Austerity Britain* (London, 2008).

McKernan, Luke, 'Diverting Time: London's Cinemas and Their Audiences, 1906–1914', in *The London Journal*, vol. 32, no. 2, July 2007.

Mash, Julian, *Portobello Road: Lives of a Neighbourhood* (London, 2014).

Wharton, Gary, *Suburban London Cinemas* (Stroud, 2008).

CHAPTER 22: THE DE LA WARR PAVILION, BEXHILL, SUSSEX

Barnett, Corelli, 'The Wasting of Britain's Marshall Aid', in *BBC History*, 3 March 2011: www.bbc.co.uk/history/british/modern/marshall_01.shtml; accessed 12 March 2022.

Brodie, Allan and Winter, Gary, *England's Seaside Resorts* (Swindon, 2007).

Cannata, Mark, 'The Repair and Alterations of the De La Warr Pavilion', in *Journal of Architectural Conservation*, vol. 12, no. 2, 2006.

Chermayeff, Serge, *Design and the Public Good: Selected Writings* (Cambridge, MA, 1982).

Fairley, Alastair, *De La Warr Pavilion* (London, 2006).

Finneran, Neil, 'Beside the Seaside. The Archaeology of the Twentieth-Century English Seaside Holiday Experience: A Phenomenological Context', in *International Journal of Historical Archaeology*, vol. 21, no. 3, September 2017.

— The Future of Seaside Towns (House of Lords Select Committee Report, London, 2019).

Porter, Julian, *Bexhill-on-Sea: A History* (Bognor, 2004).

Powers, Alan, *Serge Chermayeff* (London, 2001).

Richter, Virginia, 'Seaside Resort Blues: The English Seaside in the 1930s', in *HJEAS: Hungarian Journal of English and American Studies*, vol. 20, no. 1, 2021.

Stevens, Russell and Willis, Peter, 'Earl de la Warr and the Competition for Bexhill Pavilion', in *Architectural History*, vol. 33, 1990.

Walton, John K., *The British Seaside* (Manchester, 2000).

CHAPTER 23: CASTLE BROMWICH FACTORY, WARWICKSHIRE

Adeney, Martin, *Nuffield: A Biography* (London, 1993).

Egan, John, *Saving Jaguar* (Tenbury Wells, 2018).

Forbes, Neil, 'Democracy at a Disadvantage? British Rearmament, the Shadow Factory Scheme and the Coming of War, 1936–40', in *Economic History Yearbook*, 2014: doi.org/10.1515/jbwg-2014-0013; accessed 12 March 2022.

Glancey, Jonathan, 'Brilliant But Flawed', in *Independent*, 8 May 1996.

— *Spitfire: The Biography* (London, 2006).

Henshaw, Alex, *Sigh for a Merlin* (London, 1979).

McKinstry, Leo, 'How Labour Unrest Nearly Lost Us The Battle of Britain', in *Spectator*, 17 November 2007.

— *Lancaster* (London, 2009).

Newell, Michael, *Castle Bromwich: Its Airfield and Aircraft Factory* (Sherington, 1982).

Parissien, Steven, *The Life of the Automobile* (London, 2014).

Whyte, Andrew, *Jaguar* (Cambridge, 1980).

CHAPTER 24: 20 FORTHLIN ROAD, LIVERPOOL

Bradbury, Ronald, 'Post-War Housing in Liverpool', in *The Town Planning Review*, vol. 27, no. 3, October 1956.

Harwood, Elain, *Space, Hope and Brutalism: English Architecture 1945–75* (London – New Haven, 2014).

Malpass, Peter, 'Wartime planning for post-war housing in Britain: the Whitehall debate, 1941–5', in *Planning Perspectives*, vol. 18, no. 2, February 2011.

Niven, David, *The Moon's a Balloon* (London, 1971).

Norman, Philip, *Paul McCartney, the Biography* (London, 2016).

Sharples, Joseph, *Liverpool* (London – New Haven, 2004).

Sykes, Olivier *et al.*, 'A City Profile of Liverpool', in *Cities*, vol. 29, no. 2, 2012.

CHAPTER 25: 30 ST MARY AXE ('THE GHERKIN')

Barnes, Victoria, Newton, Lucy Ann and Scott, Peter, 'A "Quiet Victory": National Provincial, Gibson Hall, and the Switch from Comprehensive Redevelopment to Urban Preservation in 1960s London', in *Enterprise and Society*, November 2020.

Glendinning, Miles, *Tower Block* (London – New Haven, 1994).

Kynaston, David, *The City of London* (4 vols, London, 1999–2001).

Mousavi, Farshid, '30 St Mary Axe', in *Harvard Design Magazine*, no. 35, 2012.

Powell, Kenneth, *30 St Mary Axe: A Tower for London* (London, 2006).

Stamp, Gavin, 'The Battle of No. 1 Poultry', in *Apollo*, 24 April 2017.

Zaera-Polo, Alejandro, '30 St. Mary Axe: Form Isn't Facile', in *Log*, no. 4, Winter 2005.

Image Credits

Index

About the Author

Dr Steven Parissien is Director of Studies and Departmental Lecturer in Architectural History at the University of Oxford and Fellow of Kellogg College, Oxford. Born in London and raised in Chesham, Buckinghamshire, Steven obtained both his undergraduate and doctoral degrees from Oxford. He has worked in the heritage, arts and education sectors for over thirty years and has written extensively on architectural and cultural history.